DUE DILIGENCE OBLIGATIONS IN INTERNATIONAL LAW

Due diligence obligations are typically described by scholars and practitioners as 'elusive', 'weak', and difficult to pin down in the abstract. Challenging these assumptions, this book offers a systematic reconstruction of the foundations of due diligence obligations of states and explores their nature, rationale, content and scope of operation in international law. Tackling due diligence from a general perspective, this book seeks to complement scholarly studies on public international law obligations and their theory. This book will be relevant for academics, practitioners, graduate students across international law and anyone seeking to better conceptualise due diligence under international law and understand how due diligence obligations are operationalised in practice.

DR. ALICE OLLINO (Ph.D, LLM) is a postdoctoral fellow in public international law at the University of Milano-Bicocca. She is the recipient of the 2019 European Society of International Law Young Scholar Prize. She undertook her doctoral studies at the University of Milano-Bicocca and has published on public international law issues in national and international peer-reviewed journals.

AF798144

DUE DILIGENCE OBLIGATIONS IN INTERNATIONAL LAW

ALICE OLLINO
University of Milano-Bicocca

CAMBRIDGE
UNIVERSITY PRESS

CAMBRIDGE
UNIVERSITY PRESS

Shaftesbury Road, Cambridge CB2 8EA, United Kingdom

One Liberty Plaza, 20th Floor, New York, NY 10006, USA

477 Williamstown Road, Port Melbourne, VIC 3207, Australia

314–321, 3rd Floor, Plot 3, Splendor Forum, Jasola District Centre, New Delhi – 110025, India

103 Penang Road, #05–06/07, Visioncrest Commercial, Singapore 238467

Cambridge University Press is part of Cambridge University Press & Assessment,
a department of the University of Cambridge.

We share the University's mission to contribute to society through the pursuit of education, learning and research at the highest international levels of excellence.

www.cambridge.org
Information on this title: www.cambridge.org/9781009054768

DOI: 10.1017/9781009053082

© Alice Ollino 2022

This publication is in copyright. Subject to statutory exception and to the provisions of relevant collective licensing agreements, no reproduction of any part may take place without the written permission of Cambridge University Press & Assessment.

First published 2022
First paperback edition 2026

A catalogue record for this publication is available from the British Library

ISBN 978-1-316-51187-9 Hardback
ISBN 978-1-009-05476-8 Paperback

Cambridge University Press & Assessment has no responsibility for the persistence or accuracy of URLs for external or third-party internet websites referred to in this publication and does not guarantee that any content on such websites is, or will remain, accurate or appropriate.

Ai miei nonni Gianni e Mariolina
e alla memoria di mia nonna Pierina

CONTENTS

ACKNOWLEDGEMENTS

This book is a revised version of my PhD thesis in international law defended in 2018 at the University of Milano-Bicocca. I am greatly indebted to my supervisor, Professor Maurizio Arcari, who generously offered his knowledge, time, and patience throughout all these years. I am also very grateful for all the mentoring and support that I received from Professor Irini Papanicolopulu, who has been a constant source of scientific as well as personal advice. In addition, I wish to express my gratitude to Professors Beatrice Bonafè, Gina Heathcote, Enrico Milano, and Antonios Tzanakopoulos for their insightful comments which have helped me improve this book.

Over the last few years, I had the opportunity to discuss the topic of my research with a number of scholars who have contributed to sharpen my intellectual thinking about due diligence. In particular, I wish to thank Professor Makane Moïse Mbengue for having welcomed me at the University of Geneva and for providing me with valuable comments on my work. I would also like to thank Professor Anne Peters for kindly allowing me to take part in the due diligence workshop held in Berlin in 2018, and Professor Samantha Besson for taking the time to discuss and share her views on due diligence with me in The Hague. Many other scholars, friends, and colleagues have provided me with insightful feedback, and I wish to express my gratitude especially to Professor Tullio Scovazzi, Professor Giulio Bartolini, Professor Paolo Zicchittu, Dr Martina Buscemi, Dr Marco Longobardo, Dr Mariana de Andrade, Dr Federica Violi, Dr Alexia de Vaucleroy, Andrea Longo and to Daniele Mandrioli, who deserves a special mention for his invaluable help in polishing the manuscript. I am most grateful also to Giampaolo Guizzardi Righetti for his assistance in the last stages of the editing process, and to Sandra Jenkins for having proofread the text.

Last but not least, I am eternally grateful to my family, my parents Massimo and Elisabetta, my siblings Gabriele and Linda, and my partner Giuseppe. This book would have never seen the light without your immense love, patience, support, and good spirit. *Grazie*, for everything.

ABBREVIATIONS

AFDI	*Annuaire Français de Droit International*
AJIL	*American Journal of International Law*
Annuair e IDI	*Annuaire de l'Institut de Droit International*
ARSIWA	Articles on the Responsibility of States for Internationally Wrongful Acts
BYIL	*British Yearbook of International Law*
CAT	Convention Against Torture
CEDAW	Convention on the Elimination of Discrimination against Women
DARIO	Draft Articles on the Responsibility of International Organizations
ECHR	European Convention on Human Rights
ECtHR	European Court of Human Rights
EJIL	*European Journal of International Law*
GYIL	*German Yearbook of International Law*
HRC	Human Rights Committee
HRLR	*Human Rights Law Review*
IACtHR	Inter-American Court of Human Rights
ICJ	International Court of Justice
ICLQ	*International and Comparative Law Quarterly*
ICRC	International Committee of the Red Cross
ICSID	International Centre for Settlement of Investment Disputes
ILA	International Law Association
IJMCL	*International Journal of Marine and Coastal Law*
ILC	International Law Commission
ILC YB	*Yearbook of the International Law Commission*
ILM	*International Law Materials*
IJCL	*International Journal of Constitutional Law*
ITLOS	International Tribunal for the Law of the Sea
LJIL	*Leiden Journal of International Law*
MPEPIL	*Max Planck Encyclopedia of Public International Law*
NYU JILP	*New York University Journal of International Law and Politics*
RCADI	*Recueil des Course de l'Académie de Droit International de la Haye*
RGDIP	*Revue Général de Droit International Public*
RIAA	Report of International Arbitral Awards

UNCLOS	United Nations Convention on the Law of the Sea
UNTS	United Nations Treaty Series
VCDR	Vienna Convention on Diplomatic Relations
VCLT	Vienna Convention on the Law of Treaties
ZaöRV	*Zeitschrift für ausländisches öffentliches Recht und Völkerrecht*

Introduction

Already in 1981, Jean Combacau observed that '*[l]e droit international a besoin d'une théorie des obligations*'.[1] With this rather assertive remark, Combacau did not intend to argue that international law lacked studies on the foundations of obligations and the nature of international law as a *legal* system.[2] Rather, Combacau's statement derived from his critical investigation on the distinction between obligations of conduct and obligations of result provisionally adopted by the International Law Commission (ILC) in the work on the responsibility of states for internationally wrongful acts. Unsatisfied by how the ILC had construed the notions of obligations of conduct and obligations of result, Combacau contended that international lawyers needed to further elaborate '*concepts operatoires*' for adequately systematising international obligations based on their intrinsic and extrinsic modalities.[3]

1 'International law needs a theory of international obligations' (this author's translation), J. Combacau, 'Obligations de résultat et obligations de comportement: Quelques questions et pas de réponse', in *Le droit international: unité et diversité. Melanges offerts à Paul Reuter* (Paris: Pedone, 1981), 204.

2 This debate flourished during the nineteenth and the first part of the twentieth centuries, especially with the expansion of positivist schools. In a nutshell, the discussion revolved around those consent-based theories which deduced the legal nature of a rule from voluntariness and consent expressed by states and theories that placed the force of obligations outside the law, in moral or sociological bases. From this perspective, the debate on the legal nature of international obligations overlaps to a great extent with discussions over sources of international law. For an overview of the various theories and schools of thought see E. Roucounas, *A Landscape of Contemporary Theories of International Law* (Leiden: Brill, 2019), 293–8; R. Higgins, *Problems and Process: International Law and How We Use It* (Oxford: Clarendon Press, 1995), 13–16; R. Ago, 'Positive Law and International Law' (1957) 51 AJIL 691. A study that attempts to appraise all the elements making up the *bases* of obligations under international law is provided by O. Schachter, 'Toward a Theory of International Obligation' (1968) 8 *Virginia Journal of International Law* 300.

3 Combacau, 'Obligations de résultat et obligations de comportement', 204.

While studies comprehensively addressing the phenomenology of international obligations are still very few,[4] over the last thirty years, efforts toward conceptual systematisation have occurred in some areas of international law and with certain aspects of international obligations.[5] Usually, behind these dogmatic reconstructions lie two main purposes. On the one hand, systematising international obligations based on their

[4] In 2016, Pierre d'Argent gave a course at The Hague Academy of International Law on the various categories of international obligations from a phenomenological perspective, see for a brief account of the course Roucounas, *A Landscape of Contemporary Theories*, 297. Among the other works that have addressed the lack of conceptual studies on the externalities of international obligations and their categorisation M. Bennouna, 'Le droit international entre la lettre et l'esprit: Cours général de droit international public' (2017) 383 RCADI 91–110; A. Marchesi, *Obblighi di Condotta e obblighi di risultato: contributo allo studio degli obblighi internazionali* (Milan: Giuffré, 2005), 1–14; P. Reuter, 'Principes de droit international public' (1961) 103 RCADI 471–8.

[5] For example, in international human rights law doctrine, there has been an increasing interest in categorizing human rights obligations based on their object, content and scope, and modalities of operation. One of the first systematisations of obligations in the human rights framework regards the distinction between obligations to respect, obligations to protect, and obligations to fulfil, introduced by H. Shue, *Basic Rights: Subsistence, Affluence, and the US Foreign Policy* (Princeton: Princeton University Press, 1980), 52–3; S. Besson, 'Les obligations de protection de droit fondamentaux: un essai en dogmatique comparative' (2003) 1 *Revue de Droit Suisse* 49. More recently, much of the scholarly effort toward systematisation has focused on the distinction between negative and positive obligations and in particular on the scope of application of human rights positive obligations, see L. Lavrysen, *Human Rights in a Positive State: Rethinking the Relationship between Positive and Negative Obligations under the European Convention on Human Rights* (Cambridge: Intersentia, 2016), 1–347; D. Xenos, *The Positive Obligations of the State under the European Convention on Human Rights* (London: Routledge, 2012), 1–172; R. Pisillo-Mazzeschi, 'Responsabilité de l'état pour violation des obligations positives relatives aux droits de l'homme' (2008) 333 RCADI 175. At a more general level, theoretical studies on obligations and their externalities have mostly regarded elaborations and taxonomies of obligations developed by the ILC during its work on state responsibility; see A. De Vaucleroy, 'Les obligations de comportement en droit international public: Due diligence et responsabilité internationale', PhD thesis, Université catholique de Louvain (2021); Marchesi, *Obblighi di Condotta e obblighi di risultato*, 1–171; Marchesi, 'The Distinction Between Obligations of Conduct and Obligations of Result Following its Deletion from the Draft Articles on State Responsibility', in *Studi in onore di Gaetano Arangio-Ruiz* (Naples: Editoriale Scientifica, 2004), vol. 2, 827; C. Tams, *Enforcing Obligations* Erga Omnes *in International Law* (Cambridge: Cambridge University Press, 2005), 1–311; L. Sicilianos, 'The Classification of Obligations and the Multilateral Dimension of the Relations of International Responsibility' (2002) 13 EJIL 1127; M. Ragazzi, *The Concept of International Obligations* Erga Omnes (Oxford: Oxford University Press, 2000), 1–218. Other general studies which have addressed different legal aspects of obligations from a conceptual perspective include, C. Tomuschat, 'Obligations Arising for States without or against Their Will' (1993) 241 RCADI 209; T. Buergenthal, 'Self-Executing and Non-Self-Executing Treaties in National and International Law' (1992) 235 RCADI 315.

structure and modalities of operation may serve a fundamental descriptive role. Certain classifications are useful for scholars and interpreters, for they allow to clarify and better grasp the nature, the content, and the functioning of classes of primary rules. On the other hand, the purpose of classification may be normative. In this case, differentiating among typologies of international obligations is functional to ascribing to each category a different legal consequence.[6]

Among the typologies of international obligations that have recently attracted the attention of international lawyers are due diligence obligations.[7] On a highly general level, due diligence obligations are international obligations that acquire the 'due diligence' label because of the type of conduct they impose on their legal subject. Due diligence derives from the Romanistic concept of *diligentia* and describes a standard of care that a subject might deem reasonable or appropriate to take in a given circumstance.[8] Therefore, due diligence obligations are international obligations that impose a standard of behaviour normally identified as reasonable or appropriate in light of the circumstances. These obligations are recognisable almost in every area of international law and concern a wide range of states' activities.

Yet, the contours of due diligence obligations remain elusive. First, the very understanding of 'due diligence' as an *identifier* for a particular category of primary rules has been subject to much scholarly debate. As will be shown, due diligence was for a long time not conceived as a concept describing a modality of international obligations, but it was rather used as a synonym for the state's (lack of) negligence in the context of international responsibility.[9] Even after the adoption of the Articles on the Responsibility of States for Internationally Wrongful Acts (ARSIWA) – which systematised due diligence as a 'component' of certain primary rules – part of the doctrine has persisted to refrain from fully situating the concept within the theory of international obligations. Some scholars are still reluctant to identify 'due diligence obligations' or *obligations de due diligence* as a distinct typology of

[6] This is the case with many of the classifications of obligations devised by the ILC in the work on the Articles on the Responsibility of States for Internationally Wrongful Acts. These classifications ultimately serve the interpreter for the application of different legal rules. See Chapter 2.

[7] See note 13 for reference. This book adopts without distinction the terms 'due diligence obligations' and 'obligations of due diligence'.

[8] S. Valentine, R. Sprague, 'Due Diligence', in *Encyclopedia Britannica*, at www.britannica.com/topic/due-diligence. See also T. Koivurova, 'Due Diligence', MPEPIL para. 1.

[9] See Chapter 1.

international obligations and prefer to speak vaguely about the 'rule' or the 'standard' of due diligence, to underscore that the notion has no systemic function.[10]

Second, even accepting the idea of due diligence as a *qualifier* for a typology of primary rules, it is often argued that the nature and the operation of these obligations remain difficult to pin down from a theoretical standpoint. One issue is how to reconcile the category of due diligence obligations with other taxonomies of obligations and, in particular, the distinction between obligations of conduct, obligations of result, and obligations to prevent. The relationship between due diligence obligations and these categories is unclear and is often a source of confusion both in scholarship and international practice. Another problem concerns the flexibility and open-ended content of due diligence obligations. Because of their flexible nature and definite content, it is often asserted that due diligence obligations are 'weak and opaque' and have a limited reach.[11] Furthermore, due diligence obligations usually become 'concrete' only *ex post facto* and according to the circumstances of the case. This aspect may be invoked as a reason for degrading their normative value and downplaying their scope of operation in the international legal order. Finally, the idea that what is 'due' can only be defined contextually and looking at the content of the primary rule may have fostered the impression that due diligence obligations cannot be tackled from a broader perspective aimed at determining their contours a priori and in the abstract.[12]

[10] See for instance the ILA Study Group on Due Diligence in International Law, 'Due Diligence in International Law: Second Report' (Johannesburg, 2016), which uses various concepts to define due diligence, such as 'principle', 'standard of conduct', and, at times, 'obligation', refraining from speaking systematically of 'due diligence obligations'.

[11] A. Gattini, 'Breach of International Obligations', in A. Nollkaemper, I. Plakokefalos (eds.), *Principles of Shared Responsibility: An Appraisal of the State of the Art* (Cambridge: Cambridge University Press, 2014), 36; V. Stoyanova, 'Due Diligence versus Positive Obligations: Critical Reflections on the Council of Europe Convention on Violence Against Women', in J. Niemi, L. Peroni, V. Stoyanova (eds.), *International Law and Violence Against Women* (London: Routledge, 2020), 98; M. Kamminga, 'Due Diligence Mania: The Misguided Introduction of and Extraneous Concept into Human Rights Discourse' (2011) Maastricht Faculty of Law Working Paper No. 07, 6; T. Koivurova, 'What is the Principle of Due Diligence?', in J. Petman, J. Klabbers (eds.), *Nordic Cosmopolitanism: Essays in International Law for Martti Koskenniemi* (Leiden: Brill, 2003), 346, defining due diligence as a 'principle of equity'.

[12] ILA Study Group on Due Diligence, 'Second Report', 4; M. Fitzmaurice, 'Legitimacy of International Environmental Law' (2017) 77 ZaöRV 339, 364–5; V.P. Tzevelekos, 'Reconstructing the Effective Control Criterion in Extraterritorial Human Rights

The purpose of this book is to challenge these assumptions and to provide a conceptual understanding of the nature, scope, content, and operation of due diligence obligations in international law. The book wishes to demonstrate that a reconstruction of the dogmatic foundations of due diligence obligations serves both a cognitive and a normative function. It serves a cognitive role as it makes the understanding of due diligence obligations more accessible, by investigating how these obligations are operationalised in practice, and by overcoming critical arguments on their elusive nature. Yet, the book seeks also to demonstrate that a conceptual understanding of due diligence obligations plays a normative role: once obligations are construed as of due diligence, this bears consequences on international law.

I.1 Approach

Literature on due diligence in international law has grown exponentially over the past few years.[13] While the notion of due diligence first entered the international legal framework in the nineteenth century, it remained somewhat at the margin of the international legal discourse for a long time. Recently, however, scholars have rediscovered the concept, seeking to fully exploit its potential on the international plane. Arguably, the reason is twofold. On the one hand, international practice is increasingly

Breaches: Direct Attribution of Wrongfulness, Due Diligence and Concurrent Responsibility' (2014) 36 *Michigan Journal of International Law* 129, 153.

[13] Recent general studies on due diligence include: H. Krieger, A. Peters, L. Kreuzer (eds.), *Due Diligence in the International Legal Order* (Oxford: Oxford University Press, 2020); S. Besson, 'La Due Diligence en Droit International' (2020) 409 RCADI; S. Cassella (ed.), *Le standard de due diligence et la responsabilité internationale* (Paris: Pedone, 2018); N. McDonald, 'The Role of Due Diligence in International Law' (2019) 68 ICLQ 1041; J. Kulesza, *Due Diligence in International Law* (Leiden: Brill, 2016). For sectorial studies on due diligence, see among others: M. Longobardo, 'The Relevance of the Concept of Due Diligence for International Humanitarian Law' (2019) 37 *Wisconsin International Law Journal* 44; A. Berkes, 'The Standard of "Due Diligence" as a Result of Interchange between the Law of Armed Conflict and General International Law' (2018) 23 *Journal of Conflict and Security Law* 433; L. Chircop, 'A Due Diligence Standard of Attribution in Cyberspace' (2018) 67 ICLQ 643; L. Grans, 'The Concept of Due Diligence and the Positive Obligations to Prevent Honour-Related Violence: Beyond Deterrence' (2018) 22 *The International Journal of Human Rights* 733; J. Heieck, *A Duty to Prevent Genocide: Due Diligence Obligations Among the P5* (Northampton: Edward Elgar Publishing, 2018); R. Kolb, 'Reflections on Due Diligence and Cyberspace' (2015) 58 GYIL 113; R. Barnidge, *Non-state Actors and Terrorism: Applying the Law of State Responsibility and the Due Diligence Principle* (Berlin: Springer, 2008); C. Benninger-Budel (ed.), *Due Diligence and Its Application to Protect Women from Violence* (Leiden: Brill, 2008).

resorting to due diligence to construe the nature and content of certain obligations. International adjudicators have shed new light on the understanding of due diligence by pairing it with a wide range of international obligations across different areas of international law.[14] The ILC has relied on due diligence in some of its recent codification works,[15] and the concept is also permeating some international treaties.[16]

On the other hand, some structural changes underlying the international legal order have also promoted due diligence across international law. In particular, the 'rise' of due diligence has gone hand in hand with the appraisal of risk under international law.[17] Due diligence is indeed perceived as one of the fundamental legal tools to regulate, manage, and anticipate risks in international society. It has now become a truism to state that one of the principal functions of due diligence obligations is to prevent harms to other

[14] *Case Concerning Application of the Convention on the Prevention and Punishment of the Crime of Genocide (Bosnia Herzegovina* v. *Serbia and Montenegro)* (Merits) [2007] ICJ Rep 43, para. 430; *Case Concerning Pulp Mills on the River Uruguay (Argentina* v. *Uruguay)* (Merits) [2010] ICJ Rep 14, paras. 101, 186, 196, 204; *Certain Activities Carried Out by Nicaragua in the Border Area (Costa Rica* v. *Nicaragua)* [2015] ICJ Rep 665, *Construction of a Road in Costa Rica along the San Juan River (Nicaragua* v. *Costa Rica)* [2015] ICJ Rep 665, para. 153; *Responsibility and Obligations of States Sponsoring Persons and Entities with Respect to Activities in the Area (Request for an Advisory Opinion submitted to the Seabed Dispute Chamber)* ITLOS Reports 2011 paras. 117, 236; *Request for an Advisory Opinion submitted by the Sub-Regional Fisheries Commission (SRFC)* (Case No. 21) ITLOS Reports 2015 paras. 123–32, 210.

[15] Notably, due diligence was discussed in the ILC work on international liability for acts not prohibited by international law, which culminated in the ILC Draft articles on Prevention of Transboundary Harm from Hazardous Activities, with commentaries (2001) ILC YB II/2, in particular see Article 3; and in the ILC work on the non-navigational uses of international watercourse, which culminated in the ILC Draft Articles on the Law of the Non-navigational Uses of International Watercourses and commentaries thereto and resolution on transboundary confined groundwater (1994) ILC YB II/2, see Article 8. More recently, the commission has discussed due diligence in relation to the Draft Articles on the Protection of Persons in the Event of Disasters, with commentaries (2016) ILC YB II/2, see Article 9; and S. Murase, 'First Report on the Protection of the Atmosphere' (2014) ILC YB II/2 para. 51; S. Murase, 'Second Report on the Protection of the Atmosphere' (2015) ILC YB II/2 para. 56.

[16] Council of Europe Convention on Preventing and Combating Violence Against Women and Domestic Violence (adopted 11 May 2011, entered into force 1 August 2014) CETS No 210; Open-ended intergovernmental working group on business and human rights, Revised Draft of a Legally Binding Instrument to Regulate, in International Human Rights Law, the Activities of Transnational Corporations and other Business Enterprises, 16 July 2019.

[17] See for instance, S. Townley, 'The Rise of Risk in International Law' (2016) 18 *Chicago Journal of International Law* 594; M. Moïse Mbengue, *Essai sur une théorie du risqué en droit international public* (Paris: Pedone, 2009).

states,[18] to avoid or minimise risk to international public interests and global commons,[19] and to regulate the conduct of non-state actors when the latter may commit international harmful acts or carry out violations of international human rights law.[20]

Up until now, scholarly approaches to due diligence have been sector-specific, looking at due diligence as it plays out in a particular international legal area, and cross-sectorial. The latter has added a new perspective to the conceptualisation of due diligence in international law by assessing the potential of this notion in the realm of international responsibility[21] as an instrument for change in the international legal order[22] or as a principle of international law.[23] Yet, none of these general studies have tackled due diligence from the *dogmatic* perspective of obligations, treating it as a *concept operatoire* for identifying a specific category of international obligations. This book seeks to fill this gap.

The recognition that it is best to situate due diligence at the level of international obligations and examine it as an element of primary rules is not new. Riccardo Pisillo-Mazzeschi pioneered this idea in 1989 in his seminal work on due diligence in international law.[24] Prior to his study, due diligence had hardly been the object of independent examination; the concept mainly had been analysed with respect to the foundations of international responsibility and as a benchmark to assess state organs' fault in situations where the state had failed to prevent private individuals from infringing the rights of other states. Through a comprehensive

[18] *Corfu Channel (UK* v. *Albania)* (Merits) [1949] ICJ Rep 244, 22.

[19] *Responsibility and Obligations of States Sponsoring Persons and Entities with Respect to Activities in the Area*, para. 117.

[20] See for instance D. König, 'The Elaboration of Due Diligence Obligations as a Mechanism to Ensure Compliance with International Legal Obligations by Private Actors' in ITLOS (ed.), *The Contribution of the International Tribunal for the Law of the Sea to the Rule of Law: 1996–2016* (Leiden: Brill, 2018), 83; A. Seibert-Fohr, 'From Complicity to Due Diligence: When Do States Incur Responsibility for Their Involvement in Serious International Wrongdoing?' (2017) 60 GYIL 667; M. Hakimi, 'State Bystander Responsibility' (2010) 21 EJIL 341; C. Chinkin, 'A Critique of the Public/Private Dimension' (1999) 10 EJIL 387.

[21] S. Cassella, 'Le travaux de la Commission du droit international sur la responsabilité internationale et le standard de due diligence', in Cassella, *Le standard de due diligence*, 11.

[22] H. Krieger, A. Peters, L. Kreuzer (eds.), *Due Diligence in the International Legal Order* (Oxford: Oxford University Press, 2020), see in particular chapters 1 and 21.

[23] Kulesza, *Due Diligence*, 262–70.

[24] R. Pisillo-Mazzeschi, *Due diligence e responsabiitá internazionale degli stati* (Milan: Giuffré, 1989) and R. Pisillo-Mazzeschi, 'The Due Diligence Rule and the Nature of the International Responsibility of States' (1992) 35 GYIL 9, especially 41–50.

review of international practice on diplomatic protection of aliens and their property, the security of states, and international environmental law, Pisillo-Mazzeschi shifted the narrative arguing that due diligence was an element of certain international obligations and not a principle of international responsibility. Due diligence embodied an international standard of conduct applying only to certain international obligations, such as those to prevent certain harmful acts from coming to existence or obligations to punish or repress certain crimes.

The conceptualisation of due diligence as an element imbued in some international obligations is also supported by the ILC in ARSIWA.[25] The articles do not classify due diligence as a secondary rule, that is, a general condition for establishing the responsibility of a state for a wrongful act or omission. Rather, due diligence is described by the Commentary to the articles as a 'standard' that may or may not be incorporated in primary rules, that is, obligations that define the conduct of states in various areas of international law. In the words of the commission, whether due diligence is integrated into the fabric of international obligations 'is a matter for the interpretation and application of the primary rules engaged in the given case'.[26]

By interpreting due diligence as a marker for identifying a typology of international obligations, this book follows the approach of ARSIWA. Therefore, this study's overall theoretical framework for analysing due diligence is that of international obligations. The specifics of due diligence are not discussed in relation to the evolution of general rules of state responsibility, and the book does not wish to make a case for construing due diligence as an alternative ground of attribution of conduct when classical ILC rules of attribution do not fit contemporary challenges.[27] Throughout the book, ARSIWA rules are acknowledged as a given, and due diligence is not treated as a missing element of the ILC articles on international responsibility.

This does not mean that the book fails to acknowledge the close connection between due diligence and rules of international

[25] ILC Draft Articles on Responsibility of States for Internationally Wrongful Acts, with commentaries (2001) ILC YB II/2.

[26] Ibid. 34–5.

[27] On this specific aspect, see Chapter 4. Among the authors construing due diligence as a 'missing' secondary rules see for instance R. Mackenzie-Gray Scott, 'Due Diligence as a Secondary Rules of General International Law' (2021) 34 LJIL 1; Chircop, 'A Due Diligence Standard of Attribution in Cyberspace', 67; K. E. Boon, 'Are Control Tests Fit for the Future? The Slippage Problem in Attribution Doctrine' (2014) 15 *Melbourne Journal of International Law* 12.

responsibility. On the contrary, a study on the dogmatic foundations of due diligence obligations exposes the limits of a rigid conceptual separation between primary and secondary rules. It is well known that Special Rapporteur Ago introduced this distinction that eventually enabled the commission to continue with the study of the topic of state responsibility and complete the project. Before Ago, the work initiated by the ILC and by the first Special Rapporteur García-Amador did not envisage a real 'system' of state responsibility,[28] since problems related to the violation of an international obligation and its consequences were combined with substantive issues concerning the treatment of aliens.[29] Introducing a separation between primary and secondary rules allowed the ousting of questions concerning the content and definition of international obligations from issues regarding exclusively the establishment of an internationally wrongful act and its consequences, irrespective of the content of an international obligation.

While the distinction remains an important analytical tool, its significance should not be overstated. Scholarship acknowledges that the distinction does not rest on logical necessity, but is instead a functional device for singling out general propositions on international responsibility and for guiding the interpreter in determining whether a state is responsible or not.[30] In fact, the distinction between primary and secondary rules becomes slippery once it is recognised that the relationship between the two is often one of mutual influence and reciprocity. The scope and content of international obligations influence the application of secondary rules, inasmuch as one can determine whether a primary rule has been breached and what consequences follow in terms of responsibility only after examining the substance and structure of the rule in question. At the same time, secondary rules, especially those set

28 On the understanding of ARSIWA as a system, see M. Arcari, 'La responsabilité en droit international: un "systeme"?', in V. Tomkiewicz (ed.), *Organisation mondiale du commerce et responsabilité* (Paris: Pedone, 2014), 1.

29 See ILC YB (1967) II, 325–7; see also G. Gaja, 'Primary and Secondary Rules in the International Law on State Responsibility' (2014) 97 *Rivista di diritto internazionale* 981.

30 Gaja, 'Primary and Secondary Rules', 990–1; Arcari, 'La responsabilité en droit international', 16–18; A. Nollkaemper, D. Jacobs, 'Shared Responsibility in International Law: A Conceptual Framework' (2013) *Michigan Journal of International Law* 359, 410; E. David, 'Primary and Secondary Rules', in J. Crawford, A. Pellet, S. Olleson, K. Parlett (eds.), *The Law of International Responsibility* (Oxford: Oxford University Press, 2010), 27; U. Linderfalk, 'State Responsibility and the Primary-Secondary Rules Terminology: The Role of Language for an Understanding of the International Legal System' (2009) 78 *Nordic Journal of International Law* 53; J. Crawford, 'The ILC Articles on Responsibility of States for Internationally Wrongful Acts' (2002) 96 AJIL 874, 879.

out in Part I of ARSIWA, also affect the scope and understanding of primary rules; their application contributes indeed to determining the contours of international obligation whose breach amounts to an internationally wrongful act.[31]

The functional and mutual connection between primary and secondary rules is apparent in this study on due diligence. As it will be seen, to assess the functioning of due diligence obligations as a typology of primary rules one needs to construe them against the taxonomy of obligations of conduct, result, and prevention, developed in the course of ILC work on state responsibility. Similarly, one can comprehensively grasp the content and operation of due diligence obligations only when such appreciation occurs against relevant secondary rules and their scope of application.[32] Hence, the present study approaches due diligence from the perspective of primary obligations and not from that of state responsibility. However, all questions that concern the relationship between due diligence obligations and secondary rules are duly considered and critically revised.

I.2 This Study's Delimitation

Some further remarks on the methodology and scope of this book are necessary. To adequately profile the dogmatic foundations of due diligence obligations and to situate due diligence within the broader context of obligations and their theory, this book adopts a general perspective. In other words, the book draws its theoretical considerations by using an inductive method that builds on the interpretation and application of customary and treaty-based due diligence obligations in various international legal areas.[33] However, the book does so transversally and without engaging with the specificities of due diligence in each legal regime. This is reflected by the division of chapters, which build on the general phenomenological features of due diligence obligations and do not follow a *ratione materiae* approach.

[31] Gaja 'Primary and Secondary Rules', 984; Arcari, 'La responsabilité en droit international', 20.

[32] See Chapter 2 and Chapter 4.

[33] The research draws in particular on those legal areas where the international practice on due diligence is most developed, like the diplomatic protection of foreigners and their property, the security of states, international environmental law, international human rights law, international humanitarian law, and international investment law.

There are two reasons behind this choice. First, this study aims neither to map comprehensively the array of due diligence obligations across international law nor to account for how due diligence obligations operate when analysed at a micro level. In a monographic study, this would require at minimum a tremendous effort of hundreds of pages and a technical knowledge of each legal regime in which a due diligence obligation is discussed. Furthermore, recent collective works on due diligence have already performed this task, seeking to map out how due diligence acquires its relevance in each international legal area.[34]

Second, the choice of not discussing due diligence obligations across substantive regimes is driven by methodological premises and not just reasons of opportunity. When the analysis is comparative and builds on how primary rules of due diligence are operationalised in each legal area, the risk is always to give too much weight to particularism and to lose sight of the broader *fil rouge* that put these rules together. In the end, this may also generate the impression that the appraisal of due diligence in international law cannot really be tackled from the general perspective of *obligations* but needs always to be tested against the specificities of each (category of) primary rule(s). The purpose of designing a general study of due diligence obligations is precisely to argue against this assumption; this book seeks to demonstrate that, notwithstanding their own particularities, the dogmatic foundations and the operation of due diligence obligations are the same across international law.

Finally, the scope of the book is limited to due diligence obligations of states. In contemporary international law, due diligence has also acquired prominence in relation to international organisations' activities (IO) and non-state actors. As subjects equipped with international legal personality, international organisations are entrusted with rights and legal obligations, the violation of which may trigger their responsibility, as reflected by the Draft Articles on the Responsibility of International Organizations.[35] Although the extent to which certain primary rules bind international organisations remains unsettled and controversial, there is little dispute that where an IO does have an international obligation, this may be a due diligence one. From this viewpoint, many aspects addressed in this book about due diligence

[34] See in particular Krieger, Peters, Kreuzer, *Due Diligence in the International Legal Order* and Cassella, *Le standard de due diligence.*

[35] Draft Articles on the Responsibility of International Organizations (ARIO), (2011) ILC YB II/2.

obligations also apply to IOs. Specifically, general considerations that regard the nature of due diligence obligations and certain aspects of their content and scope can also be transposed to the framework of IOs.[36]

At the same time, many issues render the analysis of due diligence obligations of IOs *sui generis* with respect to states' obligations. For example, much of what this book argues about the scope of due diligence obligations builds on the concept of a state's power over the source of risk and a state's territorial control over risks emanating from its territory. It is contended that territorial control is the presumption of a state's power over the source of risk and, in this sense, the primary 'reason' for a state's duty to act with due diligence vis-à-vis certain risks. Not only is this territorial dimension absent in the case of IOs; when one deals with due diligence obligations of IOs, the very understanding of power of the source of risk must be appropriately tailored against the limited powers and functions of the organisation. Similarly, the evaluation of the content of IOs' due diligence obligations is strictly connected to questions regarding the competencies attributed to the organisation and the relationship between these competencies and member states.[37] A thorough analysis of these aspects would require broader theoretical considerations on the law of international organisations that are outside the scope of this study. Finally, one should add that it is not always clear whether the concept of due diligence as it applies to IOs refers only to a particular typology of obligations or to broader 'policies' that the organisation shall display in some of its internal functioning processes.[38]

[36] On how the conceptual understanding of due diligence obligations of states can be transposed to international organisations see *Request for an Advisory Opinion submitted by the Sub-Regional Fisheries Commission*. Approaching due diligence as an *unicum* and exploring its foundations both in relation to states and IOs see Besson, *La Due Diligence*, 167.

[37] For a critique on how the ITLOS drew an analogy between due diligence obligations of states and due diligence obligations of international organizations see E. Lagrange, 'La responsabilité des organisations internationales pour violation d'une obligation de diligence', in Cassella, *Le standard de due diligence*, 24; L. Gasbarri, 'The European Union is not a State: International Responsibility for Illegal, Unreported and Unregulated Fishing Activities' (2020) *Maritime Safety and Security Law Journal* 54; P. Palchetti, 'La violation par l'Union européenne d'une obligation de diligence', in Cassella, *Le standard de due diligence*, 150.

[38] See for instance E. Campbell, E. Dominic, S. Stadnik, Y. Wu, 'Due Diligence Obligations of International Organizations under International Law' (2018) 50 *New York University Journal of International Law and Politics* 541; H. P. Aust, 'The UN Human Rights Due Diligence Policy: An Effective Mechanism against Complicity of Peacekeeping Forces?'

There is an even stronger argument for leaving out of the present analysis the due diligence obligations of non-state actors. Some of the most recent general analyses of due diligence have indeed included in their appraisal of concept both obligations of states and IOs, and obligations of due diligence of non-state actors.[39] Due diligence obligations of non-state actors regard primarily the obligations that foreign investors hold vis-à-vis the investment done in the host state, and the human rights due diligence obligations of multinational corporations concerning corporate social responsibility. However, it is submitted that, in these contexts, due diligence does not hold the same meaning as states' due diligence obligations.

First, the very notion of *obligations* is subject to dispute: while in international investment law foreign investors may indeed have a duty to conduct due diligence,[40] in the context of corporate social responsibility, the idea that multinational corporations and business operators have human rights obligations, is still contested.[41] Second, and more fundamentally, when the term due diligence is used to define the conduct required by non-state actors, it usually refers to a *process* these actors shall undertake to identify, assess, and manage risks related to the investment or the activities. The concept of due diligence 'process' as opposed to due diligence 'obligations' is better clarified in the Chapter 1.

Due diligence as a *process* of risk management is not the target of this book, which is instead concerned with situating due diligence within the theory of international obligations. My perspective is that due diligence identifies a particular typology of international obligations, which are placed side by side with other categories, like obligations of result, obligations of conduct, and obligations to prevent. This also means that much of the theoretical framework behind this study is public international law obligations and state

(2014) *Journal of Conflict & Security Law* 61; this aspect is considered in Chapter 1, Section 1.4.

39 See A. Rajput, 'Due Diligence in International Investment Law', in Krieger, Peters, Kreuzer (eds.), *Due Diligence in the International Legal Order*, 279–84; ILA Study Group on Due Diligence, 'Second Report', 27–35.

40 A. Rajput, 'Due Diligence in International Investment Law', 27.

41 See the United Nations Human Rights Council, 'Guiding Principles on Business and Human Rights: Implementing the United Nations "Protect, Respect and Remedy" Framework' (2011) UN Doc. A/HRC/17/31; generally, A. Clapham, *Human Rights Obligations of Non-State Actors* (Oxford: Oxford University Press, 2006).

responsibility. For this reason, due diligence of non-state actors is outside the scope of this book.

I.3 Structure of the Book

This book aims to provide a conceptual understanding of due diligence obligations to understand how to operationalise them in practice and overcome common critiques on their elusive nature. As such, the book intends to demonstrate that the systematisation of due diligence obligations as a distinct typology of international obligations serves a unique cognitive and normative role since it allows better appraisal of public international law obligations and their functioning in the international legal order.

Chapter 1 sets the framework and explores the concept of due diligence under international law. The chapter retraces the history of due diligence from a notion emerging in the nineteenth century to assess the responsibility of states in connection with acts of private individuals to an element of primary rules. The purpose of this chapter is to reappraise the pedigree of due diligence and to clarify its meaning with respect to interrelated concepts, such as fault, international liability, and the notion of due diligence as a risk-management process. The chapter also addresses the question of due diligence as a principle of international law. It demonstrates that much of the difficulty of construing due diligence as a principle stems from the unsettled scope and function of general principles of international law and from the occasional confusing way in which international practice and scholarship refer to the 'principle of due diligence'. For this reason, the chapter argues that it is best to understand due diligence as a *qualifier* for a distinct typology of international obligations.

Chapter 2 discusses the nature of due diligence obligations and explores to which international obligations this notion attaches. The chapter places due diligence obligations within the broader taxonomy of obligations of conduct, result, and prevention as elaborated by the ILC in the work on state responsibility and subsequently interpreted by international practice. It is argued that using the taxonomy serves both a cognitive and a normative function; the taxonomy allows to grasp better the type of conduct that is expected by a state bound by a certain obligation and to make relevant normative considerations when the responsibility of a state for the breach of an obligation is at stake. After exploring the main structural features of due diligence obligations – which are identified in the concept of risk, in the 'conduct' nature of these obligations, and their flexible character – the chapter uses a deductive approach to map out the types of international obligations that carry the qualifying features of due diligence in their nature and content.

Chapter 3 explores the scope and content of due diligence obligations. The chapter contends that the scope of operation of a due diligence obligation depends on two essential conditions: a state's power over the source of risk linked to a due diligence rule and knowledge of the risk. The chapter thoroughly examines the different variations of power over the source of risk linked to due diligence. It distinguishes this concept from other similar abstractions, such as the notion of states' control or capacity to influence. The chapter demonstrates that a proper understanding of power over the source of risk is crucial, as it unveils the conceptual confusions that characterises in certain cases the application of due diligence obligations. The chapter then discusses the main legal and factual parameters that inform the content of due diligence obligations across international law.

Chapter 4 examines obligations of due diligence in the law of international responsibility. This chapter aims to discuss how an international wrongful act accrues from the violation of a due diligence obligation and its consequences. This chapter illustrates clearly that the relationship between primary and secondary rules is functional and not ontological in nature, and demonstrates why the category of due diligence obligations serves a normative role primarily in the realm of responsibility. One of the main problems addressed by the chapter is the relationship between due diligence obligations and Article 14(3) of ARSIWA. By retracing the genealogically of this article, the chapter argues that there is room to critically reappraise the commission's final choice and depart from the understanding that the breach of preventive obligations necessarily requires the event to occur.

Finally, Chapter 5 deals with the phenomenon of 'proceduralisation' of due diligence obligations. The chapter argues that in different areas of international law, due diligence obligations are operationalised through the progressive objectification of their flexible content into a series of procedural, substantive duties or technical standards. The chapter critically explores this phenomenon and touches upon the potentials and perils of solidifying the substance of due diligence obligations through the practice of international courts, tribunals, and technical bodies. In line with this book's underlying theme, this chapter explores the effect that proceduralisation bears on the nature and content of due diligence obligations. Drawing on two case studies, the chapter argues that proceduralisation tests the dogmatic structure of due diligence obligations and fundamentally affects some of their conceptual traits.

1

The Foundations of Due Diligence in International Law

Introduction

A book on due diligence obligations must first clarify what due diligence is under international law. Therefore, this chapter addresses the meta-question and settles the premises of this study in order to situate the notion of due diligence within the theory of international obligations. Due diligence has a long history in international law. The concept entered the international legal discourse by analogy with Roman law and the notion of *diligentia*, which described a behaviour qualified for excluding fault (*culpa*) and, consequently, responsibility.[1] The genealogy of due diligence in international law is therefore intimately linked to continental European legal traditions, which have played a great role in shaping and influencing the understanding of this concept at the international legal level as well.

In the practice of states, due diligence first emerged in the nineteenth and twentieth centuries in relation to the duty of state neutrality in maritime and land wars and the international protection of aliens and their property. In these areas, due diligence developed as a legal standard for evaluating state conduct in connection with certain international obligations. In scholarly writings, however, due diligence did not find autonomous evaluation for a long time.[2] Being invoked primarily as a benchmark for assessing state responsibility in connection with acts of private individuals, due diligence coalesced with broader theoretical questions on the nature and the foundations of state responsibility under international law. Even during the work of the International Law

[1] C. Maiorca, 'Colpa (teoria generale)', in *Enciclopedia del diritto* (Milan: Giuffré, 1960), 517–23.

[2] G. Bartolini, 'The Historical Roots of the Due Diligence Standard', in H. Krieger, A. Peters, L. Kreuzer (eds.), *Due Diligence in the International Legal Order* (Oxford: Oxford University Press, 2020), 23; J. A. Hessbruegge, 'The Historical Doctrine of Attribution and Due Diligence in International Law' (2004) 36 NYU JILP 265.

Commission (ILC) on state responsibility, which spanned almost fifty years, the commission steered clear of addressing the topic of due diligence, mostly in order to avoid critical questions on the relationship between this concept and the role of fault in international responsibility.

After the adoption of the 2001 ILC Articles on the Responsibility of States for Internationally Wrongful Acts (ARSIWA)[3] and the 2001 draft Articles on Prevention of Transboundary Harm from Hazardous Activities,[4] the conceptualisation of due diligence in international law has fundamentally changed. Both international instruments have situated due diligence at the level of primary rules, leading most scholars to acknowledge that due diligence is best understood as a component of international obligations and not a principle of international responsibility. The crystallisation of due diligence at the level of primary rules has further contributed to the migration of the concept across various areas of international law. Due diligence is now a reference notion for a wide range of international obligations in different legal areas and international courts, and tribunals and treaty bodies increasingly resort to it as a tool for operationalising primary rules. This 'propagation' of the due diligence language across various fields has led scholarship to enquire whether due diligence is a general principle of law and what function it serves in the contemporary international legal order.

This chapter traces the genealogy of due diligence and lays out its foundations in international law. This preliminary discussion functions in order to clarify the relationship between due diligence and relevant legal concepts with which the notion has traditionally been associated, such as fault, international liability, and principles of international law. Furthermore, the chapter sets the groundwork for the rest of the book and for building a theory of due diligence obligations in international law.

1.1 The Origins of Due Diligence

This section provides a short review of the origins of due diligence in international law. Due diligence is first analysed as it entered the international practice of states between the nineteenth and twentieth centuries. At that point, arbitral tribunals and claim commissions usually

[3] ILC Draft Articles on Responsibility of States for Internationally Wrongful Acts, with commentaries (2001) ILC YB II/2.

[4] ILC Draft Articles on Prevention of Transboundary Harm from Hazardous Activities, with commentaries (2001) ILC YB II/2.

resorted to due diligence to indicate the standard of conduct expected of states in the performance of their international obligations. Accordingly, Section 1.1.1 focuses on the two areas in which due diligence was mostly applied – a state's duty of neutrality in times of war and the protection of foreigners and their property.[5] If, in international practice, due diligence developed as an element of states' international obligations,[6] considerations on due diligence overlapped with broader discussions on the role of fault in international responsibility in the doctrine addressing the rudiments of international responsibility. The conceptual underpinnings of 'the duty to act with due diligence' and its corollary, 'responsibility for failure to use due diligence', rest in fact on early understandings of states' responsibility and, specifically, on the connection between state responsibility and acts of private individuals.

1.1.1 Due Diligence in the Early Practice of States

I Due Diligence and the Operation of Neutrality

Due diligence first appeared in international law in the context of neutrality in relation to the duties incumbent on a neutral state. Over the course of the nineteenth century, a rule emerged in international law whereby neutrality implied a duty of the neutral state to prevent its subjects from rendering aid or supplying arms and ammunitions to belligerent states.[7] One of the earliest examples of this duty can be found in the Alabama arbitration case. In England in 1862, a vessel built for war and supplied with guns and ammunition (called the *Alabama*) was sold to the Confederates during the American Civil War. After the war, the United States complained to Great Britain that it had suffered damages to its merchant marine from operations carried out by the *Alabama* and other vessels built in England. As a result of the dispute between the United States and Great Britain, in 1871, the parties signed the Treaty of Washington, which was a bilateral agreement aimed

[5] See Bartolini, 'The Historical Roots', 26–33.

[6] Extensively R. Pisillo-Mazzeschi, 'The Due Diligence Rule and the Nature of the International Responsibility of States' (1992) 35 GYIL 9; R. Pisillo-Mazzeschi, *Due diligence e responsabiitá internazionale degli stati* (Milan: Giuffré, 1989).

[7] See L. B. Hautefeuille, *Des droits et des devoirs des nations neutres en temps de guerre maritime*, vol. I (Paris: Guillaumin et C, Libraires, 1858), 241, 256, 269–70; L. Oppenheim, *International Law: A Treatise*, vol. II, *War and Neutrality* (London: Longmans, Green, 1912), 405–6; J. Westlake, *International Law*, Part II, *War* (Cambridge: Cambridge University Press, 1913), 214–21.

at guiding the arbitral judges in their decision. The Treaty of Washington provided for special obligations of the neutral state:

> *Firstly.* To use due diligence to prevent the fitting out, arming, or equipping within its jurisdiction, of any vessel which it has reasonable ground to believe is intended to cruise or carry on war against a Power with which it is at peace, and to use like diligence to prevent the departure from its jurisdiction of any vessel intended to cruise or carry on war as above.
>
> . . .
>
> *Thirdly.* To exercise due diligence in its waters, and as to all persons within its jurisdiction, to prevent any violation of the foregoing obligations and duties.[8]

During the arbitration dispute the parties gave different interpretations of what it would mean for a state to act with due diligence. Great Britain argued that a neutral state was only bound to exercise a reasonable degree of diligence corresponding to the efforts that a government typically provides in relation to its own domestic affairs.[9] The United States offered a more stringent definition of the concept, arguing that a neutral state had to provide a level of diligence proportional to the size of the interests of the conflicting party.[10] Eventually, the tribunal opted for the second interpretation and found Great Britain responsible for violating its obligations as a neutral power.[11]

Because of the disagreement over the meaning of 'acting with due diligence', the decision sparked criticism.[12] For example, Judge Cockburn, the British arbitrator in the case, questioned the interpretation of due diligence given by the majority of the tribunal and rejected the idea that the latter could find support in principles of international law and international jurisprudence.[13] The Alabama case was nonetheless crucial for recognising that a state's duty to prevent its subjects from aiding or assisting belligerent states entailed the exercise of some positive actions

[8] J. B. Moore, *History and Digest of the International Arbitrations to which the United States Has Been a Party* (Washington, DC: US Government Printing Office, 1943), vol. 1, 550; for a background, see T. Bingham, 'The Alabama Claims Arbitration' (2005) 54 ICLQ 1; A. Ouedraogu, 'La neutralité et l'emergence du concept de due diligence en droit international: l'affaire de l'Alabama revisité' (2011) 13 *Journal of the History of International Law* 307.

[9] Moore, *History and Digest*, 610–11.

[10] Ibid. 572–3.

[11] Ibid. 655–66.

[12] Oppenheim, *International Law*, 408–9; W. B. Lawrence, 'Opinion exprimé sur les Trois Règles de Washington' (1974) *Revue de Droit International et de Législation Comparée* 570, at 574.

[13] Moore, *History and Digest*, 660.

on the neutral state, including the exercise of vigilance over its territory and the adoption of measures to prevent harmful occurrences. In 1875, shortly after Alabama, the Institut de Droit International codified the obligations required of neutral states, noting that '*l'Etat neutre est tenu de veiller à ce que d'autres personnes ne mettent des vaisseaux de guerre à la disposition d'aucun des Etats belligérants, dans se ports ou dans les parties de mer qui dépendent de sa juridiction*'.[14] More significantly, the Hague Convention on the Rights and Duties of Neutral Powers in Naval War, adopted in 1907, contained a number of articles specifying the positive duties of neutral states in maritime war. Article 8, for example, affirmed that a neutral state shall 'employ the means at its disposal' to prevent the fitting out or arming of any vessel within its jurisdiction to be used against a belligerent state, and 'to display the same vigilance to prevent the departure from its jurisdiction of any vessel intended to cruise, or engage in hostile operations, which had been adapted entirely or partly within the said jurisdiction for use in war'.[15] Article 25 required a neutral state 'to exercise such surveillance as the means at its disposal allow' to prevent the violation of the articles of the convention prescribing the duties of the neutral power in ports or in its waters. Similarly, Article 26 of the 1928 Havana Convention on Maritime Neutrality provided that neutral states are bound 'to exert all the vigilance within their power' to prevent a violation in their ports or territorial waters of the rights set in the convention.

The idea that states must prevent the use of their territory for activities detrimental to other states did not remain confined to the issue of neutrality in maritime wars. International courts and mixed claims tribunals started to recognise that states had to diligently act to prevent raids,[16] conspiracies,[17] and acts of hostile propaganda[18] carried out by private individuals that were harmful to the sovereignty of other states.

[14] 'A neutral state shall ensure that persons do not provide military vessels to belligerent states within the ports or at sea in areas under the state's jurisdiction' (this author's translation), *Annuaire de l'Institut de Droit International*, 1877, 139.

[15] Convention (IV) respecting the Laws and Customs of War on Land and its annex: Regulations concerning the Laws and Customs of War on Land (adopted 19 October 1907, entered into force 26 January 1910) 205 CTS 299.

[16] W. E. Hall, *A Treatise on International Law* (Oxford: Oxford University Press, 1924), 77–8.

[17] P. Fauchille, *Traité de Droit International Public* (Paris: Rousseau & C, 1922), vol. 1, 245–56.

[18] P. Pradier-Fodéré, *Traité de Droit International Public Européen et Américain* (Paris: Pedone, 1885–1906), vol. 1, paras. 238–60.

For example, in 1887, in a case involving the counterfeiting of notes of a foreign bank and the possible wrongful act of a state that fails to punish this criminal act, the United States Supreme Court affirmed that the 'law of nations requires every national government to use "due diligence" to prevent a wrong being done within its dominion to another nation with which it is at peace'.[19] At the international level, in a 1908 case decided by the Central American Court of Justice involving hostile acts by foreigners in Honduras during the civil revolution, the court held that the mere fact of prejudice to the interests of a sovereign state is not sufficient for state responsibility to arise; rather, it must be proved that the conduct of the state was negligent.

Soon, it became generally acknowledged that states' sovereignty entails a corollary duty of states to protect within their territory the rights of other states.[20] Yet, this obligation does not impose an absolute duty to prevent all acts injurious to other states; it only requires the state to enact measures reasonably sufficient to prevent hostile acts or to punish them after they have occurred.[21] In 1928, in the well-known Lotus case, Judge Moore branded as 'well-settled' the principle that 'a State is bound to use due diligence to prevent the commission within its dominion of criminal acts against another nation or its people'.[22]

II The Protection of Aliens and Their Property

In addition to the neutrality arena, early international practice on due diligence developed in the context of the protection of aliens and their property. In the eighteenth century, Emmeric de Vattel wrote that 'the sovereign ought not to grant an entrance into his state for the purpose of drawing foreigners into a snare: as soon as he admits them, he engages to protect them as his own subject and to afford them perfect security, as far as depends on him'.[23] This idea progressively developed into recognising a customary obligation of states to afford protection to foreigners and

19 *United States* v. *Arjona* 120 US 479, 484 (1887). At the international level see the *Dickens's* case mentioned in Moore, *History and Digest*, vol. 3, 3037–8.

20 *Island of Palmas (Netherlands* v. *United States of America)* (1928) 2 RIAA 839.

21 C. Calvo, *Le droit international theorique et pratique* (Paris: Nabu Press, 1923), 425–6; H. Lauterpacht, 'Revolutionary Activities by Private Persons Against Foreign States' (1928) 22 AJIL 105, at 126–9.

22 *The Case of the S.S. "Lotus" (France* v. *Turkey)* PCIJ Rep Series A No 10 88.

23 E. de Vattel, *The Law of Nations, Or, Principles of the Law of Nature, Applied to the Conduct and Affairs of Nations and Sovereigns, Book II*, edited by B. Kapossy, R. Whatmore (first published 1758, Indianapolis: Liberty Fund, 2008), 313.

their property from injurious acts taking place within their territorial jurisdiction.[24]

As with the law of neutrality, due diligence emerged as an '*élément limitative*'[25] of the responsibility of states for injuries caused to foreigners and their property. Judicial practice at the end of the nineteenth century and the beginning of the twentieth century consistently referred to due diligence as the threshold for measuring the level of effort required by states to fulfil their obligations to protect. Arbitral tribunals and mixed claims commissions recognised that in the event of injuries to aliens caused by private individuals, states could be responsible for their failure to show due diligence in affording adequate protection to aliens or punishing the offenders. What distinguishes the international practice in this area and makes it richer than the practice related to the duties of neutrality is that judicial authorities assumed a creative normative function vis-à-vis due diligence. In fact, they not only consistently referred to due diligence as a standard to measure state responsibility for failure to protect or punish, but they also progressively contributed to the emergence of the international legal understanding of the duty to act with due diligence.

Practitioners usually interpreted states' responsibility to prevent injuries to foreigners as a twofold obligation comprised of the duty to prevent injury to aliens and their property in a state's territory and a state's duty to apprehend and punish those responsible for harmful acts against foreigners. As for the duty to prevent, it came to be interpreted as a state's duty to furnish adequate legislative, administrative, and judicial machinery to protect the alien against harmful acts, and the state's duty to use that apparatus effectively.[26] Particularly with regard to the latter, judicial decisions would often resort to the standard of due diligence for measuring state responsibility. For example, in a case brought before the American-Turkish Claims Commission, the commission affirmed that 'a government is not responsible for injuries caused by private persons to aliens, unless it is shown ... that the authorities failed to take reasonable care to prevent such injuries'.[27] In the Wipperman case,

[24] C. Eagleton, *Responsibility of States in International Law* (New York: New York University Press, 1928), 80.

[25] P. A. Zannas, *La responsabilité internationale des Etats pour les actes de négligence* (Montreaux: Ganguin & Laubscher, 1952), 54.

[26] *Affaire des biens Britanniques au Maroc Espagnol (Spain* v. *United Kingdom)* (1923) 2 RIAA 615; *Walter A. Noyes (United States* v. *Panama)* (1933) 6 RIAA 308.

[27] F. K. Nielsen, *American-Turkish Claims Settlement under the Agreement of December 24, 1923, and Supplemental Agreements Between the United States and Turkey, Opinions and Reports* (Washington: US Government Printing Office, 1937), 391.

which concerned the violation of the customary obligation to protect foreign representatives of states and diplomats, a mixed claim commission similarly stressed that state responsibility is excluded 'as long as reasonable diligence is used in attempting to prevent the occurrence or recurrence of such wrongs'.[28] Similar conclusions can be found in cases ranging from injuries to aliens caused by private individuals during episodes of mob violence or civil unrest,[29] to cases in which the state's failure to exercise due diligence manifested in relation to injuries carried out by rebels or revolutionary armed groups.[30]

The obligation of states to apprehend and prosecute the perpetrators of crimes committed against foreigners and their property was also understood as an obligation of due diligence. Accordingly, in a case involving the killing of two American citizens in Mexico by a group of individuals, the mixed claims commission appointed to decide the case stressed Mexico's lack of diligence in pursuing and apprehending the culprits.[31] In the same vein, the United States–Venezuelan Claims Commission affirmed that a state's responsibility in failing to protect foreigners is 'to be determined and measured by . . . [the state's] conduct in ascertaining and bringing to justice the guilty parties'. If the state 'did all that could be reasonably required in that behalf she [the state] is to be held blameless'.[32] However, not every scholar interpreted the obligation to prosecute and punish as a duty of due diligence. Some preferred distinguishing between the authorities' duty to apprehend the culprit, subject to the due diligence rule, and the duty of the judicial apparatus to prosecute and punish the responsible party, not subject to the due diligence rule, which violation amounted to a denial of justice, not a lack of due diligence.[33] Their main argument rested on the idea that while the duty to apprehend is a best-effort obligation, the duty to subject

[28] Moore, *History and Digest*, vol. 3, 3039.

[29] *Thomas H. Youmas (United States* v. *United Mexican States)* (1926) 4 RIAA 110; *Noyes* case, 308.

[30] *Sambiaggio (Italy* v. *Venezuela)* (1903) 10 RIAA 499; *Home Insurance Company (United States* v. *United Mexican States)* (1926) 4 RIAA 58.

[31] *Laura M. B. Janes et al. (United States* v. *United Mexican States)* (1926) 4 RIAA 87; *John D. Chase (United States* v. *United Mexican States)* (1928) 4 RIAA 337; *Sewell (United States* v. *United Mexican States)* (1930) 4 RIAA 626.

[32] Moore, *History and Digest*, vol. 3, 2968.

[33] Zannas, *La responsabilité internationale*, 62–3; see also the 'Draft Convention and Comments on the Responsibility of States for Injuries to Aliens and Their Territory' (1929) 23 AJIL Supplement 132, prepared by the Harvard Law School.

the offender to a foreign trial is a required duty to be enforced by the state with no margin of appreciation.

The rich international practice developed between the nineteenth and twentieth centuries constituted the basis for the discussion submitted by the Preparatory Committee for the 1930 Hague Conference for the Codification of the Responsibility of States for Damages Caused in their Territory to the Person or Property of Foreigners. The League of Nations organised the Committee in 1924 to prepare bases for discussion concerning state responsibility arising out of acts committed by private individuals that damaged foreigners or their property.[34] The document crystallised the link between due diligence and the obligation to protect foreigners and their property. For example, Basis for Discussion Number 17 provided: 'a State is responsible for damage caused by a private individual to the person or property of a foreigner if it has failed to show . . . such diligence as, having regard to the circumstances . . . could be expected from a civilized State'. In a similar fashion, Basis for Discussion Number 18 indicated international responsibility for a state's failure 'to show such diligence in detecting and punishing the author of damage, as having regard to the circumstances, could be expected from a civilized State'.

Early practice regarding the protection of aliens and their property was also instrumental in developing the contours of the due diligence standard and identifying the key factors that influenced its application. With few exceptions, most judicial decisions started to acknowledge that the level of due diligence required of a state in protecting foreigners corresponded to an international standard of conduct[35] and not to the *diligentia quam suis* that a state normally exercises in its internal affairs.[36] Furthermore, the idea clearly emerged in many decisions that the degree of effort to fulfil the due diligence standard should be connected to the notion of reasonableness. The interpretation of what is 'reasonable', however, varied depending on the case. Some decisions pointed to the substance of states' duties, engaging responsibility whenever the state had not exercised 'reasonable care' in the circumstances.[37] Others referenced

[34] For an account of the works of the committee, see H. Hackworth, 'Responsibility of States for Damages Caused in Their Territory to the Person or Property of Foreigners' (1930) 24 AJIL 500.

[35] *H. G. Venable (United States* v. *United Mexican States)* (1927) 4 RIAA 219; *L. F. H. Neer (United States* v. *United Mexican States)* (1926) 4 RIAA 60.

[36] Contrary, *Affaire des biens Britanniques au Maroc Espagnol*, 644.

[37] Nielsen, *American-Turkish Claims Settlement*, 391.

reasonableness in relation to the possibility of a state's foreseeing potential violations and reacting promptly.[38] Others construed state responsibility based on the authorities' failure to fulfil the international standard 'that every *reasonable* and impartial man would readily recognize its insufficiency'.[39] Finally, the practice on the protection of aliens and their property also contributed to the foundation for the identification of the elements influencing the standard of due diligence. In many decisions, the possibility of finding state responsibility ultimately depended on 'the particular circumstances of the case',[40] the assessment of the interests to be protected,[41] as well as the evaluation of the level of control exercised by the state in its territory.[42]

1.1.2 Due Diligence in the Early Doctrine of International Law

Although international practice started to refer to due diligence only from the late nineteenth century, the root of the concept can be traced to the writings of the founders of international law. It is useful to briefly review their theories to better understand why classical doctrinal debates on due diligence from the twentieth century onwards revolved mostly around the nature of international responsibility. Furthermore, such analysis is instrumental to illustrating how early doctrine failed to properly distinguish between state responsibility for due diligence and responsibility for being complicit in a crime.

For a long time, international responsibility was not treated as a separate legal category in international legal doctrine. Scholars mostly discussed substantial fields of international law such as the law of war, the law of the sea, and the law of diplomatic relationships, and treated questions of responsibility incidentally and mostly in a fragmented fashion.[43] Moreover, the concept of responsibility originally developed

[38] Moore, *History and Digest*, vol. 3, 3041.

[39] *Venable* case, 229 (emphasis added).

[40] See *Negrete* case in Moore, *History and Digest*, vol. 6, 962.

[41] *William E. Chapman (United States* v. *United Mexican States)* (1930) 4 RIAA 634.

[42] *The Globe Cotton Oil Mills (United States* v. *United Mexican States)* (1926) 4 RIAA 15.

[43] Authors such as Alberico Gentili and Pierino Belli and later Grotius touched on the issue fragmentedly, mostly in relation to the responsibility of the sovereign for acts of its citizens and for wrongs committed against ambassadors; P. Belli, *De Re Militari et Bello Tractactus* [A Treatise on Military Matters and Warfare], trans. by H. C. Nutting, *The Classics of International Law* (first published 1563, Oxford: Clarendon Press, 1936), 296–8; A. Gentili, *De Legationibus Libri Tres* [Three Books on Embassies], vol. II, trans. By J. Laing, *The Classics of International Law* (first published 1612, Oxford: Clarendon Press,

by these writers hindered a neat distinction between the state and individuals. International wrongful acts were not conceptualised as a form of states' wrongful conduct separate from the acts of individuals; the responsibility of the sovereign for a crime overlapped greatly with that of its nationals. It was only at the beginning of the twentieth century, thanks in particular to the writings of Heinrich Triepel and Dionisio Anzilotti, that the treatment of international responsibility as a legal concept emerged, and with that, the idea that responsibility requires conduct in violation of a rule of international law and attributable to the state.[44]

Alberico Gentili's writings demonstrate that in the course of the seventeenth century, the division between the private realm and the public sphere in which the corpus of the sovereign's activities is conveyed was still quite blurred. At some point in the *De Jure Belli*, Gentili theorised that, in principle, only acts of the sovereign could justify war, while acts of private individuals could not be charged against the community unless the sovereign had knowledge of the act and failed to prevent it. Later in his writing, however, Gentili argued that grounds for a war could still exist 'in instances in which a private individual has done wrong and his sovereign or nation has failed to atone for his fault'.[45] This proves that although Gentili already had conceived some form of separation between acts of the sovereign and individuals' crimes, the principle of non-attribution of private acts was still embryonic, for the sovereign's failure to repair the individual's crime could still give rise to an international response.

A more systematic approach to the question of international responsibility is found in the works of Hugo Grotius. Grotius applied the principles of Roman law that construed responsibility based on fault to the

1924), 72–6; H. Grotius, *De Jure Belli ac Pacis Libri Tres* [A Treatise on War and Peace], trans. by F. W. Kelsey, *The Classics of International Law* (first published 1625, Oxford: Clarendon Press 1925), vol. 2, chapter 21, para 2. See also J. Crawford, T. Grant and F. Messineo, 'Toward an International Law of Responsibility: Early Doctrine', in L. Boisson de Chazournes and M. Kohen (eds.), *International Law and the Quest of its Implementation: Liber Amicorum Vera Gowlland-Debbas* (Leiden: Brill, 2010), 377.

44 E. Triepel, *Völkerrecht und landesrecht*, trans. by R. Brunet, *Droit international et droit interne* (first published 1899, Oxford: Pedone, 1920), 325–30; D. Anzilotti, *Teoria generale della responsabilità dello Stato nel diritto internazionale*, Part I (Florence: Lumachi Libraio Editore, 1902), 102–57; Anzilotti, 'La responsabilité internationale des Etats à raison des dommages soufferts par des étrangers' (1906) 13 *Revue Générale de Droit International Public* 5.

45 Gentili, *De Legationibus*, 99.

international framework, focusing on the notion of *culpa* (or *dolus*) as a fundamental premise for the accountability of the sovereign. For Grotius, the responsibility of the sovereign derived from its failure to perform the duty to take all necessary measures to prevent an individual's crime and to arrest and punish the culprit. Distinguishing between *patientia* and *receptus*, Grotius affirmed that the sovereign is responsible under the principle of *patientia* when it knows one of its citizens plans to commit a crime but fails to prevent it.[46] Under the concept of *receptus*, the sovereign is responsible if it fails to punish or extradite the offenders or if the sovereign offers them refuge in its realm.[47] Accordingly,

> [T]o participate in a crime a person must not only have knowledge of it but also have the opportunity to prevent it. This is what the laws mean when they say that knowledge, when its punishment is ordained, is taken in the sense of toleration, so that he may be held responsible who was able to prevent a crime but did not do so.

Grotius's argument on fault played a pivotal role in shaping rules of state responsibility for acts carried out by private subjects. By limiting responsibility to situations of failure to prevent or repress a crime, Grotius moved away from previous collective and natural law concepts postulating absolute liability as the moral and legal consequence of a sovereign's duty to exercise territorial sovereignty and maintain peace and order.[48] On the contrary, a sovereign (and later, the state) would be responsible for its own omissions and not for the acts of private individuals.

Vattel further elaborated on the idea of international responsibility flowing from a failure to prevent or to punish. He argued that to allow a citizen to injure a foreign state would violate the right of independence of that state and the principle of natural law. However, he acknowledged that a state cannot regulate and control the acts of its subjects at all times and thus cannot be held responsible for every crime committed by them. Accordingly, in Vattel's opinion, responsibility can only arise if the state 'who has the power to see that his subjects act in a just manner permits them to injure a foreign nation, either the state itself or its citizens', since the state in such cases 'does no less wrong to that nation than if he injured himself'.[49] The same applied in cases of failure to punish the act of

[46] Grotius, *De Jure Belli ac Pacis*, vol. 2, para. 2.
[47] Ibid.
[48] See M. R. Garcìa Mora, *International Responsibility for Hostile Acts of Private Persons Against Foreign States* (Leiden: Martinus Nijhoff, 1962), 18.
[49] de Vattel, *Völkerrecht und landesrecht*, 72.

individuals, for 'a sovereign who refuses to repair the evil done by one of his subjects, or to punish the criminal or, finally, to deliver him up, makes himself in a way an accessory to the deed and becomes responsible for it'.[50]

Vattel's appreciation of state responsibility highlights the lack of a conceptual separation between state responsibility for participating in a crime and responsibility for merely knowing about and failing to prevent a crime. In the following passage of *The Law of Nations*, Vattel clarifies that '[i]f the nation, or its ruler, approve or ratify the act of the citizen, it takes upon itself the act, and may then be regarded by the injured party as the *real author* of the affront of which the citizen was perhaps only the instrument'.[51] The overlap between complicity and what would subsequently become known as due diligence was also reflected in later scholarship. Authors writing at the beginning of the twentieth century still conflated the case of a state that positively condones or supports the commission of a wrong by a private individual with state 'bystander' responsibility, which occurred when the state had or should have had knowledge of the crime and failed to diligently act to prevent it. In their minds, failure to prevent the crime by mere toleration amounted to implied complicity of the state. For instance, Edwin Borchard acknowledged that in the context of international responsibility, private acts are not in principle attributable to the state. However, he argued that in cases of wrongs committed by private subjects, a state could be responsible through

> manifestations of the *actual or implied complicity* of the government in the act, before or after it either by [the state] directly ratifying or approving the act, or by an implied, tacit or constructive approval in the *negligent failure to prevent the injury*, or to investigate the case, or to punish the guilty individual, or to enable the victim to pursue his civil remedies against the offender.[52]

Similarly, William Hall affirmed that when a state fails to punish the perpetrators of a wrong it becomes complicit in the crime. In cases of injuries committed by private individuals, although the connection between the individuals and the state is weaker than with its organs or

50 Ibid.

51 Ibid.

52 E. M. Borchard, *The Diplomatic Protection of Citizens Abroad* (New York: The Banks Law Publishing Company, 1915), 213 (emphasis added).

agents, responsibility can ensue from the state's failure to perform its general duty to exert control within its territory:

> [A state] can only therefore be held responsible for such of them [private acts] as it may reasonably be expected to have knowledge of and to prevent. If the acts done are undistinguishably open or of common notoriety, the state, when they are of sufficient importance, is obviously responsible for not using proper means to repress them; if they are eventually concealed or if for sufficient reason the state has failed to repress them, it has obviously become responsible, *by way of complicity* after the act, if its government does not inflict punishment to the extent of its legal powers.[53]

Hall's argument slightly differs from Borchard's. Hall recognises that a state's failure to exert control over its territory and prevent a crime would trigger responsibility, but classifies as a state's complicity only the refusal to punish the offender. In Halls' line of thinking, the state's failure to inflict punishment on the perpetrators of a crime is a more serious crime than failure to prevent, since it amounts to an act of the state's condonation of the private act. Some international cases of that time also reflected this approach, with adjudicators construing complicity as a rule of attribution of conduct. For example, in the Cotesworth and Powell case, which involved damages caused to foreigners by acts of private individuals who were granted immunity in Colombia, a British-Colombia Mixed Commission held:

> One nation is not responsible to another for the acts of its individual citizens, except when it approves or ratifies them. It then becomes a *public concern*, and the injured party may consider the nation itself the real author of the injury. And this approval, it is apprehended, need not to be in express terms; but may fairly be inferred from a *refusal to provide means of reparation* when such measures are possible: or from its pardon of the offender when such pardon necessarily deprives the injured party of all redress.[54]

Overall, scholars grappled with translating the various layers of a state's participation in acts of an individual into the concept of state

[53] Hall, *A Treatise on International Law*, 218 (emphasis added).

[54] *Cotesworth & Powell* (*Great Britain* v. *Colombia*) (1875) in Moore, *History and Digest*, vol. 2, 2082 (emphasis added); see also R. Ago, 'Fourth Report on State Responsibility' (1972) ILC YB II/2 101, querying whether 'public concern' refers indeed to the failure of the state to punish as amounting to complicity, or whether the commission intended that in the event of crimes committed to aliens by private individuals, failure to punish or granting amnesty are conduct contrary to a state's international duties.

responsibility. They often failed to clarify whether complicity arose from a state's active participation in the crime or whether complicity could also flow from a state's failure to condemn the private acts and provide redress. Originally, responsibility for complicity and responsibility for failure to exercise due diligence largely overlapped.

Furthermore, the idea of fault being linked to the responsibility of a state for injuries carried out by private persons underlined a certain confusion in the relationship between the state and the individual. It is not always clear in the early writings whether responsibility was based exclusively on the state's own acts or whether there was a special link between the individual's crime and the idea that the state 'assumes' responsibility as a result of it. This confusion, which for long time put due diligence on a sliding scale between state responsibility and individual responsibility, was still evident in international legal doctrine in the first part of the twentieth century. Many scholars of this age labelled responsibility for failure to act with due diligence as a form of indirect state liability for private acts, ranging from forms of responsibility for condonation[55] to theories of vicarious responsibility. Lassa Oppenheim, for example, branded the state's responsibility for government actions as 'original', and the state's responsibility stemming from acts of private individuals as 'vicarious'. This author also argued that once a state fails to comply with its duty to punish the perpetrator of a wrong and to repair the damage caused, its vicarious responsibility turns *ipso facto* original.[56] In this regard, although most contemporary scholars reject the opposing concepts of 'original' and 'vicarious' responsibility, a minority of authors continue to construe state responsibility for failure to exercise due diligence as a form of indirect responsibility. These positions are especially common among Anglo-American scholars and are usually developed in relation to state responsibility for failure to prevent terrorist attacks.[57]

In any case, theories of complicity, condonation, and indirect responsibility tried to strike a balance between the emergence of international responsibility as an independent category separate from individual

[55] For instance C. Hyde, 'Concerning Damages Arising from Neglect to Prosecute' (1928) 22 AJIL 140; Ago, 'Fourth Report on State Responsibility', 104.

[56] L. Oppenheim, *International Law*, 208–9. See also A. S. Hershey, *The Essentials of International Public Law* (New York: The Macmillan Company, 1912), 161–2.

[57] For example D. Brown, 'Use of Force Against Terrorism After September 11th: State Responsibility, Self-Defence and Other Responses' (2003–2004) 11 *Cardozo Journal of International and Comparative Law* 13; D. Jinks, 'State Responsibility for the Acts of Private Harm Groups' (2003) 4 *Chicago Journal of International Law* 83, at 90.

responsibility and the need to ensure international justice for certain crimes. The rise of liberal thought over the nineteenth and twentieth century facilitated their gradual replacement thanks to the solidification of the distinction between the limited sphere of state control and the private realm governed by individual freedom. Furthermore, the Italian and German doctrine at the beginning of the twentieth century was paramount in contributing to insulating international responsibility for crimes of private subjects. Triepel was one of the first scholars to ground international responsibility on an objective conception of the international wrongful act and to argue that the individual who injures another state or its citizens never violates international law.[58] Shortly after, Anzilotti famously laid the conceptual foundations for understanding state responsibility as flowing from two objective conditions, namely conduct of a representative of the state in violation of a rule of international law. His ideas had a great influence on the work of Roberto Ago as a future Special Rapporteur of the ILC and, more generally, on the entire architecture of ARSIWA.

As for the relationship between due diligence and complicity, the concepts were eventually separated during the ILC work on state responsibility. In particular, Special Rapporteur Ago developed complicity as a form of attribution of responsibility to a state for the wrongful acts of another state. He rejected the idea that a state could be complicit in the harmful act of private individuals and only recognised the possibility that the state could be responsible for its own acts or omissions. This concept led to the distinction between a state's failure to prevent giving rise to its omissions and the state's active participation in an individual's wrongful acts. Provided that such participation would reach a certain 'intensity', the participation would transform the individual's act into the conduct of the state, giving rise to state responsibility for its own action.[59]

1.2 Due Diligence in Modern International Law

Over the course of the second half of the twentieth century, due diligence struggled to find codification in international law. Part of the difficulty stemmed from the substantial confusion over the international legal boundaries of key concepts linked to due diligence, such as responsibility and fault. Even when the crystallisation of the state as an entity separate

[58] Triepel, *Völkerrecht und landesrecht*, 325–30.

[59] Ago, 'Fourth Report on State Responsibility', 120.

from private individuals was completed and international responsibility was finally severed from the connection with crimes of private subjects, the foundational elements of state responsibility were still unclear. In particular, scholars debated whether responsibility stemmed objectively from conduct of a state organ in violation of an international obligation, or whether responsibly arose only from situations in which there was fault or intent to violate international law. Thus, for long time the question on the status of due diligence in international law overlapped with debates around the nature of international responsibility.

Over the course of the twentieth century, much doctrinal scholarship focused on whether the system of state responsibility required fault before an international wrongful act could accrue. This dispute heavily influenced the approach toward due diligence and, at least until the adoption of ARSIWA, limited the discussion around this topic to the realm of international responsibility. Understanding the contours of the debate around fault is therefore crucial for reconstructing part of the genealogy of due diligence and for laying down some key points that will serve the theoretical reconstruction of due diligence obligations later in this work.

Simultaneously, attempts to codify due diligence took place during the ILC work on state liability for acts not prohibited by international law. Initially, the ILC had conceived responsibility and liability as complementary regimes respectively covering the consequences of wrongful acts and those not prohibited by international law. In this framework, due diligence was seen by many as the point of contact between the two regimes. However, it soon became clear that the complementarity between responsibility and liability was built upon shaky methodological premises, and it did not find support in international practice. With the work on liability split into two different projects – the draft articles on prevention of transboundary harm and the draft articles on allocation of loss in cases of transboundary harm – the discussion on due diligence became integral to the draft articles on the prevention of transboundary harm, and the concept was finally dedicated to the realm of primary rules.

1.2.1 Due Diligence and Fault in International Responsibility

It is difficult to summarise the scholarly debate on the place of fault in the law of international responsibility without running the risk of oversimplification. This risk stems not only from the complexity of the topic and the diversity of doctrinal positions developed through the first half of the twentieth century. Discussions on the role of fault in international responsibility are further complicated by the lack of consensus about the very premise of the debate. Any inquiry into fault and state responsibility must in fact begin with acknowledging that there is no universal agreement as to what fault is and to which subject fault should be assigned.

Much like in every other legal field, international legal scholars have attached different meanings to fault. Some understand fault in its 'classic' sense, that is, the subjective psychological mindset a subject assumes toward the effects of their actions or omissions.[60] Others steer clear of any reference to psychological elements and essentially equate fault with voluntariness or the violation of an international obligation.[61] Some adopt an intermediate position and construe fault as a concept imbued with both psychological and normative dimensions.[62]

Furthermore, the law of international responsibility typically broaches the issue of fault as a question concerning the fault of the individual-organ, whose action or omission breaches an international obligation. Essentially, the contours of the problem are limited to the relevance of the psychological mindset of the individuals acting on the state's behalf. Assessing state fault means evaluating the *mens rea* of the individual acting as an organ of the state. This approach toward fault is predominant among scholars and sometimes resurrects in the practice of international courts and tribunals.[63]

However, thinking about the *animus agendi* of the individual-organ may not be the only way to speak about fault and how it plays out in assessing state responsibility. It is indeed conceivable to construe fault not as the psychological mindset of the individual-organ acting on a state's behalf, but as fault of the state as an international legal entity.[64]

[60] R. Ago, 'Le délit international' (1939) 68 RCADI 419; Ago, 'La colpa nell'illecito internazionale', in *Scritti giuridici in onore di Santi Romano* (Padova: CEDAM, 1940), vol. 3, 175; G. Morelli, *Nozioni di diritto internazionale* (Padova: CEDAM, 1967), 344–7.

[61] See generally I. Browlie, *Principles of International Law* (Oxford: Oxford University Press, 6th ed., 2003), 424–5; the understanding of fault as a violation of an obligation emerges in J. Combacau, 'La responsabilité internationale', in H. Thierry, J. Combacau. S. Sur, C. Vallée (eds.), *Droit International Public* (Paris: Editions Mont-Chrestien, 1981), 69; and Anzilotti, *Teoria generale della responsabilità*, 102–87 (fault as voluntariness).

[62] G. Sperduti, 'Sulla colpa in diritto internazionale' (1950) 3 *Comunicazioni e Studi* 93; R. Luzzatto, 'Responsabilitá e colpa in diritto internazionale' (1968) 51 *Rivista di diritto internazionale* 53.

[63] For instance, the case of *Velásquez Rodríguez* v. *Honduras, Interpretation of the judgement of reparations and costs*, IACHR Series C no 9, 17 August 1990, para. 173.

[64] Or, better, fault of the state as a 'corporeal' entity. The idea of fault of the state as opposed to fault of the individual-organ have been developed specifically within those theories that construe the state as a 'corporeal' entity and not as a legal person defined by rules of

In his seminal study of fault in international responsibility, Giuseppe Palmisano argues that state fault does not necessarily relate to the intent or neglect of the individual-organ acting on a state's behalf. Fault may be understood as a condition attached to the state as an international legal person. Under this concept, fault is a composite notion, something that is ascribed to the state when the combination of a series of factual elements – for example, the inadequacy of certain legislation, the inefficiency of a governmental apparatus, the lack of proper administration, or the wilful or negligent omissions of certain organs – points in its entirety to negligent behaviour of the state as an international person.[65] According to Palmisano, fault is therefore a concept that resembles other subjective elements normally imputed to a state in international law, such as consent, error, or *opinio juris*.[66]

Although such approach ultimately builds upon a distinct representation of the state under international law,[67] it does feature a change of paradigm in the way in which state fault can be construed. This distinction – between fault as the psychological mindset of the individual-organ and fault of the state as an international legal entity – will be crucially

international law. In other words, this reading of state fault is intimately connected to a certain conception of the state as a subject of international law, see G. Palmisano, 'Colpa dell'organo e colpa dello Stato nella responsabilità internazionale: Spunti critici di teoria e di prassi' (1992) 19–20 *Comunicazioni e Studi* 525, 684–98; G. Palmisano, 'Fault' (2007) MPEPIL paras. 24–9; G. Arangio-Ruiz, 'Second Report on State Responsibility' (1989) ILC YB II/1 1; G. Arangio-Ruiz, 'State Fault and the Forms and Degrees of International Responsibility: Questions of Attribution and Relevance', in *Mélanges Michel Virally: Le droit international au service de la paix de la justice et du développement* (Paris: Pedone, 1991), 25; G. Arangio-Ruiz, 'State Responsibility Revisited: The Factual Nature of the Attribution of Conduct to the State' (2017) *Rivista di diritto internazionale, Supplemento al fascicolo 1*, 1, at 130–44. Speaking also of fault of the state as an international legal entity P. M. Dupuy, 'Faute de l'Etat et "fait internationalement illicite"' (1987) 5 *Droit*, 54–5; on the distinction between fault of the individual-organ and fault of the state in its entirety see also P. De Sena, 'Condotta di singoli organi e condotta dell'apparato statale in tema di colpa nell'illecito internazionale' (1988) 71 *Rivista di diritto internazionale* 525.

65 Palmisano, 'Colpa dell'organo e colpa dello Stato', 684–8, 704; Palmisano, 'Fault', para. 28.

66 Palmisano, 'Colpa dell'organo e colpa dello Stato', 705–10; Palmisano, 'Fault', para. 29.

67 This idea of state's fault derives indeed from a conception of the international personality of the state that sees the latter as a *corporeal entity*; this approach is radically opposed to the views construing the state under international law as the 'external face' of the state under national law, namely an entity defined by the collective substratum of municipal *legal rules*, see especially Arangio-Ruiz, 'Dualism Revisited: International Law and Interindividual Law' (2003) *Rivista di diritto internazionale, Estratto*, 909, 939–81; Arangio-Ruiz, 'State Responsibility Revisited', 130–44; Palmisano, 'Colpa dell'organo e colpa dello Stato', 663–78.

important in conceptualising the scope and content of due diligence obligations, as will be seen in Chapter 3.

At any rate, one can identify essentially two opposing views that dominated the early discourse about the role of fault in international responsibility. Between these two ends, a spectrum of doctrinal positions developed, influencing the debate around the topic.[68] On the one hand, there were those favouring an objective approach to state responsibility, who rejected any idea of fault being imputed to the state.[69] One of the most famous supporters of this strand is Anzilotti. In his *Teoria generale della responsabilita' dello Stato nel diritto internazionale*, Anzilotti undertook a thorough analysis of why psychological conditions relate only to individuals and could not be imputed to the state. Laying down the conceptual underpinnings of the future law of state responsibility, Anzilotti argued that an international wrongful act arises as a result of two objective conditions: i) conduct of a state organ, ii) in contravention of an international obligation.[70] Fault, as the psychological mindset of an individual, cannot be transposed to the state as a legal entity. Therefore, even when a state is found responsible in connection with the actions of private individuals, responsibility does not flow from any negligent mindset of the state. Rather, responsibility accrues as a result of the violation of a duty to prevent certain activities or to punish violations.

On the other hand, the proponents of the fault-based theory of state responsibility regarded fault as a requirement for the accrual of every international wrongful act. The origins of their positions can be traced back to Grotius, although fault-based theories established during the twentieth century developed from a more 'mature' international law and were increasingly complex. Several authors contended that, in the absence of any degree of fault on the part of a state organ, no international wrongful act could accrue.[71] Among the supporters of fault-based responsibility was Ago. In *Le délit international*, Ago maintained that intent or negligence by a state organ may be required by rules of

[68] For an overview, see Pisillo-Mazzeschi, 'The Due Diligence Rule', 10–21.

[69] Borchard, 'Theoretical Aspects of the International Responsibility of States' (1929) 1 ZAöRV 225; Anzilotti, *Teoria generale della responsabilità*, 102–87; D. Lévy, 'La responsabilité pour omission et la responsabilité pour risque en droit international public' (1961) 65 RGDIP 744; O. Schachter, *International Law in Theory and Practice* (1991) 178 RCADI 203.

[70] Anzilotti, *Teoria generale della responsabilità*, 163.

[71] Luzzatto, 'Responsabilitá e colpa', 65; Dupuy, 'Le fait générateur de la responsabilité internationale des Etats' (1984) 188 RCADI 9–183 ; Dupuy, 'Faute de l'Etat', 51.

attribution of conduct, making fault a condition for international responsibility.[72]

Against this framework, supporters of both the objective theory and the fault-based theory invoked due diligence to back their respective arguments. Proponents of the fault-based theory regarded responsibility for failing to exercise due diligence as the epitome of fault in establishing a state's responsibility. They supported their argument by referring to arbitral decisions treating lack of due diligence to prevent or repress harmful acts as evidence of a state's negligence. On the opposite side, the proponents of the objective theory invoked a state's responsibility for lack of due diligence in order to unveil the conceptual misunderstanding around this notion. For the 'objectivists', international practice on due diligence did not support fault as a prerequisite for state responsibility. Due diligence only indicated an objective standard of conduct linked to the content of some international obligations, like obligations to protect or obligations to repress harmful activities carried out by non-state actors.[73]

The oscillation between an objective standard of conduct and the presence of fault in the theory of state responsibility was also present in the history of due diligence during the ILC work on ARSIWA. García-Amador, the first Special Rapporteur nominated by the ILC, described due diligence as 'the expression *par excellence* of the so-called theory of fault',[74] reflecting an understanding of the concept as a standard for measuring negligence by a state organ.[75] For Special Rapporteur Ago, the idea that state responsibility arises as a result of two objective conditions – conduct attributable to the state and in breach of an international obligation – crystallised. And yet, Ago's reports still revealed much overlap between due diligence and the notion of state negligence. For instance, Ago's notions of obligations to prevent and of force majeure as a circumstance precluding wrongfulness harboured elements of fault and drew a connection between negligence and failure to act with due diligence.[76]

[72] R. Ago, 'Le délit international' (1939) 68 RCADI 419, 450–98.

[73] For an overview of different conceptual positions regarding the relationship between due diligence and fault, see M. Seršić, 'Due Diligence: Fault-Based Responsibility of Autonomous Standard?', in R. Wolfrum, M. Seršić, T. Šošić (eds.), *Contemporary Developments in International Law: Essays in Honour of Budislav Vukas* (Leiden: Brill, 2015), 151.

[74] F. V. García-Amador, 'Second Report on State Responsibility' (1957) ILC YB II/2 122.

[75] Ibid. 121–2.

[76] Ago, 'Seventh Report on State Responsibility' (1978) ILC YB II/2 35–6; Ago, 'Eighth Report on State Responsibility' (1979) ILC YB II/1 paras. 123–45.

1.2.2 *Due Diligence After the Adoption of the 2001 Articles on State Responsibility*

Fault is not listed by ARSIWA as a condition for the existence of an international wrongful act. Article 2 defines an international wrongful act as flowing 'objectively' from two cumulative conditions, namely, conduct attributable to the state and in breach of an international obligation. Notably, the scope of ARSIWA is limited to secondary rules of state responsibility, namely 'general conditions under international law for the State to be considered responsible for wrongful actions or omissions, and the legal consequences which flow therefrom'.[77] Definitions of the content of international obligations are left aside because 'this is the function of primary rules, whose codification would involve restating most of the substantive customary and conventional international law'.[78]

While ARSIWA exclude fault as a general secondary rule, this exclusion does not mean that fault is completely absent in the articles adopted by the commission.[79] Explicit and implicit remnants of fault can be identified in several articles, and for some commentators, the ILC formally rejected fault as a secondary issue only to sneak it in some articles through the back door.[80] Some rules, like Article 39, expressly include a state's negligence among the elements to be considered when setting the amount of reparations due.[81] Other rules include elements of fault in a more subtle way. For instance, Article 23 lists force majeure as a circumstance precluding wrongfulness and 'injects' only objective elements into the definition of this circumstance. Yet, the Commentary to this article interprets force majeure by invoking subjective components like 'voluntariness' or 'lack of free choice', which can overlap with the notion of (lack of) fault.[82]

77 ARSIWA, at 31.

78 Ibid.

79 For a critical review, see O. Diggelmann, 'Fault in the Law of State Responsibility: Pragmatism *ad Infinitum*' (2006) 49 GYIL 293; D. Bodansky, J. R. Crook, 'Symposium: The ILC'S State Responsibility Articles Introduction and Overview' (2002) 96 AJIL 773, 781; A. Gattini, 'Smoking/No Smoking: Some Remarks on the Current Place of Fault in the ILC Draft Articles on State Responsibility' (1999) 10 EJIL 397.

80 Gattini, 'Smoking/No Smoking', 397–9.

81 ARSIWA, Article 39.

82 See Commentary to Article 23 of ARSIWA. However, on the difference between fault and voluntariness see Palmisano, 'Fault', para. 19. On how fault is equated by Ago with the concept of voluntariness or *suitas*, Palmisano, 'La colpa', 658–9; De Sena, 'Condotta di singoli organi', 529.

As for due diligence, the commission eventually decided to migrate the concept to the level of primary rules. In fact, ARSIWA only briefly reference due diligence while discussing the elements of an international wrongful act. Specifically, in explaining why the articles avoid the terminology 'subjective element' and 'objective element' to describe attribution of conduct and the breach of an obligation respectively, the Commentary notes:

> Whether there has been a breach of a rule may depend on the intention or knowledge of relevant state organs or agents and in that sense may be 'subjective' . . . In other cases, the standard for breach of an obligation may be 'objective', in the sense that the advertence or otherwise of relevant state organs or agents may be irrelevant. Whether responsibility is objective' or 'subjective' in this sense depends on the circumstances, including the content of the primary rule in question. The articles lay down no general rule in that regard. The same is true of other standards, whether they involve some degree of fault, culpability, negligence or want of due diligence. Such standards vary from one context to another for reasons which essentially relate to the object and purpose of the treaty provision or other rules giving rise to the primary obligation. Nor do the articles lay down any presumption in this regard as between the different possible standards. Establishing this is a matter for the interpretation and application of the primary rules engaged in the given case.[83]

With this short passage, the ILC states that whether due diligence is part of the equation that establishes state responsibility is a matter of primary rules. From this perspective, ARSIWA rule out the classification of due diligence as a general principle of international responsibility and circumscribes its function to the level of primary rules. At the same time, the articles leave vague and uncertain the questions about the relationship between due diligence and fault. The Commentary lists 'fault, culpability, negligence or want of due diligence' as elements of primary rules without stating the extent to which these concepts differ or overlap. This uncertainty in the relationship between fault and due diligence is, at least in part, still reflected by contemporary international scholarship. Some authors have purged due diligence from any subjective element and construe it as a purely objective standard of conduct applicable to certain primary rules. Other scholars accept that fault may not be a general secondary rule of international responsibility, yet maintain that breaches of obligations to exercise due diligence amount to a form of state responsibility based on fault.

[83] ARSIWA Commentary at 34–5.

1.2.3 Due Diligence and International Liability

Another stepping stone for the crystallisation of due diligence was the ILC work on International Liability for Injurious Consequences Arising Out of Acts Not Prohibited by International Law.[84] The project began in the 1970s and was originally conceived to complement the system of international responsibility still in the making. Specifically, international responsibility would deal with obligations arising from violations of international law. The system of international liability would cover obligations arising from acts that cause significant transboundary harm but that international law did not prohibit.[85] The commission's intent was to codify a system of rules related to reparations for losses caused by lawful activities taking place in a state's territory or under its jurisdiction or control and generating significant transboundary harm.[86] Although environmental harm would later become the primary focus of rules on liability, the project initially had a broader scope and covered any transboundary harm caused by lawful activities.[87] Thus, the work of the ILC was built on the premise that the systems of responsibility and liability would work on different planes.[88] Rules on international responsibility were secondary obligations stemming from the breach of a primary rule. Rules on international liability established primary rules stemming from transboundary damage caused by lawful risk-generating activities and were unconnected to a breach of international law.[89]

Initially, the commission set up a system responsive to the occurrence of transboundary harm. In particular, causation of significant transboundary damage would trigger a 'compound' primary obligation, which included prevention, minimisation of the risk, and reparations

[84] UNGA Res. 3071 (XXVIII) (30 November 1973).

[85] ILC YB (1980) I 248. In 1978 the ILC Working Group noted that the topic on state liability was a subject worthy of separate analysis, 'Report of the Working Group on International Liability for Injurious Consequences Arising out of Acts Not Prohibited by International Law' (1978) ILC YB II/2 150.

[86] ILC Draft Articles on Prevention with commentary, Article 3.

[87] See A. Boyle, 'Liability for Injurious Consequence of Acts not Prohibited by International Law', in J. Crawford, A. Pellet, S. Olleson, K. Parlet (eds.), *The Law of International Responsibility* (Oxford: Oxford University Press, 2010), 96.

[88] R. Quentin-Baxter, 'First Report on International Liability for Injurious Consequences Arising out of Acts not Prohibited Under International Law' (1980) ILC YB II/1 253; J. Barboza, 'Fourth Report on International Liability for Injurious Consequences Arising out of Acts not Prohibited Under International Law' (1988) ILC YB II/1 draft Articles 1 and 2.

[89] Quentin-Baxter, 'Fourth Report on International Liability for Injurious Consequences Arising out of Acts not Prohibited Under International Law' (1983) ILC YB II/2 213.

for damage caused. Due diligence was conceived as part of this compound primary rule.[90] Due diligence measured the level of care that a 'good neighbouring' state had to display to balance its freedom to undertake activities on its territory with the respect for the sovereign rights of other states.[91] Hence, at the beginning, both prevention and due diligence were not conceptualised as part of a primary duty to anticipate risk. For the commission, the breach of prevention and due diligence existed without consequences in terms of international responsibility; they were both elements of the primary obligation to repair triggered in the *ex post* context of harm mitigation.[92]

However, after the first attempt to codify relevant rules,[93] the entire conceptual architecture of international liability was substantially criticised. The commission grappled with appreciating the relationship between responsibility for wrongful acts and liability for acts not prohibited by international law. To begin with, the terms 'responsibility' and 'liability' could be easily associated with the concepts of accountability for 'fault' and accountability based on 'risk' or absence of fault. The first Special Rapporteur on international liability, Quentin-Baxter, had consciously refrained from using the antinomies of 'fault' and 'no-fault' or 'risk' to describe the distinction between the two regimes,[94] and the ILC had tried to omit reference to fault in the architecture of ARSIWA. Yet, there was a real risk that due diligence – which was being discussed in both frameworks – could be construed as the silver lining for distinguishing situations of state responsibility from situations of international liability.[95]

Furthermore, it soon became clear to members of the commission and scholars that the notion of international liability derived from conceptual confusion built on the dichotomy between 'international wrongful acts' and 'activities not prohibited by international law'. The distinction on the nature of state acts had in fact created the impression of two opposing

[90] Quentin-Baxter, 'First Report on International Liability', 252.

[91] Barboza, 'Ninth Report on International Liability for Injurious Consequences Arising out of Acts not Prohibited by International Law' (1993) ILC YB II/2 189; P. S. Rao, 'First Report on International Liability for Injurious Consequences Arising out of Acts not Prohibited by International Law' (1998) ILC YB II/2, 28.

[92] L. A. Duvic-Paoli, *The Prevention Principle in International Environmental Law* (Cambridge: Cambridge University Press, 2018), 100.

[93] ILC, 'Report of the Working Group on International Liability for Injurious Consequences Arising out of Acts not Prohibited by International Law' (1996) ILC YB II/2.

[94] Quentin-Baxter, 'First Report on International Liability', para. 15.

[95] N. L. J. T. Horbach, 'The Confusion about State Responsibility and International Liability' (1991) 4 LJIL 47, 55.

systems of accountability premised on different factual grounds, respectively, a state's commission of an internationally wrongful act and a state's exercise of its sovereign rights.[96]

However, there is no legal regime for 'acts not prohibited under international law'. Conduct either breaches an international legal rule, with all the relative consequences provided by secondary rules of responsibility, or it does not, in which case no 'primary' or 'secondary' obligation arises.[97] It gradually appeared that the commission's work on international liability had dealt fundamentally with two separate issues under the same umbrella. On the one hand, there were rules on the prevention of transboundary harm, whose rationale and status as a primary duty had increasing gained recognition in international environmental law. On the other hand, the commission had attempted to identify rules on strict liability for damage, that is, rules allocating compensation for damages caused by transboundary harm.

Once the conceptual confusion was unveiled, it was agreed that international liability would be split into two topics:[98] the ILC would first focus on the 'Prevention of Transboundary Harm from Hazardous Activities' and then on 'Principles of Allocation of Loss in the Case of Transboundary Harm Arising Out of Hazardous Activities'.[99] The work on prevention led the commission to adopt, in 2001, the draft Articles on the Prevention of Transboundary Harm from Hazardous Activities, which were commended to the General Assembly. The Principles of Allocation of Loss in the Case of Transboundary Harm Arising Out of Hazardous Activities were adopted in 2006 and are meant to include principles aimed at ensuring adequate compensation for victims of transboundary damage and principles aimed at restoring the environment damaged by transboundary harm. As they are concerned with remedies and allocation of compensation for transboundary damage, the 2006 articles have little to do with due diligence, except that they

[96] Barboza, 'Second Report on International Liability for Injurious Consequences Arising out of Acts not Prohibited Under International Law' (1986) ILC YB II/1 152.

[97] Boyle, 'State Responsibility and International Liability for Injurious Consequences of Acts not Prohibited by International Law: A Necessary Distinction?' (1990) 39 ICLQ 12–15; A. Pellet, 'Les Articles de la CDI sur la responsabilité de l'État pour faits internationalement illicite : Suite – et fin?' (2002) 48 *Annuaire Français de Droit International* 1. P. Birne, A. Boyle, C. Redgwell, *International Law & the Environment* (Oxford: Oxford University Press, 3rd ed., 2009), 141.

[98] ILC YB (1997) II/2 59.

[99] ILC Draft Principles on Allocation of Loss in the Case of Transboundary Harm Arising Out of Hazardous Activities (2006) ILC YB II/2.

should apply when harm materialises and they should apply without prejudice to the rules governing state responsibility, including responsibility flowing from a breach of a due diligence rule.

The methodological shift toward prevention of transboundary harm allowed due diligence to be clarified and finally conceptualised prevention as commonly known, that is, a primary duty of anticipatory character. Specifically, the ILC took the view that the international legal system governing prevention is largely the product of the due diligence rule.[100] Due diligence was defined as the degree of effort against which the conduct of the state in preventing or minimising the risk of harm shall be assessed.[101] As such, due diligence reflects the degree of care that is expected of a good government[102] and should be proportional to the risk of transboundary harm in a given situation. Hence, when a state does not exercise due diligence, the state is failing to fulfil its obligation to prevent significant transboundary harm. This failure may result in that state's international responsibility, as it usually occurs for any violation of primary rules of international law. In any event, failure to exercise due diligence does not imply that the activity carried out in a state's territory or under its jurisdiction and control and causing harm is prohibited under international law.[103] Prohibition of a certain activity is not the necessary and inevitable outcome of responsibility for wrongful acts.[104]

Retrospectively, the contribution of the draft articles on Prevention of Transboundary Harm from Hazardous Activities has been twofold. First, the articles have solidified the status of due diligence as an element of primary rules. In the draft articles, due diligence is understood as part of the duty to prevent transboundary harm and not as an element of an accountability regime opposed to that of international responsibility. Thus, the draft articles on prevention completed the process initiated by the ILC with the work on state responsibility, which migrated due diligence from secondary to primary rules.

Second, the draft articles on prevention were the first to make due diligence a concrete concept under international law. To fulfil their

[100] Baxter, 'First Report on International Liability', 252.

[101] Rao, 'First Report on the Legal Regime for Allocation of Loss in Case of Transboundary Harm Arising Out of Hazardous Activities' (2003) ILC YB II/2 28.

[102] ILC Draft Articles on Prevention with commentary, Article 3 para. 17.

[103] Rao, 'Third Report International Liability in Case of Loss from Transboundary Harm Arising Out of Hazardous Activities' (2006) ILC YB II/2 122.

[104] This is true not only for international environmental law but for international law in general.

obligation to prevent, states are not only generically required to 'adopt appropriate measures to prevent significant transboundary harm',[105] but they are also expected to cooperate in good faith,[106] to carry out pre-emptive assessments of the possible harm derived by state's activities,[107] and to notify,[108] consult,[109] and exchange information[110] with potentially affected states. These obligations have now been largely recognised by international practice[111] and are considered to reflect components of the rule of due diligence in the environmental context. In other words, for a state to discharge its positive preventive obligation and act with due diligence, it will be necessary to prove that the commencement of an activity involving a risk of significant transboundary harm complies with certain parameters (such as environmental impact assessments, the monitoring of the risk inherent to the activity, and notification of the risk should the conditions arise).

1.3 The Status of Due Diligence in International Law

Between 2014 and 2016, the International Law Association (ILA) studied due diligence in international law. The ILA's interest in this topic was driven by the proliferation of due diligence as a standard of conduct for a variety of international obligations across international law. The Study Group on Due Diligence set up by the ILA delivered two reports and, at the end, it concluded that due diligence is as 'an evolving principle of international law'.[112] Specifically, the second report stressed that, as a principle, due diligence holds a central place in the operation of

105 ILC Draft Articles on Prevention with commentary, Article 3.

106 Ibid. Article 4.

107 Ibid. Article 7.

108 Ibid. Article 8.

109 Ibid. Article 9.

110 Ibid. Article 12.

111 *Case Concerning Pulp Mills on the River Uruguay (Argentina* v. *Uruguay) (Merits)* [2010] ICJ Rep 14, para. 102; *Certain Activities Carried Out by Nicaragua in the Border Area (Costa Rica* v. *Nicaragua)* [2015] ICJ Rep 665, paras. 101, 106; *Construction of a Road in Costa Rica along the San Juan River (Nicaragua* v. *Costa Rica)* [2015] ICJ Rep 665, para. 153; *Responsibility and Obligations of States Sponsoring Persons and Entities with Respect to Activities in the Area (Request for an Advisory Opinion submitted to the Seabed Dispute Chamber)* ITLOS Reports 2011 para. 236.

112 The ILA Study Group on Due Diligence in International Law, 'Due Diligence in International Law: Second Report' (Johannesburg, 2016), 2–3. Note however, that in the final resolution on the topic adopted by the ILA, the study group addresses due diligence as a 'relevant standard of conduct', Study Group on Due Diligence in International Law, 'Resolution No. 8/2016' (Johannesburg 2016).

a wide array of international obligations and, more generally, in global governance.[113]

The status of due diligence as a principle of international law is a point of discussion for much contemporary legal scholarship. Some authors share the conclusions reached by the ILA and interpret due diligence either as a general principle of law or a principle of international law.[114] Others see due diligence as a general standard of conduct applicable to a variety of international obligations but are sceptical about construing it as a principle of international law.[115] Some hold even more radical positions and contend that the term 'due diligence' is imbued with an array of different meanings and, as such, cannot be generally defined, let alone considered a principle or a general rule of international law.[116]

Along with the variety of different and often opposing views, it is not always clear what scholars mean when they recognise or deny the 'principle' status of due diligence. For instance, from a careful reading of the ILA's Second Report on Due Diligence, it emerges that the study group used the 'principle of due diligence' both as an articulation of the Corfu Channel dictum[117] and to refer to a concept underlining certain primary rules and providing reason and rationality to them. A cursory look at the contemporary literature on due diligence depicts a similarly spotty picture. Sometimes, the qualifying term 'principle' is attached to due diligence to highlight its nature as a general standard of behaviour applicable across international law.[118] In other cases, the 'principle' of due diligence is instead illustrated as a source of states' rights and

[113] ILA Study Group on Due Diligence, 'Second Report', 1.

[114] J. Kulesza, *Due Diligence in International Law* (Leiden: Brill, 2016), 272–6; A. Ouedraogo, 'La due diligence en droit international: de la règle de la neutralité au principe général' (2012) 42 *Revue Général de Droit* 641; T. Koivurova, 'Due Diligence' (2010) MPEPIL para. 2; R. Barnidge, 'The Due Diligence Principle under International Law' (2006) 8 *International Community Law Review* 81; L. Condorelli, 'The Imputability to States of Acts of International Terrorism' (1989) 19 *Israel Yearbook of Human Rights* 233, 241. On the differences between general principles and principles of international law see Section 1.3.1.

[115] H. Krieger, A. Peters, 'Due Diligence and Structural Change in the International Legal Order', in Krieger, Peters, Kreuzer, *Due Diligence*, 371–6; Pisillo-Mazzeschi, 'Le chemin étranger de la due diligence: d'un concept mystérieux à un concept surévalué', in S. Cassella (ed.), *Le standard de due diligence et la responsabilité internationale* (Paris: Pedone, 2018), 323.

[116] N. McDonald, 'The Role of Due Diligence in International Law' (2019) 68 ICLQ 1041.

[117] ILA Study Group on Due Diligence, 'Second Report', 5–6.

[118] C. Ryngaert, 'State Responsibility and Non-State Actors', in M. Noortmann, A. Reinisch, C. Ryngaert (eds.), *Non-State Actors in International Law* (London: Hart Publishing, 2015), 177.

obligations.[119] In view of this confusion, the next sections briefly reappraise the complex debate surrounding the question of principles of international law and then discuss the status of due diligence in the contemporary international legal order.

1.3.1 The Unsettled Scope and Role of Principles in International Law

In international law, the definition of what constitutes a general principle has been subject to much scholarly debate. Many scholars agree there is dissention on almost every aspect regarding general principles, except for their recognition as a source of international law pursuant to Article 38(1)(c) of the Statute of the International Court of Justice.[120] Disagreements concern the definition and scope of general principles, the function(s) they serve in international law, as well as the method for their identification. Catherine Redgwell has aptly observed that much of the controversy surrounding general principles stems from the divergent and often irreconcilable views that scholars hold about the nature of sources of international law, the function of lawmaking, and the role played by international courts and tribunals.[121]

A first issue of contention is on the very understanding of the term 'general principles'. Article 38(1)(c) of the Statute of the International Court of Justice lists as sources of international law 'general principles of law recognized by civilized nations'. These principles have traditionally been understood to indicate sources of law identifiable through a comparative analysis of different national legal systems, such as the principle of *res judicata*.[122] There is emerging consensus that the term 'general principles' refers not only to principles of law 'recognized by civilized nations', but also to 'general principles of international law', or '*principes du droit international*'.[123] The latter differ from 'general

[119] For instance, M. Schmitt, 'In Defense of Due Diligence in Cyberspace' (2015) 125 *Yale Law Journal Forum* 68, 69.

[120] Statute of the International Court of Justice (as annexed to the Charter of the United Nations) (26 June 1945) 1 UNTS 16.

[121] C. Redgwell, 'General Principles of International Law', in S. Vogenauer, S. Weatherill (eds.), *General Principles of Law: European and Comparative Perspectives* (London: Hart Publishing, 2017), 5.

[122] B. Cheng, *General Principles of Law as Applied by International Courts and Tribunals* (first published 1953, Cambridge: Cambridge University Press, 2006), 105, 336.

[123] In opposition to '*principes de droit international*', which would refer to principles recognised in the domestic law of states, see P. Dailler, M. Forteau, A. Pellet, *Droit International Public* (Paris: Librairie Général de Droit et de Jurisprudence, 2009), 380.

principles of law recognized by civilized nations' because they are drawn directly from the international legal system. Essentially, principles of international law are extrapolated from the international legal order and applied to situations falling outside the original scope of rules from which they are inferred.[124]

However, the boundaries of general principles of international law are much disputed. According to some authors, there is a distinction between general principles of international law falling under Article 38(1)(c) and principles that are derived from treaties or from international customary rules. Rüdiger Wolfrum, for instance, broadly defines a principle as a 'binding legal statement which describes obligations of conduct and obligations to achieve an objective'.[125] These principles, like the principle of common heritage of mankind or the principle of sustainable development, may serve different purposes, like the systematisation of legal norms, the interpretation of more concrete rules, or the development of international law.[126] As such, these principles should be distinguished, at least theoretically,[127] from 'general principles of law' provided by Article 38(1)(c) of the Statute of the ICJ, which instead comprise only norms constituting a *source* of international law. Other authors, like Giorgio Gaja, do not appear to draw a separation of this kind, noting that general principles falling under Article 38(1)(c) may also comprise abstractions from specific norms of customary or treaty law and may be used to 'affect the way in which a certain treaty rule is to be applied'.[128]

General principles of international law also raise controversy because of their relationship with customary rules. Some authors are sceptical about the very existence of general principles derived from international law as a category distinct from customary international rules.[129] Others

[124] See M. Wood, 'First Report on Formation and Evidence of Customary International Law' (2013) ILC YB II/2 16–17; See also the considerations of the commission on the topic of general principles of law, ILC YB (2019) II/2 para. 233.

[125] R. Wolfrum, 'General International Law (Principles, Rules, and Standards)' (2010) MPEPIL para. 6.

[126] Ibid.

[127] Wolfrum acknowledges in fact that the distinction between principles that serve for the systematisation of legal rules and principles that constitute a source of rights and obligations and that fall under Article 38(1)(c) is often blurred in international practice, see Wolfrum, 'General International Law', paras. 20–1.

[128] G. Gaja, 'General Principles of Law' (2020) MPEPIL paras. 22, 24.

[129] see A. Pellet, D. Müller, 'Article 38', in A. Zimmermann, C. Tomuschat, K. Oellers-Frahm, C. Tams (eds.), *The Statute of the International Court of Justice* (Oxford: Oxford University Press, 3rd ed., 2019), 925 para. 260; H. Thirlway, *The Sources of International Law* (Oxford: Oxford University Press, 2014) 94.

draw the distinction between general principles of international law and customary rules on the methods necessary to identify them. Accordingly, rules of customary international law should be grounded in general practices of states that are accepted as law.[130] They should differ from general principles of international law inasmuch as the latter usually entail wider discretion of the interpreter in deducing their existence from the international legal framework.[131] That said, it is not always clear to what extent general principles of international law can be distinguished from customary international law[132] or whether the two ultimately overlap.[133]

In light of the controversies surrounding general principles, in 2017 the ILC decided to include the topic in its programme of work. The work is still in progress, and so far only two reports have been submitted by Special Rapporteur Vázquez-Bermúdez.[134] However, relevant observations have already been made by the Special Rapporteur and by the commission with regard to fundamental issues touching upon the scope and the methodology of identification of general principles.

The focus of the ILC's work is on 'general principles of law as a source of international law'. Thus, the point of departure is Article 38(1)(c) of the ICJ Statute, analysed in relation to the practice of states and the jurisprudence of international courts and tribunals. The scope that the Special Rapporteur attaches to Article 38(1)(c) is rather broad. General principles of law are indeed defined as comprising 'general principles of

130 Note that Draft Conclusion no. 13 adopted by the Drafting Committee on the Identification of Customary International Law on second reading acknowledges that decisions of international courts and tribunals are a 'subsidiary mean' for the identification of customary international law, ILC, 'Report of the International Law Commission on the Work of its 70th session' (30 April–1 June, 2 July–10 August 2018) UN Doc. A./CN.4/L.908.

131 B. Bonafé, P. Palchetti, 'Relying on General Principles in International Law', in C. Brölmann, Y. Radi (eds.), *Research Handbook on the Theory and Practice of International Lawmaking* (Cheltenham: Edward Elgar, 2016) 165.

132 Wood, 'First Report on Customary International Law', 17.

133 For the view that principles elaborated by the ICJ are customary international rules, P. d'Argent, 'Les principes généraux à la Cour internationale de Justice', in S. Besson, P. Pichonnaz (eds.), *Les principes de droit européen* (Paris: Librairie Général de Droit et de Jurisprudence, 2011), 112–19. On the relationship between customary rules and principles of international law see also P. Palchetti, 'The Role of General Principles in Promoting the Development of Customary International Rules', in J. Wouters, M. Andenas, M. Fitzmaurice, A. Tanzi (eds.), *General Principles and the Coherence of International Law* (Leiden: Brill, 2019), 47; A. Rasi, 'Lo sviluppo dei principi generali del diritto nel tempo' (2020) 103 *Rivista di diritto internazionale* 959.

134 Last update 31 March 2021.

law derived from national legal systems' and 'general principles of law formed within the international legal system'.[135] The latter are described as a distinct category whose method of identification differs both from that required for general principles derived from national systems and from the method used for identifying rules of customary international law.[136] Of particular interest is the much looser criterion of identification that the Special Rapporteur has established to distinguish general principles of law formed within the international legal system from rules of customary international law. For a rule of customary international law to emerge, there must be a general practice, mostly of states, accompanied by its recognition as law (*opinio juris*). Some degree of logical deduction may assist in the determination of a customary rule, but the use of deductive methods should be very limited and never substitute for the two-element approach of practice and *opinio juris*. On the contrary, general principles formed within international law would rely on 'recognition' from the community of nations.[137] Such recognition may be inferred from international legal instruments or take place through deductive methods consisting of extrapolating general statements from customary and conventional rules.[138]

The broad scope attached to Article 38(1)(c) seems to also derive from the definition given by the Special Rapporteur to general principles of law formed within the international legal system. In the view of Vázquez-Bermúdez, general principles of law formed within international law are separated into three different groups, depending on their method of identification. First, principles formed within international law include principles widely recognised in treaties and other international instruments, such as the 'Principles of International Law Recognised in the Charter of the Nürnberg Tribunal' or the polluter pays principle incorporated in the field of international environmental law.[139] These principles are generally expressed by treaties and other international documents, such as resolutions of the General Assembly, and are recognised and used by the community of states as a source of rights and obligations for states.

135 M. Vázquez-Bermúdez, 'First Report on General Principles of Law' (29 April–7 June, 8 July–9 August 2019) UN Doc. A. CN.4/732; for the positions of the members of the commission in relation to this distinction ILC YB (2019) II/2 335.

136 Vázquez-Bermúdez, 'Second Report on General Principles of Law' (27 April–5 June, 6 July–7 August 2020) UN Doc. A./CN.4/741 paras. 159–71.

137 Ibid. para. 160.

138 Ibid. paras. 166, 168.

139 Ibid. paras. 122–37.

Second, general principles formed within international law include principles that underline general rules of a conventional or customary character. These principles are inferred from a deductive method that consists of extrapolating general statements from accepted rules of customary or conventional law. Essentially, the interpreter looks at specific rules provided by treaties or by customary rules and derives from these rules a general principle, which can be applied by analogy to other situations in which these treaties or customary rules are not necessarily applicable.[140] One example would be the principle of respect of human dignity, which is extrapolated from the corpus of international humanitarian law and human rights law and it has been applied as a source of state's obligations also in other contexts.[141] Finally, general principles may include those that are inherent in the basic features and fundamental requirements of the international legal system, such as the principle of consent to jurisdiction or the principle of independence and equality of states.

A fundamental point of controversy – which the ILC has yet to discuss – concerns the function served by general principles of law. Scholars generally agree that the main role of general principles of law is to fill the gaps in treaty and customary rules to ensure the completeness of the law.[142] Article 38(1)(c) was in fact designed primarily with the intent to avoid the possibility of a *non liquet* and prevent the ICJ from exercising a legislative function.[143] As just illustrated above, this gap-filling function is seen by authors like Wolfrum as the main rationale for distinguishing general principles of law from principles of international law that may assist the interpretation of customary or conventional rules or the development of international law. As gap-fillers, general principles of law are exceptional sources of rights and obligations of states and, as such, should be subject to a more rigorous method of identification.

Yet, there are those who see general principles of law that fall under Article 38(1)(c) as a tool for interpreting rules or reinforcing legal

140 Some scholars reject the idea that these are principles falling under article 38(1)(c) and argue that principles derived from treaties and customary rules fall either under Article 38(1)(a) or Article 38(1)(b), see M. Mendelson, 'The International Court of Justice and the Sources of International Law', in V. Lowe, M. Fitzmaurice (eds.), *Fifty Years of the International Court of Justice: Essays in Honour of Sir Robert Jennings* (Cambridge: Cambridge University Press, 1996), 64.

141 See Vázquez-Bermúdez, 'Second Report on General Principles of Law', paras. 143–4.

142 Redgwell, 'General Principles', 7.

143 Pellet, Müller, 'Article 38', 923; Vázquez-Bermúdez, 'First Report on General Principles of Law', para. 25.

reasoning as well.[144] Accordingly, general principles could be invoked even in the absence of a legal *lacuna*, for example, when the text of a treaty rule is unclear or open-ended and recourse to a general principle aids the interpreter in elaborating on the rationale of the rule and its meaning. In such cases, the function of a general principle is not to avoid a gap in the law but to reinforce the systemic nature of the international legal order and to reduce the fragmentation of international law.[145] For example, some scholars maintain that, by relying on general principles of law to clarify the content of rules or to resolve conflicts of norms, international courts and tribunals reduce 'the fragmentation in the approaches adopted in different sub-fields of international law . . . [and ensure] that they remain part of general international law'.[146] This approach to general principles of law is more inclusive than theories construing general principles only in their law-creating dimension. In this broader concept, there is no rigid dogmatic separation between lawmaking and interpretative function, and general principles of law are imbued with both dimensions.

In sum, much uncertainty remains around the concept of general principles of law. Much of the scope and role of general principles of law depend on one's conceptualisation and approach to international law. By and large, positivist conceptions of international law tend to circumscribe the scope of general principles of law to 'residual' sources of states' rights and obligations and have more conservative approaches to the methodology for their identification. Broader conceptualisations of general principles seem to build on the occasional collapse between sources, construed as law-identification norms, and interpretation, taken as a content-determinant technique.[147] In any case, there is clearly an intimate connection between scope, function, and methodology for the identification of legal principles. A restrictive interpretation of what constitutes a general principle of law is generally accompanied by the narrow interpretation of its function. On the contrary, the more room there is for arguing that the function of principles of law go beyond that

144 M. Andenas, L. Chiussi, 'Cohesion, Convergence and Coherence of International Law', in Wouters, Andenas, Fitzmaurice, Tanzi, *General Principles*, 10.

145 ILC, 'Report of the Study Group on the Fragmentation of International Law, Finalized by Martti Koskenniemi' (2006) ILC YB II/2 para. 28; see also Vázquez-Bermúdez, 'First Report on General Principles of Law', paras. 24–8.

146 Andenas, Chiussi, 'Cohesion, Convergence and Coherence of International Law', 10.

147 D. H. Hollis, 'The Existential Function of Interpretation in International Law', in A. Bianchi, D. Peat, M. Windsor (eds.), *Interpretation in International Law* (Oxford: Oxford University Press, 2015), 13.

of gap-fillers, the more the methods for identifying general principles tend to relax.

1.3.2 Due Diligence as a General Principle of Law?

When it comes to due diligence, there is little doubt that the concept was introduced in the international legal order by analogy with notions derived from domestic legal systems. In the Alabama claims arbitration, the pleadings of both the United States and the United Kingdom made reference to the notion of due diligence in their domestic law to define its meaning under the Treaty of Washington.[148] Likewise, early international practice shows that arbitral tribunals often tried to grasp the meaning of 'acting with due diligence' by looking at classical interpretations of the concept in domestic legal systems and Roman law in particular.[149] Yet, what most modern and contemporary scholarship has in mind when referring to the principle of due diligence is not the *diligentia quam suis* extrapolated from Roman law, but a general rule derived from the international legal system. Expressions such as 'the principle of due diligence', 'the general obligation of due diligence', the 'rule of due diligence', or the 'general standard of due diligence' generally point to a concept developed in international law that is now detached from any corresponding concept in national legal orders.[150]

The first observation is that the recognition of due diligence as a general principle is mainly the product of scholarship's elaboration. Except for some new-generation treaties which, for the most part, regard international human rights law,[151] treaty texts do not usually adopt the term due diligence, let alone refer to the concept as a principle. The same can be said about international courts, tribunals, and treaty bodies. The ICJ for example has eschewed reference to the principle of due diligence and, like other international courts and tribunals, normally invokes the concept either as a qualifier for a primary rule (the due diligence obligation 'x') or in a neutral way (e.g., speaking of a 'notion').

Furthermore, what many authors have in mind when referring to due diligence as a general principle is the no-harm rule. In other words, the

[148] Moore, *History and* Digest, vol. 1, 600–1.

[149] *Affaire des biens Britanniques au Maroc Espagnol*, 644.

[150] See, in general, ILA Study Group on Due Diligence, 'Second Report', 6–22.

[151] For instance Council of Europe Convention on Preventing and Combating Violence Against Women and Domestic Violence (adopted 11 May 2011, entered into force 1 August 2014) CETS No 210.

principle of due diligence is used as a shorthand expression for states' obligation not to knowingly allow their territory to be used for acts contrary to the rights of other states. This approach derives from the articulation of the no-harm rule before the ICJ in the Corfu Channel case and, more recently, in Pulp Mills. The Corfu Channel case involved a dispute between the United Kingdom and Albania. On 22 October 1946, two British warships were struck by mines and were heavily damaged while sailing the Corfu Channel in Albania's territorial waters. The court found that Albania was responsible under international law for the explosion that had occurred in its territorial waters and for the damage and loss of life that followed. It declared that Albania's responsibility ensued from its failure to notify the United Kingdom of the existence of mines in its territorial waters. The court extrapolated the duty to notify based on 'certain general and well-recognized principles', including 'every State's obligation not to allow knowingly its territory to be used for acts contrary to the rights of other States'.[152]

In the more recent Pulp Mills case, the question brought before the court regarded Uruguay's responsibility for violations of environmental obligations under a 1975 bilateral treaty with Argentina. In order to interpret the extent of Uruguay's obligations under this treaty, and in particular, Uruguay's obligation to preserve and protect the ecosystem of the San Juan River, the court looked at the customary obligation to prevent transboundary environmental harm, noting:

> [T]he *principle* of prevention, as a *customary rule*, has its *origins in the due diligence* that is required of a State in its territory. It is "every State's obligation not to allow knowingly its territory to be used for acts contrary to the rights of other States" (*Corfu Channel* (*United Kingdom* v. *Albania*), Merits, Judgement, ICJ Reports 1949, p. 22).[153]

Both the Corfu Channel and Pulp Mills decisions shed light on the ICJ's use of general principles, and, interestingly, on the relationship between general principles of international law and customary rules. In Corfu Channel, the court did not base Albania's duty to notify the United Kingdom on a customary or conventional obligation, given that the Hague Convention of 1907 – which provides for the duty of notification of a neutral power – was not applicable to the circumstances of the case. Instead, the ICJ judges resorted to general principles as the source of Albania's obligation to notify. As for the no-harm rule, it is open to

[152] *Corfu Channel Case (UK* v. *Albania)* (Merits) [1949] ICJ Rep 15, 22.
[153] *Pulp Mills*, para. 101 (emphasis added).

interpretation whether the court effectively deduced it as a general principle from the corpus of international legal rules or whether the term 'principle' was used as equivalent to a customary rule.[154] In any case, while at the time of the judgment the status of the no-harm rule may have been unclear, states' obligation to not knowingly allow their territory to be used for acts contrary to the rights of other states is now part of customary international law.[155] With regard to Pulp Mills, the judgement illustrates how deductive methods can permeate the identification of customary rules, or how general principles may be used for lowering the threshold of evidence required for establishing custom.[156] Indeed, the ICJ did not infer the customary nature of prevention in international environmental law based on the rigorous two-steps approach required to identify custom. The court identified the customary status of prevention based on the application of a general principle of due diligence extrapolated from the Corfu Channel dictum and applied to the environmental context.[157]

From the perspective of due diligence however, it does not appear that the court used due diligence per se as a free-standing source of obligations for states. In the Corfu Channel case, the ICJ judges inferred Albania's duty to exercise due diligence by way of notification from a combination of established rights (the right of innocent passage) and obligations (the *alienum non laedas* obligation).[158] In Pulp Mills, the court appeared to invoke due diligence as a shorthand expression for identifying the no-harm rule and the underlying *nature* of the conduct that this obligation imposes on states. Both in the Corfu Channel and

[154] See A. Shibatam 'The Court's Decision *In Silentium* on the Sources of International Law', in K. Bannelier, T. Christakis, S. Heathcote (eds.), *The ICJ and the Evolution of International Law: The Enduring Impact of the Corfu Channel Case* (London: Routledge, 2012), 207.

[155] According to Pellet, general principles are indeed a transitory source of international law, since they are inevitably going to be absorbed into rules of customary international law, Pellet, Müller, 'Article 38', 939–40; see also Palchetti, 'The Role of General Principles', 48–50.

[156] See S. Talmon, 'Determining Customary International Law: The ICJ's Methodology between Induction, Deduction and Assertion' (2015) 26 EJIL 417, especially 423–7; Palchetti, 'The Role of General Principles', 57–8.

[157] Supporting the idea that the 'principle' of due diligence was invoked by the ICJ in Pulp Mills to affirm the existence of the customary obligation of prevention of environmental harm, Y. Kerbrat, 'Le standard de due diligence, catalyseur d'obligations conventionnelles et coutumières pour les Etats', in Cassella, *Le standard de due diligence*, 27.

[158] S. Heathcote, 'State Omission and Due Diligence: Aspects of Fault, Damage, and Contribution to Injury in the Law of State Responsibility', in Bannelier, Christakis, Heathcote, *The ICJ and the Evolution of International Law*, 299.

Pulp Mills decisions, the duty to exercise due diligence was indeed highly contextualised and construed in relation to the general principles and obligations (the primary rules) to which it applied.

This does not mean that there is no commonality of understanding when speaking about due diligence in international law. When courts and tribunals invoke due diligence, they usually point to a common substratum that informs the interpretation and application of international rules. Still in relation to ICJ case law, the court has resorted to due diligence in a few other cases.[159] The most illustrative one is probably the 2007 Bosnian Genocide case, in which the court spoke of the 'notion of due diligence' as being of 'critical importance' for the interpretation of Serbia's obligation to prevent genocide in Srebrenica.[160] The court did not treat due diligence as a free-standing source of obligations for Serbia. Yet, the judges of the world court clearly had a certain substratum in mind when they employed due diligence to operationalise the nature and scope of the obligation to prevent genocide and to clarify its meaning. A similar approach was adopted by the ITLOS in its 2011 advisory opinion on the Responsibility and Obligations of States Sponsoring Persons and Entities with Respect to Activities in the Area. The tribunal used the notion of 'obligations of due diligence' to describe the nature of sponsoring states' obligations in the Area and to shed light on their content and scope.[161] Like in the ICJ Bosnian Genocide case, the ITLOS judges did not invoke due diligence as a free-standing source of rights and obligations for states in relation to activities in the Area. At the same time, they clearly alluded to a well-developed concept in international law which, once invoked, allowed them to better operationalise the primary rules under scrutiny. Investment arbitral tribunals, human rights courts, monitoring treaty bodies, and the practice of states appear to employ due diligence in the same fashion.[162] Reference to due

[159] In the Armed Activities case, the court resorted to the notion of 'vigilance', rather than due diligence, to define the nature and content of human rights and humanitarian obligations falling upon Uganda. However, it is submitted that the substance of these two concepts is the same, see *Case Concerning Armed Activities on the Territory of the Congo (Democratic Republic of the Congo* v. *Uganda)* (Merits) [2005] ICJ Rep 168, paras. 179, 189.

[160] *Case Concerning Application of the Convention on the Prevention and Punishment of the Crime of Genocide (Bosnia Herzegovina* v. *Serbia and Montenegro)* (Merits) [2007] ICJ Rep 43, para. 430.

[161] *Responsibility and Obligations of States Sponsoring Persons*, para. 117.

[162] Human Rights Committee, 'General Comment No. 31: The Nature of the General Legal Obligation Imposed on State Parties to the Covenant' (2004) UN Doc CCPR/C/21/

diligence is typically made in relation to specific primary rules either to provide concreteness to them or to underscore the nature and type of conduct that certain international obligations expect.

An overview of international practice suggests that due diligence is an international legal notion assisting the operationalisation of international rules of a conventional or customary character. Due diligence can be defined as a principle if, by the word 'principle', one intends an abstract concept originally extrapolated by analogy from domestic legal orders – and which has now acquired its own meaning in the international legal system – serving the interpretation of certain international rules by providing them with substance and rationale. Legal theorists sometimes speak of principles as general legal statements or as standards that underlie a class of rules and give them systematic meaning.[163] Ronald Dworkin for instance has famously described principles as general standards that serve a certain requirement but, different from rules, are not applicable in an all-or-nothing fashion. Principles help judges operationalise rules and determine the exact scope of legal obligations.[164] In a similar manner, Neil McCormick has construed principles as general norms that inform certain classes of rules and contribute by their application to the coherence of a legal system. McCormick explains that 'when we are in doubt about the proper meaning of the rule in a given context, reference to the principle may help us to explain how it is to be understood'.[165] Due diligence serves exactly this purpose: it identifies the nature of conduct required of a primary rule and explains how a rule is to be understood.

The only contexts in which the designation of due diligence as a principle alludes to a source of rights and obligations for states are the Corfu Channel dictum and the international environmental field. The no-harm rule extrapolated in the Corfu Channel case is now part of customary international law, yet it is often referred to as the 'principle of due diligence'. This obligation was originally deduced and enforced in relation to the duty of neutrality among states but has now been

Rev.1/Add.13 para. 8; Human Rights Committee, 'General Comment No. 36 (2018) on Article 6 of the International Covenant on Civil and Political Rights, on the Right to Life' (2018) UN Doc. CCPR/C/GC/36 para. 21; Committee Against Torture, 'General Comment No. 2' (2008) UN Doc. CAT/C/GC/2 para. 18.

163 N. McCormick, *Legal Reasoning and Legal Theory* (Oxford: Clarendon Press 1978), 152–6; see also R. Dworkin, 'The Modes of Rules I', in *Taking Rights Seriously: New Impression with a Reply to Critics* (London: Duckworth, 1977), 22–5.

164 Dworkin, 'The Modes of Rules I', 25.

165 McCormick, *Legal Reasoning*, 152–3.

transposed and applied to a variety of different situations, from the protection of the environment to the security of states in cyberspace, and possibly, human rights.[166] In the international environmental field, due diligence law is a notion at the boundary between a 'component' of primary rules (typically obligations to prevent) that helps their operation in practice and a principle source of obligations for states. On the one hand, the concept points to a specific standard of behaviour incorporated in treaties and various international environmental instruments that postulates a specific approach toward environmental risks. On the other, due diligence has also been invoked in the environmental context as a source for the identification of other duties, such as the general obligation of states to conduct an environmental impact assessment.[167]

To summarise, due diligence is not a free-standing obligation that is, per se, a source of rights and duties for states. It is a notion that is necessarily 'attached' to primary rules, whether customary or conventional, and that depends on these rules to be clearly defined. Yet, due diligence in international law works as a tool for assisting in the identification of certain classes of (primary) rules, their interpretation, and their operation in practice. It is, in this sense, a principle, if by principle one intends a 'cohesive force' for the convergence of a set of international obligations that acquire a specific meaning and rationale when read through the due diligence lens.[168]

Conceptualising the principle of due diligence in this manner does not imply that the concept points inevitably to a unique standard of behaviour applicable to all primary rules imbued with this notion.[169] As this book will illustrate, the understanding of what is 'due' by a primary

[166] Inter-American Court of Human Rights, *Environment and Human Rights*, Advisory Opinion OC-23/17 (2017) para. 101. In the same vein, HRC, 'General Comment No 36 (2018) on Article 6 of the International Covenant on Civil and Political Rights, on the Right to Life' (2018) UN Doc CCPR/C/GC/36 para. 22. The impression is that, by requiring states to regulate activities within their territory or under their jurisdiction in a way that does not negatively affect the human rights of individuals located abroad, these pronouncements provide a vertical dimension to the Corfu Channel principle. For a critical reappraisal of these pronouncements in light of the foundations of due diligence obligations, see Chapter 3, Section 3.1.2.

[167] *Construction of a Road*, para. 217.

[168] For the understanding of general principles as a cohesive force reinforcing the systemic nature of international law, Andenas, Chiussi, 'Cohesion, Convergence and Coherence of International Law', 9.

[169] Arguing against the recognition of due diligence as a general principle of law in the view, inter alia, of not imposing a uniform standard of behaviour, Krieger, Peters, 'Due Diligence and Structural Change', 376.

obligation of due diligence always relies on the content of the obligation and the legal regime to which the obligation belongs. What is due is, therefore, always highly contextualised. This notwithstanding, this book will show that there is indeed a common substratum in the international legal notion of due diligence. Such common substratum not only serves the identification of a certain typology of international obligations but also informs their content, their scope, and their application in practice.

1.4 Due Diligence as a *Qualifier* for Primary Rules and Due Diligence as a *Process*: Setting the Difference

There is a final caveat in the understanding of due diligence as unitary concept assisting the interpretation and operation of certain primary rules. In fact, the genealogy of due diligence as elaborated throughout this chapter points to a legal concept originally linked to state fault and then associated with international obligations of states. Yet, in contemporary international law, due diligence is also a reference notion for international organisations and in relation to activities carried out by certain non-state actors, such as private investors or businesses and multinational corporations. Reference to due diligence in these areas is not always tantamount to the international legal notion originated in the Alabama claims and developed through states' practice.

There are at least two meanings attached to due diligence in the contemporary international legal order. The first concerns an international standard of conduct or, as this book suggests, an *identifier* for certain international obligations, all sharing common elements in terms of nature, content, and scope of application. In the wording of ARSIWA, this variation of due diligence corresponds to an element of primary rules. The second meaning attached to due diligence describes a procedure in the policy sphere aimed at identifying risks and mitigating them with the view of ensuring responsible decision making. This form of due diligence – also defined as a 'due diligence audit'[170] or 'doing due diligence'[171] – is borrowed from the private business sector, where the concept traditionally refers to a process of investigating the risks to a company before executing a project. When due diligence is used in the international legal sphere in this second variation, it usually points to

[170] Ibid. 372.
[171] McDonald, 'The Role of Due Diligence', 1041.

a particular *process* of risk mitigation and not to a qualifier for singling out a particular category of international obligations.

Due diligence as a process of risk mitigation in the international legal order is commonly applied with regard to non-state actors, and for the most part, in the contexts of business and sustainable development.[172] At the UN level, one of the first documents to incorporate due diligence as an investigation and risk-mitigating process was the Guiding Principles on Business and Human Rights, adopted by the Human Rights Council in 2011. The principles address the relationship between businesses and human rights and set forth a non-binding legal framework for ensuring respect and protection of international human rights law by both states and private business operators. The principles identify several due diligence obligations among the obligations required of states to ensure the protection of human rights against business-related activities.[173] However, the principles do not expressly use the notion of due diligence for these duties. Instead, the expression 'human rights due diligence' recurs throughout the document in relation to the obligations of private business operators. For example, Principle 15 states that in order to meet their responsibility to respect human rights, businesses should adopt appropriate policies, including 'a human rights due diligence process to identify, prevent, mitigate and account for how they address their impact on human rights'.[174] Human rights due diligence is then defined as a process that should include 'assessing actual and potential human rights impacts, integrating and acting upon the findings, tracking responses, and communicating how impacts are addressed'.[175] Thus, due diligence for private business operators does not mark a standard of behaviour linked to a particular primary rule. The term is not employed to shape the *conduct* of a particular *obligation* but to indicate an audit process aimed at addressing a policy.[176]

A similar use of due diligence also occurs in international investment law and in relation to the law applicable to international organisations. In

[172] See United Nations Human Rights Council, 'Guiding Principles on Business and Human Rights: Implementing the United Nations "Protect, Respect and Remedy" Framework' (2011) UN Doc. A/HRC/17/31. For an overview of the meaning of due diligence in the Guiding Principles, see J. Bonnitcha, R. McCorquodale, 'The Concept of "Due Diligence" in the Guiding Principles on Business and Human Rights' (2017) 28 EJIL 899.

[173] See for instance 'Guiding Principles on Business and Human Rights', Principles 1, 4, 25. For the classification of these states' obligations as of due diligence, see Chapter 2.

[174] 'Guiding Principles on Business and Human Rights', Principle 15.

[175] Ibid. Principle 17.

[176] Krieger, Peters, 'Due Diligence and Structural Change', 372.

international investment law, due diligence may either identify a particular type of obligation falling upon the host states – in which case due diligence is used in its 'first' version – or indicate the process that risk-assessment investors have to undertake to be aware of the risks connected to their investment.[177] As for the law applicable to international organisations, a distinction is necessary between the due diligence obligations that may bind an international organisation as an entity with international legal personality, and the due diligence audits that may be part of an organisation's internal policy. As entities endowed with international legal personality separate from member states, international organisations are bound by a wide range of primary rules, including obligations of due diligence.[178] Although there are some differences between due diligence obligations as they apply to states and international organisations,[179] most of what is discussed in this book regarding states' due diligence obligations also applies to the due diligence obligations of international organisations.[180]

Due diligence is also used in the realm of international organisations to suggest a particular type of process or policy internal to the organisation, aimed at achieving a particular result – including compliance with a legal rule. There are several examples of this use of due diligence in practice.[181] An illustrative one is the 2013 UN Due Diligence Policy adopted by the UN as part of its efforts to comply with international human rights law, humanitarian law, and refugee law in the context of peacekeeping missions.[182] Although the document fits into the broader framework regarding the human rights *obligations* of the UN and its peacekeeping personnel, the UN Due Diligence Policy is a tool designed to ensure that the organisation conducts a risk-assessment of potential violations of human rights and humanitarian law prior to cooperating with non-UN forces. In other words, due diligence here encompasses a series of

177 M. Paparinskis, *The International Minimum Standard and Fair and Equitable Treatment* (Oxford: Oxford University Press, 2013), 256.

178 See the construction of EU due diligence obligations in the *ITLOS Request for an Advisory Opinion submitted by the Sub-Regional Fisheries Commission*, paras. 168–73.

179 See Introduction.

180 Supporting the analogy between international organisations and states due diligence obligations S. Besson, 'La Due Diligence en Droit International' (2020) 409 RCADI 167–79.

181 For instance, D. A. Desierto, 'Due Diligence in World Bank and Project Financing' in Krieger, Peters, Kreuzer, *Due Diligence*, 329.

182 UNGA, 'Human Rights Due Diligence Policy on United Nations Support to Non-United Nations Security Forces', (2013) UN Doc. A/67/775-S/2013/110.

measures and procedures which should ensure that the UN does not commit grave breaches of human rights and other norms.[183]

Finally, at least in some areas, the dimension of due diligence as a policy laid out to avert negative outcomes is increasingly connected to the practice of states. For instance, in the context of human rights and sustainable development, UN institutions have made increasing efforts to push states toward adopting 'due diligence policies'. This is demonstrated by the proliferation of 'human rights impact assessments' that states are encouraged to undertake in a variety of situations, such as prior to concluding trade agreements or before imposing economic sanctions on other states.[184] Human rights impact assessments are often framed as part of a broader policy of due diligence through which states should assess the potential negative impact of their financial, economic, and investment policies on human rights. States are therefore called upon to conduct impact assessments to identify and address the human rights risk that would arise from international economic policies or from proposed trade and investment agreements. Human rights impact assessments have been framed as a 'tool to ensure consistency and coherence between the obligations of States under international [human rights] law, and other international agreements to which they are parties, and thus to overcome, or at least mitigate, the problems resulting from the fragmentation of international law'.[185]

In any case, the legal boundary of these due diligence policies is often blurred. At times, rather than being framed as types of 'good practices' and policies, impact assessments are construed as components of states' primary obligations to ensure human rights. In other words, they are perceived as *duties* imposed on states as part of their human rights obligations, including obligations of international assistance and cooperation and positive obligations to protect human rights. In these situations, there is an overlap between due diligence as process involving risk governance and a state's obligations to protect that may impose, as part of due diligence, a requirement to undertake impact assessments.[186]

[183] N. D. White, 'Due Diligence, the UN, and Peacekeeping', in Krieger, Peters, Kreuzer, *Due Diligence*, 232.

[184] UNGA, 'Guiding Principles on Human Rights Impact Assessment of Economic Reforms' (2018) UN Doc. A/HRC/40/57; UNGA, 'Report of the Special Rapporteur on the Negative Impact of Unilateral Coercive Measures on the Enjoyment of Human Rights' (2017) UN Doc. A/HRC/36/44; UNGA, 'Guiding Principles on Human Rights Impact Assessments of Trade and Investment Agreements' (2011) UN Doc. A/HRC/19/59 Add.5, principle 1.

[185] Commentary to the Guiding Principles of Trade and Investment Agreements, para. 1.1.

[186] On the due diligence nature of obligations to protect see Chapter 2.

Concluding Remarks

This chapter has traced the genealogy of due diligence in international law. Ever since its emergence in international law, due diligence has been entwined with the responsibility of states in connection with acts of private individuals. The history of due diligence has been part of dogmatic discussions on the foundations of international responsibility. In this regard, the ILC codification work has greatly contributed toward conceptualising and systematising due diligence in international law. International practice and most international legal scholarship widely acknowledge that due diligence is an element of primary rules and not a general principle of responsibility. This is not to say that the question of due diligence in international law is now unhooked from broader responsibility issues, nor that the relationship between due diligence and secondary rules is smooth and uncomplicated. On the contrary, this relationship continues to resurrect in scholarship as one that is ambiguous and calls for persistent reconsideration of the boundary between primary and secondary rules. For this reason, even if one wishes to adhere to the orthodoxy of ARSIWA, any study of due diligence in international law cannot be approached simply from the perspective of primary rules and without dealing with issues of secondary norms.

In any case, this chapter has illustrated the journey of due diligence from the realm of international responsibility to that of primary rules and has clarified the relation between due diligence and relevant concepts such as fault and international liability. With respect to fault, it has been argued that there is an intimate connection between due diligence and the notion of state fault. Although ARSIWA do not list fault as a general condition necessary for an international wrongful act to accrue, it leaves open the possibility of construing responsibility for breaches of due diligence obligations as forms of responsibility based on fault. With regard to international liability, this chapter has explained why it is better to construe due diligence as an element of the general obligation to prevent transboundary harm from hazardous activities, and not as a 'shared' link between responsibility and liability. First, the concept of liability was eventually abandoned by the ILC because it was the source of great misunderstanding. Second, conceptualising due diligence as an element of a primary rule to prevent transboundary harm fits well the notion that due diligence is not limited to acts prohibited by international law but is an element linked to a variety of primary rules across international law.

Finally, this chapter has attempted to clarify the understanding of due diligence as a principle. Inasmuch as general principles are narrowly construed as a source of states' rights and obligations that fill legal *lacunae*, this author agrees that due diligence is not a principle of international law. Apart from situations in which the 'due diligence principle' is used as a shorthand reference for the no-harm rule, due diligence is not a free-standing obligation but something that always 'attaches' to a primary rule. However, a looser approach to 'principle' may indicate general legal statements that assist in the interpretation of classes of rules that give them meaning and rationale. From this perspective, due diligence works as a principle because it helps operationalise certain international obligations by providing them with meaning, content, and scope. As the following chapters will illustrate, the notion of due diligence operates as a qualifier for a specific class of international obligations, which all share common characteristics in terms of nature, scope, content, and relationship with secondary rules. Hence, invoking due diligence often serves the interpreter by allowing identification of the rule and its nature, clarifying its content, and operationalising it in practice. This understood, the principle of due diligence must be clearly distinguished from other concepts that, while sharing the same name and common origins, serve a much different function in the international legal order. Specifically, this chapter has underscored that due diligence, as applied to international obligations of states, differs substantially from the due diligence that is applicable to non-state actors like private investors and multinational corporations.

2

The Nature of Due Diligence Obligations

Introduction

This chapter asks to which international obligations the notion of due diligence applies and consequently, what type of conduct is required of the state to fulfil those obligations. Identifying due diligence obligations is an exercise of interpretation. Hence, this chapter builds primarily on international case law and treaty practices to examine the extent to which due diligence is incorporated into primary rules.

Categorising primary rules under the due diligence notion allows considerations of the type of conduct that is expected when a state is bound by certain international obligations. This may have consequences in terms of international responsibility. When conduct associated with an international obligation is recognised to have a specific character, this may affect whether an international wrongful act has occurred and the exact time of the breach. Thus, this chapter will map due diligence obligations to examine the nature of conduct required by these obligations and lay the groundwork for the discussion on how due diligence operates in determining international responsibility.[1]

To this end, it is necessary to reappraise the notions of obligations of conduct and obligations of result as well as concisely reassess the usefulness of this taxonomy in the theory of international obligations. Hence, the first part of the chapter considers the distinction between obligations of conduct and obligations of result. This is the grid used not only by the International Law Commission (ILC) for classifying obligations depending on the moment of the breach, but also by international courts and tribunals to construe due diligence obligations. Therefore, the analysis of

[1] While this chapter will outline some of the responsibility issues that arise from the categorisation of certain obligations as of due diligence, the relationship between due diligence obligations and international responsibility is addressed in Chapter 4.

this distinction precedes the rest of the chapter because it sets out the theoretical framework for identifying due diligence obligations. Furthermore, a preliminary account of the value of this taxonomy is warranted, in light of the debates that arose during the ILC work on the draft Articles on Responsibility of States for Internationally Wrongful Acts (ARSIWA)[2].

The chapter then uses an inductive method to conceptually grasp the structural features of due diligence obligations. The purpose is twofold. First, this chapter builds on international case law to establish to which international obligations due diligence normally attaches and why adjudicators and interpreters resort to due diligence to construe certain primary rules. Second, by analysing the structural traits of due diligence obligations, the chapter delves into treaty practices to identify clusters of international obligations that are imbued with the due diligence notion. Overall, this chapter provides the framework for the discussion in the rest of the book. Once it is established *which* international obligations due diligence serves and what nature these obligations share, it will be possible to examine *how* they operate, *what* due diligence entails in terms of content for obligations imbued with this notion, and *why* the due diligence parameter is used to provide them meaning.

2.1 Taxonomy in the Theory of International Obligations

Taxonomy can be defined as the grouping of entities into classes that can function in or facilitate the formation of scientific laws.[3] Classifications can be created based on different criteria, depending on the question they answer in a particular field of knowledge. On a very general level, however, taxonomy creates systems for organising knowledge.

Legal doctrine uses taxonomy to pinpoint different aspects of the international legal order.[4] One area of international law that commonly uses classifications is that related to the theory of international obligations.[5] First, taxonomy is used to distinguish international

[2] ILC Draft Articles on Responsibility of States for Internationally Wrongful Acts, with commentaries (2001) ILC YB II/2.

[3] See D. Hull, 'Taxonomy', in E. Craig (ed.), *Routledge Encyclopedia of Philosophy* (London: Routledge, 1998).

[4] The very organisation of international law as a body of knowledge in international legal manuals (the sources of international law, the subjects of international law, the substance of international law, etc.) is an exercise of taxonomy.

[5] On a general note, international law lacks a comprehensive study on the theory of international obligations. International obligations are normally considered by scholars

obligations according to their sources, whether they are customary or conventional, or based on a general principle, a binding judicial decision, or a unilateral act.[6] Classifications are also used to emphasise phenomenological aspects of international obligations, such as their extrinsic modalities and the type of behaviour they mandated on the international plane. Accordingly, one common distinction classifies obligations based on whether they consist of some degree of state action (a positive obligation) or whether they require state organs to abstain (a negative obligation), whereas another distinguishes obligations based on the way in which they are given effect within domestic legal orders, that is, whether they are self-executing or non-self-executing.[7]

In relation to state responsibility, the ILC discussed different taxonomies during the work on ARSIWA. The ILC construed these

in relation to some of their specific aspects, such as their sources, their effects, or the consequences of their breach. Dogmatic considerations on the concept of obligation and its legal foundations are provided by H. Kelsen, *Principles of Public International Law* (New York: Rinehart & Company, 1952), 7–9, according to which

> [t]he delict is neither a violation nor a negation of the law. It is conduct determined by the law as a condition of the sanction, likewise determined by the law. . . . If a conduct is the specific condition of a sanction, the contrary conduct is the content of a legal obligation. An individual is legally obligated to conduct himself in a definitive way if a sanction is provided for the contrary conduct.

See also R. Quadri, *Diritto internazionale pubblico* (Naples: Liguori, 1968), 585–6, for whom 'an obligation is nothing else than a mean of representing the consequence of the functioning of an objective legal order: the imposition of sanctions as a result of wrongful conduct' (*L'obbligo giuridico non è che un modo di rappresentarsi la conseguenza del funzionamento generale dell'ordinamento giuridico obbiettivo: scatto della sanzione in seguito alla condotta illecita*). For Quadri, obligations do not have autonomous existence, for they can be logically derived from sanctions and situations of responsibility. See also O. Schachter, 'Toward a Theory of International Obligation' (1968) 8 *Virginia Journal of International Law* 300, theorising the legal basis and the processes necessary for the establishment of legal obligations under international law. Older studies have also explored the notion of obligation in legal theory, see, for example G. Perassi, *Introduzione alle scienze giuridiche* (Cittá di Castello: Unione Arti Grafiche, 1938), and G. Sperduti, *Contributo alla teoria delle situazioni giuridiche soggettive* (Milan: Giuffé, 1944); for a discussion of the object and purpose that the reconstruction of a general theory of obligations may serve in international law, see A. Bleckmann, 'General Theory of Obligations under Public International Law' (1995) 38 GYIL 26.

6 A different classification that still looks at the source of obligations is the one offered by Tomuschat, which distinguishes between obligations arising out of states' consent and obligations that fall on states without their consent or against their will, C. Tomuschat, 'Obligations Arising for States without or against Their Will' (1993) 241 RCADI 209.

7 On this T. Buergenthal, 'Self-Executing and Non-Self-Executing Treaties in National and International Law' (1992) 235 RCADI 315.

classifications from the perspective of secondary rules, yet they reflect different aspects of international obligations.[8] For example, Special Rapporteur Ago articulated a distinction based on international crimes, international delicts, and breaches of a 'less serious' character.[9] Although this idea later radically changed, Chapter III, Part II of ARSIWA provides for special responsibility for serious breaches of obligations 'arising under a peremptory norm of general international law'.[10] The rules on invoking responsibility also reflect a distinction between the *statuses* of the breached obligations. Thus, Article 42(a) deals with obligations having a bilateral structure, whose breach individually injures the state to which they are owed. Article 42(b)(ii) deals with 'interdependent' obligations, which are owed to a group of states and whose breach may be of such a character 'as to radically change the position of all the other States' to which the obligation is owed. Obligations *erga omnes partes* are those owed to a group of states and established for the protection of the collective interest of the group. States especially affected by their breach are considered injured states (Article 42(b)(i)), while other states are states other than the injured one (Article 48(1)(a)). Finally, breaches of obligations *erga omnes* entitle states other than the injured one to invoke the conditions provided by Article 48(2), namely cessation, a guarantee of non-repetition, and reparation in the interest of the injured state (Article 48(1)(ii)).

This chapter focuses on a specific classification used by the ILC in early phases of the work of ARSIWA – the distinction between obligations of conduct and obligations of result.[11] The distinction was introduced to identify the conduct that constitutes an international wrongful act and the moment of the breach. It was eventually abandoned because governments and the ILC were sceptical as to its value. Specifically, it was argued that not all obligations can be classified as ones of conduct or result, and the only way to ascertain the existence of a breach is to look at the content and importance of the primary rule. Before delving into the details of this dichotomy, it is necessary to critically reappraise its function. Some of the

[8] See ILC YB (1973) II/2 184.

[9] ILC YB (1976) II/2 draft Article 19 at 26.

[10] ILC Draft Articles on Responsibility of States for Internationally Wrongful Acts (ARSIWA) with commentaries (2001) ILC YB II/2 Article 40(1).

[11] An exception to the lack of comprehensive studies on the phenomenology of international obligations and in particular on the distinction between obligations of conduct and obligations of result is A. Marchesi, *Obblighi di condotta e obblighi di risultato: Contributo allo studio degli obblighi internazionali* (Milan: Giuffrè, 2005).

arguments raised during the work of ARSIWA and against the distinction may in fact generate the idea that there is little if no added value in resorting to such classification. The purpose of the next two paragraphs is to rebut this thesis and to illustrate the cognitive function that taxonomy serves in interpreting primary rules.

2.1.1 Taxonomy as a Normative Tool in the Work of the International Law Commission on State Responsibility

During the ILC work on state responsibility, Special Rapporteur Ago introduced the problem of classification of obligations into the commission's agenda. Ago argued that the analysis of different categories of international obligations was useful for identifying different aspects of the 'objective element' of an international wrongful act and developing the notion of 'breach of an international obligation'.[12] Ago noted that the issue of breach must determine

> in what circumstances and on what conditions it must be concluded that a State has committed such a breach or ... infringed an international subjective right of one or more other States. The aim is also to define, on the basis of the conclusions thus established, the characteristics, in the different hypothesis envisaged, of such a breach and such an infringement.[13]

Ago sought to have the commission consider the way international obligations impose their requirements upon states and how to ensure their fulfilment.[14] For Ago, distinguishing obligations based on this criterion served two essential purposes. The first was to help determine the *existence* of the breach. In his sixth Report to the ILC, Ago set forth his belief that 'a difference should be established between obligations whose content is such that a breach is revealed by the simple fact that the State engages in conduct different from that expressly required of it', and obligations 'whose breach is only manifested when the conduct of the State is accompanied by an external event that the State should have prevented'.[15] Second, the distinction served to provide the *legal criteria* necessary for assisting the identification of the *tempus commissi delicti*, that is, the time and duration of the breach.[16]

[12] R. Ago 'Fifth Report on State Responsibility' (1976) ILC YB II/1 4.
[13] Ibid.
[14] Ago, 'Sixth Report on State Responsibility' (1977) ILC YB II/1 4.
[15] Ibid. 5.
[16] Ago noted that although the determination of the time of the breach of an international obligation 'is a question of verifying facts', such operation necessarily requires the

Prior to the ILC work, Ago had already attempted to classify different categories of international wrongful acts (*faits international illicites*) in 'Le délit international'. Building on the type of conduct required for a breach to arise, Ago had distinguished between *le fait illicite international d'omission* and *le fait illicite international d'action.* The first arose from a breach of a state's positive obligation to act, whereas the second arose out of the breach of a state's obligation to refrain from undertaking certain conduct.[17] A second classification was between cases where wrongfulness ensued from state conduct contrary to an international obligation and cases where the breach of an obligation required a wrongful state's wrongful conduct and the occurrence of a given (external) event.[18] Finally, 'Le délit international' also proposed a distinction between *délits internationaux simples* and *délits internationaux*

application of legal rules. Indeed, in discussing breaches of preventive obligations, Ago argued:

> Equally dependent on the application of legal criteria is the task of determining the *tempus commissi delicti* in the case ... where, in order for the breach of international obligation to exist, an external event must occur in addition to negligent conduct on the part of State organs. Indeed, in such cases the choice between the period during which the negligent conduct was adopted and the time at which the event rendered possible by that conduct occurred can only be made in the light of legal principles.

Ago, 'Eighth Report on State Responsibility' (1979) ILC YB II/1 37. This demonstrates that, for the Special Rapporteur, the taxonomy of obligations served a normative function, for its application had legal consequences in terms of wrongfulness and responsibility.

17 Ago, 'Le délit international' (1939) 68 RCADI 446–7.

18 As for the first category, Ago illustrated that *'Si un organe d'Etat insulte le Drapeau d'une nation avec laquelle son pays entretient des relations pacifiques, la conduit de l'organe es ten elle-même une lésion de la deuxième nation dans son droit au respect de son emblème, et elle est par là suffisante pour former la base objective d'un fait illicite international'* ('If an organ of the state insults the national flag of another state with which it undertakes peaceful relations, the conduct of this organ amounts in itself to the violation of the right of the second state, and it is sufficient to constitute an international wrongful act'). On the opposite end, Ago noted: *'Mais pour que l'on puisse dire qu'un Etat belligérant a violé l'obligation juridique de ne pas bombarder un hôpital... il faut aussi que cet objectif ait été effectivement attaint: qu'à la conduit de l'aviateur s'ajoute l'élément extérieur, le fait que l' hôpital a été attaint par des bombes'*, ('however, in order to conclude that a belligerent state has violated the obligation to refrain from bombing a hospital, it is necessary that the conduct of the aviator is coupled with an external event, i.e., the fact that the hospital has in fact been bombed') see Ago, 'Le délits, 447–8. The distinction between *délit internationaux simples* and *délits internationaux complexes* resembles the dichotomy in criminal law between *délits de pure conduite* and *délits d'événement.* In international law it was also elaborated by G. Morelli, *Nozioni di diritto internazionale* (Padua: CEDAM, 1967), 348–9.

complexes. Les délits internationaux simples arose from breaches of international obligations specifying the means (legislative, judicial, administrative) necessary to fulfil them; *les délits internationaux complexes* arose from breaches of obligations that left the state freedom to decide how to pursue the objective of the obligation. Specifically,

> *nous pouvons établir la possibilité de* deux modes différents de realisation d'un fait illicite international. *Le premier mode sera caractérisé, s'il s'agit d'un délit d'omission, par le fait de ne pas avoir exercé l'activité qui était spécifiquement demandée; et s'il s'agit d'un délit d'action, par le fait d'avoir exercé l'activité qui était spécifiquement défendue. Le deuxième mode, au contraire, sera caractérisé, en toute hypothèse, par la circonstance que le résultat concrètement voulu par l'obligation internationale n'a pas été finalement atteint.*[19]

The classifications set in 'Le délit' were reappraised and further elaborated upon during Ago's work as Special Rapporteur on ARSIWA. A tripartite classification was introduced that included obligations of conduct, obligations of result, and obligations to prevent (a given event). Obligations of conduct were defined as obligations requiring the state to adopt a particular course of conduct, for they determined the means of attaining the result set by the obligation in question. Their breach would arise by virtue of a state's adopting a course of conduct different from that specifically required by the obligation.[20] Obligations of result, being 'concerned with respect for the internal freedom of the State',[21] merely required the state to ensure a particular result. A breach would arise if, in exercising freedom of choice as to the means to be adopted, the state did not achieve the required result.[22] Finally, breaches of obligations to prevent would require the occurrence of the event to be prevented coupled with negligent conduct on the part of state organs.[23]

With the sole exception of preventive obligations, whose codification was partially retained by the ILC, the distinction between obligations of conduct and obligations of result was subject to much criticism that

[19] 'We can identify two different modalities for international wrongful acts to occur. The first consists of non-performance of the activity specifically required by the rule, which is the case of the *délit d'omission*, or performance of the activity proscribed by the rule, which is the case of the *délit d'action*. The second modality consists of not attaining the concrete result which was required by the obligation' (this author's translation) Ago, 'Le délit', 506–8 (emphasis added).

[20] Ago, 'Sixth Report', Proposed Article 20 at 8.

[21] Ibid.

[22] Ibid. 20.

[23] Ago, 'Seventh Report on State Responsibility' (1978) ILC YB II/1 32.

eventually prompted the ILC to abandon it. Ago's classifications were critiqued on three major grounds. First, this taxonomy of international obligations triggered a boundary problem between primary and secondary rules. During his work as a Special Rapporteur, Ago had acknowledged that issues on the existence, modality, and time of the breach of international obligations could overstep the domains of responsibility and cross into the realm of primary rules.[24] Initially however, the commission supported the view that the classification should be retained nonetheless. The ILC had concluded that while criteria for establishing when international law imposes obligations of conduct, result, or prevention remained confined to the stage of formation of primary rules, the conditions in which international obligations are breached belonged to the sphere of secondary rules.[25] This approach shifted during the revision of the draft articles adopted on the first reading. Specifically, the ILC eventually argued that the taxonomy of international obligations strayed too far in the field of primary obligations.[26] Its retention would have lessened the separation between primary and secondary rules and impinged on the domain of state responsibility, which was primarily devoted to consequences, effects, and results.[27]

In retrospect, the argument on the primary rule nature of Ago's taxonomy stands as one of the less convincing critiques set forth by the ILC. The current Part i of ARSIWA builds entirely on a functional rather than on an ontological distinction between primary and secondary rules. All the elements that play a role in determining the international wrongful act reflect substantive aspects of primary obligations. Chapter III of ARSIWA (breach of an international obligation) possibly reveals the highest degree of contiguity with the realm of primary rules. Furthermore, what at the end of the ARSIWA process influenced the ILC in deciding what would be labelled a secondary rule or classified as a primary norm were opportunity costs rather than dogmatic issues.[28] Thus, either one opts for discarding the entire Part I of ARSIWA, or one must admit that the nature of the conduct-result distinction is no more 'primary' than other codified rules on the breach and existence of the international wrongful act.

[24] Ago, 'Fifth Report', 5.
[25] ILC YB (1977) II/2 13.
[26] ILC YB (1999) II/2 51.
[27] Ibid. 60–1.
[28] ILC YB (1999) II/2 57–63.

The second string of critiques to including Ago's taxonomy into a project on international responsibility concerned substantive aspects of Ago's distinction. These will be further analysed in the following sections. In sum, some governments and members of the commission argued that the distinction between obligations of conduct and obligations of result was unnecessarily complex and could lead to unwanted results.[29] Others pointed to its confusing language, given that the dichotomy of conduct and result is normally used in French and other civil law systems to describe aspects of obligations that are not related to the choice of means necessary to fulfil them.[30] It was also suggested that not every international obligation can be classified as one of conduct, result, or prevention as international law is full of obligations of a hybrid nature.[31]

The final string of critiques related not to substance but to the normative function of the taxonomy in the framework of international responsibility. First, there had been concerns over whether the taxonomy of obligations devised for ARSIWA could effectively guide interpreters toward deciding on the existence of an international wrongful act. After reviewing relevant international case law, Special Rapporteur Crawford had in fact concluded that Ago's distinction was not necessarily decisive in answering questions of breach:

> In each case [under review] the question was one of interpretation of the relevant obligation, and the value of the distinction lies in its relevance to the measure of discretion left to the respondent State in carrying out the obligation. That discretion was necessarily constrained by the primary rule, and the crucial issue of appreciation was, to what extent? The distinction may help in some cases in expressing conclusions on this issue: whether it helps in arriving at them is another matter.[32]

Second, and most importantly, Crawford had argued that retaining the taxonomy ran the risk of transforming Ago's distinction into a substitute for the interpretation of the primary rule.[33] This was a powerful argument, one that justifies the benefit of overlooking the classification of obligations in the final version of ARSIWA. Had the distinction between obligations of conduct and result been maintained, it would have

29 ILC, 'Comments and Observations Received by Governments' (1998) UN Doc. A/CN.4/488 at 46–8.

30 Ibid. 67.

31 J. Crawford, 'Second Report on State Responsibility' (1999) II/1 27.

32 Ibid. 24.

33 Ibid. 26.

essentially operated as an intermediary in establishing international responsibility. The effect of providing normative value to a taxonomy of obligations is in fact to turn categorisation into a preliminary and necessary step for evaluating responsibility. In other words, if codified, the conduct-result taxonomy would have become a necessary 'intermediate process' in the establishment of breach and existence of the international wrongful act.[34] Yet, in a project strongly marked by pragmatic considerations, it was neither practical nor desirable to 'encase' international obligations into a rigid and predetermined grid. As will be shown in the following sections, there is still much inconsistency in international practice as to the meanings that conduct and result (and to some extent prevention) acquire when used to construe primary obligations. Furthermore, the wide array of formulations of international obligations in treaties makes it hard to always categorise obligations either as 'of conduct' or 'result'. Many primary rules portray structural features that would fail to be adequately captured within the distinction originally proposed by Ago. For these obligations, retaining the taxonomy would have added a further layer of complexity to the operation of responsibility, possibly rendering the question of breach even more arduous.

2.1.2 Taxonomy as a Cognitive Tool for Assisting in Interpreting Primary Rules

The fact that a taxonomy between obligations of conduct and obligations of result proved unsuitable for the purpose of codification should not undermine its authority and efficacy in international law. 'Conduct' and 'result' are parameters that scholars, arbitral tribunals, human rights courts, and the International Court of Justice (ICJ) still regularly employ to construe international obligations. The ILC's choice to drop the distinction in ARSIWA has not affected their use in practice. On the contrary, and taking the ICJ as a case study, the use of the conduct-result dichotomy seems to be increasing greatly, and it is certainly employed much more than it was during and before the ILC work on ARSIWA.[35]

The conduct-result taxonomy primarily serves a cognitive function and is instrumental to helping interpreters and adjudicators grasp the

[34] Ibid.

[35] The instances in which the ICJ used the notions of conduct or result remain relatively low, but the number of cases in which the court has used the distinction more than doubled after the adoption of ARSIWA. For a brief review of practice, see Section 2.2.4.

nature of international obligations. For example, in the Dispute Concerning Access to Information Under Article 9 of the OSPAR Convention between Ireland and the United Kingdom, the issue brought before the Arbitral Tribunal concerned the interpretation of Article 9(1) of the Convention for the Protection of the Marine Environment of the North East Atlantic (OSPAR),[36] which calls upon the contracting parties 'to ensure that their competent authorities are required to make available the information described in paragraph 2 of this Article to any natural legal person, in response to any reasonable request . . . as soon as possible and at least within two months'. Ireland used the category of obligations of result to contend that under this article, the contracting parties have to ensure that the information requested by a person is delivered by competent authorities.[37] The state wished to stress that it was not sufficient for the United Kingdom to merely provide a domestic regulatory framework dealing with information disclosure, since it is the 'result' – the delivery of the information requested – that matters.

The cognitive function of the dichotomy emerged also in the 2007 ICJ Bosnian Genocide case. In particular, when the court in this case interpreted the obligation to prevent genocide as an obligation of conduct, it did so to emphasise the structural elements of such obligation. The court noted that the obligation to prevent genocide 'is one of conduct, and not one of result, in the sense that a State cannot be under an obligation to succeed, whatever the circumstances, in preventing its commission of genocide'. Labelling the duty to prevent genocide as an obligation of conduct allowed the ICJ judges to argue that states bound by this obligation are required 'to employ all means reasonably available to them, so as to prevent genocide so far as possible'.[38] The conduct-result dichotomy assisted the court in interpreting a primary rule and outlining foundational traits linked to its nature.

Ian Brownlie had illustrated this function noting that the taxonomy 'should be regarded as a useful tool of analysis, as a servant and not a master' in interpreting primary rules.[39] This must certainly be the case

[36] Convention for the Protection of the Marine Environment of the North-East Atlantic (OSPAR) (adopted 22 November 1992, entered into force 25 March 1998) 2354 UNTS 67.

[37] *Dispute Concerning Access to Information Under Article 9 of the OSPAR Convention (Ireland v. United Kingdom) (*2003*)* 13 UNRIAA para. 147.

[38] *Case Concerning Application of the Convention on the Prevention and Punishment of the Crime of Genocide (Bosnia Herzegovina* v. *Serbia and Montenegro)* (Merits) [2007] ICJ Rep 43, para. 430.

[39] I. Brownlie, *System of the Law of Nations, State Responsibility*, Part I (Oxford: Oxford University Press, 1983), 241.

if one were to avoid using the distinction as an 'intermediate process of classification' for establishing responsibility, as the ILC had originally envisaged. In other words, the conduct-result distinction can guide interpreters when determining the content of primary rules, but it should not be used as a fixed predetermined grid to assess the breach of obligations in each and every case.

At the same time, the idea that taxonomy functions as a 'servant' and not a 'master' should not give way to misleading considerations on its genuine value. On the one hand, there is certainly truth in former Special Rapporteur Crawford's argument that distinguishing between conduct and result may not always be a determinant for establishing wrongfulness. The conduct-result dichotomy has served in some instances simply to better describe the content of primary rules, without necessarily entailing consequences for achieving a solution in terms of responsibility.[40] On the other hand, the assertion that the taxonomy between conduct and result is not in any away imbued with normative value should also be rejected. If the taxonomy serves to identify the nature of primary rules, it is clear that the structural elements of a primary obligation will bear on the way in which such obligation is breached. The nature and structure of international obligations necessarily influence the nature and form of international responsibility. In the Bosnian Genocide case, the classification of the obligation to prevent genocide as a best-effort obligation affected the way in which Serbia's responsibility for failing to prevent genocide was established. To argue that Serbia had failed to prevent genocide, the ICJ did not simply found that the occurrence of genocide in Srebrenica constituted Serbia's violation of Article 1 of the Genocide Convention. The court evaluated Serbia's efforts to prevent genocide in light of all of the circumstances of the case and determined the existence and content of Serbia's responsibility by classifying the duty to prevent genocide as an obligation of conduct.

In sum, while the ILC may have rightly opted out of *codifying* the dichotomy, that cannot be seen as a distinction carrying a solely descriptive value. The conduct-result classification may in some circumstances affect the way in which breach of an international obligation is determined. The impression, which will emerge more clearly in the course of

[40] Special Rapporteur Crawford reviewed case law to determine in which cases the conduct-result distinction elaborated by the ILC had effectively helped interpreters decide responsibility, see Crawford, 'Second Report', 22–4.

the analysis, is that much of the normative value of the conduct-result dichotomy depends on the *meaning* that interpreters attach to these notions. In international law, there are at least two different ways to intend the distinction between obligations of conduct and obligations of result. One is the Ago distinction. The other is the meaning of the distinction between 'conduct' and 'result' in civil law systems. While Ago's distinction may not have proved to be the determinant for the question of breach, the distinction between conduct and result in civil law systems does impinge on the way in which responsibility for breaches of certain primary rules is determined. Hence, much of the criticism over the value of the distinction stems from the fundamental disagreement over what distinguishes an obligation of conduct from an obligation of result. Such disagreement often creates confusion both in doctrine and practice in the way in which the dichotomy is used and consequently, its normative function in terms of responsibility.

2.2 The Distinction between Obligations of Conduct and Obligations of Result

Against this backdrop, it is necessary to look more specifically at the substantive facets of the distinction between obligations of conduct and obligations of result, for this will contribute to a better conceptual understanding of the nature of due diligence obligations. The outset of this chapter has briefly introduced the meaning of conduct and result as elaborated by Special Rapporteur Ago. This section explores in detail the specifics of the distinction, starting from the definitions endorsed by the ILC in the work on state responsibility. It then reappraises the distinction critically, and in particular, against its alternative counterpart, namely the distinction between obligations of conduct and obligations of result derived from civil law doctrines.

2.2.1 The ILC Distinction between Obligations of Conduct and Obligations of Result

Draft Articles 20 and 21, adopted by the ILC on the first reading, articulated the distinction between obligations of conduct and obligations of result as follows:

> *Article 20: Breach of an international obligation requiring the adoption of a particular course of conduct*

> There is a breach by a State of an international obligation requiring it to adopt a particular course of conduct when the conduct of that State is not in conformity with that required of it by that obligation.
>
> *Article 21: Breach of an international obligation requiring the achievement of a specific result*
>
> 1. There is a breach by a State of an international obligation requiring it to achieve, *by means of its own choice*, a specific result if, by the conduct adopted, the State does not achieve the result required of it by that obligation.
>
> 2. When the conduct of the State has created a situation not in conformity with the result required by it by an international obligations but the obligation allows that this or an equivalent result may nevertheless be achieved by subsequent conduct of the State, there is a breach of the obligation only if the State also fails by its subsequent conduct to achieve the result required of it by that obligation.[41]

Based on these definitions, the distinguishing criterion between conduct and result rests on the extent to which international law encroaches upon the state machinery by instructing state organs to conform to a particular behaviour.[42] Obligations of conduct specify the means or the course of action to be taken by the state to comply with the content of the primary rule. It is true that every international obligation imposes on the state a certain conduct (including obligations of result) and that every international obligation provides for an object or 'a result' to be achieved (including obligations of conduct). Yet, as noted in the Commentary to the draft Articles, what characterises obligations of conduct 'is not that obligations "of conduct" or "of means" do not have a particular object or result, but that their object or result must be achieved through *action, conduct or means "specifically determined" by the international obligation* itself'.[43]

The most illustrative examples of obligations of conduct are international obligations consisting of the approval or the repeal by legislative or other regulatory powers of specific laws and regulations. For instance, Article 4(1) of the ILO Convention on the Worst Forms of Child Labour Convention (no. 182), provides that the worst forms of child labour as defined in Article 3(d) of the Convention 'shall be determined by national laws or regulations or by the competent authority ... taking into consideration relevant international standards'.[44] This is an obligation of

41 ILC Draft Articles on State Responsibility with Commentaries Thereto Adopted by the International Law Commission on First Reading (1996) ILC YB II/2 draft Article 23.

42 Ago, 'Sixth Report', 8.

43 ILC, 'Commentary to the Draft Articles', 135 (emphasis added).

44 ILO Convention (no 182) Concerning the Prohibition and Immediate Action for the Elimination of the Worst Forms of Child Labour (adopted 17 June 1999, entered into force 19 November 2000) 2133 UNTS 161.

conduct because it obligates the state to adopt legislation to prohibit the worst forms of child labour. Non-conformity with the conduct specifically required by this primary rule – that is, failure to adopt the legislation required – results in a breach by the state party to Article 4(1) of the ILO Convention.

As argued by Ago and initially endorsed by the ILC, a specific course of conduct may also be imposed in the form of omission. Hence, the right of innocent passage in Article 17 of the United Nations Convention on the Law of the Sea (UNCLOS)[45] gives rise to a state's obligation to adopt a specific course of conduct, namely to refrain from any action that may interfere with a foreign ship's right of innocent passage through the state's territorial sea. This poses a problem concerning the degree of precision required for an obligation to be classified as one 'of conduct'. In fact, it may not always be entirely clear whether the content of an obligation designates the specific course(s) of conduct required of the state. Some obligations clearly lay down the types of actions/omissions to be complied with, but many others only point to a detailed objective to be reached, leaving the state free to decide on the specific means to fulfil this objective. For example, the Commentary to the draft Article 20 mentioned Article 33 of the Charter of the United Nations, under which states must settle their international disputes by peaceful means, some of which are specified by the rule. If one applies the same rationale of Article 17 of UNCLOS, this provision may be interpreted as an obligation of conduct, since it imposes states a particular course of conduct – to settle international disputes by peaceful means. However, the ILC Commentary stressed that this is an obligation of result, for states remain free to choose the peaceful means they consider most appropriate for settling disputes between them. In any case, Ago had acknowledged the issue of the degree of precision required for construing an obligation as 'of conduct', noting that 'difficulty may arise in a particular case in determining what in fact was the conduct of the State organs, and questions may always arise regarding the verification of the exact content of the obligation incumbent upon the State'.[46]

When the international obligation does not encroach upon state machinery and leaves the state free to determine how to achieve the objective set by the content of the primary rule, the obligation is one of

[45] United Nations Convention on the Law of the Sea (UNCLOS) (adopted 10 December 1982, entered into force 16 November 1994) 1833 UNTS 3.

[46] ILC, 'Commentary to the Draft Articles', 135.

result. Thus, obligations of result include a wide range of primary rules. They encompass obligations that entirely leave it to the state to choose between the means available to achieve the given result, such as many preventive obligations or obligations 'to adopt all the necessary measures' to attain a given result;[47] obligations that leave the freedom to choose to the state yet indicate a preference as to the means to be adopted to produce the required result;[48] and obligations that do not expressly provide for any measure to be adopted, yet their *raison d'être* lies in the state's assurance that the goal set by the obligation will be secured.[49]

Draft Article 21, paragraph 2, also provided for a specific category of obligations of result, which would be later be described as 'extended obligations of result'.[50] Ago had originally conceptualised these obligations noting that in some cases, despite an initial course of conduct incompatible with the result set by the obligation, the state is allowed to remedy the effects of this incompatibility either through adopting an alternative conduct or through adopting a subsequent conduct equivalent to the first. If the state attains the alternative result, this obliterates the consequences of the initial conduct. Hence, under these two options, it is only when there is failure to achieve the alternative or equivalent result that the obligation is breached. According to Ago, extended obligations of result applied to some international obligations in the field of human rights protection or the treatment of aliens and their property. For instance, in the case of the customary obligation to prevent unlawful attacks against the person or property of foreigners, Ago noted that if a state in a concrete case has been unable to prevent unlawful attacks against

47 One of the examples provided by Ago is Article 2(1) of the Convention on the Elimination of All Forms of Racial Discrimination (adopted 7 March 1966, entered into force 12 March 1969) 660 UNTS 195, which provides that 'State Parties condemn racial discrimination and undertake to pursue by all appropriate means and without delay a policy of eliminating racial discrimination in all its forms'; see Ago, 'Sixth Report', 9.

48 Ibid. 10, where one of the examples provided by the Special Rapporteur regards Articles 12, 16, 22(1) of the International Covenant on Civil and Political Rights (ICCPR) (adopted 16 December 1966, entered into force 23 March 1976) 999 UNTS 171.

49 Ago provides the example of Article 3(1) of the General Agreement on Tariffs and Trade (GATT) (adopted 30 October 1947, entered into force 30 May 1950) 64 UNTS 187 which states: 'The contracting parties recognize that internal taxes and other internal charges . . . should not be applied to imported or domestic products so as to afford protection to domestic production'. See also Ago, 'Sixth Report', 11.

50 Crawford, 'Second Report', 24.

an alien, the state can still discharge its obligation by offering reparation for the damage suffered.[51]

As for the relationship between the international wrongful act and the nature of the obligations, the Commentary to the draft Articles yielded the following conclusions. With regard to obligations specifically requiring the state to adopt a certain measure, it was noted that 'the mere fact of not adopting that measure constitutes in itself a breach of the international obligation in question'.[52] In relation to breaches of obligations of result, the ILC acknowledged that the task of determining their breach was more complex than in cases of obligations of conduct. As obligations of result were only concerned with the actual achievement, whatever the means, of the particular objective provided by the obligation, their breach required a failure of the state, *in concreto*, to achieve the desired result. In other words, the mere adoption by the state of measures abstractly in conflict with the result set by the obligation was not sufficient for determining responsibility.[53] As for breaches of extended obligations of result, the Commentary provided many concrete examples as to how

[51] In the draft Articles adopted on the first reading, the category of 'extended obligations of result' is linked to the question of exhaustion of local remedies. For Special Rapporteur Ago, the possibility of successfully invoking local remedies constituted the 'alternative' or 'subsequent' conduct capable of 'wiping out' the effects of the initial wrongful conduct. Draft Article 22 dealt with exhaustion of local remedies in the context of treatment of aliens and their property, see ILC, 'Commentary to the Draft Articles', draft Article 22. In the reports of Special Rapporteur Ago however, the question of exhaustion of local remedies was tackled not only in the context of treatment of aliens and their property, but also in relation to the protection of human rights.

[52] ILC, 'Commentary to the Draft Articles', 138.

[53] Ago, 'Sixth Report', 14–15. The fact that the breach would occur only in case of a state's failure *in concreto* to achieve the result set by the obligation was crucial for Ago, for it allowed the Special Rapporteur to explain the distinction between cases where mere failure to adopt legislation results in the breach of the obligation (when the obligation is 'of conduct'), and cases where lack of legislation must be accompanied by the circumstance that, in practice, the state has failed to ensure the desired result (when the obligation is 'of result'). Ago writes:

> The difficulties experienced by certain writers seem to us to be really due to the fact that they have not borne in mind the distinction to be made between the different types of obligation, and that have taken an undifferentiated position on the whole question whether the promulgation of a law 'contrary to international' is in itself a breach of its obligation by the State, or whether the breach only occurs later, when the law is applied in practice. . . . The writers who have based their solution of the problem on the distinction between the breach of obligations 'of conduct, and the breach of obligations 'of result' are undoubtedly those who have provided the valid criterion for deciding the question we are considering.

these obligations could effectively be breached. However, this was the category that would receive the greatest critiques from later doctrine, with scholars pointing to their confusing and unacceptable outcomes.[54]

On the whole, the core of the distinction between conduct and result as developed by the ILC concerned the relationship between international law and a state's domestic legal system.[55] A review of Ago's reports and the ILC Commentary demonstrates indeed that most of the examples regarding duties of conduct focused on obligations that required the state to enact domestic laws or adopt actions to be taken by executive or judicial state organs. Examples of obligations of result were instead much more diverse, ranging from obligations that set out general principles, to obligations of a preventive nature or obligations of progressive realisation of goals. The Commentary sought to provide guidance for the distinction in the following terms: obligations of conduct were described as those in which the action required of the state is typically to be taken at the level of direct relations between states. On the opposite, obligations of result predominate when states are required to bring about a certain situation within their internal systems.[56]

At any rate, it was because of the direct impingement of international law on domestic legal orders that Ago had understood obligations of conduct as more demanding than their counterpart. For Ago, the more stringent nature of obligations of conduct depended on the lack of a state's international freedom as to the means to be used to comply

[54] Combacau critically appraises Ago's construction of extended obligations of result by referring back to the Special Rapporteur's example of Article 9 of the ICCPR. In his reports, Ago had argued that if a state fails to achieve the result provided by Article 9(1) of the ICCPR ('no one shall be subject to arbitrary arrest or detention'), the state can still discharge its obligation by ensuring the remedies provided by Article 9(5) ('Anyone who has been the victim of unlawful arrest or detention shall have an enforceable right to compensation'). Combacau notes that, should this be really the case, Article 9 of the ICCPR could simply be interpreted in the following manner: '*Nul Etat ne peut, sans lui offrir de reparation, arrêter ou détenir arbitrairement un individu*' ('no state can arrest or detain arbitrarily an individual without offering compensation'), see J. Combacau, 'Obligations de résultat et obligations de comportement: quelques questions et pas de réponse', in *Le droit international: unité et diversité. Melanges offerts à Paul Reuter* (Paris: Pedone, 1981), 191–2. Essentially, the problem with Ago's conceptualisation is that it construes as alternative ('*alternatives*') obligations those that are in reality '*conjonctives*', since they '*portent sur deux objects distincts qui sont également dus*', see J. Salmon, 'Le fait étatique complexe: un notion contestable' (1982) 28 AFDI 709, 728–9.

[55] See P. M. Dupuy, 'Le fait générateur de la responsabilité international des États' (1984) 188 RCADI 50; B. Conforti, 'Obblighi di mezzo e obblighi di risultato nelle convenzioni di diritto uniforme' (1989) 25 *Rivista di diritto privato e processuale* 373–6.

[56] ILC, 'Commentary to the Draft Articles', 134.

with the primary rule. Obligations of result did not carry this stringency in their nature, since they respected the state's internal freedom by not imposing any particular means of compliance. Ago regarded them as the common standards in international law.[57]

In view of these considerations, one understands why critical arguments predicated on Ago's confusion with the meaning of conduct and result are not fully convincing.[58] Ago was well aware that in civil law, the distinction between obligations of conduct and obligations of result point to a different aspect of their nature and not to the greater or lesser determinacy of the content of the primary rule. Obligations of conduct in civil law systems are usually less demanding than obligations of result, for they only require the state 'to endeavour' towards the pursuit of a certain goal without the guarantee of its attainment. To clear up any source of misunderstanding with this latter dichotomy, Ago noted:

> 'it might ... be wiser to speak more precisely, with regard to the first category, of "obligations of specific conduct" and, consequently, of "international wrongful acts of specific conduct", for even in the case of "obligations of result" it is still the conduct of the State which is required in order to ensure the desired result'.[59]

This shows that Ago's distinction can hardly be classified as 'confused' or 'reversed in its meaning', as later contended by scholars.[60] Rather, his was a dichotomy built on earlier doctrinal works, including those of Triepel, Anzilotti, and Donato Donati, all of which concerned the relationship between international law and a state's internal legal order.[61] Donati's work in particular inspired Ago to draw a distinction between obligations of conduct and obligations of result. In his examination of the

[57] See Ago, 'Sixth Report', 4; see also ILC YB (1977) II/2 13.

[58] See Crawford, 'Second Report', 21, stating that the distinction proposed by Ago is predicated upon determinacy and not risks. For a critique of Ago's distinction in scholarship Combacau, 'Obligations de résultat et obligations de comportement', 198; Salmon, 'Le fait étatique complexe', 724–5; Dupuy, 'Reviewing the Difficulties of Codification: On Ago's Classification of Obligations of Means and Obligations of Result in Relation to State Responsibility' (1999) 10 EJIL 371, 375–6.

[59] Ago, 'Sixth Report', 8.

[60] Crawford, 'Second Report', 21.

[61] See Ago, 'Sixth Report', 4, fn. 3. Triepel and Anzilotti did not expressly distinguish between conduct and result; however, they both acknowledged that international law may either specify the type of domestic legal activity required of a state to perform its obligations, or it may leave to the state's internal legal order the choice of means to execute them, E. Triepel, *Völkerrecht und landesrecht*, trans. by Brunet, *Droit international et droit interne* (first published 1899, Oxford: Pedone, 1920), 296; D. Anzilotti, *Teoria generale della responsabilità dello Stato, Parte prima* (Florence: Lumachi Libraio Editore, 1902), 114–15.

effects of treaties on domestic constitutional systems, Donati noted that 'treaties provide States with rights and duties which consist of permitting, imposing or prohibiting to the State the execution of certain activities'.[62] He had conceptualised a first distinction among obligations arising out of treaties, by separating situations where international law *directly* requires the state to make changes to its internal legal system and situations where these changes are only imposed *indirectly*. For Donati,

> often treaties do not impose on a State the duty or the right to execute selected activities belonging to one of the State's three fundamental functions [legislative, administrative, judicial]; they simply impose the duty or the general right to execute activities that may produce a specific effect. Often treaties . . . grant or simply require to carry out activities functional to attaining a given objective . . . leaving the State free to determine or choose – in as much as this choice is permitted – the nature and form of such activities.[63]

Hence, Ago's conceptualisation of obligations of conduct and result was not based on a simple transposition of civil law analogies. It corresponded to an original aspect of the international legal order.

2.2.2 *The Critique: The Spectrum Argument*

One critique of the ILC's distinction between obligations of conduct and obligations of result regards the lack of a neat dichotomy between conduct and result. It has been noted that the distinguishing criterion between obligations of conduct and obligations of result consists of the greater or lesser determinacy as to the means that international law imposes to fulfil the obligation. Yet, determinacy is a relative concept that varies in degree depending on its basis of comparison.

[62] This author's translation is taken from D. Donati, *I trattati internazionali nel diritto costituzionale* (Turin: Unione tipografico-editrice torinese, 1906), 343: '*l'effetto dei trattati stipulati dallo Stato può essere o di imporre o di vietare o di consentire allo Stato stesso l'esplicazione di un'attività o legislativa o amministrativa o giurisdizionale*'.

[63] Ibid., this author's translation:

> *spesso dai trattati non deriva agli Stati contraenti il dovere o il diritto di esplicare un'attività specificatamente determinata per la sua appartenenza all'una o all'altra delle tre ricordate funzioni statuali fondamentali, ma deriva semplicemente il dovere o il diritto generico di esplicare quell'attività che può valere a raggiungere un determinato effetto. Spesso i trattati . . . concedono o impongono semplicemente allo Stato lo svolgimento di quella attività che è necessaria per il raggiungimento di un dato scopo . . . lasciando poi lo Stato libero di determinare o scegliere – in quanto tale scelta sia possibile – la natura materiale e la forma di tale attività.*

Take the example of Article 17 of UNCLOS, which was classified above as an obligation of conduct. The specific course of conduct required by this obligation consists of the peculiar act of refraining from interfering with the right of ships of all states to enjoy the innocent passage through a state's territorial sea. But this obligation may also be construed as an obligation of result, for one may argue that so long as the result is ensured – that is, that all ships are guaranteed the right of innocent passage and that the sovereignty of other states is not intruded upon – states remain free to decide how to conduct their activities. And indeed, this conundrum emerges in the readings of the ILC work on state responsibility. At some point in the Commentary to the draft Articles adopted on the first reading, the ILC provides the example of the general obligation of states not to interfere with the sovereignty of other states. The commission argued that this was an obligation of conduct, since a state's police and armed forces are prevented from adopting specific courses of conduct, all of which are identifiable *ex ante* (not to enter the territory of another state without its consent, not to make arrest there, etc.).[64] In a different section of the same commentary however, the prohibition against slavery and arbitrary arrest set by Article 4(1) and Article 5(1) of the European Convention on Human Rights (ECHR),[65] which are predicated upon the same logic of non-interference, are defined as obligations of result. The ILC notes: 'It is implicit in these provisions that the State is free to choose whatever means it considers best, calculated to ensure that no one can be held in slavery, that everyone's security is assured, etc.'[66]

The arbitrariness of the distinction between obligations of conduct and obligations of result also surfaces from a different angle. In Ago's original conceptualisation of conduct and result, determinacy rests upon the relationship between international law and domestic law. Essentially, the obligation is one 'of conduct' when international law lays out the domestic legal means or the internal legal organ called upon to fulfil the content of the obligation. But many primary rules in international law require the adoption of specific means at the international rather than the national level.[67] Take the case of obligations 'to negotiate' or 'to cooperate', which focus on particular international

64 Ago, 'Sixth Report', 6, supported by the commission in the ILC YB (1977) II/2 at 15.
65 European Convention for the Protection of Human Rights and Fundamental Freedoms (adopted 4 November 1950, entered into force 3 September 1953) 213 UNTS 221.
66 ILC YB (1977) II/2 at 20, fn. 66.
67 Combacau, 'Obligations de résultat et obligations de comportement', 209.

means that states must employ to pursue given goals. On the one hand, cooperation and negotiation are specific forms of actions that qualify the course of conduct states must adopt. From this viewpoint, they may be classified as obligations of conduct. This is especially apparent when such obligations stress the goal toward which negotiation and cooperation shall be oriented. In the Legality of the Threat or Use of Nuclear Weapons, the ICJ elaborated upon the meaning of Article VI of the Treaty of the Non-Proliferation of Nuclear Weapons, which requires states 'to pursue negotiations in good faith on effective measures relating to cessation of nuclear arms race . . . and on a treaty on general and complete disarmament[.].' The court argued that this is an obligation 'to achieve a precise result – nuclear disarmament in all its aspects – *by adopting a particular course of conduct*, namely, the pursuit of negotiations on the matter in good faith'.[68] On the other hand, one may argue that obligations to cooperate and negotiate are obligations of result, since states are required to ensure negotiation or cooperation but remain free to determine the means through which they perform.

These examples explain why the distinction between obligations of conduct and obligations of result were later defined by Special Rapporteur Crawford as 'not a dichotomy but a spectrum'.[69] Many primary rules are framed in ways that combine aspects of both conduct and result and intertwine them 'to such a degree that the different components can hardly be separated from one other'.[70] With the few exceptions of obligations clearly stating the degree of permissiveness provided by the duty, that is, to enact a *specific law or regulation* in the case of obligations of conduct or to '*prevent*' or '*adopt all the necessary measures*' to attain a given goal in cases of obligations of result, one grapples with the implementation of the distinction. If the ILC's ultimate goal of using the dichotomy was indeed to provide consequences in terms of responsibility, the relativity of its nature made this purpose clearly more challenging.

68 *Legality of the Threat or Use of Nuclear Weapons* (Advisory Opinion) [1996] ICJ Rep 226, para. 20.

69 Crawford, 'Second Report', 27.

70 C. Tomuschat, 'What Is a "Breach" of the European Convention on Human Rights?', in R. Lawson, M. de Blois (eds.), *The Dynamics of the Protection of Human Rights in Europe: Essays in Honour of Henry G. Schermers* (Leiden: Martinus Nijhoff, 1994), 324; Combacau, 'Obligations de résultat et obligations de comportement', 200.

2.2.3 *The Critique: Obligations of Conduct and Result in the Civil Law Doctrine*

As anticipated above, there is another relevant dichotomy between conduct and result that needs to be considered when discussing international obligations. Specifically, the distinction between international obligations of conduct and international obligations of result holds an alternative meaning if considered from the perspective of French legal doctrine[71] and other civil law systems.

In its 'domestic' and 'classical' versions, the conduct-result dichotomy builds on the concept of risk. Obligations of conduct are obligations 'to endeavour', only requiring a party to display its best effort toward the achievement of a particular result, without the guarantee of success. On the contrary, obligations of result are obligations to guarantee the result set by the obligation. Obligations of conduct are typically the ones that a doctor assumes in relation to a patient. While there is a duty incumbent upon the former to exercise their medical activity in conformance with the best standards of practice and with maximum effort, there is no strict expectation that the doctor will succeed in healing the patient. This also explains why the criteria for the distinction between conduct and result lay in the different degree of risk inherent in the object of the agreement. Contracts that impose obligations of result are premised on the assumption that the attainment of the goal set forth in the agreement does not involve a particular risk of failure on the part of the obligated party. Instead, in contracts that impose obligations of conduct, the goal provided by the obligation depends to a certain extent on conditions outside of the party's sphere of control. The obligated party is only required to display its best effort in trying to fulfil its obligation because this obligation carries a certain degree of *alea* as to its fulfilment.

Another direct consequence of the domestic distinction is that, with obligations of result, failure to achieve the goal releases the debtor only in cases of force majeure. Instead, failure to achieve the goal provided by an obligation of conduct does not necessarily involve the responsibility of the obligated party. In this case, responsibility will accrue should it be established that the debtor failed to exercise due diligence in seeking to

[71] The distinction between obligations of conduct and obligations of result was introduced for the first time by R. Demogue, *Traité des Obligations en General* (Paris: Libraire Arthur Rousseau, 1925), 536.

attain the result. In sum, responsibility arises only when fault of the debtor is proved.[72]

Against this background, it emerges why the ILC's understanding of conduct and result was later defined 'almost the opposite' of the domestic approach,[73] with Special Rapporteur Crawford arguing that draft Articles 20 and 21 had 'reversed' the effects of the distinction. In the civil law version of the dichotomy, obligations of result are perceived as more onerous than obligations of conduct because they are obligations 'to attain'. Conversely, obligations of conduct are generally less onerous because they are *only* best-effort duties that are not premised upon the guarantee that the result will be attained.

The distinction between obligations of conduct and obligations of result in the domestic context has also relevance on the international plane. Many primary rules in international law focus indeed on the efforts that states need to display toward results which cannot be absolutely guaranteed. These include international obligations focusing on a state's duty to prevent certain circumstances from materialising (e.g. transboundary environmental damage) or obligations requiring states to ensure that private activities taking place on their territory do not cause damage to other states or individuals. Usually, these obligations do not expect states to absolutely guarantee that the event to be prevented will not materialise or that private activities taking place on their territory will never damage other states. What these obligations require is for states to 'endeavour' to achieve a result, to exercise their best effort to ensure that these events will not occur.

Obligations to prevent or to protect internationally recognised values also fall into this category, as they usually expect states to enact all means necessary to ensure prevention and protection with no guarantee of the results. When analysed from the perspective of international responsibility, the crux of these obligations is not freedom of the state as to the choice of internal means to fulfil them. Simultaneously, the fact that the state may have failed to achieve the result is typically not the decisive element for a breach of such obligations. Rather, what counts is whether the state has taken all reasonable efforts to achieve the result, even if the latter was not eventually attained. Responsibility for breaches of these obligations depends on the state *not having chosen* the means – or not having exercised due diligence – that would have guaranteed the result (e.g. prevention of damage).

72 Combacau, 'Obligations de résultat et obligations de comportement', 195.
73 Dupuy, 'Reviewing the Difficulties of Codification', 375.

The problem with Ago's classification of international obligations is that it failed to allow for a proper understanding of obligations 'to endeavour', or obligations of conduct in the civil law sense. This gap was already identified and discussed by the members of the ILC after Ago's proposal of Articles 20 and 21. During the debate within the commission, some members had raised doubts on whether the Special Rapporteur's classification of conduct-result duly considered obligations of conduct based on risk.[74] In particular, their concern was that Ago's dichotomy did not capture situations in which the result set by the primary rule is not achieved – mainly because the result to be attained was not entirely within the state's sphere of control – but the state exercised all reasonable efforts toward it.[75]

The commission's initial criticism was partially addressed by Ago with his conceptualisation of obligations to prevent. Along with the distinction conduct-result, Ago had in fact proposed a 'third' category of international obligations whose object was the prevention of certain events. Specifically, draft Article 23 proposed by the Special Rapporteur and later adopted by the ILC on the first reading described obligations to prevent as follows: 'when the result required of a State by an international obligation is the prevention, by means of its own choice, of the occurrence of a given event, there is a breach of that obligation only if, by the conduct adopted, the State does not achieve that result'.

A full reading of Ago's report and comments before the ILC on this Article demonstrates that the Special Rapporteur did acknowledge the existence of international obligations in which the result depends on conditions outside of the state's strict sphere of control. For instance, in a passage of his eighth report, Ago noted in relation to the obligation to prevent an attack by private persons on a foreign embassy: 'It goes without saying that the preventive action required of the State consists essentially of surveillance and vigilance with a view to preventing this event, *in so far as it is materially possible*'.[76] Similarly, in the Commentary to draft Article 23 there were references to the concept of obligations to endeavour. The commission affirmed that, in assuming obligations to prevent 'States are not underwriting some kind of insurance to cover contracting States . . . against the occurrence of the event even regardless of any material possibility of the State's preventing it from occurring in

[74] ILC YB (1977) I see generally meetings 1455th, 1456th, 1457th, 1460th, 1462nd and in particular the comments of Mr Reuter, Mr Calle y Calle, Mr Verosta, and Mr Ushakov.

[75] Ibid. meeting 1457th para. 17.

[76] Ago, 'Eighth Report', 32.

a given case'.[77] Breaches of obligations to prevent would occur 'only when the event has occurred because the State has failed to prevent it by its conduct'.[78]

This notwithstanding, Ago did not conceive preventive obligations as 'pure' obligations of conduct in the 'domestic' mean. In particular, in the domestic conception of the distinction conduct-result, what matters for establishing whether the obligation of conduct has or has not been fulfilled is conduct adopted by the obliged party. In other words, if a state is bound to exercise best effort to prevent a given result, the important element for establishing a breach of such obligation is the violation of the best-effort duty, not the result actually achieved. However, this was not how Ago and, at least initially, the commission understood breaches of obligations to prevent. While acknowledging their best-effort nature, the Commentary to draft Article 23 affirmed indeed that, in relation to the breach, 'if the result which the obligation [to prevent] requires . . . is that one or another event should not take place, the key indication of breach . . . is the occurrence of the event, just as the non-occurrence of the event is the key indication of fulfilment of the obligation'.[79]

This approach toward obligations to prevent basically turned them into 'negative obligations of result'.[80] Neither the dichotomy conduct-result nor obligations to prevent as conceptualised by Ago fully accommodated 'pure' obligations of conduct (in the civil law meaning), whose featured element rests on the best-effort duty, and not the 'event' or the result to be achieved.[81] As will be discussed in more detail later on in this book,[82] failure to devote individual consideration to these obligations left an enduring impact both

[77] ILC, 'Commentary to the Draft Articles', 173.

[78] Ibid.

[79] ILC, 'Commentary to the Draft Articles', 172–3.

[80] This is indeed confirmed by Ago, see ILC YB (1978) I meeting 1477th para. 9: 'There was no question . . . that when the obligation was formulated in such a way as to require that the State prevent the occurrence of a certain event, by means of its choice, the obligation incumbent upon it was one of result.'

[81] This is mainly because, for Ago, due diligence obligations were either grouped under obligations to prevent, hence obligations of 'negative' result, or they were considered as obligations requiring the adoption of a particular course of conduct. On the issue of the lack of proper conceptualisation of 'pure' obligations of conduct in Ago's taxonomy see the comment of Mr Reuter, ILC YB (1978) meeting 1478th, para. 7. On how Ago conceptualised due diligence obligations see also A. Gattini, 'Breach of International Obligations', in A. Nollkaemper, I. Plakokefalos (eds.), *Principles of Shared Responsibility: An Appraisal of the State of the Art* (Cambridge: Cambridge University Press, 2014), 35–7.

[82] See Section 2.4.1; on the breach of obligations of due diligence and specifically on the breach of preventive obligations see chapter 4.

on the appreciation of the ILC's taxonomy and on a proper conceptualisation of due diligence obligations under international law.

As for the ILC's taxonomy, during the second reading of the draft Articles on State Responsibility, the commission's initial support for Ago's classification of obligations was called into question also because it overlooked obligations to 'endeavour' or 'of conduct' in the civil law variation.[83] The ILC members agreed since Ago's classification failed to cover all the externalities of international obligations and created confusion with the classic civil law distinction, that it was best to drop the conduct-result distinction all together.

As for how the ILC's codification work has affected the conceptualisation of due diligence obligations, suffice it to say here that the ILC work created a contradiction between due diligence and obligations to prevent as understood by the commission. This contradiction occasionally emerges in scholarship and international practice, and it is one of the reasons why in international law the dogmatic foundations of due diligence obligations are still hard to trace.

2.2.4 A Cursory Glance at the Use of Conduct and Result in International Practice

Before moving to the conceptual analysis of due diligence obligations in international law, it is useful to provide a brief reappraisal of the use of the concepts 'obligations of conduct' and 'obligations of result' in international practice. Although it is not the purpose of this book to conduct a comprehensive analysis of how international courts and tribunals apply the taxonomy of international obligations, a cursory look at some areas of practice can help draw relevant observations on the importance of the dichotomy in current international law. In particular, a focus on the practice of the ICJ suggests that the conduct-result dichotomy is alive and well and is used by the court in its various meanings.

First, despite being heavily criticised, Ago's version of the distinction between conduct and result still finds application in practice. A clear reference to it was made in the Immunity from Legal Process advisory

[83] Later, authoritative scholars would even suggest that if the categorisation of international obligations had to be preserved in ARSIWA, it should have been the civil law categorisation between obligations to 'endeavour' (or 'of conduct' in the civil law variation) and obligations to 'attain a given result' as duties to reach a certain goal, see Dupuy, 'Reviewing the Difficulties of Codification', 379, 382. More extensively on the debate within the ILC see Chapter 4, Section 4.1.2.

opinion by the government of Malaysia in relation to the obligation set forth in Article VI, Section 22, of the Convention on the Privileges and Immunities of the United Nations. This rule provides that

> Experts . . . performing missions for the United Nations shall be accorded such privileges and immunities as are necessary for the independent exercise of their functions during the period of their missions . . . In particular they shall be accorded: . . . (b) in respect to words spoken or written and acts done by them in the course of the performance of their mission, immunity from legal process of any kind.

The question submitted to the ICJ centred around Malaysia's failure to inform its judicial authorities that Mr Cumaraswamy, UN Special Rapporteur of the Commission on Human Rights, enjoyed immunity from legal process and could not be arrested for words spoken in the course of the performance of his mission. Malaysia contended that Article VI, Section 22 is 'an obligation of result and not of means to be employed in achieving that result'. Therefore

> Malaysia has complied with its obligation under Section 34 of the General Convention, which provides that a party to the Convention must be 'in a position under its own law to give effects to [its] own terms', by enacting the necessary legislation; finally, it contends that the Malaysian courts have not yet reached a final decision as to Mr Cumaraswamy's entitlement to immunity from legal process.[84]

It appears that the phrase obligation of result was used according to Ago's understanding of the term. Malaysia argued indeed that failure to inform its judicial authorities could not by itself constitute an international wrongful act since Article VI, Section 22 can only be breached once a final decision as to immunity from legal process is taken by competent state organs.[85] The court in its findings did not elaborate upon the notion of obligations of result and the classification provided by Malaysia. However, it argued that Article VI, Section 22 requires that state authorities immediately notify their judicial authorities of immunity from legal process of UN representatives and that Malaysia had therefore not complied with this obligation.[86]

Another example where the ICJ made use of Ago's distinction is the Interim Accord case, where the court addressed the question on the

[84] *Difference Relating to Immunity from Legal Process of a Special Rapporteur of the Commission on Human Rights* (Advisory Opinion) [1999] ICJ Rep 62, para. 58.

[85] In particular, Malaysia appears to refer to the obligation set forth in Article IV, Section 22 as an 'extended obligation of result'.

[86] *Difference Relating to Immunity from Legal Process*, paras. 57–62.

nature of Article 11(1) of the 1995 Interim Accord between Greece and the Former Yugoslav Republic of Macedonia (FYROM). The first part of paragraph 1 of Article 11 provides that the Hellenic Republic 'agrees not to object to the application by or the membership of the Party of the Second Part [FYROM] in international, multilateral and regional organizations and institutions' of which Greece was a member. The ICJ noted that the obligation 'not to object' did not require Greece to actively support FYROM's admission to international organisations and that the parties agreed that such obligation is one of conduct.[87]

The ICJ has also employed the distinction between conduct and result in its civil law understanding. In the 2007 Bosnia Genocide case, the court notably used the concept of obligations of conduct to construe the nature of the obligation to prevent genocide as a best-effort obligation. In stressing that a state cannot guarantee against the commission of genocide in any circumstance but is only asked to employ all means reasonably available to prevent it, the Court opted for construing such obligation as a duty to endeavour.[88]

Less clear was the use of conduct and result that the court made in the Pulp Mills case. At some point in the decision – which famously regarded the environmental consequences of the construction of two mills on the River of Uruguay – the court was asked to make a pronouncement on the nature of Articles 36 and 41 of the 1975 Statute of the River of Uruguay between Argentina and Uruguay. In relation to Article 36 (obligation to coordinate measures to avoid changes in the ecological balance of the river) the ICJ affirmed that this Article 'imposes an obligation on both States to take positive steps to avoid changes in the ecological balance. These steps consist not only in the adoption of a regulatory framework ... but also in the observance and enforcement by both Parties of the measures adopted'.[89]

Argentina claimed that this was an obligation of result. The court noted that Article 36 'prescribes the *specific* conduct of coordinating

[87] *Application of the Interim Accord of 13 September 1995 (The Former Yugoslav Republic of Macedonia* v. *Greece)* [2011] ICJ Rep 644. The court seems to refer to notion of obligations of conduct as obligations to adopt a particular course of conduct at the international level. Macedonia's submission to the court confirmed this, noting that 'the obligation is violated if the objection occurs at any point once the Applicant initiates the process for joining a particular organization or institution', see *Memorial of the Former Yugoslav Republic of Macedonia*, para. 4.18.

[88] *Genocide* case, para. 430.

[89] *Case Concerning Pulp Mills on the River Uruguay* (*Argentina* v. *Uruguay*) (Merits) [2010] ICJ Rep 14, para. 185.

the necessary measures . . . to avoid changes in the ecological balance' and that an 'obligation to adopt regulatory or administrative measures either individually or jointly and to enforce them is an obligation of conduct'.[90] It is not clear what the court meant by obligations of conduct, but the reference to specific conduct consisting in the adoption of regulatory framework and enforcement points to Ago's understanding of the notion. Yet, in relation to Article 41 (obligation to prevent pollution and to preserve the aquatic environment) the court seems to use a different taxonomy. Argentina claimed that the obligation to prevent pollution and preserve the aquatic environment was one of result, while Uruguay maintained that these were obligations of conduct. The court did not use the conduct-result dichotomy, but it noted that this obligation was one of due diligence, because Article 41 entails 'the adoption of appropriate measures and a certain level of vigilance in their enforcement'. The court also stressed that 'the responsibility of a party . . . would . . . be engaged if it was shown that it had failed to act diligently and take all the appropriate measures to enforce its relevant regulation'. The understanding of Article 41 as a best-effort obligation, breached only in cases of failure to exercise due diligence, points to the civil law distinction between conduct and result.

This interchangeable use of the dichotomy is even more apparent in cases where the ICJ has effectively merged the distinctions, comparing, for example, the concept of obligations of conduct in Ago's sense with obligations of result in the civil law version. One example is the already mentioned passage of the Legality of the Threat or Use of Nuclear Weapons, where the ICJ was confronted with the meaning of Article VI of the Treaty of the Non-Proliferation of Nuclear Weapons (TNP). The court noted that the legal import of the obligation to undertake to pursue negotiation in good faith on effective measures related to the cessation of the nuclear arms race 'goes *beyond* that of a *mere* obligation of conduct; the obligation involved here is an *obligation to achieve a precise result* – nuclear disarmament in all its aspects – by *adopting a particular course of conduct*, namely the pursuit of negotiations on the matter in good faith'.[91]

The court appears to refer to obligations of result in their civil law version as obligations to guarantee a particular result. Yet, this notion is opposed to an understanding of obligations of conduct that carries

[90] Ibid. para. 77.

[91] *Legality of the Threat or Use of Nuclear Weapons*, para. 100.

a twofold meaning. On the one hand, when the court says that the obligation to negotiate goes *beyond* that of a *mere* obligation of conduct, it is implicitly referring to obligations of conduct as obligations 'to endeavour'; on the other hand, reference to the obligation to adopt a particular course of conduct is clearly an allusion to Ago's distinction. Similar observations can be made in relation to the recent Jadhav case. The dispute concerned the nature of Pakistan's obligation 'to provide effective review and reconsideration' of the conviction and sentence of Mr Jadhav following Pakistan's breach of Article 36(1) of the Vienna Convention on Consular Relations. The ICJ stated:

> The Court notes that the obligation to provide effective review and reconsideration can be carried out in various ways. The choice of means is left to Pakistan. . . . Nevertheless, freedom in the choice of means is not without qualification. . . . The obligation to provide effective review and reconsideration is 'an obligation of result' which 'must be performed unconditionally' . . . Consequently, Pakistan shall take all measures to provide for effective review and reconsideration, including, if necessary, by enacting appropriate legislation.[92]

Here the court appears to merge the two different versions of obligations of result. By stating that the obligation to provide effective review 'requires a specific outcome' and 'must be performed unconditionally' the court resumes the notion of obligations of result as obligations to attain (in the civil law variation). In particular, in the Request for Interpretation of the Avena case judgment, the court stressed that the obligation to provide effective review and reconsideration 'must be met within a reasonable amount of time' and that, even serious efforts by a state, should they fall short of providing review and reconsideration, 'would not be regarded as fulfilling this obligation of result'.[93] At the same time, by noting that the obligations to carry an effective review leaves to the state the choice of means to ensure effectiveness, the court appears also to abide by Ago's interpretation of obligations of result.

Finally, an interesting approach to the merging of the different meaning of conduct and result is offered in the Gabčíkovo-Nagymaros case. Here the ICJ pointed to the existence of three different types of obligations arguing that, through the Treaty on the Construction and Operation of the Gabčíkovo-Nagymaros Project, Hungary and Slovakia

92 *Jadhav* case *(India* v. *Pakistan)* (Merits) [2019] ICJ Rep 231, para. 146.

93 *Request for Interpretation of the Judgement of 31 March 2004 in the Case Concerning Avena and Other Mexican Nationals (Mexico* v. *United States of America)* (Merits) [2009] ICJ Rep 3, para. 27.

had undertaken 'obligations of conduct, obligations of performance, and obligations of result'.[94] Specifically, the court held that Articles 15, 19, and 20 – which respectively required the parties to 'ensure, by means specified in the joint contractual plan, that the quality of the water in the Danube is not impaired as a result of construction and operations'; to 'ensure compliance with the obligation to protect nature'; and to 'take the appropriate measures' for the protection of fishing interests'

> [d]o not contain specific *obligations of performance* but require the parties, in carrying out their obligations . . . to take new environmental norms into consideration when agreeing upon the *means* to be specified in the Joint Contractual Plan. . . . The obligations . . . are, by definition, general and have to be transformed into *specific obligations of performance* through a process of consultation and negotiation.[95]

While the court did not clarify the meaning of obligations of conduct and obligations of result, a plausible interpretation is that they were intended in the civil law meaning. In fact, the court recognises that Articles 15 and 19 are duties that 'impose a continuing – and thus necessarily evolving – obligation on the parties' to maintain the quality of the water in the Danube and to preserve the environment. The ICJ did not explicitly link these duties with the concept of best-effort obligations, yet it did connect them with the concepts of *vigilance* and *prevention* inherent in the field of environmental protection.[96] This would suggest a reading of the obligations to protect the environment and to ensure no damage to the Danube waters as obligations of endeavour, a conclusion that the court explicitly reaches in Pulp Mills. Yet, the notion of obligations of performance used by the court seems to correspond to Ago's understanding of obligations of conduct. This is supported by the court's argument that obligations of performance are *specific* obligations that should consist of the adoption of new environmental standards agreed upon through a process of consultation and negotiation.

This brief reappraisal of practice suggests the following. First, seeking to discern from practice which conduct-result taxonomy is more valuable seems a futile exercise. The ICJ continues to use the distinction two ways and often does so by overlapping the distinctions without much methodological rigour. Rather than using the confusion over the meaning of conduct and result to suggest that the dichotomy should be relinquished

94 *Gabčíkovo-Nagymaros Project (Hungary* v. *Slovakia)* (Merits) [1997] ICJ Rep 7, para. 135.
95 Ibid. paras. 111–12.
96 Ibid. para. 140.

all together, one may start by acknowledging that both versions carry analytical value.[97] After all, once it is apparent to the reader and the interpreter that these two taxonomies are based on different distinguishing criteria, each version can prove useful to grasp different aspects of primary rules. Thus, when courts really want to stress that the fulfilment of the goals set by the primary rule depends on the *specific* course of conduct agreed by states at the international level, they will opt for the concept of Ago's obligation of conduct. When they want to emphasise that the breach of an obligation does not depend on simply failing to ensure the objective set by the primary rule but rather on failing to adopt measures within a state's power to pursue that goal, they will resort to the civil law version of the dichotomy.

Furthermore, the lack of any codified rule as to the meaning of conduct and result facilitates the use of both taxonomies in practice. If there is no formal indication of which distinction should be preferred, interpreters and adjudicators can efficiently use both versions. In particular, it appears that the ICJ often leans on a 'tripartite' classification that includes obligations of conduct and result in their civil law version, and obligations to adopt a particular course of conduct.[98] Admittedly, obligations of conduct (or 'to endeavour') are extremely useful tools to analyse due diligence obligations, which are traditionally seen as best-effort obligations. At the same time, the notion of obligations 'to adopt a particular course of conduct' can be of significant value when one wishes to pinpoint to the more or less 'determinacy' of a legal rule, or make a comparison between rules in order to assess which is more stringent

[97] From this viewpoint, conduct and result are not necessarily exhaustive categories if one's aim is to provide a comprehensive classification of international obligations. Other criteria may highlight the specific features of international obligations, some of which may not be adequately reflected through the conduct-result dichotomy. See in this regard R. Wolfrum, 'Obligations of Result Versus Obligation of Conduct: Some Thoughts About the Implementation of International Obligations', in M. H. Arsanjani, J. Cogan, R. Sloane, S. Wiessner (eds.), *Looking into the Future: Essays on International Law in Honor of W. Michael Reisman* (Leiden: Brill, 2010), 353–83; in the context of human rights; see R. Pisillo-Mazzeschi, 'Responsabilité de l'état pour violation des obligations positives relatives aux droits de l'homme' (2008) RCADI 333, construing various categories of international obligations.

[98] On the opportunity to resort to the tripartite classification for covering all externalities of international obligations, A. Marchesi, 'The Distinction between Obligations of Conduct and Obligations of Result Following its Deletion from the Draft Articles on State Responsibility', in *Studi in onore di Gaetano Arangio-Ruiz* (Naples: Editoriale Scientifica, 2004), vol. 2, 827; and, more extensively, Marchesi, *Obblighi di condotta e obblighi di risultato*, 116–22.

in terms of means of compliance.[99] From this perspective, one can, at least for now, set aside the question of which distinction the ILC should have preferred for the purpose of international responsibility and acknowledge that both taxonomies are practical tools for legal analysis.

2.3 The Conceptual Understanding of Due Diligence Obligations

In contemporary international law, it is a well-established fact that due diligence only attaches to certain categories of international obligations. The Commentary to ARSIWA acknowledges this truth implicitly when it states that whether or not a primary obligation requires due diligence depends on the interpretation of the rule and its content. But even before the adoption of ARSIWA, Riccardo Pisillo-Mazzeschi had illustrated this aspect so clearly in his seminal work on due diligence in international law, that there is no reason to devote further analysis to the issue.[100] Hence, the intention of this section is not to demonstrate that due diligence has a limited scope of application in the theory of international obligations. Rather, this section investigates the extent to which due diligence operates vis-à-vis primary rules in order to conceptually grasp the characteristics of international obligations imbued with this notion.

To this end, it is useful to start with the description of due diligence obligations provided by the Seabed Dispute Chamber of the International Tribunal for the Law of the Sea (ITLOS) in the 2011 advisory opinion on the Responsibility and Obligations of States Sponsoring Persons and Entities with Respect to Activities in the Area. In discussing the nature of states' obligations 'to ensure' that activities carried out in the Area are in conformity with the obligations set in Part XI of the UNCLOS, the tribunal noted:

> 110. The sponsoring State's obligation to 'ensure' is *not an obligation to achieve, in each and every case, the result* that the sponsored contractor complies with the aforementioned obligations. Rather, it is an *obligation to deploy adequate means, to exercise the best possible efforts, to do the utmost, to obtain this result.* To utilize a terminology current in international law, this obligation may be

[99] On how the tripartite classification can assist the interpretation of due diligence obligations see Chapter 5, Section 5.2.1.

[100] Pisillo-Mazzeschi, 'The Due Diligence Rule and the Nature of International Responsibility of States' (1992) 35 GYIL 9, 46–9 and, more extensively, Pisillo-Mazzeschi, *Due diligence e responsabiitá internazionale degli stati* (Milan: Giuffré, 1989).

characterized as an *obligation of 'conduct'* and not 'of result', as an obligation of 'due diligence'.

117. The content of 'due diligence' obligations may not be easily described in precise terms. Among the factors that make such a description difficult is the fact that *'due diligence' is a variable concept*. It may change over time as measures considered sufficiently diligent at a certain moment may become not diligent enough in light, for instance, of new scientific and technological knowledge. *It may also change in relation to the risk involved in the activity.*[101]

These two passages identify the main structural features of due diligence obligations. These are: i) the association of the obligation with the concept of risk, ii) the 'conduct' nature of due diligence obligations, and iii) the flexible character of obligations imbued with due diligence.

2.3.1 The Risk Associated with Due Diligence Obligations

At the end of his analysis on the status of due diligence in international law and after a comprehensive review of practice on the security of foreign nationals and their property, the security of foreign states, and the conservation of the environment, Pisillo-Mazzeschi notes that 'the empirical examination of practice confirms that the obligations which contain the "diligence" factor are precisely those in which the result pursued by the obligation is conditioned by a particular latitude of risk'.[102]

While the author focuses mostly on case law of the early twentieth century, more recent practice confirms his findings. In the 2011 advisory opinion of the Seabed Dispute Chamber, the tribunal noted that due diligence obligations are obligations not requiring the debtor 'to achieve, in each and every case, the result' provided by their content, but rather to do the utmost to obtain it. Hence, states are not expected to guarantee that a violation by the sponsored contractor of the international rules and regulations prescribed by UNCLOS and the International Authority of the Seabed Area will not occur.[103] They are only asked to act with due

[101] *Responsibility and Obligations of States Sponsoring Persons and Entities with Respect to Activities in the Area (Request for an Advisory Opinion submitted to the Seabed Dispute Chamber)* ITLOS Reports 2011 paras. 110, 117.

[102] Pisillo-Mazzeschi, 'The Due Diligence Rule', 49.

[103] *Responsibility and Obligations of States Sponsoring Persons and Entities with Respect to Activities in the Area*, para. 109.

diligence in carrying out their duties, so as to minimise the risk that a violation will indeed take place. This structural element of due diligence obligations was also clearly identified by the ICJ in the Bosnian Genocide case. Linking the obligation to prevent genocide to due diligence, the court argued: '[A] State cannot be under an obligation to succeed, whatever the circumstances, in preventing the commission of genocide: the obligation of State parties is rather to employ all means reasonably available to them, so as to prevent genocide so far as possible. A State does not incur responsibility simply because the desired result is not achieved.'[104]

The understanding that responsibility for breaches of due diligence obligations does not arise simply because the result (that sponsored contractors will comply with rules of UNCLOS; that genocide will be averted) is not achieved depends on the association of these obligations with the concept of risk. Certain primary rules presuppose that the state may not always be in a position to guarantee that the result set by the content of the obligation will be attained. They only expect the state to exercise its best effort, since the risk linked to the obligation may prevent the reaching of the result. For example, in the context of the protection of diplomats, a state is required to abstain from entering the premises of a diplomatic mission but is not required through its organs to protect the premises of the mission *in an absolute manner*. Intrusions may still occur, and state organs need not provide absolute guarantee from any disturbance of the peace of the mission.[105] Similarly, international law can impose on the state the duty to immediately notify other states of an imminent danger of damage to the marine environment, but it could not impose an absolute obligation of protection and prevention from pollution.[106]

Mainly, what links these examples is the fact that the result set by the primary rule (to protect the premises of the diplomatic mission; to prevent pollution of the marine environment) is associated with conditions outside the state's strict control. In the first case, a state may adopt all the necessary measures to protect the premises of a diplomatic mission, yet disturbances may still occur following unpredictable actions of third parties. In the second case, the type of activity carried out by the state at sea may carry a certain degree of environmental risk, and the state

[104] *Genocide* case, para. 430.

[105] See Article 22 of the Vienna Convention on Diplomatic Relations (VCDR) (adopted 18 April 1961, entered into force 24 April 1964) 500 UNTS 95.

[106] Article 194 of UNCLOS.

cannot be expected to completely erase the possibility that such risk materialises. Thus, unless we completely obliterate the public/private distinction[107] and accept states' absolute liability for wrongs falling outside their sphere of control,[108] the rationale is that the state is only asked to exercise due diligence.

It should not be at all surprising that the international legal notion of due diligence is linked to the concept of risk. As Chapter 1 has illustrated, due diligence was first invoked in the twentieth century regarding the protection of foreigners and the security of other states, but then resurfaced in modern international law mostly in connection to states' activities that cause a significant risk of transboundary harm, primarily in the environmental realm. It was during the ILC work on international liability that the idea emerged of a legal regime for states' activities not prohibited by international law but nevertheless giving rise to an appreciable *risk* of transboundary harm.[109] Throughout the work of the commission, liability was largely considered the product of the duty of care or a state's duty to exercise due diligence.[110] The 2001 draft Articles on Prevention of Transboundary Harm from Hazardous Activities clearly reflect this, drawing a triangular relationship between risk, prevention, and due diligence. States' general obligation to prevent significant

[107] See the *Request for an Advisory Opinion submitted by the Sub-Regional Fisheries Commission (SRFC)* (Case No. 21) ITLOS Reports 2015 para. 146 noting:

> [T]he liability of the flag State does not arise from a failure of vessels flying its flag to comply with the laws and regulations of the SRFC Member States concerning IUU fishing activities in their exclusive economic zones, as the violation of such laws and regulations by vessels is not per se attributable to the flag State. The liability of the flag State arises from its failure to comply with its 'due diligence' obligations.

From this perspective, the possibility of holding a state responsible for failure to exercise due diligence vis-à-vis harmful activities carried out by non-state actors and outside its sphere of control is inextricably linked to the issue of attribution of conduct; on this, and specifically on the function served by due diligence, see C. Chinkin, 'A Critique of the Public/Private Dimension' (1999) 10 EJIL 387.

[108] This is of course possible and indeed provided for by some specific primary rules, for example Convention on International Liability for Damage Caused by Space Objects (adopted 29 March 1972, entered into force 1 September 1972) 961 UNTS 187 Article II; see also ILC Draft Principles on the Allocation of Loss in the Case of Transboundary Harm Arising Out of Hazardous Activities (2006) YB II/2.

[109] J. Barboza, 'Fourth Report on International Liability for Injurious Consequences Arising Out of Acts Not Prohibited Under International Law' (1988) ILC YB II/1 draft Article 1, 254.

[110] R. Quentin-Baxter, 'First Report on International Liability for Injurious Consequences Arising Out of Acts Not Prohibited Under International Law' (1980) ILC YB II/1 252.

transboundary harm is construed as an obligation to *minimise* the risk, which is 'to be taken objectively, as denoting an appreciation of possible harm resulting from an activity which a properly informed observer had or ought to have had'.[111] The duty to prevent is declared as 'one of due diligence', that is 'the standard basis for the protection of the environment from harm', with a source in international environmental conventions, resolutions, and international conferences.[112] From a broader structural perspective that goes beyond environmental transboundary harm, due diligence has in fact been regarded as one of the fundamental tools to address normatively the rise of risk in international law.[113]

Generally, one can define the risk connected to due diligence obligations as the probability that the object or result set by the primary rule will not be attained. Such risk finds a variety of sources, depending on the content of the rule and its regime of application. Certain 'sources' of risk however are typically linked to duties of due diligence.

First, the notion of due diligence attaches primarily to international obligations identifying the risk with the action of third subjects, in particular private parties. Common examples include due diligence obligations in the context of human rights, the protection of foreign investments, or the security of states from acts of private armed groups. These obligations' connection with the source of risk lies in the circumstance that the state cannot absolutely prevent harmful acts of third parties or ensure that third parties will always abide by international regulations.

[111] ILC Draft Articles on Prevention of Transboundary Harm from Hazardous Activities, with commentaries (2001) ILC YB II/2 151.

[112] Ibid. 154.

[113] See M. Moïse Mbengue, *Essai sur une théorie du risqué en droit international public* (Paris: Pedone, 2009); S. Townley, 'The Rise of Risk in International Law' (2016) 18 *Chicago Journal of International Law* 594, and M. Ambrus, R. Rayfuse, W. Werner (eds.), *Risk and the Regulation of Uncertainty in International Law* (Oxford: Oxford University Press, 2017). In any case, due diligence is not the only legal instrument to address the risk in international law. For example, another legal tool accommodating this concept is the precautionary approach/principle. Generally, the distinction between prevention and precaution in international law can be defined as follows: '*le principe de prévention s'applique aux risques pleinement appréhendés, ou au moins probables, c'est-à-dire potentiels objects d'une mise en equation ou au minimum d'une representation mathématique. En revanche, le principe de précaution intervient dans le situations de risques possibles, soupçonnès, mais ni connus, ni "probabilisables"*' ('the principle of prevention applies to risks fully foreseeable, or at least probable, i.e., risks which can be put into an equation or can be assessed in mathematical terms. On the contrary, the principle of precaution applies to situations where risks are possible, under doubt, and are neither known nor measureable through probability'), see J. Cazala, *Le principe de précaution en droit international* (Paris: Librairie générale de droit et de jurisprudence, 2006), 10.

Many human rights due diligence obligations find their connection with the risk in harmful violations carried out by private subjects. In the famous case of Velásquez Rodriguez v. Honduras, the Inter-American Court of Human Rights (IACtHR) drew a clear link between state parties' obligation to prevent human rights violations carried out by private persons and due diligence:

> An illegal act which violates human rights and which is initially not directly imputable to the State (for example, because it is the act of a private person or because the person responsible had not been identified) can lead to international responsibility of the State, not because of the act itself, but because of the lack of due diligence to prevent the violation or to respond to it as required by the Convention.[114]

Although resorting mainly to the notion of 'obligations of conduct' rather than 'due diligence',[115] the ECtHR has reached similar conclusions. The court has repeatedly stated that positive obligations may arise when 'the authorities are under a duty to protect the life of an individual where it is known, or ought to have been known to them in view of the circumstances, that he or she was at real and immediate risk from the criminal acts of a third party'.[116] Similar statements have also been made by international human rights bodies with reference to a wide range of human rights obligations to prevent harmful acts of third parties.[117]

[114] *Velásquez Rodríguez* v. *Honduras*, Interpretation of the judgement of reparations and costs, IACHR Series C no 9, 17 August 1990, para. 172.

[115] The court uses the term 'obligations of conduct' or 'obligations of means' to indicate obligations of a best-effort nature, as opposed to obligations requiring the state to guarantee absolute results, see *Georgel and Georgeta Stoicescu* v. *Romania* (Judgment) [2011] App no 9718/03 para. 59; *Blumberga* v. *Latvia* (Judgment) [2001] App no 70930/01 para. 67; *Osman* v. *United Kingdom* (Judgment) (GC) [1998] App no 23452/94 para. 116. Furthermore, the parameters developed by the court to assess the fulfilment of obligations of means correspond to the classical due diligence parameters, see Chapter 3.

[116] *Osman* v. *United Kingdom*, para. 115; *Öneryldiz* v. *Turkey* (Judgment) (GC) [2004] App no 48939/99 paras. 107–9; *Kemaloglu* v. *Turkey* (Judgment) [2012] App no 19986/06 para. 33, referring back to previous decisions in which the court linked the obligation of state authorities to act with due diligence with the risk of human rights violations.

[117] Human Rights Committee, 'General Comment No. 36 (2018) on Article 6 of the International Covenant on Civil and Political Rights, on the right to life' (2018) UN Doc. CCPR/C/GC/36 paras. 7, 21; UN Committee for the Elimination of All Forms of Discrimination against Women, 'General Recommendation no 35 on Gender-Based Violence Against Women, Updating General Recommendation No 19', UN Doc. CEDAW/C/GC/35 para. 24(b).

Other examples of sources of risk deriving from the activities of private parties belong to the regime of foreign investment protection. In one arbitral case for instance, the tribunal held:

> A well-established aspect of the international standard of treatment is that states must use 'due diligence' to prevent *wrongful injuries* to the person or property of aliens *caused by third parties* within their territory. ... It should be emphasised that the obligation to show 'due diligence' does not mean that the State has to prevent each and every injury. Rather, the obligation is generally understood as requiring that the State takes reasonable actions within its power to avoid injury when it is, or should be, aware that there is *risk of injury*.[118]

In the context of the security of foreign states and the principle of non-intervention, states' due diligence obligations normally relate to the prevention of harmful acts by third parties, including terrorist and other private armed groups. This is not only the case of customary law, such as a state's obligation not to knowingly allow their territory to be used for acts contrary to the rights of other states[119] or a state's duty not to supply arms and other assistance to military and paramilitary groups operating in the territory of other states.[120] In addition, in relation to conventional obligations, the risk of terrorist acts and the correlated preventive duties falling upon states have long been subject to the due diligence rule.[121]

Sometimes, the risk linked to a due diligence obligation does not find source in the conduct of private parties but relates to the nature of the activity carried out by the state in its territory or under its jurisdiction or control. For example, in the case of obligations to prevent or not to cause

118 *El Paso Energy International Company* v. *The Argentine Republic*, ICSID Case no ARB/03/15, 31 October 2011 (Award) para. 523 (emphasis added). See also *Tulip Real Estate and Development Netherlands B.V.* v. *Republic of Turkey*, ICSID Case no ARB/11/28, 10 March 2014, para. 433.

119 *Corfu Channel (UK v. Albania)* (Merits) [1949] ICJ Rep 244, 22.

120 *Case Concerning Military and Paramilitary Activities In and Against Nicaragua (Nicaragua* v. *United States of America)* (Merits) [1986] ICJ Rep 14, para. 157.

121 For example, UN Declaration on Measures to Eliminate International Terrorism, UNGA Resolution 72/124 (2017) paras. 5, 11; International Convention for the Suppression of Terrorist Bombings (adopted 16 December 1997, entered into force 23 May 2001) 2149 UNTS 256, Article 7; International Convention for the Suppression of the Financing of Terrorism (adopted 9 December 1999, entered into force 10 April 2002) 2178 UNTS 197, Article 18. In doctrine see T. Becker, *Terrorism and the State: Rethinking the Rules of State Responsibility* (Portland: Hart Publishing, 2006), 140–1; K. Trapp, *State Responsibility for International Terrorism. Problems and Prospects* (Oxford: Oxford University Press, 2011), 64–5.

environmental harm, sources of risk linked to due diligence are usually activities that are inherently dangerous for the environment. Likewise, there may be circumstances in which the activity undertaken by the state, based on current scientific and technological developments, entails a significant risk of harm and therefore the obligation placed upon the state to conduct this activity is one of due diligence. Generally speaking, sources of risk linked to due diligence obligations are those activities taking place in a state's territory or under its jurisdiction or control that carry a qualified risk of harm (so-called hazardous activities), or activities for which danger is rarely expected but that cause grave consequences if such danger materialises (so-called ultra-hazardous activities).[122]

At any rate, due diligence obligations can also build upon risks that are not necessarily associated with private parties or dangerous activities.[123] In this this regard, a relevant question is whether due diligence can be used to construe primary rules in which the source of risk is 'internal' to the state apparatus and refers to the relationship between the state as an international legal entity and the activity carried out by its organs.

In principle, scholars tend to reject this possibility, based on the idea that due diligence is traditionally linked to sources of risk external to the state and out of its strict control, and in particular to (harmful) acts carried out by private third parties.[124] According to these positions, state responsibility for failure to exercise due diligence is primarily a form of responsibility in connection with harmful acts not attributable to the state: when the risk lies in the conduct of state organs and is caused by them, there is no need to resort to due diligence, for the conduct of a state organ is state conduct. On the one hand, these are strong arguments that help steer clear of theoretical confusion between the concept of responsibility for failure to exercise due diligence and attribution of conduct as per secondary rules.[125]

122 Draft Articles on Prevention with commentary, 149–50.

123 Arguably, the risk linked to a due diligence obligation may also derive from a circumstance which makes it impossible for the state to predict and ensure that the result envisaged by the primary rules will be achieved; this may be the case of obligations to investigate or punish the responsible of a crime, or obligations to negotiate or cooperate toward certain aims. In the latter case, states may be required to negotiate but they cannot guarantee that the goal of negotiation will be attained.

124 See generally Pisillo-Mazzeschi, 'The Due Diligence Rule', 46–9; E. De Brabandere, 'Host States' Due Diligence Obligations in International Investment Law' (2015) 42 *Syracuse Journal of International and Comparative Law* 319, with reference to the duty to protect foreign investments.

125 An example of this confusion is offered in *Nuhanović* v. *Netherlands*, [2011] Court of Appeal of The Hague, ECLI:NL:GHSGR:2011:BR0133, para. 5.19 where the Court of Appeal of the Hague read 'failure to act to prevent' within the question of attribution of conduct. On this

On the other hand, these positions fail to capture the whole picture of international obligations with respect to which the standard of due diligence may be invoked. For example, in the international humanitarian context, some obligations require the exercise of due diligence vis-à-vis actions carried out by state organs, such as a state's own military forces.[126] Furthermore, many primary rules provided in treaties and conventions are framed in a way that reflects, to some extent, due diligence language in the relationship between the state and its legal, administrative, or judicial apparatus. Instead of imposing direct results on the state, these rules leave to the state much latitude as to measures it must adopt by only requiring the state 'to ensure' certain undertakings by its domestic authorities.[127] In some circumstances, international courts have leaned toward the interpretation of these obligations as best-effort duties to be assessed through a due diligence standard.[128]

2.3.2 The 'Conduct' Nature of Due Diligence Obligations

The second relevant feature of due diligence obligations is their nature as obligations of conduct. When the ITLOS framed the relationship between due diligence and obligations of conduct in 2011, it actually did so in rather ambiguous terms. The tribunal stated that 'the notion of "obligations of due diligence" and "obligations of conduct" are connected'.[129] This ambiguity also emerges in the Bosnian Genocide case when the ICJ asserted that the obligation to prevent genocide is an

see critically P. D'Argent, 'State Organs Placed at the Disposal of the UN, Effective Control, Wrongful Abstention and Dual Attribution of Conduct' (2014) 1 *QIL-Questions of International Law* 27–8.

126 See Protocol Additional to the Geneva Convention of 12 August 1949 (adopted 8 June 1977, entered into force 7 December 1978) 1125 UNTS 3, Article 57; See also ICRC Commentary on the First Geneva Convention (2016) Article 15, para. 1499; ICRC Commentary on the Second Geneva Convention (2017) Article 12, para. 1406. In the context of international human rights, the ECtHR sometimes applies the theory of positive obligations to assess whether authorities have exercised sufficient diligence and taken precautions in law enforcement operations involving the use of lethal force, see *Giuliani and Gaggio* v. *Italy* (Judgment) [2011] App no 23458/03, 58–68. However, it is better to read the test adopted by the ECtHR in these cases as the proportionality test, rather than a test assessing whether the state has used due diligence to make sure its authorities did not use excessive force.

127 For instance, OSPAR Convention, Article 9(1); Convention for the Suppression of Terrorist Bombings, Article 7(1).

128 See Section 2.4.2.

129 *Responsibility and Obligations of States Sponsoring Persons and Entities with Respect to Activities in the Area*, para. 111.

obligation of conduct requiring the state to employ all means reasonably available to prevent genocide so far as possible.[130] The court noted that 'in this area, the notion of "due diligence", which calls for an assessment *in concreto*, is of critical importance'.[131] By qualifying the link between due diligence and obligations of conduct in terms of 'connection' and 'importance', it is not clear whether the two concepts perfectly overlap for the ICJ and the ITLOS.

The answer to this question should be affirmative. Shortly after the advisory opinion on the responsibility of sponsoring states in the Seabed Area, the ITLOS in 2015 dwelt again on the meaning of due diligence by pairing it with a flag state's obligation to ensure that vessels flying its flag do not engage in illegal, unreported, and unregulated fishing in the exclusive economic zone of other states. On this occasion, the tribunal argued that 'as an obligation of conduct, this is an obligation of due diligence, not an obligation of result', suggesting that all obligations of conduct are due diligence obligations.[132] The understanding of obligations of conduct as obligations of due diligence is in fact coherent with the taxonomy of international obligations described above. In their 'domestic' version, obligations of conduct are obligations 'to endeavour' or obligations of best-effort nature, which usually imply a connection with the concept of risk.

From this perspective, one should bear in mind that international courts and tribunals often give divergent interpretations of the meaning of conduct and result. As explained above, the notion of obligations of conduct is at times used by courts and interpreters not to refer to obligations linked to concepts of risk and best effort, but rather to a specific type of conduct to be adopted by the state. Hence, when conduct is intended in its domestic interpretation, the nature of obligations of conduct as due diligence obligations should be automatically recognised. The standard of diligence may vary for these obligations depending on the circumstances and the legal regime, yet compliance with them always requires a minimum degree of effort against which state conduct shall be assessed. If conduct is instead intended as an obligation 'to adopt a particular course of conduct' – as in the original understanding of Ago and the ILC – then not all obligations of conduct can be construed through the due diligence notion.[133]

[130] *Genocide* case, para. 430.

[131] Ibid.

[132] *Request for an Advisory Opinion submitted by the Sub-Regional Fisheries Commission*, para. 129.

[133] For example, the obligation to adopt a given piece of legislation is an obligation of conduct according to Ago, but it is not an obligation of due diligence.

Two corollaries attach to the assimilation of due diligence obligations as obligations of conduct. First, as obligations of conduct, due diligence obligations are primary rules which imply action on the part of the state. In the words of the African Court of Human and People's Rights, '*La doctrine de diligence raisonnable est ... une façon de décrire* le seuil d'action et d'effort *qu'un Etat doit démontrer pour s'acquitter de sa résponsabilité*'.[134] The 'threshold of action and effort' linked to due diligence presupposes indeed a duty of positive character to be discharged by the state to comply with the primary rule. The second corollary of the conduct nature of due diligence obligations is their continuing character. As best-effort duties, primary rules of due diligence are normally predicated upon the idea that states continuously operate to identify sources of risk, to monitor those sources, to minimise the risk, and to act upon the risk if it materialises.[135] An example are preventive obligations in the field of environmental protection. In Pulp Mills, the ICJ stated that the obligation of due diligence in the context of transboundary environmental harm 'is an obligation which entails not only the adoption of appropriate rules and measures, but also a *certain level of vigilance* in their enforcement and the exercise of administrative control applicable to public and private operators, such as the monitoring of activities undertaken by such operators'.[136]

Clearly, the fact that the notions 'obligations of conduct' and 'obligations of due diligence' overlap does not mean that all primary rules imbued with due diligence are always worded as duties of conduct nature. In other words, as a general statement, we can affirm that primary rules framed as duties of conduct (in the 'domestic' sense) are obligations of due diligence, since they impose the exercise of best effort and are linked to the concept of risk. However, there are circumstances where a rule codified or worded as an obligation 'of result' incorporates also a duty to exercise due diligence. Take, for example, the customary rule that states must refrain from organising, instigating, assisting or participating in acts of civil strife or terrorist acts in another state and refrain from acquiescing in organised activities within its territory.[137] This is an

134 *Zimbabwe Human Rights NGO Forum* v. *Zimbabwe*, Merits, Communication no 245/2002 (ACHPR 2006) IHRL para 147 (emphasis added).
135 A thorough analysis of the content of due diligence obligations is provided in Chapter 3.
136 *Pulp Mills*, para. 197.
137 Declaration on Principles of International Law Concerning Friendly Relations and Cooperation Among States in Accordance with the Charter of the United Nations, UNGA Res 2526(XXV) (24 October 1970).

obligation codified as a duty 'of result' and primarily as an obligation to abstain from certain activities. Yet, it is a rule which is also imbued with a duty to exercise due diligence, inasmuch as it is normally interpreted as encompassing a state's obligation to adopt measures and exercise vigilance to prevent the toleration of the use of its territory as a base of operation by armed and terrorist groups against another state.[138] Like states' obligation to refrain from instigating organised armed groups to operate in another state, other primary rules are enunciated in treaties as obligations of result that also incorporate duties of due diligence.[139] Thus, the fact that a primary rule is not framed as a prima facie duty of conduct nature does not exclude that this rule may also require due diligence.

2.3.3 Flexibility

The third distinctive feature of due diligence obligations is flexibility. Flexibility of due diligence is twofold. First, it regards the very nature of due diligence as a principle or international standard of conduct applicable to a wide range of international obligations across international law. From its 'original' use in the context of the security of states, aliens and their property, and then in relation to transboundary environmental harm, due diligence is proving a concept with a great capacity for adaptation; it has been invoked in a variety of different legal areas, from human rights to investment law, from the law of the sea to humanitarian law. It also covers a wide range of international obligations to prevent and protect as well as obligations of other characters.[140]

Yet, flexibility primarily refers to the content of primary rules to which the concept of due diligence applies. In the words of the ITLOS, the content of due diligence obligations 'may change over time as measures considered sufficiently diligent at a certain moment in time may become not diligent enough in light, for instance, of new scientific or technological knowledge'.[141] In the Bosnian Genocide case, the ICJ argued that

[138] *Case Concerning Military and Paramilitary Activities in and Against Nicaragua*, paras. 83–6. In relation to the duty of the state to refrain from acts of exploitation of natural resources of other states, see also *Case Concerning Armed Activities on the Territory of the Congo (Democratic Republic of the Congo* v. *Uganda)* (Merits) [2005] ICJ Rep 168, paras. 226–8.

[139] Protocol Additional to the First Geneva Convention, Article 57.

[140] See Section 2.4.1.

[141] *Responsibility and Obligations of States Sponsoring Persons*, para. 117.

the obligation to act with due diligence to prevent genocide 'calls for an assessment *in concreto*' and that '[v]arious parameters operate when assessing whether a state has duly discharged the obligations concerned'.[142] The court listed several parameters, including the capacity to influence the action of persons likely to commit genocide, the geographical distance of the state from the scene of the events, and the strength of the political and other links between the state and the actors of the events. When applying these criteria to the facts of the case, the ICJ noted:

> [D]uring the period under consideration, the FRY was in a position of influence over the Bosnian Serbs who devised and implemented the genocide in Srebrenica . . . owing to the strength of the political, military and financial links between the FRY on the one hand and the Republika Srpska and the VRS on the other. . . . [T]he Court recalls that although it has not found that the information available to the Belgrade authorities indicated, as a matter of certainty, that genocide was imminent . . . they could hardly have been unaware of the serious risk of it once the VRS forces had decided to occupy the Srebrenica enclave. . . . In the view of their undeniable influence and of the information, voicing serious concern, in their possession, the Yugoslav federal authorities should, in the view of the Court, have made the best efforts within their power to try and prevent the tragic events. . . . Yet the Respondent has not shown that it took any initiative to prevent what happened.[143]

Factual criteria and the assessment of state conduct in light of the particular circumstances of the case shape the degree of diligence required of a state to discharge its obligations. These factual conditions contribute to the understanding of due diligence obligations as flexible duties, for what may be considered as diligent in a certain case may not be so under different facts. This does not mean however that the flexible character of due diligence may not be eroded over time. On the contrary, the development of international standards and 'procedural' duties may progressively 'objectify' the content of certain primary obligations of due diligence, thereby reducing the flexibility traditionally engrained in this notion.[144]

Flexibility also emerges from how primary rules of due diligence are often worded in treaties and other international instruments. In some instances, the level of diligence required of the state exists in the adoption

[142] *Genocide* case, para. 430.
[143] Ibid. paras. 434–6, 438.
[144] See, in particular, Chapter 5.

of '*all appropriate measures*' for the pursuit of particular goals,[145] measures deemed *necessary*,[146] or *considered appropriate* by the state,[147] or measures deemed *effective*[148] or *reasonable*[149] in relation to the circumstances of the case. Sometimes flexibility also emerges from the fact that states are required to fulfil their duties *in so far as possible*,[150] *in accordance with the state's capability*,[151] using the *best practical means at the state's disposal*,[152] or *in light of different national circumstances*.[153]

The use of different qualifying terms may raise the question of whether variation in the wording of the primary rule is legally relevant for classifying an obligation as one 'of due diligence'. In other words, can due diligence be used as an 'umbrella' notion encompassing different standards of care (reasonableness, appropriateness, effectiveness, etc.), or should the concept be confined to describe only *certain* obligations of conduct across international law? In this regard, it cannot be excluded that different degrees of flexibility provided by the primary rule entail different legal consequences in terms of the scope and content of the latter. Accordingly, international obligations requiring states 'to adopt all necessary measures' to prevent certain harmful events may require a more stringent standard of effort than obligations only imposing those measures that states deem 'most appropriate'. At the same time, a distinction in the wording of standards of effort should always be

[145] Convention on the Elimination of All Forms of Discrimination against Women (CEDAW) (adopted 18 December 1979, entered into force 3 September 1981) 1249 UNTS 13, Article 2; VCDR Article 22.

[146] UNCLOS Article 117; Convention Against Torture and Other Cruel, Inhuman or Degrading Treatment or Punishment (CAT) (adopted 10 December 1984, entered into force 27 June 1987) 1465 UNTS 85 Article 5.

[147] Convention for Protection of Cultural Property in the Event of Armed Conflict (adopted 14 May 1954, entered into force 7 August 1956) 249 UNTS 215 Article 3.

[148] CAT Article 2; Measures to Eliminate International Terrorism, UNGA 72/123 (18 December 2017) UN Doc. A/RES/72/123 para. 10.

[149] See *Case of E and Others* v. *United Kingdom* (Judgment) [2003] App no 33218/96 para. 88.

[150] Convention for the Protection of the World Cultural and Natural Heritage (adopted 16 November 1972, entered into force 17 December 1975) 1037 UNTS 151 Article 5; Convention on Wetlands of International Importance especially of Waterfowl Habitats (RAMSAR) (adopted 2 February 1971, entered into force 21 December 1975) 996 UNTS 245 Article 2.

[151] Convention on Biological Diversity (CBD) (adopted 5 June 1992, entered into force 29 December 1993) 1760 UNTS 79 Article 6.

[152] Convention on the Protection of the Underwater Cultural Heritage (adopted 2 November 2001, entered into force 2 January 2009) Article 2(4).

[153] United Nations Framework Convention on Climate Change (Paris Agreement) (12 December 2015, entered into force 4 December 2016) Article 4(19).

treated with caution, for it may not necessarily give rise to different legal effects. A notable example of this is the decision of the ICJ in the 1974 Fisheries Jurisdiction case. In this case, the court de facto equated the standard of 'reasonable regard' with that of 'due regard'. Specifically, the court noted: 'The *principle of reasonable regard* for the interest of other States enshrined in Article 2 of the Geneva Convention on the High Seas of 1958 requires Iceland and the United Kingdom to have *due regard* to each other's interests, and to the interests of other States, in those resources.'[154]

The court did not seem to attach legal consequence to the fact that the Geneva Convention on the High Seas opted for the term 'reasonable' instead of 'due', and ultimately paired the two concepts.[155] This arguably applies to due diligence. The term can be used to construe obligations that are all flexible but, at the micro-level, embody standards of care which may vary and diverge from one another. Furthermore, as it will be better explained in Chapter 3, the fact that due diligence is used as an identifier for primary rules incorporating different standards of efforts does not mean that there is no commonality of understanding (i.e., a 'common substratum', as hinted in Chapter 1) in the use of this notion. On the contrary, resorting to the notion of due diligence to construe primary rules typically entails that a number of common legal and factual parameters are at play in operationalising the rule in question.

2.4 The Mapping of Due Diligence Obligations in Treaty Practice

Once the qualifying traits of due diligence obligations are identified, it is useful to examine in more detail the types of international obligations to which the notion is usually attached. For this reason, this section maps obligations of due diligence by looking at treaty practices and the array of primary rules that are typically construed through this notion. The investigation of rules incorporated in treaties provides a good opportunity for a cross-sectorial examination of due diligence obligations in practice. In particular, this interpretation exercise does not aim to discuss the particular contexts where due diligence obligations are applied. Rather, the purpose is to clarify the scope of operation of due diligence by looking at the types of primary rules that carry its qualifying elements

[154] *Fisheries Jurisdiction (United Kingdom* v. *Iceland)* (Merits) [1974] ICJ Rep 3, para. 68 (emphasis added).

[155] On this aspect also M. Forteau, 'The Legal Nature and Content of "Due Regard" Obligations in Recent International Law Case' (2019) 34 IJMCL 25.

in their nature and content. Thus, the following is a list that comprises both international obligations traditionally interpreted through the due diligence prism, as well as obligations whose due diligence character is less definite. The list is clearly not exhaustive and only furnishes a practical grid for a better understanding of due diligence obligations.

2.4.1 Obligations Aimed at Avoiding a Risk from Arising or Reducing the Risk

I Obligations to Prevent

There is little doubt that the concept of due diligence attaches to international obligations of prevention. The most authoritative decision in this regard is the Pulp Mills case and the obligation to prevent transboundary harm. The court famously stated that 'the principle of prevention, as a customary rule, has its origins in the due diligence that is required of a State in its territory'.[156] Similarly, in the Bosnian Genocide case, prevention was linked to due diligence, with the court noting that the obligation to prevent genocide is an obligation of conduct which calls for the application of due diligence. Many treaties also incorporate preventive obligations whose interpretation rests on due diligence. Traditionally, preventive obligations imply due diligence when prevention is required to protect international legal values from harmful acts of non-state actors, like in the context of human rights,[157] the security of states against terrorism,[158] organised crime,[159] or in international humanitarian law.[160] But preventive obligations predicated upon due diligence are also very common in the context of the protection

[156] *Pulp Mills*, para. 101.

[157] HRC, 'General Comment No. 31 on the Nature of the General Legal Obligation Imposed on State Parties to the Covenant' (2004), UN Doc. CCPR/C/21/Rev./Add.13, para. 8, interpreting Article 2(1) of the ICCPR; Protocol to Prevent, Suppress and Punish Trafficking in Persons, Especially Women and Children (Palermo Protocol) (adopted 15 November 2000, entered into force 25 December 2003) 2237 UNTS 319, Articles 2, 9(1)(a), 11(1).

[158] Council of Europe Convention on the Prevention of Terrorism (adopted 15 May 2005, entered into force 1 June 2007) CETS 196 Articles 2, 3(1).

[159] United Nations Convention against Transnational Organized Crime (adopted 15 November 2000, entered into force 29 September 2003) 2225 UNTS 209 Articles 1, 9(2), 31; Protocol Against the Smuggling of Migrants by Land, Sea and Air (adopted 15 November 2000, entered into force 28 January 2004) 2241 UNTS 507, Articles 2, 7, 11(1)(2).

[160] Convention for the Protection of Cultural Property in the Event of Armed Conflict, Article 4(3).

of natural resources[161] and the environment,[162] where prevention may be required both against the activities of private actors as well as the state.[163]

What deserves more scrutiny therefore is not the understanding that prevention requires due diligence, but rather the propositions that seek to establish a 'special' relationship between the two. Some scholars suggest that preventive obligations are *sui generis* due diligence obligations, and that their difference rests in the normative value of the *event* engrained in primary rules of prevention. In particular, as 'authentic' best-effort duties, obligations of due diligence focus on conduct states must adopt to attain the object set by the primary rule of due diligence. Breaches of these obligations therefore accrue the moment the state fails to act in conformity with conduct required by due diligence, regardless of whether the result has materialised. Differently, preventive obligations are partly codified by Article 14(3) of ARSIWA, which states that a breach of an obligation to prevent a given event occurs when the event occurs. Thus, obligations to prevent are sui generis due diligence obligations inasmuch as for their breach to accrue it is not sufficient that the state has failed to adopt the necessary measures that would have prevented the event from occurring; the event itself has to materialise.

For now, I will not delve into the genealogy of Article 14(3) and the problem of breaches of preventive obligations. This aspect will be thoroughly discussed in Chapter 4, which applies the law of state responsibility as codified by ARSIWA to due diligence obligations. At this point, my interest lies in addressing the relationship between due diligence and obligations to prevent. In this regard, Crawford contends that 'despite the close the relationship between obligations of prevention and those of due diligence (which also usually apply in the context of prevention), the latter were omitted from draft Article 23 [of the Articles on State Responsibility adopted on the first reading]'.[164]

To substantiate the argument, Crawford refers to the Bosnian Genocide case. As noted above, the court there classified the obligation to prevent genocide as an obligation of conduct requiring due diligence.

[161] UNCLOS Article 117.

[162] Basil Convention on the Control of Transboundary Movements of Hazardous Wastes and Their Disposal (adopted 22 March 1989, entered into force 5 May 1992) 1673 UNTS 57, Article 2(c); Convention on the Protection of the Black Sea Against Pollution (adopted 21 April 1992, entered into force 15 January 1994) ILM 10, Article 1(1).

[163] For example, Convention on the Protection of the Underwater Cultural Heritage, Article 5.

[164] J. Crawford, *State Responsibility: The General Part* (Cambridge: Cambridge University Press, 2013), 227–8.

Yet, after resorting to the concept of best-effort obligation, the court declared

> [A] State can be held responsible for breaching the obligation to prevent genocide only if genocide was actually committed. It is at the time when commission of the prohibited act (genocide or any of the other acts in Article III of the Convention) begins that the breach of an obligation of prevention occurs. In this respect, the Court refers to a general rule of the law of State responsibility, stated by the ILC in Article 14 paragraph 3, of its Articles on State Responsibility.[165]

This passage allows Crawford to recognise that 'the Court's formulation of the obligation to prevent genocide as an obligation of conduct . . . is preferable to the view that obligations of prevention are obligations of result'. At the same time, according to the former Special Rapporteur, 'although the Court acknowledged that due diligence is an important factor in discharging the obligation of prevention, *the latter cannot be categorized as an obligation of due diligence per se, because such an obligation would be breached by a state's party failure to take action, regardless of whether the prohibited event in fact took place*'.[166]

Thus, Crawford's argument is that there is a fundamental difference between due diligence obligations and obligations to prevent. This position finds origin in a distinction that was incidentally proposed by Ago during his work as a Special Rapporteur to the commission and subsequently reprised by Crawford during the articles' second reading.[167] The idea is that obligations to prevent should be differentiated between so-called obligations of 'pure' prevention and preventive obligations 'of conduct nature'. Obligations of pure prevention are those regulated by Article 14(3) since, as Crawford explains, they require a conduct of best effort on the part of the state but cannot be breached unless the event to be prevented occurs. Preventive obligations of conduct nature are instead 'classic' due diligence obligations, since their breach can accrue even if the event has not materialised, once it is established that the state has failed to take action.

The problem with this distinction is that it is hard to justify conceptually and it raises more questions than it answers when applied in practice. First, there is clearly a 'paradox',[168] in stating that obligations to prevent (or pure preventive obligations) are best-effort duties and then

[165] *Genocide* case, para. 431.

[166] Crawford, *State Responsibility*, 231–2 (emphasis added).

[167] See Ago, 'Seventh Report', 35–6; Crawford, 'Second Report', para. 134.

[168] The term is borrowed by Dupuy, 'Reviewing the Difficulty of Codification', 379.

maintaining that the decisive element for their breach is the non-achievement of the result (and not actual state conduct). Still in the Bosnian Genocide case, after noting that a violation of preventive obligations requires the event to occur, the court affirmed:

> This obviously does not mean that the obligation to prevent genocide only comes into being when the perpetration of genocide commences; that would be absurd, since the whole point of the obligation is to prevent, or attempt to prevent, the occurrence of the act. In fact, *a State's obligation to prevent, and the corresponding duty to act, arises the instant that the State learns of, or should normally have learned of, the existence of a serious risk that genocide will be committed.*[169]

Hence, according to the court, a duty to prevent genocide arises the moment the state has knowledge of a serious risk of genocide, but if the state fails to take measures from that moment onwards, responsibility cannot accrue unless genocide is committed. To a certain extent, this construction of the obligation to prevent genocide resembles Ago's much-criticised category of 'extended obligations of result'.

Second, if one reads carefully the ILC work on state responsibility and the Special Rapporteurs' reports that assert the distinction between pure obligations to prevent and the preventive obligation of conduct nature (i.e. obligations of due diligence), one finds a series of contradictions. For instance, Special Rapporteur Ago contends that Article 22 of the Vienna Convention on Diplomatic Relations (VCDR) is a pure obligation to prevent which necessarily requires the event to be prevented – for instance a disruption to the diplomatic premises of the mission – in order to be breached. However, Special Rapporteur Crawford, in line with the ICJ's Teheran Hostage case, defines Article 22 as preventive obligation of conduct nature, or as a pure obligation of due diligence. Notably, in the Teheran Hostage case, the court found that Iran had failed to take appropriate steps to protect the premises, staff, and archives of the United States embassy in Teheran from attacks carried out by a group of Iranian militants in November 1979. In this circumstance, the ICJ had not referred to the occupation of the embassy as a normative condition for breaches of Article 22. It had simply declared that the 'inaction of the Iranian Government *by itself* constituted clear and serious violation of Iran's obligations to the United States'.[170] Other similar contradictions are detectable

[169] *Genocide* case, para. 431 (emphasis added).

[170] *United States Diplomatic and Consular Staff in Teheran (United States of America* v. *Iran)* (Merits) [1980] ICJ Rep 3, para. 33.

not only through Ago's and Crawford's reports but also by reading the debates within the ILC on the nature of obligations to prevent.[171]

If one wishes to stick to Crawford's distinction, it may be argued that while the object of the obligation 'to undertake to prevent . . . genocide' is *prevention*, the object of the obligation to 'take all appropriate steps to protect the premises of the mission against any intrusion' is to *take appropriate steps*. The first obligation emphasizes the event to be prevented, whereas the second focuses on the adoption of appropriate measures.[172] But even this fine literal distinction raises doubts since it implies a substantive distinction between obligations requiring states *to prevent* certain occurrences and obligations *to adopt all the appropriate measures to prevent* – a distinction that does not seem to find support in practice.

Overall, it seems that, if not for the fact that breaches of preventive obligations require the event to occur whereas due diligence does not, there is no relevant difference between the two. In fact, the purported distinction between due diligence and prevention collapses before one of the most classic obligations to prevent, that is, the duty to prevent transboundary environmental harm. It is true that the ICJ has so far construed such obligation *à la Crawford*, maintaining that there is no breach of the substantive obligation to prevent transboundary harm unless environmental damage occurs.[173] Yet, to state that the only focus of this obligation is for damage not to occur would greatly overlook the international legal developments of the past fifty years as well as the ultimate aim of this rule, which is to *anticipate* risk of harm through appropriate action.[174] One may even say that the whole theory of procedural environmental obligations recently developed by the ICJ is a strategy for holding states responsible vis-à-vis violations that have yet to result in significant transboundary environmental damage but arise from a failure to adopt adequate measures.[175]

171 See generally the debate within the commission on the nature of obligations to prevent, meetings 1476th, 1477th, 1478th; see in particular, comment of Mr Ushakov at meeting 1476th para. 25.

172 In fact, Crawford argues that the obligation to prevent genocide is within the category of preventive obligations, while Article 22 of the VCDR is an obligation of due diligence.

173 *Pulp Mills*, 180, 214; *Certain Activities Carried Out by Nicaragua in the Border Area (Costa Rica* v. *Nicaragua)* [2015] ICJ Rep 665, *Construction of a Road in Costa Rica along the San Juan River (Nicaragua* v. *Costa Rica)* [2015] ICJ Rep 665, paras. 192, 196, 207, 213, 216–17.

174 See in particular, ILC draft Articles on Prevention with commentaries.

175 See Chapter 5.

For all these reasons, a distinction between obligations to prevent and due diligence obligations does not appear conceptually sound. From the perspective of their nature, obligations to prevent share all the structural components of due diligence obligations and therefore, they are to be classified as such.

II Obligations to Protect

The distinction between preventive obligations and obligations 'to protect' is not clear-cut. Obligations requiring the state to protect internationally recognised values often also entail the adoption of duties of a preventive nature. In the international human rights context for instance, it is generally recognised that states' obligations to protect individuals from human rights violations encompass duties of a preventive character.[176]

Many obligations to protect are framed as obligations that prima facie imbue due diligence elements. As just indicated above, Article 22 of the VCDR which provides for the obligation to take all appropriate steps to protect the premises of the mission against any intrusion is one example. Like Article 22, other obligations to protect impose protection from external sources of risks, pointing to the adoption of 'necessary measures', 'appropriate steps', and 'appropriate measures' which may ensure such protection. For instance, Article 2(1) of the Vienna Convention for the Protection of the Ozone Layer provides that the 'Parties *shall take appropriate measures . . . to protect* human health and the environment against adverse effects resulting or likely to result from human activities which modify or are likely to modify the ozone layer'.[177]

Similar considerations can be made about protection against harmful acts of private parties, such as in the field of human rights and the

[176] See also UNCLOS Article 192 providing for a general obligation 'to protect and preserve the marine environment'. To fulfil the obligation to protect set by Article 192, Article 194 provides that states 'shall take, individually or jointly as appropriate, all measures consistent with this Convention that are necessary to prevent, reduce and control pollution of the marine environment from any source'.

[177] Vienna Convention for the Protection of the Ozone Layer (adopted 22 March 1985, entered into force 22 September 1988) 1513 UNTS 293 Article 2(1) (emphasis added). As for the due diligence character of this obligation, the commentary to the draft convention linked the obligation to protect the ozone layer with Principle 21 of the Stockholm Declaration and the principle *sic utere tuo ut alienum non laedas*, see UNEP/WG.78/2, at 7. See also Council of Europe Convention on Prevention on Terrorism (adopted 16 May 2005, entered into force 1 June 2007) CETS 196 Article 13; Council of Europe Convention on the Conservation of European Wildlife and Natural Habitats (adopted 19 September 1979, entered into force 1 June 1982) CETS 104, chapter III.

protection of foreign investments. States' obligations under Article 1 of the ECHR 'to secure to everyone within their jurisdiction' the rights and freedoms defined in the convention includes the obligation to protect individuals against interferences that are not directly caused by state agents but come from private parties.[178] Likewise, the full protection and security standard (FPS) required by investment treaties is commonly understood as providing a state's obligation to protect foreign investments against acts of third parties.[179] These obligations are typically assessed through due diligence, as they require the state to display its efforts to protect individuals and investments from the interference of third parties.[180]

The relationship between measures required to ensure protection and the understanding of obligations to protect as obligations with a due diligence nature should be elucidated. Some treaties contain obligations to protect that impose protection as their ultimate objective, at the same time spelling out in their content the specific duties to be undertaken by states to assure such protection. One illustrative example is Article 3 of the Protocol on Environmental Protection to the Antarctic Treaty,[181] which establishes the obligation of state parties to the protocol to protect the Antarctic environment. To this end, Article 3(2) provides a rather detailed list of measures that states are required to undertake to comply with their duty to protect the Antarctic environment. Not every single protection duty is necessarily one of due diligence since measures states must adopt may encompass legislation or regulations of an administrative, policy, or financial character.[182] Another example is Article 24 of the United Nations Convention against Transnational Organized Crime. This provision establishes that state parties shall take appropriate measures to provide protection for witnesses in criminal proceedings giving

178 *Osman v. United Kingdom*, para. 115. See similarly, Article 2(1) of the ICCPR, providing for state parties' obligations to exercise due diligence to prevent and protect from harm caused by non-state actors. See also, Human Rights Committee, 'General Comment No. 31', para. 8; see also 'General Comment no 36 on the right to life', para. 7.

179 S. M. Blanco, *Full Protection and Security in International Law* (Berlin: Springer, 2018), 206–69.

180 *Eastern Sugar B.V.* v. *The Czech Republic*, SCC Case no 088/2004, 27 March 2007 (Partial Award) paras. 203–4; *Koch Minerals Sàrl and Koch Nitrogen International Sàrl* v. *Bolivian Republic of Venezuela*, ICSID Case no ARB/11/19, 30 October 2017 (Award) 8.46.

181 See Protocol on Environmental Protection to the Antarctic Treaty (adopted 4 October 1991, entered into force 14 January 1998) 2941 UNTS 6.

182 Ibid. Article 2 and especially Article 3.

testimony on offences covered by the convention. While the obligation to adopt appropriate measures to ensure protection is clearly one of due diligence, the duty to relocate witnesses – which is indicated by Article 24(2)(a) as one of the measures that states may adopt to comply with their duty to protect – is a duty of result. Hence, the overall nature of the obligation to protect is one of due diligence, but the content of this duty indicates with more precision the measures to be adopted, among which there also may be duties of result.

Obligations to protect human rights and to protect foreign investments from external interference should also be read against this backdrop. As for states' obligation to protect individuals from human rights violations, scholars often draw a distinction between states' positive obligations *to adopt* legislation and to maintain an adequate legal and administrative apparatus to protect from and address violations, and obligations *to use* such apparatus in the face of interference by third parties or other risks.[183] Only the latter are regarded as due diligence duties. States' obligations to enact legislation and to provide for an adequate apparatus are seen as duties of result. Likewise, in the context of the obligation to ensure full protection and security of foreign investments, distinctions are made between a *duty to possess* a minimum legal and administrative protective apparatus, and the *duty to use* that apparatus diligently against injuries committed by third parties.[184] Yet, these artificial separations add an unnecessary layer of complexity to the understanding of obligations to protect human rights or foreign investment.[185] While duties to enact legislation or to possess adequate legal and administrative apparatus are not strictly of due diligence, they often constitute the precondition that the state act diligently in using its apparatus. Conceptually, they can be construed as part of the state's

[183] See for example Pisillo-Mazzeschi, 'The Due Diligence Rule', 46–9; Pisillo-Mazzeschi, 'Responsabilité de l'état pour violation des obligations positives', chapters III and IV, adopting an interpretation of due diligence obligations more restrictive than this author's.

[184] This distinction finds support mostly in early practice, where a separation was often made between the duty to have an adequate apparatus and the duty to use that apparatus with due diligence to protect aliens and their property. See Pisillo-Mazzeschi, 'The Due Diligence Rule', for a review of this practice. Also supporting this view is De Brabandere, 'Host States' Due Diligence Obligations', 319, 325, 341–5.

[185] See also P. M. Dupuy, 'La diligence due dans le droit international et la résponsabilité', in Organization for Economic Co-operation and Development (ed.), *Aspects juridiques de la pollution transfrontière* (Paris: OECD, 1977), 379.

general obligation to act with due diligence in ensuring that individuals and investments are protected against external interference.

2.4.2 Obligations Aimed at Ensuring the Realisation of Particular Goals

Aside from preventive and protective obligations, due diligence can be invoked in relation to certain international obligations aimed at pursuing the realisation of specific goals. Relevant examples include Article 139(1) and Article 58(2) of UNCLOS as recently interpreted by the ITLOS. As for states' obligation to ensure that activities in the area conducted by the sponsored contractors are in conformity with regulations set in UNCLOS, it has already been noted that the tribunal construed this obligation as one of due diligence. Similarly, in relation to Article 58(2), the ITLOS has held that states' obligation to have due regard to the rights and duties of the coastal state includes the obligation 'to ensure that State nationals engaged in fishing activities in the EEZ of another State comply with the conservation measures and other conditions established in its laws and regulations'.[186] The ITLOS judges have confirmed that a state's obligation 'to ensure' is a due diligence obligation to deploy adequate means and to do the utmost to prevent illegal, unreported, and unregulated (IUU) fishing by ships flying its flags.[187]

To better grasp why the notion of 'obligation to ensure' should be paired with due diligence, it is useful to exactly report the argument made by the tribunal in its 2011 advisory opinion:

> The expression 'to ensure' is often used in international legal instruments to refer to obligations in respect of which, while it is not reasonable to make a State liable for each and every violation committed by persons under its jurisdiction, it is equally not considered satisfactory to rely on mere application of the principle that conduct or private persons or entities is not attributable to the State under international law (see ILC Articles on State Responsibility, Commentary to Article 8, paragraph 1).[188]

This is true for many international obligations whose duty to ensure a particular goal is linked to conduct of private individuals or entities not

[186] The ITLOS held that this is an obligation that arises from a combined reading of Article 58(2), Article 62(4), and Article 109 of UNCLOS.

[187] The ITLOS's findings were confirmed in *The Matter of the South China Arbitration (The Republic of the Philippines* v. *People's Republic of China)* (2016) ICGJ 495 at paras. 287–97.

[188] *Responsibility and Obligations of States Sponsoring Persons*, paras. 110–12.

attributable to the state. These are, for example, human rights obligations to ensure that certain conditions are fulfilled within society in the relations between individuals,[189] or international obligations that call upon states to ensure that entities and persons within their jurisdiction or control comply with international standards,[190] regulations,[191] or particular objectives set by treaties.[192] The characteristic of these rules is that they require action to be taken by the state; these actions are often spelled out through requiring the state to adopt measures or to endeavour to ensure particular results. At the same time, the responsibility of the state for 'failure to ensure' does not arise out of mere failure by private parties to respect human rights or to comply with international standards and regulations.[193] Responsibility arises out of a state's failure 'to endeavour', 'to adopt appropriate measures', or to act with due diligence in striving to achieve a particular goal.

When the objective to be ensured by the obligation is connected to activities of private parties, we are within the traditional sphere in which due diligence has been applied. The duty to ensure translates into the duty 'to act with due diligence' when the risk of 'not ensuring' stems from conditions outside state's the strict control. But due diligence may also be

[189] CEDAW Articles 3, 5(b), 8, 10, 13; Convention on the Rights of Persons with Disabilities (adopted 13 December 2006, entered into force 3 May 2008) 2515 UNTS 3 Articles 4(1), 6, 7.

[190] Arms Trade Treaty (adopted 2 April 2013, entered into force 24 December 2014) 3031 UNTS 7 Articles 7(5), 9; UNCLOS Article 94(5); Convention on International Trade in Endangered Species of Wild Fauna and Flora (CITIES) (adopted 3 March 1973, entered into force 1 July 1975) 993 UNTS 243 Article 8(3).

[191] Convention on International Civil Aviation (adopted 7 December 1944, entered into force 4 April 1947) 15 UNTS 295 Article 12; UNCLOS Article 73(1), 94(4); Revised Draft Text of an Agreement under the United Nations Convention on the Law of the Sea on the Conservation and Sustainable Use of Marine Biological Diversity of Areas Beyond National Jurisdiction (18 November 2019) UN Doc A/CONF/232./2020/3 Article 10(2).

[192] WHC Article 4; UNCLOS Article 117; Convention on the Prohibition of the Development, Production, Stockpiling and Use of Chemical Weapons and on their Destruction (adopted 3 September 1992, entered into force 29 April 1997) 1975 UNTS 45 Article VI(2), and also Article IV(11) which regards a duty to ensure in connection to conduct of third states.

[193] See *Request for an Advisory Opinion submitted by the Sub-Regional Fisheries Commission*, para. 129:

> This means that this is not an obligation of the flag State to achieve compliance by fishing vessels flying its flag in each case with the requirement not to engage in IUU fishing in the exclusive economic zone of the SFRC Member States. The flag State is under the 'due diligence obligation' to take all the necessary measures to ensure compliance and to prevent IUU fishing by fishing vessels flying its flags.

attached to obligations whose duty to ensure is not connected to conduct of private parties and rather concerns activities to be undertaken by domestic authorities. These may include obligations requiring states to ensure that competent national authorities make certain information available;[194] obligations of states to take measures to ensure that certain conduct is criminalised under domestic law or that legal entities are made liable for certain offences;[195] and obligations requiring states to ensure that individuals or other states have access to relevant legal procedures,[196] assistance, or information through competent domestic authorities.[197] Examples include Article 8(1) of the Arms Trade Treaty, which provides that each state party shall 'take measures to ensure that appropriate and relevant information is provided, upon request, pursuant to its national laws, to the exporting State Party,' and Article 15(1) of the Council of Europe Convention on the Prevention of Terrorism, which obligates state parties to take such measures as may be necessary under their domestic law to investigate persons who are suspected to have committed an offense covered by the convention.

194 OSPAR Article 9(1); Arms Trade Treaty Article 8(1).

195 See for example Article 6 of the International Convention for the Suppression of Terrorist Bombings and Article 7 of the Convention Against the Financing of Terrorism. Many provisions in the Convention for the Suppression of Terrorist Bombings are framed so as to require states 'to adopt such measures as may be necessary' to ensure certain objectives. Arguably, not all these obligations are of a due diligence nature, specifically, those that actually only require states to adopt criminal provisions into their domestic legal framework. For example, Article 4 obligates states to 'adopt measures as may be necessary' to establish as criminal offences under their domestic law the offences covered by the convention. This is better construed as a duty of result and not as a duty of best efforts. However, there are other provisions, such as Article 6, whose interpretation may lean toward the concept of 'best-effort' nature obligations. The provisions within the Convention for the Suppression of Terrorist Bombings were originally drafted based on the rules contained in the Convention Against the Taking of Hostages and the IMO Convention for the Suppression of Unlawful Acts Against the Safety of Maritime Navigation. Interestingly, Article 2 of the Convention Against the Taking of Hostages, from which Article 4 has been drafted, simply provides that 'States shall make the offences set forth in Article 1 punishable by appropriate measures', reflecting the nature of this obligation as a duty of result. Instead both Article 5 of the Convention Against the Taking of Hostages and Article 6 of the IMO Convention for the Suppression of Unlawful Acts Against the Safety of Maritime Navigation – from which Article 6 of the Convention for the Suppression of Terrorist Bombings has been drafted – requires states 'to take such measures as may be necessary to establish jurisdiction' over the offences covered by both conventions, which reflects due diligence language. See UNGA, UN Doc. A/52/37 at 23. See also Article 11 Convention on Transnational Organized Crime.

196 Palermo Protocol Article 6(2)(b).

197 CBD Article 17(1); Palermo Protocol Article 6(2)(a).

The due diligence nature of some of these obligations is well known. Such is the case of states' obligations to ensure that domestic authorities investigate and punish those responsible for certain crimes.[198] States are required to exercise due diligence in ensuring that persons responsible for certain violations of human rights are arrested and brought to justice, yet they are not required to guarantee conviction in every case.[199] As for other obligations however, their nature as obligations of conduct is more contentious. On the one hand, they look prima facie to be imbuing due diligence because of their focus on state's efforts, and the flexibility granted to the state in the pursuit of the obligation's goal. On the other hand, their interpretation often oscillates between due diligence and obligations of result.[200]

Another relevant issue is whether due diligence can be used to construe obligations that target the progressive realization of particular goals. These obligations are typical, but not exclusive,[201] in the human rights context, and are found particularly in social, economic, and cultural rights treaties.[202] Article 2(1) of the International Covenant on Economic,

198 *LFH Neer and Pauline Neer (USA* v. *United Mexican States)* (1926) 4 RIAA 62; *L. M. B. Janes et al. (USA* v. *United Mexican States)* (1925) 4 RIAA 87; *Mustafa Tunç and Fecire Tunç* v. *Turkey* (Judgment) (GC) [2015] App no 24014/05 para. 173.

199 In these cases, one may say that the source of risk is the possibility that investigative authorities do not identify and punish those responsible for the death of the individual.

200 See for example *LaGrand (Germany* v. *United States)* (Merits) [2001] ICJ Rep 466, paras. 111–12, where the ICJ noted that the United States' obligation 'to take all the necessary measures at its disposal to ensure that Walter LaGrand is not executed pending the final decision' of Arizonian authorities did not create an obligation of result; the court appears to interpret this obligation as a duty of best-effort, in particular, see para. 112 where it states:

> The Court observes, nevertheless, that the mere transmission of its Order to the Governor of Arizona without any comment, particularly without even so much as a plea for a temporary stay and an explanation that there is no general agreement on the position of the United States that orders of the International Court of Justice on provisional measures are non-binding, was certainly less than could have been done even in the short time available.

But see *Dispute Concerning Access to Information Under Article 9 of the OSPAR Convention*, para. 147, where the tribunal interpreted Article 9(1) as an obligation of result; however, one of the members of the tribunal, Michael Reisman, made a separate declaration to the decision in which, while not explicitly resorting to the concept of due diligence, he did interpret Article 9(1) as a duty of best-effort.

201 CBD Articles 12(b), 13(a), 15(2); Paris Agreement Article 3.

202 See International Covenant on Economic, Social and Cultural Rights (adopted 16 December 1966, entered into force 3 January 1976) 993 UNTS 3 Article 2(1); Convention of Persons with Disabilities Article 4(2); Convention on the Right of the

Social and Cultural Rights (ICESCR) establishes that state parties *shall take steps*, individually or through international cooperation, to the maximum of their resources, 'with a view *to achieving progressively the full realization of rights*' recognised in the covenant by all appropriate means.

Certain authors construe obligations like Article 2(1) of the ICESCR as belonging to an autonomous category of obligations and refrain from resorting to the notion of due diligence. For instance, it has been argued that Article 2(1) '*n'a ni la nature juridique des obligations de résultat ni celles des obligations de* due diligence, *mais qu'elle a plutôt un peu la nature des deux categories, car elle requiert de l'Etat un effort de diligence en vue d'atteindre un résultat final déterminé*'.[203] This appears to be a rather restrictive interpretation of what amounts to a due diligence obligation. First, with regard to the nature of Article 2(1), the Committee on Economic, Social and Cultural Rights has noted:

> The principal obligation of result reflected in article 2(1) is *to take steps* 'with a view to achieving progressively the full realization of the rights recognized' in the Covenant. The term 'progressive realization' is often used to describe the intent of this phrase. The concept of progressive realization constitutes a recognition of the fact that full realization of all economic, social and cultural rights will generally not be able to be achieved in a short period of time. . . . Nevertheless, the fact that realization over time, or in other words progressively, is foreseen under the Covenant should not be misinterpreted as depriving the obligation of all meaningful content. It is on the one hand a necessary flexibility device. . . . On the other hand, the phrase must be read in the light of the overall objective, indeed the raison d'être, of the Covenant which is to establish clear obligations for States parties in respect of the full realization of the rights in question. It thus imposes an obligation *to move as expeditiously and effectively as possible towards that goal.*[204]

The comment emphasises that this is essentially a conduct nature obligation that implies a continuous effort toward achieving a certain goal. From this viewpoint, there is no distinction from more 'classic' due diligence obligations. The only criteria that appear to separate the two are

Child (adopted 20 November 1989, entered into force 2 September 1990) 1577 UNTS 3 Article 4 second part.

[203] 'Article 2(1) is neither an obligation of result nor an obligation of due diligence, but shares the characteristics of both, since it requires of a State an effort with the view of attaining a particular result' (this author's translation), see Pisillo-Mazzeschi, 'Responsabilité de l'état pour violation des obligations positives', 442, and more generally 438–43.

[204] Committee on Economic, Social and Cultural Rights, 'General Comment No. 3: The Nature of States Parties' Obligations' (1990) UN Doc. E/1991/23 para. 9.

i) the temporal dimension of Article 2(1), and ii) the fact that the progressive steps states must adopt for realising economic, social, and cultural rights may translate at a certain point in time into the adoption of concrete and specific duties of result.[205] As for the temporal dimension, that actions to be taken may stretch over time and may not be of an 'immediate' character does not seem a determining factor to the discarding of the due diligence nature of these obligations. As for the second distinguishing criterion, the circumstance that obligations of progressive realisation may at some point translate into specific obligations (both of conduct and result) should not be seen as an oddity. Rather, this is a peculiarity of many due diligence obligations, whose content can in time be 'proceduralised' or transformed into more specific obligations.[206]

2.4.3 Other International Obligations with Due Diligence Elements

There are other types of primary norms that can be grouped under the due diligence notion. Like obligations of progressive realization of goals, these are not 'classic' due diligence obligations, yet their content normally reflects a best-effort dimension or it carries some of the distinctive elements which define an obligation of due diligence.

First, within the framework of obligations to pursue the attainment of particular goals, one may cite obligations to cooperate or obligations to negotiate toward the achievement of certain results. As for obligations to

[205] See also the Committee on the Elimination of Discrimination Against Women, 'General Recommendation no 28 on the Core Obligations of States Parties under Article 2' (2010) UN Doc. CEDAW/C/2010/47/GC.2 para. 9, regarding state's obligations in relation to Article 2 of the convention. The committee notes:

> The obligation to fulfil requires that States parties take a wide variety of steps to ensure that women and men enjoy equal rights de jure and de facto, including, where appropriate, the adoption of temporary special measures in line with article 4, paragraph 1, of the Convention and general recommendation No. 25 on article 4, paragraph 1, of the Convention on the Elimination of All Forms of Discrimination against Women, on temporary special measures. This entails obligations of means or conduct and obligations of results. States parties should consider that they have to fulfil their legal obligations to all women through designing public policies, programmes and institutional frameworks that are aimed at fulfilling the specific needs of women leading to the full development of their potential on an equal basis with men.

[206] On the due diligence nature of obligations of progressive realisation of goals see also S. Forlati, 'L'objet des différentes obligations primaires de diligence: prévention, cessation, répression . . . ?', in S. Cassella (ed.), *Le standard de due diligence et la responsabilité internationale* (Paris: Pedone, 2018), 54–6.

cooperate, they may be framed in rather broad terms, like the case of Article 8 of the Convention on the Non-Navigational Use of Watercourses, setting a general obligations of states 'to cooperate on the basis of sovereign equality, territorial integrity, mutual benefit and good faith, in order to obtain optimal utilization and adequate protection of international watercourses'. In other cases, the object to be pursued through cooperation and the mechanisms through which states shall cooperate are described with considerable precision. For example, Article 197 of UNCLOS establishes that states shall cooperate 'on a global basis, and as appropriate, on a regional basis, directly or through competent international organizations, in formulating and elaborating international rules, standards and recommended practices ... for the protection and preservation of the marine environment'.

It is not easy to grasp the nature of a state's obligation to cooperate.[207] On the one hand, cooperation points to a duty of a procedural nature that is 'a label for an entire range of obligations'.[208] The fulfilment of a duty to cooperate often involves the undertaking of a series of 'sub-obligations', which are both content-dependent and may consist of specific duties of conduct and result.[209] At the same time, if taken as a whole, cooperation points to an obligation of means calling for best effort to attain the objective of cooperation. Its implementation is always context-dependent, as it needs to be assessed against the factual circumstances of the case. Accordingly, in the 2015 advisory opinion on fisheries, the ITLOS affirmed that the obligation to cooperate under Article 64(1) of UNCLOS, which requires states to cooperate with a view to ensuring conservation and sustainable management of shared fish stocks, is a due diligence obligation. The tribunal noted that this is an obligation requiring good faith consultations that 'should be meaningful in the sense that substantial effort should be made by all States concerned'.[210]

[207] Reference here is to the nature of obligations to cooperate as provided by customary or treaty rules, and not the nature of cooperation as a general principle of international law. On this last issue, see Wolfrum, 'International Law of Cooperation', in R. Bernhardt (ed.), *Encyclopedia of Public International Law* (Heidelberg: Encyclopedia of Public International Law, 1995), II 1242–47; see also the discussions during the work of the ILC on the Law of the Non-Navigational Uses of International Watercourses in ILC YB (1987) I on draft Article 10 and the duty to cooperate.

[208] ILC YB (1987) II/2 75.

[209] Ibid. 76.

[210] *Request for an Advisory Opinion submitted by the Sub-Regional Fisheries Commission*, para. 201.

Similar observations can be made in relation to obligations to negotiate within a certain framework of rules. In the Maritime Delimitation between Ghana and Cotê d'Ivoire, the ITLOS affirmed that the obligation to render the delimitation of the continental shelf between states with opposite or adjacent coasts effected by an international legal agreement includes an obligation to negotiate. The tribunal construed the obligation to negotiate in good faith as 'an obligation of conduct and not one of result', noting that the 'violation of this obligation cannot be based only upon the result expected by one side not being achieved'.[211] The tribunal's reference to obligations of conduct was clearly intended in the civil law meaning and recalls the notion of due diligence: negotiation toward a goal does not necessarily require the attainment of said goal.[212]

Yet, this is not the only way to interpret obligations to pursue negotiations in good faith. When in 2016 the Marshall Islands brought a case before the ICJ against India for the latter's alleged violation of Article VI of the TNP, they intended the obligation to negotiate as a duty of result. The Marshall Islands did contend that India had breached its obligations by failing 'to pursue in good faith and *bring to a conclusion* negotiations leading to nuclear disarmament'.[213] This interpretation of the obligation to pursue negotiation relied on the ICJ's dictum in the 1996 advisory opinion on the Legality of the Threat or Use of Nuclear Weapons. Here the court had affirmed that Article VI of the TNP imposes an obligation to negotiate, which is not a mere obligation of conduct, but rather imposes the achievement of a precise result, that is, nuclear disarmament in all its aspects.[214] Specifically, the court argued that this is a twofold obligation *to pursue and to conclude negotiations.*[215]

Besides cooperation and negotiation, other international obligations with a goal-oriented *esprit* may exhibit elements of due diligence in the way they are worded. Some of them do not place upon the state a duty 'to ensure', yet they are framed in a way that emphasises their conduct

[211] *Dispute Concerning Delimitation of the Maritime Boundary Between Ghana and Côte d'Ivoire in the Atlantic Ocean* (Case 23) ITLOS Reports 2017, para. 604.

[212] See P. Reuter, 'De l'obligation de negocier' (1975) 14 *Comunicazioni e Studi* 711.

[213] *Obligations Concerning Negotiations Relating to Cessation of the Nuclear Arms Race and to Nuclear Disarmament (Marshall Islands* v. *India)* (Admissibility) [2016] ICJ Rep 833, para. 261. The case did not reach the merits stage however.

[214] *Legality of the Threat or Use of Nuclear Weapons*, para. 99.

[215] Ibid 199–200. The court was confronted with the question of the nature of the obligation to negotiate also in the *Obligation to Negotiate Access to Pacific Ocean (Bolivia* v. *Chile)* (Preliminary Objections) [2015] ICJ Rep 507, para. 592, but even in this circumstance the case did not reach the merits stage.

nature and the flexibility granted to the state to pursue the required goal. These include obligations calling upon states 'to endeavour' to pursue certain objectives,[216] undertake certain policies,[217] or cooperate toward certain results.[218] Other international obligations may set general and overarching goals to be pursued through the adoption of 'appropriate' or 'necessary' measures that are left to states' discretion. For example, they may require states to adopt measures to reduce the vulnerability of certain groups to human rights violations, such as trafficking,[219] to reduce social and cultural practices regarding discrimination,[220] stereotypes, and other harmful practices;[221] to 'take appropriate measures' to enforce the obligations set into a convention,[222] or to take measures to promote compliance by nationals of other states with international agreements or to consult with other states with the view of guaranteeing protection to internationally recognised values.[223] There may also be cases where the content of the obligation requires states to adopt measures with the view of promoting or facilitating the attainment of certain goals in a way that resembles obligations of progressive realisation of goals.[224]

Generally, what links this heterogeneous group of obligations to due diligence is the spirit of best-effort obligations emerging from their wording and the fact that their content leaves the state much latitude as

216 Ramsar Convention Articles 3(1), 4(5) and 5; CBD (n 378) Article 8(i); Article 7 Convention on the Protection and Promotion of the Diversity of Cultural Expression (adopted 20 October 2005, entered into force 18 March 2007) 2440 UNTS 311; UNCLOS Article 194(1); Palermo Protocol Article 9(2).

217 WHC Article 5.

218 Convention on the Prohibition of the Development, Production, Stockpiling and Use of Chemical Weapons Article IV(12).

219 Council of Europe Convention on Actions Against Trafficking Article (adopted 16 May 2005, entered into force 1 February 2008) CETS 197 Article 5(5), Article 10(2).

220 Article 4(b)(e) Convention on the Rights of Persons with Disabilities; Article 7 CEDAW Convention; Article 2(c) Convention on Elimination of All Forms of Racial Discrimination.

221 Article 5 CEDAW Convention; Article 7 Convention on the Elimination of All Forms of Racial Discrimination.

222 CITIES Article 8.

223 Articles 22, 25 Convention on Civil Aviation (n 418); Article VII of the Agreement on the Conservation of Polar Bears (adopted 15 November 1973, entered into force 26 May 1976) 2898 UNTS 243.

224 Article 3(1) Council of Europe Convention Conservation of European Wildlife; Article 3(4) Council of Europe Convention on Prevention of Terrorism; Articles 22, 25 Convention on Civil Aviation; Article VII of the Agreement on the Conservation of Polar Bears.

to the means to fulfil them. In some cases, the implementation of these obligations implies, among other things, the duty of the state 'to exercise vigilance' over certain activities, which is a distinctive trait of more 'traditional' due diligence obligations. At the same time, their content often differs substantially from classic due diligence obligations aimed at avoiding or minimising risk, and therefore it is difficult to give them the same label.

Finally, one should mention obligations whose formulation does not provide, at least prima facie, any distinctive element of due diligence, but that still incorporate a duty of due diligence. It has been noted above that some obligations of result entail a duty to exercise due diligence, such as in the case of the obligation not to provide assistance to belligerents operating in the territory of other states. Another example concerns the obligation to have due regard as provided in Article 58(3) of UNCLOS. As construed by the ITLOS, this is a primary rule that includes the obligation of a state to exercise due diligence to ensure that nationals flying its flag do not engage in IUU fishing in the Exclusive Economic Zone of other states. Thus, while the obligation of due regard has an autonomous existence in the UNCLOS framework, the standard of due regard may at times encompass or equate with that of due diligence.[225]

Concluding Remarks

This chapter has examined the scope of application of due diligence by inquiring to which international obligations due diligence attaches. It has shown that a firm grasp of the nature of due diligence obligations requires a prior understanding of the conduct-result dichotomy and of its value in the theory of international obligations.

Ago's distinction between conduct and result is a prerequisite to fully making sense of why the ILC eventually deemed the taxonomy of international obligations impractical for a project on responsibility. Not only was the use of conduct and result considered not a determining factor for establishing wrongfulness, it was also concluded that a fixed grid on its use would have operated as a necessary intermediary in the process of assessing responsibility, possibly making the latter even more complex.

[225] See *The Matter of the South China Arbitration*, paras. 287–97. On the legal nature of due regard obligations, see T. Treves, '"Due Regard" Obligations under the 1982 UN Convention on the Law of the Sea: The Laying Cables and Activities in the Area' (2019) 34 IJMCL 167.

Yet Ago's distinction still carries its own value and reflects aspects that are typical and unique of the international legal order.

The civil law distinction between obligations of conduct and obligations of result is instrumental for identifying primary rules imbued with due diligence. These are indeed obligations that carry a flexible character and oblige states 'to endeavour', to do the utmost to attain certain results. The analysis of due diligence obligations through the civil law dichotomy also clarifies why due diligence is the standard reference for primary rules linked to activities of non-state actors and the concept of risk. Being obligations of conduct, duties that obligate states to do their utmost without guaranteeing the result are primarily found in situations where states are obligated to ensure results outside their strict sphere of control. Hence, the traditional area of application of due diligence encompasses obligations requiring the state to prevent, to protect from harmful activities of private parties, and to ensure that private parties comply with international regulations and that lawful activities carrying an intrinsic risk of harm do not injure other states. The survey of treaty practices has shown that, along with this 'classic' field of application, there is room to use to due diligence also to interpret other international obligations with a best-effort nature and rather flexible content. Some of these primary rules may not necessarily be linked to the concept of risk external to the state. However, they are premised on the idea that states are left with a margin of discretion as to the means they adopt, and that non-achievement of the result set in the obligation is not automatic proof of a state's failure to comply with it.

Obviously, licence to use both taxonomies of international obligations does not take away the fact that preference accorded to one of them by the ILC did have an impact on the normative value of the other. Specifically, Ago's classification of international obligations had a long-lasting effect on the significance of its civil law counterpart and ultimately on the understanding of due diligence obligations. This chapter has begun to unveil that the understanding of due diligence obligations as best-effort obligations clearly collides with some of the findings of ARSIWA. This aspect will emerge even more clearly in the following chapters, which will query the value of the 'event' (result) connected to due diligence obligations and discuss more critically the conclusions of ARSIWA in relation to preventive obligations.

3

The Scope and Content of Due Diligence Obligations

Introduction

This chapter discusses the scope and content of due diligence obligations. It asks how the concept of due diligence operates and affects the substance of obligations of this nature. The premise of this chapter is the same that runs through the entire book. As a qualifier for a class of primary rules, due diligence provides meaning and rationale to international obligations imbued with this concept. As such, due diligence not only identifies the nature of conduct required of a primary rule, but it also informs the scope and content of the rule.

Discussing the scope and content of due diligence obligations naturally implies looking at the substance of primary rules. It is only through investigating the content of an obligation imbued with due diligence that one can effectively grasp *when* is 'diligence' due, *what* does it entail, and *how far* a state should exercise it. For this reason, it is appropriate to set the boundaries of the following analysis to understand the extent to which this chapter digs into the content of primary rules. First, the chapter is not divided according to 'substantive' regimes and does not review the scope and content of due diligence obligations *ratione materiae*.[1] Although the chapter engages with the substance of (some) primary rules of due diligence across various fields, the analysis is functional to discussing the overarching operational issues, parameters, and variables affecting these obligations' scope and content. In this regard, the only section focusing on obligations in a particular area (human

[1] This type of analysis can be found in H. Krieger, A. Peters, L. Kreuzer (eds.), *Due Diligence in the International Legal Order* (Oxford: Oxford University Press, 2020); S. Cassella (ed.), *Le standard de due diligence et la responsabilité internationale* (Paris: Pedone, 2018), part I; and S. Besson, *La Due Diligence en Droit International* (2020) 409 RCADI (chapter IV); see also The ILA Study Group on Due Diligence in International Law, 'Due Diligence in International Law: First Report' (2014).

rights) does so with the intention of better clarifying a general condition for the operation of *all* primary rules of due diligence.

Second, since the purpose of the chapter is to explore the *modus operandi* of due diligence obligations from a general perspective, more specific questions regarding the peculiarity of these obligations in some international legal regimes are left aside. Addressing these questions would necessarily imply broader and deeper considerations on each regime's content, function, and scope, something which is outside the scope of this book.

Third, and more fundamentally, it is true that the identification of the due diligence nature of an obligation speaks to its *interpretation* in terms of content and scope. Yet, this does not undermine in any way the specificity of the primary rule. In other words, due diligence is a catalyst for giving substance to a primary rule and helps the judge or the interpreter establish the standard of behaviour expected of a state by that rule in a particular circumstance. However, priority in interpreting the rule should always be given to the specific *content* provided by a treaty text or custom. Hence, every general inquiry into the scope and content of due diligence obligations comes with the caveat that each primary rule may dictate its specific conditions, variables, and parameters. This is a straightforward yet fundamental consideration, often too easily forgotten when due diligence is analysed from a general perspective.

3.1 The Conditions of Due Diligence Obligations

Regardless of the specific international obligation in question, the exercise of due diligence is always premised upon certain factual conditions. Sometimes, the primary rule identifies with more precision the circumstances upon which a state needs to activate its apparatus and act diligently.[2] In other cases, primary rules are silent on these aspects and only incorporate general duties of due diligence nature (prevention, protection, duty to ensure or endeavour to ensure particular outcomes). For example, common Article 1 of the Geneva Conventions requires states 'to ensure respect' of the conventions in all circumstances;[3] the way

[2] For instance Rule 6 of the *Tallinn Manual 2.0* on the international law applicable to cyber operations, in M. Schmitt (ed.), *Tallinn Manual 2.0 on the International Law Applicable to Cyber Operations* (Cambridge: Cambridge University Press, 2017).

[3] Convention (I) for the Amelioration of the Condition of the Wounded and Sick in Armed Forces in the Field (First Geneva Convention) (adopted 12 August 1949, entered into force 21 October 1950) 75 UNTS 31; Convention (II) for the Amelioration of the Condition of

this rule is framed does not clarify *when*, *how*, and *in relation to whom* states shall act diligently 'to ensure respect'. In this and other similar circumstances, questions arise when the duty to act is triggered, in relation to which risks a state should act, and how far the state should fulfil its duty.

Whether or not the primary rule explicitly provides it, a state's exercise of due diligence depends on at least two factual conditions. First, the state must hold a certain power over the source of the risk linked to the primary rule. As Chapter 2 has illustrated, the connection with the concept of risk generally characterises primary rules of due diligence.[4] This depends on the fact that the *object* of a due diligence obligation – that is, prevention or protection from a harmful event; realisation of a specific outcome – cannot be absolutely guaranteed. Coming back to Article 1 of the Geneva Conventions, states can use all their efforts to 'ensure' that non-state armed groups, private military contractors, or other states respect the Geneva Conventions. Still, they cannot guarantee that these actors will effectively do so. Thus, risk can be defined as the probability that the object or purpose of a due diligence primary rule will not be achieved. Sources of risk are entities, persons, activities, or even circumstances that bring such probability into effect. The second condition of due diligence obligations is knowledge of the risk. States must indeed be aware of the risk about which they shall exercise due diligence; they cannot be expected to act upon risks that were unknown or that they could not have foreseen at the time they were bound by the primary rule.

3.1.1 *Power over the Source of Risk as the First Condition of Due Diligence Obligations*

The first condition for triggering a duty to act with diligence is that the state holds power over the source of risk (PSR) linked to the due diligence primary rule. If a state must protect the premises of a diplomatic mission from intruders, a duty to act exists as long as the state holds power over the intruders. To a certain degree, this is intuitive. Possibility is what

the Wounded, Sick, and Shipwrecked Members of the Armed Forces at Sea (adopted 12 August 1949, entered into force 21 October 1950) 75 UNTS 85; Convention (III) Relative to the Treatment of Prisoners of War (adopted 12 August 1949, entered into force 21 October 1950) 75 UNTS 135; Convention (IV) Relative to the Protection of Civilian Persons in Time of War (adopted 12 August 1949, entered into force 21 October 1950) 75 UNTS 287.

[4] Chapter 2, Section 2.3.1.

postulates due diligence obligations. Due diligence means requiring the state to display best efforts toward a certain result, not to attain a result outside the state's possibility to guarantee. If a state has no PSR, the state lacks the capacity to affect the situation that the primary rule of due diligence intends to change or manage. Hence, PSR informs states' capacity to affect a certain outcome. Capacity to affect creates possibility for the state to act.

The concept of PSR needs further clarification. First, a state's power vis-à-vis the source of risk means *capacity* or *ability* to produce some effects over this source.[5] From this perspective, a state's power over the source of risk is a dispositional concept and not the manifestation of a particular state's action. A state can hold power over the source of risk and have the capacity to affect it even if such capacity is not actually *exercised* in a given case and only remains a potential. In this sense, power differs from control. While power reflects an ability but can remain a potential, control is normally taken as the *outcome* of an exercise of power.[6] For instance, to affirm that a state had a duty to act with due diligence to prevent intruders from entering the premises of a diplomatic mission in a given case, it is unnecessary to verify whether actions were taken by the state vis-à-vis these intruders. For a duty to act to be established, it is sufficient to show that, at the time of the harmful events, the state had capacity to act upon the intruders and a potential to stop their action.

As the next sections will illustrate, the foundations of a state's PSR are multifaceted and vary depending on the primary rule and the circumstances in which the rule applies. In relation to many and mostly 'traditional' due diligence obligations, PSR is usually inferred by a state's territorial control. A state's control over the territorial area within which sources of risk operate is often the primary indication of the existence of a certain state's power over these sources. Yet, the foundation

[5] On power as ability or capacity to effect and how power differs from concepts like influence and control P. Morriss, *Power: A Philosophical Analysis* (Manchester: Manchester University Press, 1987), 8–36; on the conceptualisation of power in the context of international responsibility A. Nollkaemper, 'Power and Responsibility', in A. di Stefano (ed.), *Un diritto senza terra? Funzioni e limiti del principio di territorialitá nel diritto internazionale e dell'Unione Europea ? A Lackland Law? Territory, Effectiveness and Jurisdiction in International and European Law* (Turin: Giappichelli, 2014), 19; see also M. S. McDougal, 'Law and Power' (1952) 46 AJIL 102.

[6] As such, control is a consequence of power, a manifestation of it, something that follows power and cannot precede it, see Morriss *Power*, 20–2, stressing the importance of distinguishing between power and control.

of PSR may be unconnected to territory and rest only on a state's jurisdictional competence over sources of risks or activities linked to these sources. For example, in the environmental context, many due diligence obligations to protect the environment presuppose that a state has to exercise due diligence as far as the state has jurisdiction or control over potentially harmful activities. Finally, in some circumstances, a state's PSR may be deduced neither by territorial control nor by a jurisdictional competence and build upon other forms of power.

As to the meaning of 'source of risk', the latter is defined on a case-by-case basis and by the primary rule's content. On a highly general level, sources of risk linked to due diligence commonly refer to a subject – a private person or a group,[7] an entity,[8] a state or an international organisation[9] – or to an activity.[10] Hence, having power over the source of risk means having power over person(s), entities, states, international organisations, or activities.

In this regard, it is often the case that PSR manifests itself in the exercise of some forms of states' *control* over them.[11] For example, a state' s power over a paramilitary group – and a corresponding duty to act with due diligence to prevent their illicit conduct – may be inferred by the fact that this state exercised some control over this group through military operations or financial links. Control over the source of risk can thus operate as an indication of state's PSR. Yet, this control must not be confused with other forms of control relevant to international law. Control functional to proving PSR is typically a form of *diffuse* control over persons, entities, or activities and not control over an *act* or an *operation.*[12] Control over the source of risk refers to a manifestation of the state's power to effect change over persons, entities, or activities and is

7 Vienna Convention on Diplomatic Relations (adopted 18 April 1961, entered into force 24 April 1964) 500 UNTS 95 Article 22.

8 UNSC Res 2370 (2 August 2017) UN Doc. S/RES/2370 para. 1.

9 On how a state may have due diligence obligations requiring to act upon international organisations K. Daugirdas, 'Member States' Due Diligence Obligations to Supervise International Organizations', in Krieger, Peters, Kreuzer, *Due Diligence*, 59.

10 Vienna Convention for the Protection of the Ozone Layer (adopted 22 March 1985, entered into force 22 September 1988) 1513 UNTS 293 Article 2(1).

11 See Section 3.3.4.

12 Nollkaemper argues that 'effective control' for the purpose of attribution, coercion, direction and control, are forms of 'compulsory power' that allow the state to shape in a concrete situation the conduct of another subject. In the context of due diligence, control is usually not exercised over the actor in a particular instance, but it is a manifestation of 'institutional power' of the state that can or cannot be effected, Nollkaemper, 'Power and Responsibility', 30.

functional to demonstrating that, in a particular circumstance, a state's duty to act with due diligence existed. This control, therefore, differs from control for attribution of conduct. Control for attribution purposes belongs to the realm of secondary rules. It refers to the (effective) control exercised by the state over a specific act or operation carried out by private subjects.

The following subsections identify the various foundations of a state's PSR. Their division in some ways reflects the history of due diligence in international law. Traditionally, due diligence has emerged as a concept applied to primary rules with actual territorial dimensions. With the development of international law, especially international environmental law, the principle of due diligence has been progressively detached from its territorial character and linked to a state's exercise of jurisdiction over certain activities.[13] More recently, there has been growing consensus that, at least for some primary rules with no territorial limitations, the scope of a state's duty to act extends so long as the state has the capacity to affect the situation addressed by the rule.

The purpose of this and the next sections is to illustrate the foundations of PSR and to show that PSR informs the scope of a duty to act with due diligence. If there is no PSR, there cannot be a duty to act in the circumstances of the case since the state cannot affect the situation linked to the rule of due diligence. Of course, this does not mean that all primary rules of due diligence can be interpreted alike nor that, whenever a state has power over the source of some risks, the state has a duty to act vis-à-vis them. The understanding of the extent to which a primary rule imposes a duty to act with due diligence depends on this rule's nature, its interpretation, and, if conventional, the treaty regime that contains it. As it will be seen, the legal interests protected by the primary rule may also influence the extent to which a state is expected to act upon certain risks.[14] Hence, in relation to primary rules established to safeguard interests deemed fundamental to the international community, the scope of a state's duty to act may be much greater than for other primary rules.

[13] On the detachment of due diligence from its territorial dimension see also O. Corten, 'La complicité dans le droit de la responsabilité internationale: un concept inutile?' (2011) 57 AFDI 57, 70.

[14] See Section 3.3.2.

I Power over the Source of Risk as Corollary of Territorial Control

For primary rules of due diligence with a territorial dimension, a state's PSR is typically presumed in the state's control over its territory. This assumption derives from the long-standing principle that territorial sovereignty entails rights and a duty to protect within a state's territory the rights of other states.[15]

The most illustrative example of the relationship between territory and sources of risk emanating within it is the Corfu Channel case. This case involved Albania's alleged responsibility for the explosions of mines in its territorial waters, which resulted in damage caused to two British warships. Albania denied having laid the mines and argued that it had not known about their presence in its waters and could not have acquiesced to their laying by a third party. While much of the argument put forward by the International Court of Justice (ICJ) built around the requisite of Albania's knowledge of the minelaying and evidence to prove it, the court also emphasised the link between territory and power over risks emanating within it. It affirmed that a state in whose territory or in whose waters an act contrary to international law has occurred might be called upon to give an explanation.[16] The court also noted that although territorial control cannot imply a state's knowledge of every single risk emanating within it, it presupposes a certain state's ability to prevent and manage risks.[17]

Territorial control works as the foundation of state's PSR because when this control is lacking, PSR is usually disputed. This emerges clearly in the early practice of due diligence regarding states' obligation to protect foreigners and their property. When damage to foreigners occurred at the hands of revolutionary groups or private individuals operating in a state's territorial area far from or outside the control of state authorities, arbitral commissions tended to exclude the existence of a duty to act. For example, in one arbitral case it was affirmed that a state's duty to protect aliens and their property ceases 'inside the territory held by the insurgents from the time such territory was withdrawn by war from the control of that government, and until her authority and

[15] *Island of Palmas (Netherlands* v. *United States)* (1928) 2 RIAA 839.

[16] *Corfu Channel Case (UK* v. *Albania) (Merits)* [1949] ICJ Rep 244, 18.

[17] Ibid. See also ILC Draft Articles on Prevention of Transboundary Harm from Hazardous Activities, with commentaries (2001) ILC YB II/2, 150.

jurisdiction were again established over it'.[18] In another case, a British-Mexican claim commission affirmed:

> no Government of a country . . . with scarce population, of a mountainous character and with great difficulty of communication, can be expected to furnish adequate military protection to all the isolated oil-fields, mines, haciendas and factories scattered over the territory. The oil camp where the murder was committed is in a very remote situation, and its connection with the rest of the country are scarce and arduous. . . . it was *outside the power of the Government* forces to operate in the region, which was practically in the hands of others.[19]

It would be more difficult in today's international law to justify the lack of territorial control based on a state territorial area's remoteness. However, contemporary practice on due diligence continues to consider the absence of this control indicative of the state's lack of PSR.[20] This applies especially when the loss of control over territory occurs due to occupation, administration, or *de facto* control exercised by another state.[21] In these circumstances, the state that loses control over part of its territory is considered to have no capacity to act over risks emanating from within and, *in principle*, no duties to exercise due diligence. On the

[18] Prat case in J. B. Moore, *History and Digest of the International Arbitrations to which the United States Has Been a Party* (Washington: US Government Printing, 1943), vol. 3, 2890–1.

[19] Buckingham case in G. Hackworth, *Digest of International Law* (Washington: US Government Printing, 1943), vol. 5, 480; see also *Boyd (USA* v. *United Mexican States)* (1928) 4 RIAA 380; *F.M. Smith (USA* v. *United Mexican States)* (1928) 4 RIAA 469. For a review of practice in this area R. Pisillo-Mazzeschi, *Due diligence e responsabilità internazionale degli stati* (Milan: Giuffré, 1989), 254–88.

[20] *Case Concerning Military and Paramilitary Activities in and against Nicaragua (Nicaragua* v. *United States of America) (Merits)* [1986] ICJ Rep 14, paras. 154–7.

[21] 'Physical control over territory, and not sovereignty or legitimacy of title, is the basis of State liability for acts affecting other States', *Legal Consequences for States of the Continued Presence of South Africa in Namibia (South West Africa) Notwithstanding Security Council Resolution 276 (1970)* (Advisory Opinion) [1971] ICJ Rep 16, para. 118. Broadly speaking, also in the human rights context, loss of state control over territory entails no duty to act upon sources of risks emanating within it, see *Loizidou* v. *Turkey (Preliminary Objections)* [1995] App no 15318/89 para. 62. Yet, human rights are a rather *sui generis* context when it comes to the relationship between loss of territorial control and lack of PSR. First, for many human rights due diligence obligations, states' lack of PSR in situations of loss of territorial control does not ensue from territorial loss *in itself* but from lack of jurisdiction. Second, in human rights practice the idea that a state losing control over territory has no PSR is not a hard-and-fast rule, see *Ilaşcu and others* v. *Moldova and Russia* (Judgment) [2004] App no 48787/99 at 75–7; generally M. Milanović, T. Papić, 'The Applicability of the ECHR in Contested Territories' (2018) 67 ICLQ 779.

contrary, it is the responsibility of the controlling or occupying state to 'control' sources of risks emanating from the occupied territory and to act diligently upon them. In the Armed Activities in the Territory of the Congo, the ICJ affirmed that since Uganda was the occupying power of the Ituri province in the Democratic Republic of the Congo, Uganda's responsibility was engaged 'for any lack of vigilance in preventing violations of human rights and international humanitarian law by other actors in the occupying territory, including rebel groups acting on their own account'.[22]

At any rate, I say that loss of territorial control only *in principle* entails no duty to act because, in reality, it may be much more difficult to assess whether this lack of control justifies a state's impossibility to act. There may indeed be circumstances where loss of territorial control points to a state's *inability* to regain it. In these cases, it is correct to assume that a state which is *unable* to regain control of its territory is unable to regulate and manage sources of risk emanating from within, and thus its responsibility for failure to act should be precluded. However, it may also happen that lack of territorial control will ensue from a *lack of effort* on the part of the state to regain such control. While inability is the limit of due diligence obligations, lack of effort constitutes conduct in contravention with a due diligence duty.[23]

As stated at the outset, PSR is a disposition and, as such, is often difficult to observe. When a state fails to act, it essentially fails 'to activate' or 'effect' its power over the source of risk, which remains hypothetical. From this perspective, territorial control serves both as the foundation of

[22] *Case Concerning Armed Activities on the Territory of the Congo (Democratic Republic of the Congo* v. *Uganda)* (Merits) [2005] ICJ Rep 168, para. 179.

[23] In the early due diligence practice on protection of foreigners and their property, some decisions of arbitral tribunals established in fact that a state which has no control over its territory but fails to take diligence efforts to *regain* it is responsible for its lack of effort, see *Elmer Elsworth Mead (USA* v. *United Mexican States)* (1939) 4 RIAA 653. In the context of international human rights, a state's lack of control over territory is usually under intense scrutiny and may fail to justify impossibility to act. The ECtHR for instance is usually strict in the type of loss of territorial control that justifies absence of a duty to act, see *Assanidze* v. *Georgia* (Judgment) [2004] App no 71503/01 paras. 137–50. Furthermore, although the distinction between *inability* and *lack of efforts* is not always easy to grasp, it does have crucial consequences in certain circumstances. For example, when a state's lack of territorial control has enabled non-state actors to carry out armed attacks against another state, whether lack of territorial control depends on inability or unwillingness is crucial for assessing the victim state's right to resort to the use of force against these actors in the territory of the first state, see A. Tancredi, 'Doctrinal Alternatives to Self-Defence Against Non-State Actors' (2017) 77 ZaöRV 69.

PSR and as primary evidence of its existence. Yet, the fact that a state is presumed to have power over sources of risks under territorial control does not mean the state *will be able* to act upon all these sources at any time and in any place. In other words, territorial control confers upon a state a general power over sources of risks linked due diligence obligations. However, the extent to which this power will *effectively* exist depends on the circumstances in which the state finds itself.[24] Accordingly, if a state proves that, despite territorial control, it lacked the capacity to act upon certain risks in a given case and that this lack of capacity did not ensue from the state's wrongful conduct, there will be no responsibility for failure to act.

In this regard, in the early practice of due diligence, arbitral commissions would exclude state responsibility for failing to protect foreigners when injuries occurred due to unpredictable accidents that the state could not have foreseen.[25] Likewise, if it were established that acts of insurgents had caused injury to a foreigner state and that the territorial state harbouring them could not have prevented their action in any way, responsibility was usually set aside.[26] Contemporary practice in the human rights context supports this aspect. It is well-established that obligations to protect human rights include the duty of a state to prevent non-state actors from violating individuals' rights under state's jurisdiction. When a person is under a state's jurisdiction and their human rights are at risk, the scope of the state's duty to prevent is always determined against the state's *actual* power to act upon these risks. As underscored by the European Court of Human Rights (ECtHR) in the notorious Osman case, not every risk of violation to an

24 To better understand this idea, it is useful to distinguish between power as *ability* and power as *ableness*. Power as ability indicates the propriety of the actor regardless of the environment, whereas power as ableness refers to an ability coupled with the conditions encountered by the agent at the time we are interested in. Therefore, if I have learned how to ride a bike, I have the *ability* to ride it. Yet, I am not *able to* ride it unless I have it with me in the circumstances of the case. Translated to our context, territorial control generally provides *ability* of the state to act over PSR, yet whether a state will effectively *be able* to act upon these sources will depend on a state's ability coupled with the conditions in which the state finds itself. On the distinction between ability and ableness Morris, *Power*, 80–3.

25 *Wippermann case* in Moore, *History and Digest*, vol. 3, 3040–1.

26 R. Ago, 'Eighth Report on State Responsibility' ILC YB II/1 64 ft 291. By exclusion of responsibility, I intend here that when the harmful event is accidental and the state could not have prevented it, the state had effectively no PSR and therefore the scope of its duty to exercise due diligence did not cover that event. Hence, exclusion of responsibility in this context does not refer to circumstances precluding wrongfulness. On why lack of PSR should not be construed as a circumstance precluding wrongfulness see Chapter 4.

identified individual entails a positive duty to act, but only real and immediate risks and which state authorities knew or ought to have known.[27]

The ECtHR's practice is rich in cases where responsibility for failure to protect has been excluded due to lack of state's *actual* power over sources of risk. In some cases, (lack of) causality between a state's conduct and the harmful event has been used by the court to infer lack of PSR.[28] For example, in the case of *Mastromatteo* v. *Italy*, the applicant contended that the killing of his son by individuals granted temporary leave from Italian prisons was due to Italy's failure to properly regulate that leave and exercise proper diligence in its enforcement. After finding that Italian legislation on alternative measures to imprisonment did not violate the general duty to protect life of society at large, the court had to evaluate whether Mastromatteo's death arose out of Italy's failure to protect him in the particular circumstances of the case. To this end, the ECtHR drew on causality and noted that 'a mere condition *sine qua non* does not suffice to engage the responsibility of the State under the Convention'.[29] The court concluded that although the Italian judge's decision to grant the temporary leave had sparked the chain of events leading to the killing, the authorities could have neither foreseen nor predicted the attack.[30] In other cases, the court has simply excluded that the state had the power in the specific circumstances to act upon sources of human rights risks. For instance, in a case involving the death of a woman committing suicide in fear of being evicted from her house, it was argued that 'self-immolation as a protest tactic cannot be *reasonably considered predictable* in the context of eviction from an illegally occupied dwelling'.[31] Similarly, the court has affirmed that the responsibility of a state for failing to protect is engaged only if there is a 'sufficient nexus' between state omission and the harmful event;[32] when it was within the capacity of the state to 'have significant influence on the course of the events' leading to the violation;[33] when the action of the state

27 *Osman* v. *United Kingdom* (Judgment) (GC) [1998] App no 23452/94 para. 116.

28 On the relationship between power and causality R. A. Dahl, 'The Concept of Power' (1957) 2 *Behavioural Science* 201; on the link between due diligence obligations and causality A. Ollino, 'A "Missed" Secondary Rule? Causation in the Breach of Preventive and Due Diligence Obligations', in G. Kajtar, B. Çali, M. Milanovic (eds.), *Secondary Rules of Primary Importance - Attribution, Causality and Evidentiary Rules in International Law* (Oxford: Oxford University Press, in press).

29 *Mastromatteo* v. *Italy* (Judgment) [2002] App no 37703/97 para. 74.

30 Ibid. para. 76.

31 *Mikayil Mammadov* v. *Azerbajan* (Judgment) [2009] App no 4762/05 para. 111.

32 *Fadeyeva* v. *Russia* (Judgment) [2005] App no 55723/00 para. 92.

33 *E. and others* v. *United Kingdom* (Judgment) [2003] App no 33218/96 para. 100.

'could have had a real prospect of altering the outcome or mitigating the harm'.[34]

These examples serve to illustrate that while PSR is anchored in a state's territorial control, a state cannot be expected to have power over all sources of risks only by virtue of this control. Factual conditions and the circumstances in which the state finds itself may *curtail* (or *increase*) the size and extent of this power and define consequently the exact scope of a duty to act with due diligence.[35] From this perspective, territorial control should be regarded as a rebuttable presumption of state's PSR.

A final question is whether it is still appropriate to treat territorial control as a presumption of a state's PSR at least in relation to certain due diligence obligations. The question is salient in relation to cyberspace. Specifically, one may query whether the presumption that states bear power over risks emanating from their territory is fallacious when applied to a state's obligation to ensure that its territory is not used for unlawful cyber operations against other states. This book does not wish to discuss the suitability of international law for the cyber context,[36] nor intends to enter the debate on whether cyber operations require a *sui generis* application of specific primary and secondary rules.[37] However, this book accepts the idea that among the primary rules applicable to cyber operations is states' customary obligation not to knowingly allow their territory to be used for acts contrary to other states. The applicability of this rule is not only supported by a large number of scholars,[38] but it appears to be upheld by states.[39]

[34] *Opuz* v. *Turkey* (Judgment) [2009] App no 33401/02 para. 136.

[35] For a more extensive account of the relationship between PSR and the correlative scope of a duty to act in the context of human rights obligations V. Stoyanova, 'Causation between State Omission and Harm within the Framework of Positive Obligations under the European Convention on Human Rights' (2018) 18 HRLR 309; in relation to the obligation to protect foreign investments S. Mantilla Blanco, *Full Protection and Security in International Investment Law* (Berlin: Springer, 2018), 457–9.

[36] F. Delerue, *Cyber Operations and International Law* (Cambridge: Cambridge University Press, 2020); M. Schmitt, 'Sovereignty in Cyberspace: *Lex Lata Vel Non*' (2017) 111 AJIL *Unbound* 213; H. Krieger, G. Nolte, 'The International Rule of Law: Rise or Decline? Points of Departure' (KFG Working Paper Series No 1 2016), 12.

[37] L. Chircop, 'A Due Diligence Standard of Attribution in Cyberspace' (2018) 67 ICLQ 643; A. Bonfanti, 'Attacchi cibernetici in tempo di pace e intrusioni nelle elezioni presidenziali alla luce del diritto internazionale' (2019) 102 *Rivista di diritto internazionale* 694.

[38] R. Kolb, 'Reflections on Due Diligence Duties in Cyberspace' (2015) 58 GYIL 114; E. Talbot Jensen, 'Cyber Sovereignty: The Way Ahead' (2015) 50 *Texas International Law Review* 275; N. Tsagourias, 'State Obligations in Cyber Operations' (2015) 14 *Baltic Yearbook of International Law* 71.

[39] UNGA 70/237 (2015) UN Doc. A/Res/70/237.

In this regard, the *Tallinn Manual 2.0* – so far the most authoritative documents on applying international law to cyber operations – recognises that states shall not allow their territory or cyberinfrastructures under their control to be used for acts contrary to other states.[40] The manual integrates the territorial principle into the application of this rule. Accordingly, states should ensure both that i) harmful cyber operations are not carried out by non-state actors operating on their territory; and ii) that cyberinfrastructures situated in their territory are not used for harmful cyber operations against other states. Yet, the presumption that territorial control implies a certain PSR resulting in harmful cyber operations is challenging. Due to their characteristics, harmful cyber operations can take a variety of forms. In some cases, a cyberattack may be *launched* by non-state actors operating on a state territory and using either this state's infrastructure or another state's infrastructures. In other cases, a cyber operation launched by non-state actors operating in a foreign state may be *routed* through the territorial state's cyber infrastructures.

The presumption of states' power and control over sources of risk is not problematic in the first scenario, that is, when non-state actors launch a cyber operation on the territory of the state. In this case, the clear physical dimension between the state and the operation justifies *possibility*, hence the duty to act diligently to respond to territorial threats. However, in cases where the alleged responsibility of a state is engaged because a cyber operation was routed through its infrastructures,[41] it is more difficult to sustain that territorial control (over infrastructures) presupposes PSR. Cyber operations often take place in a very short time, and the remote use of a foreign state's infrastructure by non-state actors may be a matter of few seconds. One may at least doubt that, in this circumstance, just because the state had control over its cyberinfrastructures, the state also had the capacity to affect cyber risks. This may explain why some scholars see the application of this primary rule to cyber operations as controversial. Upholding the territorial presumption may eventually incentivise states to strengthen their control over risks arising out of their territory (for instance through systems of mass-surveillance and cyber monitoring) at the expenses of human rights.

[40] Schmitt, *Tallinn Manual 2.0*, Rule 6.

[41] On the application of this customary obligation to these circumstances Schmitt, *Tallinn Manual 2.0*, 32–3.

II Power over the Source of Risk beyond Territorial Control

A Jurisdiction over Areas or Activities For many primary rules of due diligence, a state's jurisdictional *competence* over entities, activities, or areas constitutes the foundation of PSR. This should not be surprising. Jurisdiction in international law is intimately connected to the concept of state power.[42] Jurisdiction is indeed a form of the state's constitutive power (power to legislate, enforce, or adjudicate) recognised as legal under international law. Thus, it is only natural that the foundation of a state's PSR linked to a due diligence rule may rest in the states' constitutive power to regulate activities, entities, or areas from which sources of risk emanate.

Jurisdiction operates as the foundation of PSR precisely when the scope of the primary rule of due diligence transcends territorial boundaries and implies a state's duty to act outside a state's territory. Paradigmatic examples of PSR expressed through the state's exercise of jurisdiction can be found in primary rules of due diligence linked to environmental protection or the law of the sea context. Concerning the protection of the environment, it is well known that the general obligation to prevent transboundary harm encompasses the duty to exercise due diligence in relation to activities undertaken in a state's territory and 'activities within the state's jurisdiction or control'.[43] The commentary to the ILC work on prevention of transboundary harm argues that 'jurisdiction over an activity' concerning the duty to prevent must be understood as competence.[44] Hence, a state's exercise of prescriptive jurisdiction over a ship that may cause significant transboundary harm triggers the state's duty to act with due diligence.

Many conventional obligations in the field of environmental protection are structured alike. Primary rules in multilateral environmental agreements (MEAs) often subordinate the performance of the state's obligations provided in MEAs to the state's exercise of jurisdiction. Sometimes, it is the exercise of jurisdiction over the *activity* or a *subject* that defines the scope of the duty;[45] other times, it is jurisdiction over

[42] F. A. Mann, 'The Doctrine of Jurisdiction in International Law' (1964) 111 RCADI 9–10.

[43] The Rio Declaration on Environment and Development (Rio de Janeiro, June 1992) UN Doc. A/CONF.151/26 (vol. I), Principle 2; *Legality of the Threat or Use of Nuclear Weapons* (Advisory Opinion) [1996] ICJ Rep, para. 29; ILC Draft Articles on Prevention with commentary, Article 3.

[44] ILC Draft Articles on Prevention with commentary, 151.

[45] Convention for the Protection of the Ozone Layer, Article 2(2)(b); Protocol on the Environmental Protection to the Antarctic Treaty (adopted 4 October 1991, entered into force 14 January 1998) 2941 UNTS 9 Article 3.

a *process* that triggers the duty to act.[46] More complex is the understanding of 'control' that triggers due diligence. As illustrated above, the ILC draft articles on preventing transboundary harm affirm that the duty to prevent extends to activities within a state's jurisdiction *or control.* In the Commentary, the notion of 'control over the activity' is given a territorial dimension. Specifically, the commission interprets control by referencing the 'effective control' exercised by a state over a territorial area, which triggers a state's duty to act diligently vis-à-vis activities located in this area and causing significant harm.[47] More unclear is whether effective control exercised *only* over the activity – but not on the territory – may be sufficient to justify the duty to act diligently.[48] Put differently, does effective control over the activity, devoid of any legal competence, triggers a duty to act toward that activity? The problem not only regards the customary obligation to prevent transboundary harm but concerns, more generally, several other obligations contained in MEAs. The latter often use the formula state's 'exercise of jurisdiction or control' over the activity to define the scope of a state's duty to act.[49]

Another area in which the duty to act diligently is normally linked to a state's jurisdictional competence is the law of the sea context. Notably, the international law of the sea allocates jurisdiction based on the functions performed by a state at sea. The reason is that the division of marine spaces in international law does not mirror the division on land, where spaces are divided according to the exclusive territorial sovereignty of each state. In the seas, the division of spaces follows the 'zonal approach' reflected in United Nations Convention on the Law of the Sea (UNCLOS),[50] and rights

[46] Convention on Biological Diversity (adopted 5 June 1992, entered into force 29 December 1993) 1760 UNTS 79 Article 4(b).

[47] ILC Draft Articles on Prevention with commentary, 151.

[48] For instance, in the ILC work on protection of the atmosphere, Special Rapporteur Murase seems to suggest that 'control' may also refer to 'factual capacity of effective control over *activities* outside the jurisdiction of the State', but then, to support this finding, he quotes the ICJ *Namibia* case, which grounded 'control' on *territory*, see S. Murase, 'Third Report on the Protection of the Atmosphere' (2016) ILC YB II/1 para. 33; on this aspect see also F. Violi, 'The Function of the Triad "Territory", "Jurisdiction" and "Control" in Due Diligence Obligations', in Kriegers, Peters, Kreuzer, *Due Diligence*, 82–4.

[49] In general, on the extraterritorial application of MEAs and how 'jurisdiction' and 'control' over activities may be interpreted M. Vordermayer, 'The Extraterritorial Application of Multilateral Environmental Agreements' (2018) 59 *Harvard International Law Journal* 59.

[50] United Nations Convention on the Law of the Sea (UNCLOS) (adopted 10 December 1982, entered into force 16 November 1994) 1833 UNTS 3. UNCLOS divides marine water spaces into six categories (internal waters, territorial sea,

and obligations of states are granted according to the function states perform in each zone. Thus, depending on whether the state is operating in one zone as the flag state, the coastal state, the port state, or the sponsoring state, UNCLOS recognises different forms of jurisdictional powers. From the perspective of due diligence, this means that due diligence primary rules in the context of the law of the sea are linked to the recognition of state's jurisdiction. For instance, the *possibility* for the coastal state to act to ensure that marine living resources in the exclusive economic zone (EEZ) are conserved and managed in a way that does not subject them to over-exploitation,[51] premises upon the jurisdictional functions granted by UNCLOS to the coastal state in the EEZ. The assumption is the same that applies to the environmental context: the exercise of jurisdictional powers over certain areas, persons, or activities taking place at sea implies power over sources of risks linked to these areas, persons, or activities.[52]

Jurisdiction over areas of activities as the foundation of a state's PSR is not limited to primary rules of due diligence in the environmental and law of the sea context. International obligations that ground PSR upon the recognition of jurisdictional powers can be found across international law.[53] Furthermore, the relationship between jurisdiction and PSR mirrors the relationship between territory and PSR. Jurisdiction over an entity, activity, or area is the basis and primary indication of state's PSR linked to due diligence. However, the *effective* measure of this power and *the extent to which* a duty to act with due diligence arises will depend on the circumstances of the case.

For example, according to Article 62(4) of UNCLOS, states other than the coastal state have the duty to ensure that their nationals engaged in fishing activities within the EEZ of the coastal state comply with the conservation measures and the conditions established by the latter. The jurisdiction that a state exercises over ships flying its flag certainly provides the state with *power* over them and the capacity to affect how these ships engage in fishing activities in the EEZ of the coastal state. At

archipelagic waters, contiguous zone, exclusive economic zones, and high seas) and marine underwater areas in two categories (the continental shelf and the area).

51 UNCLOS Article 61(2).

52 For a comprehensive analysis of due diligence obligations in the international law of the sea and why this legal area provides for many due diligence rules see I. Papanicolopulu, 'Due Diligence in the Law of the Sea' in Krieger, Peters, Kreuzer, *Due Diligence*, 147.

53 For example Arms Trade Treaty (adopted 2 April 2013, entered into force 24 December 2014) 3031 UNTS 7 Article 10; Convention on International Civil Aviation (adopted 7 December 1944, entered into force 4 April 1947) 15 UNTS 295 Article 3 bis (d), Article 12.

a minimum, this power will entail a state's duty to adopt laws and regulations that will incentivise ships to abide by the coastal state's rules. However, the extent to which the state will *effectively* be able to exert this power over a ship flying its flag and engaged in illegal fishing activities in the EEZ of the coastal state will depend on the circumstances of the case. For instance, a state may effectively have power to prevent the act of illegal fishing by a ship because its authorities were made aware of these activities or because an official state's vessel was in the proximity of the ship or had control over it when the activity took place. Thus, recognition of the state's jurisdiction is only a condition for the exercise of due diligence. It *presumes* the possibility (thus obligations) for a state to adopt laws, regulations, and other necessary measures. The 'intensity' of this power and the extent to which it shall be effected toward the source of risk is instead a separate question, one that may be more difficult to answer.

B Other Forms of Power over the Source of Risk Both territorial control and jurisdiction over sources of risk operate as presumptions of a state's PSR and thus conditions for the corresponding duty to act diligently. Yet, a duty to exercise due diligence may be wholly detached from a state's control over its territory and the recognition of jurisdiction. Other forms of power or control may provide evidence of a state's PSR linked to a due diligence rule and trigger a state's duty to act diligently upon them.

Examples of due diligence duties existing beyond territorial boundaries and regardless of jurisdiction over sources of risks have already been provided above. In discussing the link between territorial control and PSR, it was argued that states' control over a territorial area without title to that area could be sufficient to engender the link between the state and sources of risk emanating from within. In the example of the Armed Activities case, the ICJ placed on Uganda, as the occupying power of an area of the DRC, the duty to prevent violations of human rights and international humanitarian law by third actors operating in the occupied zone.[54] Similarly, the ECtHR has a long track record of cases in which PSR has been *inferred* by the control or influence over another state's territorial area.[55] On the one hand, these examples show that a state's PSR

[54] *Armed Activities*, para. 179.

[55] *Catan and others* v. *Moldova and Russia* (Judgment) [2012] App no 43370/04, 8252/05, 18454/06 paras. 111–23; *Chiragov and others* v. *Armenia* (Judgment) [2015] App no 13216/05 paras. 169–80.

may be linked neither to title to territory nor a competence accorded by international law. On the other hand, these cases still build the connection between the state and PSR on territorial control.

There are cases in international practice which derive PSR from other links. The most notable and cited example is undoubtedly the Bosnian Genocide case. It is common knowledge that when the ICJ in 2007 faced the issue of Serbia's responsibility for the genocide in Srebrenica, the court grappled with the nature of the factual link between Serbia and the militia groups effectively carrying out acts of genocide. Serbia was not an occupying power in Srebrenica, nor exercised effective control over the territorial area where genocide occurred. Nonetheless, having the court excluded that the acts of genocide committed by the militia were attributable to Serbia pursuant to rules of attribution of conduct,[56] the question remained whether Serbia was still under the obligation to prevent genocide in the area. The court notoriously concluded that a duty to act diligently to prevent genocide had arisen due to the political, military, and financial links between Serbia and the militia groups.[57] Expressly, the ICJ judges affirmed that the strength of those political and other links between the authorities of Serbia and the main actors in the event had informed the state's '*capacity to influence effectively* the action of persons likely to commit, or already committing, genocide'.[58]

The Genocide case is a representative example of a duty to act which finds a source exclusively in the state's power (political, military, and financial) over the source of risk. Serbia's political, financial, and military power over the militia carrying out genocide triggered the foundation of due diligence, that is, the *possibility* for the state to act and capacity to affect the outcome of such control. While this remains the most paradigmatic case of a duty to act linked neither to territory nor to competence, it is not the only case. For instance, in 2016, the International Committee of the Red Cross (ICRC) updated its commentary to the First Geneva Convention, whose Article 1 provides that states undertake to respect and *ensure respect* for the present Convention in all circumstances. The ICRC has classified the obligation 'to ensure respect' as embodying duties of due diligence nature.[59] The commentary stresses that the obligation 'to ensure respect' is composite and requires action vis-à-vis various actors to a conflict. First, Article 1 embodies the state's duty to act

[56] *Case Concerning Application of the Convention on the Prevention and Punishment of the Crime of Genocide (Bosnia Herzegovina* v. *Serbia and Montenegro)* (Merits) [2007] ICJ Rep 43, paras. 380–3, 395, 412–14.

[57] Ibid. para. 434.

[58] Ibid. para. 430.

[59] ICRC Commentary on the First Geneva Convention (2016) Article 1, paras. 150, 154, 165.

diligently to prevent violations of the convention by its armed forces, persons or groups acting on state's behalf,[60] and private persons or groups over which a state exercises authority.[61] Read against our analytical framework, this confirms that states have to act diligently when sources of risk (armed forces or other groups violating the convention) emanate from their territory or are under states' authority[62] or jurisdiction.[63] More importantly, the commentary also argues that states have a duty to act to prevent violations by others that are party to a conflict, including non-state parties and other states.[64] Duties to act diligently arise, for instance, for a 'third' state participating in the financing, equipping, or arming of a state party's arm forces to a conflict, or when a state finances and trains a paramilitary group operating in a non-international arm conflict (NIAC).[65] In these cases – and drawing on the ICRC commentary – duties to act exist so long as a state is in the 'position to influence' the behaviour of those responsible for the breach of the Convention.[66] This 'position to influence' will ensue from some forms of state's power over these actors. For example, in the case of a state financing and equipping a paramilitary group operating in a NIAC, it will be the strength of the military and financial links between the state and the group that substantiates state's position to influence the group and its capacity to prevent 'foreseeable risks' of violations.

3.1.2 Power of the Source of Risk in the Human Rights Context

States' PSR as the condition of a duty to act diligently has been hardly the object of systematic studies by the literature.[67] Yet, the importance of

60 On the classification of the state's duty 'to ensure respect' of the convention by its own arm forces as a due diligence duty see Chapter 2.

61 ICRC Commentary on the First Geneva Convention, para. 150.

62 For instance, non-state armed groups or private persons whose conduct is not attributable to the state but who are under its occupation.

63 For example, a duty to act diligently to prevent violations of the convention may arise for home states in whose jurisdiction a private military or security company is based, see H. Tonkin, *State Control over Private Military and Security Companies in Armed Conflict* (Cambridge: Cambridge University Press, 2011), 229–58.

64 ICRC Commentary on the First Geneva Convention, para. 154.

65 Accordingly, *Case Concerning Military and Paramilitary Activities in and Against Nicaragua*, para. 220. On the scope of Article 1 and its relationship to due diligence see M. Longobardo, 'The Relevance of the Concept of Due Diligence for International Humanitarian Law' (2019) 37 *Wisconsin International Law Journal* 44, 58–65; O. A. Hathaway et al., 'Ensuring Responsibility: Common Article 1 and State Responsibility for Non-State Actors' (2017) 95 *Texas Law Review* 539.

66 ICRC Commentary on the First Geneva Convention, paras. 164–8.

67 Exceptions are Violi, *The Function*, 75; Besson, *La Due Diligence*, 239–45.

addressing the concept emerges by the tendency of recent strands of scholarship and practice to confound it with other types of control that a state may hold toward other 'subjects' of a due diligence rule. This is particularly true in the human rights field, where the overlapping of PSR with control for jurisdictional purposes testifies to the lack of adequate conceptualisation of due diligence obligations.

Commenting about human rights due diligence obligations naturally requires broaching the question of jurisdiction. That is because almost all international human rights instruments tie the scope of states' human rights obligations to an exercise of the state's jurisdiction vis-à-vis the individual. Jurisdiction is, in a nutshell, the trigger of a state's obligations in the human rights context. If the state has no jurisdiction toward the individual, the state holds no human rights obligations vis-à-vis that individual. This emerges clearly in the ECtHR jurisprudence, which often defines jurisdiction as the 'threshold criterion' for the application of the rights guaranteed by the convention.[68]

How the jurisdictional link between the state and the individual is conceptualised varies significantly across international legal scholarship. Some scholars see jurisdiction only as a yardstick that, once attained in reality, gives rise to a state's human rights obligations in a particular context.[69] Others construe jurisdiction not just as a benchmark to determine the existence of certain obligations but very much as the fundamental linkage *justifying* why a specific duty-bearer (the state) should be allocated duties to a particular right-holder (the individual).[70] Regardless of the position one wishes to adopt, jurisdiction is about the connection between a state and the individual. The UN Human Rights Committee expressed this neatly in one of its earliest individual complaints, where it argued that the reference to 'individuals subjects to its jurisdiction' in

[68] *Al-Skeini and others* v. *United Kingdom* (Judgment) (GC) [2011] App no 55721/07 para. 130.

[69] Positions vary even within this approach; see M. Scheinin, 'Just Another World? Jurisdiction in the Roadmaps of State Responsibility and Human Rights', in M. Langford, W. Vandenhole, M. Scheinin (eds.), *Global Justice, State Duties: The Extraterritorial Scope of Economic, Social and Cultural Rights in International Law* (Cambridge: Cambridge University Press, 2013), 212, who sees jurisdiction as a shorthand expression for attribution of conduct; M. Milanovic, *Extraterritorial Application of Human Rights Treaties* (Oxford: Oxford University Press, 2011), understanding jurisdiction as a threshold criterion only for positive human rights obligations.

[70] S. Besson, 'The Extraterritoriality of the European Convention on Human Rights: Why Human Rights Depend on Jurisdiction and What Jurisdiction Amounts To' (2012) 25 LJIL 857; L. Raible, *Human Rights Unbound: A Theory of Extraterritoriality* (Oxford: Oxford University Press, 2020).

Article 1 of the Optional Protocol of the International Covenant on Civil and Political Rights 'is not to the place where the violation occurred, but rather *to the relationship between the individual and the State* in relation to a violation of any rights set forth in the Covenant'.[71]

There is another element to be borne in mind when discussing jurisdiction in international human rights law. Given that what matters for establishing jurisdiction is the relationship between the state and the individual, acts of jurisdiction in international human rights law are not limited to a state's exercise of power under rules of international law. Put differently, a state does not incur human rights violations only when it acts in its territory or lawfully outside of it, for example, because a rule of international law has recognised power to the state to arrest beyond its territorial boundaries.[72] Jurisdiction in international human rights law also exists *de facto*, that is, when the exercise of power by the state falls outside its legal competence. No court or human rights body would deny a state's responsibility vis-à-vis a person captured or detained by state agents in the course of an enforcement operation carried out in another state's territory, because capture occurred without the latter state's consent. Accordingly, jurisdiction has been found in situations where a state had occupied a foreign territory,[73] exercised some forms of control over a territorial area,[74] or when a state's authorities exercised control over an individual despite the absence of legal rule prescribing power to exercise such control.[75] In short, jurisdiction in human rights practice is made dependent on the *power* (and its exercise) of a state toward the individual.

Given this book's scope, there will be no further inquiry into the notion of jurisdiction in human rights law. The only additional element worth

[71] *Lopez Burgos* v. *Uruguay* (1981), IHRL 2796, Human Rights Committee, para. 12.2

[72] Take the case of the right of the coastal state to arrest a vessel that is wilfully polluting the territorial sea.

[73] *Legal Consequences of the Construction of a Wall in the Occupied Palestinian Territory* (advisory opinion) [2004] ICJ Rep 136, para. 111.

[74] *Loizidou* v. *Turkey*, para 62; *Catan*, paras. 111–23; *Chiragov*, paras. 169–80.

[75] *Al-Skeini*, para. 149. Literature on extraterritorial jurisdiction in human rights is vast; see among others P. De Sena, *La nozione di giurisdizione statale nei trattati sui diritti dell'uomo* (Turin: Giappichelli, 2002); R. Wilde, 'Compliance with Human Rights Norms Extraterritoriality: Human Rights Imperialism?', in L. Boisson de Chazournes, M. Kohen (eds.), *International Law and the Quest for Its Implementation: Liber Amicorum Vera Gowlland-Debbas* (Leiden: Brill, 2010); Milanovic, *Extraterritorial Application*; Besson, 'The Extraterritoriality of the European Convention'; C. Mallory, *Human Rights Imperialists: The Extraterritorial Application of the European Convention on Human Rights* (London: Hart Publishing, 2020).

stressing is that the definition of what amounts to power (and its exercise) giving rise to the human rights obligations of a state is still subject to much debate in scholarship and practice. The ECtHR, the body with the richest and most established case law on jurisdiction, still struggles to develop a principled notion of jurisdiction applicable across the board. The court has famously developed the dichotomy between the 'spatial' model of jurisdiction – according to which state's effective control over an area triggers jurisdiction vis-à-vis the individuals in that area – and the 'personal' model – according to which the exercise of a state's authority over an individual triggers jurisdiction.[76] Yet, some cases before the court move away from this dichotomy and build jurisdiction based on other grounds.[77] The Human Rights Committee has instead argued that a state party must secure human rights to anyone within 'power or effective control' of that state party, at times interpreting these notions more broadly than the ECtHR.[78]

Similarly, human rights scholarship has offered different and often opposing views on what kind of state's power toward the individual should qualify for jurisdiction. Some contend that power should be assessed mainly by taking into account the level of control exercised by a state over territory or people abroad or the state's capacity to fulfil human rights.[79] Others vest power with more than factual control over territory or individuals, claiming that jurisdiction requires 'de facto political and legal authority',[80] or at least political power over areas of human activities achieved by applying legal principles and rules.[81]

Moving to the core of our analysis, it emerges from the above that state's PSR in human rights due diligence obligations (HRDDO hereafter) is also linked to the concept of jurisdiction.[82] If there is no jurisdiction over the individual, there are no human rights obligations. With

[76] See *Al-Skeini*, paras. 130–42.

[77] See for instance *Güzelyurtlu and others* v. *Cyprus and Turkey* (Judgment) (GC) [2019] App no 36925/07 para. 188.

[78] Human Rights Committee, 'General Comment No. 31 on the Nature of the General Legal Obligation Imposed on State Parties to the Covenant' (2004) UN Doc. CCPR/C/21/Rev.1/add.13 para 10.

[79] Y. Shany, *The Extraterritorial Application of International Human Rights Law* (2020) 409 RCADI 29–30, 141–8.

[80] Besson, 'The Extraterritoriality of the European Convention', 857.

[81] Raible, *Human Rights Unbound*, 132.

[82] Of course, this occurs at least for those obligations whose application is linked to the recognition of states' jurisdiction over individuals, such as the International Covenant on Civil and Political Rights, the European Convention on Human Rights, or the Inter-American Convention on Human Rights.

no human rights obligations, there cannot be a duty for the state to act diligently to protect from certain violations of human rights.

However, power over the source of risk in HRDDO and jurisdiction do not necessarily overlap. First, the tests required to assess them are distinct and belong to a separate analysis. The test for jurisdiction pertains to the relationship between the right-holder and the duty-bearer and regards the existence of the HRDDO. The test for assessing PSR typically follows the question of state responsibility.[83] It relates to the exercise of a state's power toward persons, entities, or activities that may 'generate' human rights violations. These tests' difference is also underscored by the fact that power over the source of risk in HRDDO and jurisdiction may not find a *cause* in the same kind of power. Sometimes, the power 'source' of jurisdiction and the power 'source' of the state's control over risk do coincide, for instance, when they both rest on territorial control over an area. But in other cases, they do not. Take the case of an individual held in custody by state agents operating in an extraterritorial setting who loses his life while in custody. Jurisdiction in this case finds its source in physical power exercised by state agents over the individual. As for the state's duty to act diligently to investigate his death,[84] power over the source of risk[85] derives from a state's *power to legislate* and put in place a judicial, administrative, and operative apparatus capable of ensuring effective and adequate investigations.

The problem is that some recent strands of human rights practice seem to confound these different notions and to 'derive' jurisdiction from a state's power over the source of human rights risk. However, this approach is flawed because it conflates the test for assessing an obligation's existence with the test for determining the scope of the duty arising out of that obligation.[86] Let us illustrate more plainly why.

[83] In reality, the question concerning PSR in due diligence obligations regards the *scope* of a duty to act with due diligence. Yet, this scope is normally assessed *ex-post facto* in relation to a state's responsibility for failure to act.

[84] Obviously, the *existence* of this duty still depends on a state's jurisdiction over the individual.

[85] In this case, the source of risk is the possibility that investigative authorities do not identify and punish those responsible for the death of the individual.

[86] Actually, there is at least one other argument against this conflation, namely that having 'power' and 'control' over sources of human rights risk does not necessarily mean having 'power' or 'control' over individuals and the enjoyment of their human rights. Due to space constraint, this argument will not be pursued further here; for a distinction of the notion of power, control, and influence in relation to human rights jurisdiction see Raible, *Human Rights Unbound*, 103–29.

In 2017, the Inter-American Court of Human Rights adopted an advisory opinion regarding the reach of state parties' obligation to protect the lives of individuals from significant environmental transboundary harm. More specifically, the court was requested to clarify whether state parties to the American Convention are under the duty to protect from significant environmental harm individuals outside state's territory, yet affected by the activities carried out in state's territory and generating transboundary harm. To answer affirmatively, the court had to dig into the scope of jurisdiction as per Article 1 of the American Convention. The court noted:

> Regarding transboundary damage, a person is subject to the jurisdiction of the State of origin, if there is a *causal connection* between the incident that took place on its territory and the violation of the human rights of persons outside its territory. The exercise of jurisdiction arises when the State of origin exercises effective control of the activities that caused the damage and consequent violations of human rights.[87]

In short, the court opened the door to recognising jurisdiction when a state fails to regulate activities under its effective control, and these activities cause human rights violations of individuals abroad.

Recently, the Human Rights Committee has also provided for a similar interpretation of jurisdiction. General Comment no. 36, adopted in relation to the right to life, affirms that jurisdiction arises when a state exercises power or effective control over the enjoyment of rights' of individuals: this may occur when a person is outside the territory of the state and her right to life is *impacted* in a direct and reasonably foreseeable manner by the activities originating in the state's territory, including activities carried out by non-state actors.[88] Referring to multinational corporations (MNCs) that operate in 'host' states, and to the obligations that 'home' states may bear toward individuals in 'host' states affected by the violations of these corporations, the Comment noted that the duty to protect life requires 'home' states: "to take appropriate legislative and other measures to ensure that all activities taking place in whole or in part within their territory and in other places subject to their [de jure] jurisdiction, but having a direct and foreseeable impact on the right to

[87] *Environment and Human Rights*, Advisory Opinion OC-23/17 of November 15 (2017) IACHR para. 101 (emphasis added).

[88] Human Rights Committee, 'General Comment No. 36 (2018) on Article 6 of the International Covenant on Civil and Political Rights, on the right to life' (2018) UN Doc. CCPR/C/GC/36 para. 63.

life of individuals outside their territory ... are consistent with article 6."[89]

Saying that jurisdiction exists if a state's fails to (diligently) regulate activities in its territory or under its effective control and causing direct and foreseeable violations to individuals abroad, is equal to say that as long as a state has power over sources of risks of violations the state has jurisdiction toward individuals affected by these violations. What links a 'territorial' state to the violations suffered by individuals abroad is the state's *capacity to affect* these individuals' enjoyment of rights. This capacity to affect originates from the state's power over sources of human rights risks. Hence, under this jurisdictional model, if a private company operating in state A (or under its effective control) produces transboundary environmental harm significantly impacting the right to life of individuals located in state B, A has jurisdiction toward these individuals, provided that harm is the direct and foreseeable consequence of the company's activity. State A's jurisdictional link arises because A has power or control over the company's activity and consequently the capacity to affect individuals' rights located in state B.

It should be clear from the analysis conducted so far that the state's PSR and the correlative capacity to affect situations linked to such risks pertain to the *scope* of a duty to act. This is also true for HRDDOs. A state's duty to act to protect the right to life extends as far as the state has power over sources of risk to individuals' lives. Essentially, this means that states not only have to 'anticipate' known risks by putting in place an adequate legislative and regulatory framework that targets them. States also need to act to prevent violations from materialising when they have some form of power or 'control' over *specific* risks of violations. For example, when state authorities know that a targeted individual's life is in danger, they have to act to prevent harm when their action would be neither impossible nor disproportionally burdensome. Thus, if an individual loses his life but it is proved that the state could not prevent this loss because it had no capacity to affect the situation in question, state responsibility is excluded. Yet, responsibility is ruled out not because the obligation to protect life was *non-existent* in the circumstances of the case, but because the state's duty to act *did not extend* to the point of covering this particular loss.

The jurisdictional model proposed by the IACtHR and the HRC reverses this operation. It uses the state's control over sources of harm

[89] Ibid. para. 22 (emphasis added).

not as a *condition* tailoring the extent of a duty to act diligently but rather as the *genuine link* between the state and the individual affected by this harm. Ultimately, this translates into saying that human rights *obligations* exist only if and to the extent that states have control over sources of harm. In the author's view, such an approach is problematic. The assessment of whether an obligation exists *in abstracto* is substituted and arguably preceded by evaluating the scope of a duty to act. Furthermore, jurisdiction is de facto rendered meaningless under this new model since there is no prior evaluation of the relationship between the state and the individual. It is assumed that power and control over sources of harm equate to power and control over individuals affected by it.

3.1.3 Knowledge of the Risk as the Second Condition of Due Diligence Obligations

The second condition that defines a duty to act with due diligence is knowledge of the risk. If the discriminating factor between due diligence obligations and other obligations is the connection with a risk, it is common sense that a duty to act is contemplated as long as risks are known or, at least, knowable. Knowledge of the risk is also linked to the concept of possibility, around which due diligence obligations are postulated. Possibility derives from PSR but also exists to the extent that a state can foresee risks addressed by the primary rule.

There is no need to survey international practice to demonstrate that duties to act with due diligence are dependent on a state's knowledge or constructive knowledge of the risk to which they are associated. To be sure, the ICJ had illustrated this plainly in the Corfu Channel case by building Albania's obligation to notify the United Kingdom upon knowledge of the minelaying in its waters and affirming that knowledge of the risk is a parameter on its own that cannot be inferred simply by a state's control over its territory.[90] The Bosnian Genocide case has confirmed this when arguing that the duty to act concerning the obligation to prevent genocide arises the moment 'the State learns of, or should normally have learned of, the existence of a serious risk that genocide will be committed'.[91] Scholarship on sectorial areas and the general literature on due diligence have examined the link between due diligence

[90] *Corfu Channel*, 16–17, 22.

[91] *Genocide* case, para. 431.

primary rules and knowledge so clearly that there is no reason to dwell on it further.[92]

There are, however, some issues that are still worth approaching from a general perspective. The first is the relationship between (constructive) knowledge of the risk and fault. In particular, it may be queried whether knowledge as a condition of due diligence obligations is the transposition of the state's fault at the level of primary rules. Chapter 1 explained how the International Law Commission in the work on ARSIWA rejected the idea of fault as a secondary element of international responsibility and conceptualised the international wrongful act 'objectively', as ensuing simply from conduct attributable to the state in breach of an international obligation. Yet, the commission did not leave out the possibility that fault may still play a role in relation to primary rules' content. The commentary to the ARSIWA recognises that

> whether there may a breach of a rule may depend on the intention or knowledge of relevant State organs or agents and in that sense may be 'subjective'... [however] whether responsibility is 'objective' or 'subjective' ... whether ... involve some degree of fault, culpability, negligence or want of due diligence ... is a matter for the interpretation and application of the primary rules engaged in a given case.[93]

The ILC did not clarify what it meant by intention or knowledge of relevant state organs, nor whether fault or 'want of due diligence' are essentially equivalent or refer to different standards – this would have signified, indeed, discussing matters of primary rules.

[92] Generally on the requirement of knowledge for due diligence obligations P. De Sena, 'La "due diligence" et le lien entre le sujet et le risqué qu'il faut prévenir: quelques observations', in Cassella, *Le standard de due diligence*, 243; O. Corten, O. Klein, 'The Limits of Complicity as a Ground for Responsibility: Lessons Learned from the Corfu Channel Case', in K. Bannelier, T. Christakis, S. Heathcote (eds.), *The ICJ and the Evolution of International Law* (London: Routledge, 2012), 315; The ILA Study Group on Due Diligence in International Law, 'Due Diligence in International Law: Second Report' (Johannesburg 2016); for a review of practice in relation to human rights due diligence obligations L. Lavrysen, *Human Rights in a Positive State* (Cambridge: Intersentia, 2017), 131–7; L. Seminara, 'Risk Regulation and the European Convention on Human Rights' (2016) 4 *European Journal of Risk Regulation* 733; in relation to obligations to protect foreign investments Blanco, *Full Protection and Security*, 459–65; E. De Brabandere, 'Host States' Due Diligence Obligations in International Investment Law' (2015) *Syracuse Journal of International Law and Commerce* 319; in relation to states' obligation to prevent terrorism T. Becker, *Terrorism and the State: Rethinking the Rules of State Responsibility* (Portland: Hart Publishing, 2006), 133–6.

[93] ILC Draft Articles on Responsibility of States for Internationally Wrongful Acts (ARSIWA) with commentaries (2001) ILC YB II/2 at 34–5.

Be that as it may, one can construe knowledge of risk as manifestation of a state's fault and, consequently, argue that primary rules of due diligence do require fault for assessing breach. The issue lies mainly in the understanding of 'fault'. In this regard, fault is not to be taken as the individual's psychological attitude acting as a state organ. As Chapter 1 has illustrated, the theory that construes fault of the state as fault of the individual-organ presents a number of shortcomings which were already identified by international legal scholars of the early twentieth century.[94] Furthermore, and limiting the scope of the analysis to due diligence obligations, a state individual-organ's fault is irrelevant when appraising states' knowledge of risks. For instance, if a man takes a woman's life and it is queried whether the state failed to protect her, the *animus agendi* of the police authorities at the time she had complained of her life being in danger is irrelevant for assessing the state's knowledge. What matters, in such case, is not the psychological attitude of the individual-organ, but rather knowledge of the state as an *entity*. Knowledge refers indeed to all those external conditions in the circumstances of the case that, taken together, lead one to conclude that the state's *apparatus* in its entirety (including police authorities) was aware of a targeted risk to the life of an individual.[95] Hence, if we speak of fault in relation to breaches of a duty to act, we speak of fault of the state as an international legal person.

As argued in Chapter 1, scholars like Giuseppe Palmisano have shown that the criticism around fault and the resistance to consider it an element of an international wrongful act have derived, at least in part, from the interpretation of fault as the psychological attitude of the

94 See Chapter 1, Section 1.2.1.

95 Dupuy writes:

> *Pour prendre la mesure exacte de la diligence due par un gouvernement conscient de ses devoirs ... dans une situation donnée, le juge s'assurera notamment des conditions dans lesquelles les fait qu'il convenait de prévenir se son déroulés, afin de se faire une idée précise de la nature et du nombre des informations dont l'Etat disposait, étape nécessaire à l'appréciation des négligences que l'on pourra éventuellement lui imputer.* (To establish which measure of due diligence a good government should enforce in a particular situation ... the judge will evaluate the factual conditions under which the event to be prevented has taken place, so as to have a clear idea of the nature and the amount of information at the State's disposal, and to appreciate the degree of the State's negligence.)

P. M. Dupuy, 'Faute de l'Etat et "fait internationalement illicite"' (1987) 5 *Droit*, 55.

individual-organ.[96] However, much as international lawyers conceive of other psychological mindsets of the state (i.e. when they speak of *error of* the state in connection with the invalidity of a treaty or when they implicitly refer the conscience of a state in relation to *opinio juris*), they can similarly envisage fault as referring to the state-entity and not to the individual-organ.[97]

Once this premise is clarified, it should also be pointed that fault is not to be confused with the *content* of the state's negligence. The content of the state's negligence refers in fact to the substance of due diligence (i.e., the measures required and the degree of care established by the primary rule, whose contravention forms the content of the state's negligence), whereas fault is the state's psychological mindset as an entity.[98] In this regard, one cannot but accept that, for an omission to give rise to responsibility for lack of due diligence, it is not sufficient to say that the state has failed to take the measures required by the primary rule (the substance of due diligence). An omission is unlawful only if state conduct was designed by will or freedom of choice, in the sense that the state must have at least foreseen the *possibility* to act and *voluntarily* chosen not to do, in contravention with what is required by the rule.[99] If this were not

[96] See G. Palmisano, 'Fault' (2007) MPEPIL para. 19; Palmisano, 'Colpa dell'organo e colpa dello Stato nella responsabilitá internazionale: Spunti critici di teoria e di prassi' (1992) 19 *Comunicazioni e Studi* 623. Chapter 1 already stressed that the question of a state's fault or wilful intent is inevitably intertwined with how one understands the personality of the state from the perspective of international law; for a view of the state as a juristic entity (*personne morale*) to which fault can be attributed based on a rule of international law see R. Ago, 'La colpa nell'illecito internazionale', in *Scritti Giuridici in Onore di Santi Romano* (Padua: CEDAM, 1939), vol. 3; contrary, for a view of state fault as a question of facts descending from the concept of the state as a corporeal entity see G. Arangio-Ruiz, 'Second Report on State Responsibility' ILC YB 48–53 and more generally G. Arangio-Ruiz, 'State Responsibility Revisited: The Factual Nature of the Attribution of Conduct to the State' (2017) *Rivista di diritto internazionale* 129–44.

[97] Palmisano, 'Colpa dell'organo e colpa dello Stato', 682–4.

[98] The distinction is not always easy to grasp; for instance, in criminal law when wrongs are committed through negligent omission there is always a certain overlapping between the identification of the agent's material conduct – failure to exercise the diligence due to prevent the harmful event – and his psychological attitude to the crime, see G. Fiandaca, E. Musco, *Diritto Penale: Parte Generale* (Bologna: Zanichelli Editore, 7th ed., 2014), 341, 615–20.

[99] This, in my view, is the limit of purely 'objectivist' theories, which reject any notion of the state's fault and contend that for a violation of due diligence to accrue, it is sufficient to demonstrate that the state acted in contravention to the measures required by the primary rule. While the latter is surely a necessary step to assess responsibility for failure to exercise due diligence, it is not a sufficient one. Responsibility can only arise once it is demonstrated that the state had possibility to act and, therefore, it *voluntarily* decided to

the case, and a failure to act were assessed with no regard to the state's mindset and merely by lack of measures adopted, responsibility would turn into a form of liability. Thus, only omissions falling within the sphere of voluntariness and freedom of choice of the state can be attributed to the latter.

From this perspective, a state's voluntariness to perform conduct in contravention to what expected by the primary rule cannot be achieved unless the state has knowledge, or should have had knowledge, of risks linked to such rule. Hence, knowledge is not only a prerequisite for a state to act; it is also the manifestation, when a harmful event occurs which may point to a breach of due diligence, that the state voluntarily decided to direct its conduct in a way contrary to what the primary rule required. This understood, knowledge is an indication of a state's fault when violations of due diligence obligations are at stake.[100]

Setting the issue of fault aside, another problem lies in whether knowledge relevant for creating possibility to act is that of the situation in which the state finds itself, or whether a state shall acquire knowledge of risks emanating from its territory, jurisdiction, or control. Recently, this issue seems particularly contentious in relation to certain primary rules, such as the general obligation not to allow states' territory to be used for acts contrary to other states and its application in the cyber context. There is debate on whether this obligation requires a state to act diligently vis-à-vis risks of cyberattacks that the state *happens to* be aware of in a particular case – or should be aware of under normal circumstances[101] – or if the state is under a duty to monitor all the cyber activities originating from its territory or jurisdiction *in order to* acquire knowledge of risks.[102]

direct its conduct in contravention to what is required by the rule. On this specific point see Palmisano, 'Colpa dell'organo e colpa dello Stato', 670 fn. 97.

100 I acknowledge that the way I have portrayed fault may foster the conviction, in the reader, that fault equates to voluntariness. On the one hand, I am aware of those scholarly critiques that point to the differences between and notion of fault and that of voluntariness, see Palmisano, 'Colpa dell'organo e colpa dello Stato', 688–98; F. Paddeu, *Justification and Excuses in International Law* (Cambridge: Cambridge University Press, 2018), 124–6. On the other hand, there is certainly a connection between these two concepts, one that is particularly useful to explore in the context of due diligence obligations.

101 Constructive knowledge implies that, up to a certain point, a state shall use its means and acquire information about risks of cyberattacks in its territory.

102 On this issue see Delerue, *Cyber Operations*, 358–62.

There is no general answer to this question. Whether a state is required to act only vis-à-vis risks that it knows or foresees in a particular situation or whether the duty to act requires it to acquire knowledge of risks previously unknown depends on the content of primary rule. For example, regarding obligations to protect in the human rights context, they are normally interpreted as requiring diligence vis-à-vis risks known or foreseeable at the time the state is bound by the obligation. Indeed, both general measures aimed to protect society at large and operative measures to be taken to protect the rights of targeted individuals are postulated upon risks that are either *actually* known or objectively knowable through a (diligent) use of the state's resources and available information.[103]

This may change, however, in relation to other obligations. In some cases, actual knowledge of risk may not be sufficient. States may be expected to take measures to identify risks that are still unknown or uncertain and, after identification, to act upon them. Primary examples are international obligations in the environmental context, especially obligations to prevent harm. As to the customary obligation to prevent transboundary harm, the ILC draft articles stress that a duty to act 'cannot be confined to activities which are already properly appreciated as involving such risk'. The obligation 'extends to taking appropriate measures to *identify* activities which involve such risk'.[104] The ICJ has confirmed this principle in the Certain Activities Carried out by Nicaragua in the Border Area, noting that 'a State must, before embarking on an activity having the potential adversely to affect the environment of another State, *ascertain* if there is a risk of significant transboundary harm, which would trigger the requirement to carry out an environmental impact assessment'.[105] The idea that a state has to identify or ascertain risks that are yet to be objectively determined testifies a more proactive approach that states should display toward knowledge and its scope.

These considerations apply equally to primary rules of due diligence subject to the precautionary principle. It is outside the scope of this book to enter the debate on the status of the precautionary principle in international law.[106] Generally, however, precaution differs from

[103] See generally V. Stoyanova, 'Fault, Knowledge and Risk within the Framework of Positive Obligations under the European Convention on Human Rights' (2020) LJIL 1.

[104] ILC Draft Articles on Prevention with commentary, 153–4.

[105] *Certain Activities Carried Out by Nicaragua in the Border Area (Costa Rica* v. *Nicaragua)* [2015] ICJ Rep 665, para. 104.

[106] It is even debated whether precaution has indeed achieved the status of principle of international law or whether is 'mainly' an approach, T. Treves, 'Environmental Impact

prevention (which implies due diligence), for it entails confronting risks when available technology and scientific evidence do not suffice to consider these risks objective and scientific facts. Hence, while prevention presupposes action toward at least identifiable risks, precaution applies when there is lack of scientific certainty about a risk.[107]

It may be that the principle of precaution is integrated into a primary rule of due diligence. The effect of such 'integration' alters the relationship state – knowledge of risk: part of the state's duty to act with due diligence will be to take into account risks that may still be uncertain or partially unknown.[108] The clearest illustration of this dynamic is found in the 2011 advisory opinion of the International Tribunal of the Law of the Sea (ITLOS) on the Responsibility and Obligations of States Sponsoring Persons and Entities with Respect to Activities in the Area. The opinion affirms that the precautionary approach is an integral part of the sponsoring state's due diligence obligation to prevent damage that might result from the activities of contractors that they sponsor. To clarify what the 'integration' of the precautionary approach means for due diligence, the tribunal noted: 'This obligation applies in situations where scientific evidence concerning the scope and potential negative impact of the activity in question is insufficient but where there are plausible indication of potential risks. A sponsoring State would not meet its obligations of due diligence if it disregarded those risks.'[109]

Overall, the content of the primary rule of due diligence, the area where the rule applies, and the legal interest protected by the

Assessment and the Precautionary Approach: Why Are International Courts and Tribunal Reluctant to Consider Them as General Principles of Law?', in M. Andenas, M. Fitzmaurice, A. Tanzi, J. Wouters (eds.), *General Principles and the Coherence of International Law* (Leiden: Brill, 2019), 379.

107 For an overview of precaution in the context of international environmental law see P. Birnie, A. Boyle, C. Redgwell, *International Law and the Environment* (Oxford: Oxford University Press, 3rd ed., 2007), 152–8; for a distinction between prevention and precaution and what it implies for international law M. Moïse Mbengue, *Essai sur une théorie du risque en droit international public* (Paris: Pedone, 2009), 75–95, 159–78; P. De Sena, 'La "due diligence" et le lien entre le sujet et le risqué qu'il faut prévenir: quelques observations', in S. Cassella (ed.), *Le standard de due diligence et la responsabilité internationale* (Paris: Pedone, 2018), 243.

108 Birnie, Boyle, Redgwell, *International Law and the Environment*, note that part of the difficulty of grasping the precautionary principle in international environmental law stems from failure to distinguish the identification of risks from the question on how to respond to them, at 155–6.

109 *Responsibility and Obligations of States Sponsoring Persons and Entities with Respect to Activities in the Area (Request for an Advisory Opinion submitted to the Seabed Dispute Chamber)* ITLOS Reports 2011 para. 131.

obligation[110] are all elements factored into assessing the relationship between the state and knowledge of the risk.

Finally, there is undoubtedly some overlapping in how knowledge of the risk and PSR linked to due diligence are assessed. Take the example of primary rules of due diligence that apply to a state's territory. In these cases, a state's actual power over the source of a specific risk linked to due diligence is often premised upon knowledge of it. The practice of human rights due diligence obligations is again very illustrative of this. The territorial state is presumed to have a certain power over sources of human rights risks and the capacity to affect generalised risks to human rights violations, which triggers the state's duty to put in place an adequate legal and administrative system to protect from them. Yet, once a state authority knows of targeted risks of violations to an individual's right, they are deemed to have, to a certain extent, power over their sources.[111] In a similar fashion, PSR can also inform knowledge that a state develops over risks linked to the due diligence rule.[112]

That is why when state conduct is evaluated to establish responsibility for the failure of due diligence, PSR and knowledge of the risks are hardly the object of separate tests. While the question of responsibility for due diligence obligations is treated in a separate chapter, we can anticipate that in some cases, the assessment of the existence of one condition (e.g. knowledge) is considered sufficient for establishing the other (e.g. PSR). In other circumstances, PSR and knowledge of risk are conflated into one single test of foreseeability, which is imbued with both knowledge and causality elements.

3.2 The Substance of Due Diligence

Having established when and how far a duty to act is triggered, it is now time to move to the substance of due diligence. As stated at the outset, it is the type and content of the primary rule that dictates what a state needs to accomplish to act diligently.[113] The international law area where the rule is applied may also have a bearing on the diligence required by the rule. The fact that a due diligence obligation belongs to the environmental regime or international humanitarian law can undoubtedly affect the

110 See Section 3.3.

111 For instance *Taner Kiliç* v. *Turkey* (Judgment) [2007] App no 70845/01 para. 51.

112 Most notably, *Corfu Channel*, 18.

113 The ILA concludes in its report that there is no single standard of due diligence that applies to primary rules, ILA Study Group on Due Diligence, 'Second Report', 20.

content of due diligence. Yet, when a judge or the interpreter construe a primary rule 'of due diligence', this usually implies that a minimum standard of care defined according to specific variables will be required to evaluate state conduct. Thus, although it is for the primary rule to establish precisely what is 'due', the expression due diligence imbues at minimum general parameters informing the content of the obligation. Clearly, the more the primary rule specifies the requirements to fulfil diligence, the less will be the space left to the operation of these general criteria. On the contrary, in the absence of more detailed requirements, the general parameters will operate as guiding lights in giving meaning to the primary rule.

3.2.1 A Standard of Conduct Defined by International Law

The first account of the content of due diligence in international law is in the Alabama case. It will be recalled from Chapter 1 that this case concerned demand for damages sought by the United States from the UK for the attack that the Confederate cruiser *Alabama*, a vessel built in the UK, had carried out against ships of the Union. The arbitral tribunal called to settle the dispute found the UK responsible for failing to exercise due diligence in the performance of the neutral obligations provided in the Treaty of Washington. During the proceeding, the UK had affirmed that for a state to manifest a failure to exercise due diligence it was necessary to show: 'a failure to use, for the prevention of an act which the government was bound to endeavour to prevent, such care as governments *ordinarily employ in their domestic concerns*, and may reasonably be expected to exert in matter of international interest and obligation'.[114]

The United States had instead defended a more stringent interpretation of due diligence, noting that under the Treaty of Washington, a state was required to exercise 'a diligence proportionate to the magnitude of the subject and to the dignity and strength of the power which is to exercise it'.[115] For the United States, 'no diligence short of this would be 'due:' that is, *commensurate with the emergency or with the magnitude of the results of negligence*'.[116] The tribunal eventually upheld the United

[114] Moore, *History and Digest*, vol. 1, 610–11.
[115] Ibid. 572–3.
[116] Ibid.

States' interpretation of due diligence, noting that insufficiency of domestic means of action could not justify lack of prevention by a state.[117]

For a long time, the debate on the content of due diligence oscillated between the two alternatives advanced in the Alabama case. On the one hand, for part of early scholarship and practice, the standard of conduct required by a primary rule of due diligence corresponded to the *diligentia quam suis* derived from Roman law. Roman law distinguished between *diligentia diligentis patris familias* (*culpa in abstracto*), which corresponds to the degree of care that an ideal person of good business would exercise under all circumstances; and *diligientia quam suis* (*culpa in concreto*), taken as the degree of care commonly used by a person in its own affairs.[118] Late Roman scholars developed the notion of *diligentia quam suis* from the doctrine of *commodatus*, whereby in a contract of gratuitous loan of a corporeal thing, the borrower-debtor is expected to use the level of care that he employs in his own affairs.[119] When applied to international law, *diligentia quam suis* was typically interpreted as requiring the state to fulfil its due diligence obligation with the 'usual' course of conduct employed in its own domestic affairs.[120]

On the other hand, the practice on the protection of foreigners and their property of the late nineteenth to early twentieth century predominantly construed due diligence as a standard of conduct *defined by* international law. According to this practice, a state's responsibility would usually be assessed against a standard of behaviour of the typical 'civilised' or 'well-organised' state. Accordingly, a state would defeat a claim for loss or damage sustained by a foreigner only by showing that the level of protection afforded to this person was that of an international standard, and not the level usually employed by the state toward its nationals.[121]

In contemporary international law, it is not disputed that due diligence refers to a standard of conduct set by rules of international law. Judges and interpreters consistently shape the content of due diligence

[117] Ibid. 656.

[118] V. Arangio-Ruiz, *Istituzioni di Diritto Romano* (Naples: Jovene Editore, 15th ed., 2006), 385–6.

[119] Initially, this was a standard used not necessarily to shrink the responsibility of the debtor, but also to enlarge it, Arangio-Ruiz, *Istituzioni di Diritto Romano*, 385.

[120] *Affairs des biens britanniques au Maroc espagnol (Spain* v. *United Kingdom)* (1925) 2 RIAA 615, 644; Institut de droit international, 'Responsabilité internationale des États à raison des dommages causés sur leur territoire à la personne ou au biens des étrangers (XIII Commission)' (1927) 33 *Annuaire de l'Institut de Droit International* 332.

[121] For a review of practice Pisillo-Mazzeschi, *Due Diligence*, 254–88.

obligations according to international legal rules and without giving thought to a state's internal apparatus or legal system. This is abundantly clear in practice across international law, including, inter alia, the international investment context, international environmental law, the human rights area, the security of other states, and international humanitarian law.[122] There is no doubt that to require a state to display due diligence means to compare states' behaviour with a standard of conduct determined by international law.

Yet, to say that due diligence implies an international legal standard of conduct does not exclude that, in some instances, the characteristics of a state be taken into account in assessing the standard. There are indeed due diligence obligations that subordinate the *diligence due* by a primary rule to a state's capabilities, that is, the degree of resource, economic or technological development possessed by a state. When this occurs, the due diligence standard is liable to *subjective* variations. States may be required to use *more or less* diligence depending on their economic development, the degree of technological resources, or the level of their financial capacity.[123] Some authors regard the level of states' capabilities as the contemporary expression of *diligentia quam suis.*[124] They go as far as arguing that for primary rules of due diligence imposed on a state to use 'all means at disposal',[125] the level of expected diligence cannot entail going beyond a state's resource capacity since this would imply *impossibility* to act.[126]

As argued above, due diligence obligations are indeed postulated around the possibility to act. In this sense, a state without sufficient resource capacity may not be able to meet the standard of behaviour of wealthier states. However, this does not mean that a state's financial, technological, or economic resources will always affect the level of

122 For ease of reference, I refer here in general to works on due diligence that survey the *content* of due diligence obligations across various areas of international law see Krieger, Peters, Kreuzer, *Due Diligence*, and Cassella, *Le standard de due diligence*.

123 The ILA Second Report on due diligence uses indeed the notion of 'subjective variations' to refer to a state's capabilities as a variable influencing the standard of due diligence required by a primary rule; however, under the umbrella 'subjective variations' the report conflates the question of a state's capabilities with the issue of control over the source of risk, at 13–17.

124 De Brabandere, 'Host States' Due Diligence Obligations', 357–8.

125 On the use of this formula for due diligence obligations see Chapter 2, Section 2.3.3.

126 De Brabandere, 'Host States' Due Diligence Obligations', 357–8; A. Newcombe, L. Paradell, *Law and Practice of Investment Treaties: Standards of Treatment* (Alphen aan den Rijn: Kluwer Law International, 2009), 310.

diligence due by the primary rule. Nor does it signify that all due diligence obligations imposing the use of means at the state's disposal shall be interpreted as not going beyond one state's resource capacity. It is sufficient to note that certain due diligence obligations while imposing the use of 'all means at a state's disposal', do expect states to acquire these means if they have not yet done so. For these rules, if a state fails to act appropriately because it did not dispose of the means expected, responsibility can still accrue.[127] In other words, what determines whether or not a state's capabilities are part of the equation in regulating the standard of diligence is the content of the primary rule. The degree of the state's capability is just one *possible* variable of the substance of due diligence.

Clearly, saying that an international standard of conduct defines due diligence does not clarify much of the concept. On the one hand, this depends on the fact that the substance of due diligence is highly contextualised, being contingent upon the content of the primary rule and the areas of international law in which the rule applies. On the other hand, due diligence is also a highly flexible concept:[128] what is understood as 'due' by an obligation may change over time and according to the circumstances of the case.

This notwithstanding, when a primary rule of due diligence is defined, this usually implies a reference to some common parameters which inform the substance of a state's 'diligent' conduct. While it may remain impossible to pin down a precise definition of due diligence, these general criteria harness the concept and provide concreteness to it. Arguably, it is very much the existence of such criteria that contributes to the idea of a core minimum standard of due diligence across international law.

In this regard, the first criterion defining due diligence's substance is undoubtedly the 'positive' content of the primary rule imbued with due diligence. The substance of due diligence is 'positive' in the sense that due diligence always requires a proactive approach toward the risk, whether in the form of legislation, vigilance, monitoring, or physical action. The second criterion links to flexibility. The content of due diligence obligations escapes a precise definition since it may vary with time and

[127] This is the case of a plethora of human rights due diligence obligations: while they are often construed by judges as requiring a state to use 'all means at its disposal', the idea is that there is a minimum legal and administrative apparatus that a state needs to achieve, see 4.2 and Chapter 5; on this aspect and in relation to the security of states see Pisillo-Mazzeschi, *Due Diligence*, 254–5.

[128] On the meaning of flexibility in relation to due diligence see Chapter 2.

depend on the circumstances of the case. However, it is generally accepted that what is 'due' should not fall short of what is *reasonable* under the circumstance. The second criterion of the substance of due diligence is reasonableness, to which Section 3.2.2 is dedicated.

3.2.2 Reasonableness

Reasonableness is the overarching parameter against which the content of due diligence obligations must be assessed. Reference to reasonableness in relation to the substance of due diligence is abundant since the early international practice on due diligence. For example, in the context of the protection of aliens and their property, arbitral commissions consistently held that the duty to prevent injuries to aliens calls for *reasonable* care or diligence in attempting to prevent the occurrence of such wrongs.[129]

Widespread contemporary practice on due diligence obligations also refers to the concept of reasonableness. For instance, the ILC has described the obligation to prevent transboundary harm from hazardous activities as one requiring '*reasonable efforts* by a State to inform itself of factual and legal components that relate foreseeably to a contemplated procedure and to take appropriate measures, in a timely fashion, to address them'.[130] Investment tribunals often characterise the obligation to provide full protection to foreign investments as requiring *reasonable measures of prevention* or at least *reasonable action* according to the circumstances of the case.[131] In international human rights practice, international courts and monitoring bodies often call on reasonableness to pin down the content of states' due diligence obligations.[132] In its final report on due diligence's status under international law, the ILA argues

[129] *Wipperman* case in Moore, *History and Digest*, vol. 3, 3033; *Buckingham (Great Britain* v. *United Mexican States)* (1931) 5 RIAA 288; *The Home Insurance Co (USA* v. *United Mexican States)* (1926) 4 RIAA 172.

[130] ILC Draft Articles on Prevention with commentary, Article 3 para. 10.

[131] *El Paso Energy International Company* v. *The Argentine Republic*, ICSID Case No ARB/03/15, 31 October 2011 (Award) para. 523; for an overview of practice in international investment law Blanco, *Full Protection and Security*, 441–9.

[132] *Case of Velásquez Rodríguez* v. *Honduras*, Interpretation of the judgment of reparations and costs, IACHR Series C no 9, 17 August 1990, para. 174; *González et al (Cotton Field)* v. *Mexico*, IACHR Series C no 205, 16 November 2009, paras. 283–4; *E. and Others* v. *United Kingdom*, para. 88; *Stanev* v. *Bulgaria* (Judgment) (GC) [2012] App no 36760/06 para. 120.

that reasonableness is 'the golden thread in determining which measures States should take to act in a duly diligent manner'.[133]

The link between reasonableness and due diligence must be better clarified. In certain cases, reasonableness is precisely the standard used to solidify the substance of the primary rule, either because the rule itself expressly requires 'reasonableness';[134] or because the rule is silent on the standard of care to be adopted but the interpreter resorts to reasonableness to substantiate it. In other cases, the content of the primary rule of due diligence imposes a standard of care different from reasonableness. Chapter 2 highlighted that several obligations of due diligence are framed in international treaties as requiring states to adopt 'all appropriate measures', take 'all practical measures', exercise 'all possible efforts', or use 'all means at a State's disposal'.[135] It may be queried how these standards relate to reasonableness and whether reasonableness is the overarching parameter structuring all due diligence obligations.

Drawing on international practice, sometimes there is no distinction between reasonableness and other standards. For example, Article 139 of UNCLOS calls upon sponsoring states to take 'all necessary and appropriate measures' to ensure that activities in the Seabed Area are carried out in conformity with international regulations, including Annex III, Article 4(4) of UNCLOS. This latter provision reads: 'A sponsoring State shall not, however, be liable for damage caused by any failure of a contractor sponsored by it to comply with its obligations if that State Party has adopted laws and regulations and taken administrative measures which are ... *reasonably appropriate* for securing compliance by persons under its jurisdiction.'[136]

In the 2011 advisory opinion on the responsibility of sponsoring states in the area, the Seabed Dispute Chamber, being asked to clarify the content of Article 139, equated the expression 'all necessary and appropriate measures' with the duty to take measures within a state's legal system that are 'reasonably appropriate'. The chamber concluded that reasonableness is the hallmark of any action taken by the sponsoring state.[137]

133 ILA Study Group on Due Diligence, 'Second Report', 8.

134 United Nations Convention on Contracts for the International Sale of Goods (adopted 11 April 1980, entered into force 1 January 1988) 1489 UNTS 3 Article 77 (The party who relies on a breach of contract must take such measures as are reasonable in the circumstances to mitigate the loss ... resulting from the breach).

135 See Chapter 2, Section 2.3.3.

136 UNCLOS, Article 4(4).

137 *Responsibility and Obligations of States Sponsoring Persons,* paras. 120, 210, 230.

In other cases, differences in the terminology used by the primary rule may point to different degrees of effort required of a state.[138] For example, the ECtHR usually interprets the positive obligations under the provisions of Articles 2 (right to life), Article 3 (prohibition of torture), and Article 4 (prohibition of slavery and forced labour) of the European Convention on Human Rights as imposing states to take 'all appropriate steps', to act 'by all means at a State's disposal',[139] and to take 'all adequate measures' that are 'effective' for ensuring protection.[140] These terms may suggest more robust degrees of protection than when the court only asks states to take 'every reasonable step' toward protecting certain rights.[141] However, it is clear from the court's case law that even when the use of terms suggests a more substantial degree of state efforts, the standard chosen by the court will still be evaluated in light of the overarching parameter of reasonableness. In this regard, the court usually argues that positive obligations need to be interpreted 'in such a way as to not impose an excessive burden on the authority, bearing in mind, in particular, the unpredictability of human conduct and operational choices that must be made in terms of priority and resources'.[142]

Another example of the link between reasonableness and other standards is Article 15 of the First Geneva Convention of 1949, requiring parties to a conflict 'to *take all possible measures* to search for and collect

[138] See for instance the discussion during the *travaux préparatoires* of Article 27 of the Protocol Additional to the Geneva Convention of 12 August 1949, relating to the Protection of Victims of International Armed Conflict (adopted 8 June 1977, entered into force 7 December 1978) 1125 UNTS 3. Article 27(2) part II provides that when a medical aircraft is recognised as such by the adverse party to a conflict, that party 'shall make *all reasonable efforts* to give the order to land or to alight on water'. During the *travaux préparatoires* related to this article, discussions arose as to whether it would be better to opt for asking the adverse party to a conflict to 'respect, *as far as possible*' the medical aircraft or asking the party to 'take *all reasonable efforts*'. It was noted by the representative of Bangladesh that that expression 'as far as possible' did not take into account the reality of war, or that it was too general, see *Official Records of the Diplomatic Conference on the Reaffirmation and Development of International Humanitarian Law Applicable in Armed Conflict*, Geneva 1974–7, vol. XI 526–31; on the other hand, the expression 'all reasonable efforts' pointed to a more precise and concrete legal concept, see vol. VI at 95.

[139] *Öneryildiz* v. *Turkey* (Judgment) (GC) [2004] App no 48939/99 para. 91

[140] *Fernandes de Oliveira* v. *Portugal* (Judgment) (GC) [2017] App no 78103/14 para. 105 (Article 2); *O'Keefee* v. *Ireland* (Judgment) [2011] App no 35810/09 para. 144 (Article 3); *S. M.* v. *Croatia* (Judgment) (GC) [2020] App no 60561/14 paras. 284–8 (Article 4).

[141] *Fociac* v. *Romania* (Judgment) [2005] App no 2577/02 para. 78 (Article 6); for the thesis that the use of different terminology by the court points indeed to different standards of care see Lavrysen, 'Human Rights in a Positive State', 163–4.

[142] *O'Keeffe* v. *Ireland*, para. 144.

the wounded and sick' and to 'ensure their adequate care'. To take 'all possible measures' implies a stronger effort than to employ 'reasonable' ones. However, the ICRC commentary to this article suggests that *possibility* should be read in light of reasonableness. The commentary indeed specifies that '[t]he exhortation to take all possible measures demands that Parties to a conflict do everything that *can reasonably be expected of them* in the circumstances to provide appropriate care'.[143]

In his study on reasonableness in the international legal order, Olivier Corten has identified two main functions served by the concept. The first, termed the 'technical function', serves the international legal order as a system of law and provides a method for operationalising the legal rule and a procedure for delivering the judicial decision.[144] As a method for the operationalisation of the legal rule, reasonableness offers a technique in law-making that provides the legal system with rules flexible in character and adaptable across time.[145] As a technical procedure serving the judicial process, the concept of reasonableness enables the judge to adjust the law to social reality and fill legal lacunae that may threaten the 'completeness' of the legal order.[146]

The technical function served by reasonableness is apparent in relation to primary rules of due diligence. Reasonableness works both as a minimum threshold of due diligence and a limit in the level of efforts expected of the obliged state. As a minimum threshold, reasonableness delimits the degree of care below which state conduct would not be deemed in compliance with a due diligence obligation. The judge or the interpreter usually invoke reasonableness in this sense to provide substance to a state's due diligence obligation and to set out the minimal level of effort required of state conduct. For example, in the 2011 advisory opinion of the responsibility of sponsoring states in the area, the ITLOS argued that any failure on the part of the sponsoring state 'to act reasonably' could be challenged before the Seabed Chamber and engage the responsibility of the state involved.[147] At the same time, reasonableness operates as a safeguard to the obliged state. As long as sufficient diligence will be display by the state in the performance of its duties, one cannot expect a state's institutional and operational choices to go beyond what is

[143] ICRC Commentary on the First Geneva Convention (2016) Article 15, para. 1503.

[144] Corten, *L'utilisation du "raisonnable" par le juge international: Discours juridique, raison et contraditions* (Brussels: Bruylant, 1997), 137–62.

[145] Ibid. 137–41.

[146] Corten, 'Reasonableness', para. 8.

[147] *Responsibility and Obligations of States Sponsoring Persons*, para. 230.

perceived as *rational*, sustained by *reason*, and *just* in the context where the primary rule applies.[148]

Within this perimeter, the state is allowed flexibility in the choice of means and actions to fulfil its obligation. Using reasonableness to channel the substance of due diligence obligations allows states, judges, and interpreters to maintain these rules' elastic nature while defining only their outer limits. Since what is reasonable 'depends on the circumstances' and cannot be precisely defined a priori,[149] also what is *due* by the obligation of due diligence will change and adjust according to the circumstances of each case. Furthermore, the ambiguity with which the notion of reasonableness is imbued allows the interpretation of a due diligence obligation to change across time and space, without formally renegotiating the content of the rule.[150]

In any case, although resorting to reasonableness to solidify the substance of due diligence obligations certainly preserves the flexible nature of these rules, the notion has progressively acquired specific meaning in this context. As a minimum standard of effort, reasonableness is generally equated with the concept of 'good government'. When a state acts with due diligence, the interpreter assumes that the state adopts measures that a 'good government' would take in the same circumstances. In this regard, acting as a 'good government' goes beyond acting with good faith and implies, at minimum, the enactment and enforcement of relevant measures. For instance, in the early practice on the protection of foreigners and their property, arbitral commissions would often describe due diligence as the level of care that a *normal*[151] or *civilized*[152] government would employ in similar circumstances, or the 'usual order which is the duty of every State to

[148] On how reasonableness connects to these concepts see generally J. Rawl, 'The Idea of Public Reason Revisited' (1997) 64 *The University of Chicago Law Review* 765; C. Perelman 'The Rational and the Reasonableness', in Perelman (ed.), *The New Rhetoric and the Humanities* (Berlin: Springer, 1989), 117; for a reading of reasonableness in international law as an 'ordering' criterion rather than an 'evaluating' criterion see E. Cannizzaro, 'Considerazioni in merito al ruolo della ragionevolezza e della proporzionalitá nel diritto internazionale' (2002) 7 *Ars Interpretandi* 347, 370.

[149] *Continental Self (Tunisia* v. *Libyan Arab Jamahiriya)* [1982] ICJ Rep 18, para. 60.

[150] Salmon underlines that the ambiguity of reasonableness lies in its capacity to incorporate divergent interpretations of a legal rule see J. Salmon, 'Le Concept de raisonnable en droit international public', in *Le droit international, unite et diversité: mélanges offerts à Paul Reuter* (Paris: Pedone, 1981), 447; see also Corten, 'The Notion of "reasonable" in International Law: Legal Discourse, Reason and Contradiction' (1999) 48 ICLQ 613, 620.

[151] *Thomas H. Youmans (USA* v. *United Mexican States)* (1926) 4 UNRIAA 115.

[152] *Mary Hall (USA* v. *United Mexican States)* (1929) 4 UNRIAA 541–2.

maintain within its territory'.[153] The generally recognised idea was not to level good governance against the criterion of the 'perfect' state (in which no harm to foreigners would be committed), but to leave a margin of tolerance typical of a state apparatus's functioning under normal conditions.[154] The notion of good governmentality is still the reference standard in contemporary practice on due diligence obligations. Parameters such as that of 'civilised state' are no longer in use, yet the understanding of what is reasonable is usually decided against the parameter of the 'well-administered' or 'well-organised' state.[155]

Corten's second function of reasonableness is termed 'ideological' and serves not the legal system itself but the (international) legal actor. In short, reasonableness can be of use to legitimise a legal actor's position vis-à-vis the receivers of its legal discourse.[156] When an actor adopts a solution to a legal problem by describing it as 'reasonable', they are vesting their choice with legal authority and the idea of rationality and non-arbitrariness.[157] This function of reasonableness benefits the judge, since by resorting to reasonableness the judge often legitimises their decision-making process and discretionary power to define international law rules.

The use of reasonableness in primary rules of due diligence also supplies this ideological function. Many treaty texts that contain due diligence obligations only establish the object of the duty to be pursued by the state (e.g. prevention or protection from a harmful event), with no indication of the required measures to pursue this object. The solidification of what due diligence entails for these rules is often achieved through a court, a tribunal, or a technical body.[158] When these actors 'spell out'

[153] *Kennedy (USA* v. *United Mexican States)* (1927) 4 UNRIAA 198.

[154] Harvard Law School Project, 'The Law of Responsibility of States for Damage Done in Their Territory to the Persons or Property of Foreigners' (1929) AJIL 131 Article 4, Article 9; 'Responsabilité internationale des États à raison des dommages causés sur leur territoire à la personne ou au biens des étrangers (XIII Commission)', 458.

[155] *Asian Agricultural Products Ltd* v. *Sri Lanka*, ICSID Case No ARB/87/3, 27 June 1990 (Award) para. 77; *El Paso* v. *Argentina*, para. 522: *Hesham Talaat Al-Warraq* v. *Indonesia*, UNCITRAL, 15 December 2014 (Award) paras. 625–8.

[156] Corten, *L'utilisation du "raisonnable"*, 260–2.

[157] If what is reasonable is perceived as non-arbitrary, this means that what is reasonable is also objective and neutral. Yet, such neutrality is an illusion, as aptly underscored by Salmon, 'Les notions à contenu variable en droit international public', in C. Perelman, R. Vander Elst (eds.), *Les notions à contenu variable en droit* (Brussels: Bruylant, 1984), 267–8. Critically on the link between reasonableness and neutrality and what this entails for due diligence obligations see Chapter 5.

[158] See Chapter 5.

the substance of due diligence and describe it as reasonable, they legitimise their discretionary choice vis-à-vis the obliged parties to the obligation, that is, states. For instance, if a harmful event occurs and there was a duty to prevent it on the part of a state, a judge may be appointed to establish whether such event happened because the state failed to prevent it. In evaluating state conduct, the judge may be required to clarify measures considered necessary to satisfy prevention, both in general terms and in the circumstances of the case. These measures may be neither explicitly provided by the text of the primary rule, nor by the treaty containing it. Yet, by labelling these measures 'reasonable', the judge imbues their choice with elements of 'normality' and 'rationality', thus validating their decision before the parties of the dispute. Resorting to reasonableness to 'spell out' the content of due diligence enables the interpreter to legitimise their understanding of what is *due* by the primary rule.

This process acquires even more importance when the intervention of the judge, the interpreter or a technical body in defining due diligence comes close to the creation of a legal rule.[159] In contemporary practice, the due diligence content of many primary rules is now filled with much specificity. When this happens, states are not deemed to have acted with the diligence due unless they have complied with a series of specific duties, standards or procedures. The most classic example of this phenomenon is international environmental law and states' obligation to prevent transboundary environmental harm. Here the notion of 'good governmentality' has acquired much specificity. A state proves to have acted with due diligence if it complies with some specific duties, including the duty to conduct an environmental impact assessment, the duty to notify the potentially affected party of a significant risk of transboundary harm and the duty to consult with the affected state. At any rate, the progressive 'technicalisation' of good governmentality and the 'breaking down' of due diligence into sets of specific duties, standards, and procedures is not limited to environmental obligations and invests primary rules of due diligence across international law.

[159] Corten underlines how the use of reasonableness by a judge serves in many cases the creation of a rule of international law; more generally, on the law-making power of the judge in the creation of the legal rule A. Boyle, C. Chinkin, *The Making of International Law* (Oxford: Oxford University Press, 2007), 268–9; contrary C. Focarelli, *International Law as Social Construct: The Struggle for Global Justice* (Oxford: Oxford University Press, 2012), 317–18.

While the question of 'proceduralisation' of due diligence obligations and the problem it raises are addressed in Chapter 5, suffice to say here that this phenomenon is often the result of the interpretative practice of judicial organs or technical treaty bodies. In the context of human rights, for instance, judicial organs like the ECtHR and technical bodies like the Human Rights Committee have given technical definitions to 'good governmentality' in relation to states' positive obligations to protect human rights. For example, under contemporary human rights practice, a state would not comply with the obligation to protect life under Article 2 of the ECHR unless a set of minimal duties was fulfilled, including i) the duty to put in place a legislative and regulatory framework to protect individuals against human rights violations; ii) the duty to set up an effective and independent judicial system capable of investigating violations and provide remedies to the victims; iii) the duty to adopt relevant criminal provisions for certain crimes; and iv) the duty to be equipped with an effective law-enforcement machinery.[160] Hence, when due diligence is crystallised through the 'spelling out' of typical measures and its scope 'enlarged' by identifying specific duties, grounding the foundations of this process on reasonableness vests the intervention of the interpreter with more legitimacy.

3.3 The Variables of Due Diligence

This final section deals with the variables of due diligence obligations. It has been argued above that the content of due diligence obligations is typically defined by the parameter of reasonableness and good governmentality. Yet, what is reasonable depends on the circumstances of the case and cannot only be defined *in abstracto*. Accordingly, the content of due diligence obligations is always contingent upon factual circumstances and is never wholly defined a priori. The diligence required of a state to fulfil its duty to protect the premises of a foreign diplomatic mission is clearly different when the threat is immediate and comes from a powerful and well-known terrorist organisation, rather than when threat is still a potential or comes from a bunch of unorganised private citizens.

In assessing whether the state's efforts were effectively reasonableness according to the circumstances, international courts and tribunals

[160] *Nicolae Virgiliu Tanase* v. *Romania* (Judgment) (GC) [2019] App no 41720/13 para. 135; *Fernandes de Oliveira* v. *Portugal* (Judgment) (GC) [2017] App no 78103/14 para. 66.

generally lean on some common variables. These include the degree of risk linked to the primary rule, the value to be protected or ensured through due diligence, the state's level of control over the source of the risk, and the degree of the state's capability. The extent to which these variables play a role in regulating the substance of due diligence depends on the type of primary rule. For instance, some primary rules make the content of due diligence contingent upon the level of the state's financial or economic resources. Others may instead regard the level of the state's capability as irrelevant in defining the required efforts expected by the rule.

3.3.1 *The Degree of Risk Linked to the Primary Rule*

Certain primary rules of due diligence submit the exercise of a duty to act only to *qualified* risks. For these rules, not every risk linked to a state's due diligence obligation requires the state to activate its apparatus and diligently act upon it. The scope of a duty to act may be 'reduced' only to risks that exceed a specific threshold. For example, regarding the customary obligation to prevent transboundary harm, it is generally accepted that the scope of a states' duty to act with due diligence extends only to risks of 'significant' transboundary harm, that is, risks that are more than detectable but need not be at the level of seriousness or substantial.[161] Similarly, in the Bosnian Genocide case, the ICJ held that the duty to act related to the obligation to prevent genocide arises when the state learns of the existent of a 'serious' risk that genocide will be committed.[162] With regard to protective human rights obligations under the European Convention, the ECtHR normally provides that states' duties to act with due diligence vis-à-vis targeted individuals at risks of human rights violations arise when these risks are 'real and immediate'.[163]

As usual, the primary rule's content dictates whether the scope of the duty to act stretches to *all* risks linked to the rule or whether a minimum threshold is required for the duty to arise.[164] The interpretation of a rule

[161] ILC Draft Articles on Prevention with commentary, 151–2; *Certain Activities*, paras. 104–5; *Construction of a Road in Costa Rica along the San Juan River (Nicaragua* v. *Costa Rica)* [2015] ICJ Rep 665, paras. 146–52.

[162] *Genocide* case, para. 431.

[163] *Osman*, para. 116.

[164] See for instance states' obligation to prevent cyberattacks against the rights of other states, which extends to all cyber operations with 'serious adverse consequences', Schmitt, *Tallinn Manual 2.0*, 36–7.

as requiring action only vis-à-vis *certain* risks may well also result from balancing opposing interests. For example, in the context of prevention of transboundary harm, it is clear that action against *all* risks of environmental harm could significantly impair the course of productive and other activities within a state. Hence, a balance should be struck between the liberty of a state to conduct activities and stimulate industrial and technological processes and other states' rights to be free from harm that could affect them.[165]

The level of risks may also play a role in intensifying the substance of due diligence obligations. Risk severity may increase the level of effort required by the state in a specific circumstance. An illustrative example is the ILC work on the prevention of transboundary harm from hazardous activities. The commentary to the draft articles underscores that:

> The *standard* of due diligence against which the conduct of the State of origin should be examined is that which is generally considered appropriate and proportionate to the degree of risk of transboundary harm in the particular instance. . . . activities which may be considered ultrahazardous require a much higher standard of care in designing policies and much higher degree of vigour on the part of the State to enforce them.[166]

The ITLOS Seabed Dispute Chamber confirmed this principle in 2011 in the advisory opinion on the responsibility of sponsoring states in the Area. The tribunal argued that the due diligence obligation arising out of Article 139 of UNCLOS is an obligation whose content changes in relation to the risks involved in the activity performed in the Area. The tribunal noted that prospecting activities in the Area – activities aiming at identifying relevant mineral resources to be later explored or exploited by states – are generally less risky than exploration and exploitation activities. Simultaneously, the type of mineral sought may also affect the risk associated with the activity in question. For these reasons, the tribunal concluded that 'the standard of due diligence has to be more severe for riskier activities'.[167]

That greater risks may entail greater due diligence is not a trait exclusive of primary rules of due diligence linked to environmental hazards. Due diligence obligations arising in other contexts may also calibrate the level of efforts to be exercised by a state depending on the magnitude of risks involved or the significance of certain risks at a specific moment in

165 For a discussion see ILC YB (1981) II/2 146–9.

166 ILC Draft Articles on Prevention with commentary, 154.

167 *Responsibility and Obligations of States Sponsoring Persons*, para. 117.

time. For instance, more significant risks of human rights violations may imply heightened duties to protect individuals from these risks.[168] Similarly, great contemporary threats posed by terrorist non-state actors may significantly heighten the threshold of diligence expected by states in relation to their obligation to refrain from supporting or acquiescing in organised activities directed toward other states.[169]

3.3.2 The Nature and Value of the Legal Interest Protected by Due Diligence

The nature or value of the legal interest protected by a primary rule of due diligence is another factor that can affect the substance of due diligence. In some cases, for example, if a primary rule is established for preventing specific harmful acts, it may be that the degree of diligence expected of a state is greater when the *beneficiary* of the state's preventive conduct belongs to a 'special category'. In the early practice on the protection of foreigners and their property, a higher level of due diligence in relation to the obligation to protect foreigners was expected toward consuls, ambassadors, and public ministers. These individuals were treated as deserving special respect and protection due to their public character. Hence states were required to 'exercise greater vigilance in respect to their security and safety'.[170] Similarly, many contemporary obligations to protect in the human rights context entail a heightened degree of diligence when protection must be ensured toward especially vulnerable categories of individuals, such as children or women, or groups of persons at particular risks of violations.[171]

The nature of the *legal interest* protected by the primary rule may also expand the scope of a state's duty to act with due diligence. For example, suppose a due diligence obligation is established to protect or ensure an interest that is considered fundamental to the international community. In that case, the degree of due diligence expected of a state may be more

[168] HRC, 'General Comment no 36', arguing that the duty to protect the life of individuals 'requires special measures of protection toward persons in situations of vulnerability whose life has been placed at a particular risk because of specific threats or pre-existing patterns of violence'; this may include human rights defenders, official fighting corruption, humanitarian workers, journalists, etc.' at 6.

[169] Generally on this issue see I. Österdahl, 'Due Diligence in International Anti-Terrorism Law: Developments in the Resolutions of the UN Security Council', in Peter, Krieger, Kreuzer, *Due Diligence*, 234.

[170] *Mallén (USA* v. *United Mexican States)* (1927) 4 UNRIAA 175–6.

[171] See for instance HRC, 'General Comment no 36', 25.

robust than for other primary rules of the same character. In this regard, the prevailing interpretation of the obligation to ensure respect of the convention set by Article 1 of the First Geneva Convention is that a state's duty 'to ensure respect' arises toward its organs, non-state actors engaged in an armed conflict as well as other states. Essentially, a state's duty to act with due diligence to ensure respect of the First Geneva Convention arises regardless of territorial limitations or the state's status as a party to a conflict. This duty exists and extends so long as the state has the capacity to influence the conduct of other states or non-state armed groups. Such a large scope of application of Article 1 may be explained by its *erga omnes* nature, which results in a heightened degree of due diligence expected by states.[172] After all, few other primary rules of due diligence aimed at protecting specific legal interests have so far been interpreted by international practice as implying duties to act irrespective of territorial control or jurisdiction over sources of risks.[173]

From this perspective, one may also read the ICJ's interpretation of Article IV of the Treaty of Non-Proliferation of Nuclear Weapons as a court's attempt to strengthen the (due diligence) nature of the obligation to negotiate in good faith nuclear disarmament. Chapter 2 illustrated that in the advisory opinion on the Legality of the Threat or Use of Nuclear Weapons, the ICJ did not construe the obligation to negotiate as an obligation of due diligence.[174] Instead, the court argued that this obligation 'goes beyond that of a mere obligation of conduct' and requires 'to achieve a precise result – nuclear disarmament in all its aspect – by adopting a particular course of conduct, namely the pursuit of negotiation in good faith.[175] As Chapter 2 has attempted to demonstrate, the ICJ's use of the classification between obligations of conduct

[172] See G. Gaja , 'Do States have a Duty to Ensure Compliance with Obligations *Erga Omnes* by Other States?', in M. Ragazzi (ed.), *International Responsibility Today: Essays in Memory of Oscar Schachter* (Leiden: Brill, 2005), 31.

[173] The obligation to prevent genocide is another example of a duty that requires states to act upon sources of risks that are neither connected to territorial control nor to state's authority or jurisdiction, see Section 2.1.2; an example of a human right duty of due diligence that is larger in scope than other positive human rights obligations is the duty to prevent torture. According to the jurisprudence of both the ECtHR and the Committee on the Convention Against Torture, states have a duty to prevent torture of individuals under a their jurisdiction when there is a serious risks that the applicant will be subject to torture if transferred or expelled to another state, *Soering* v. *United Kingdom* (Decision) (European Comm.) [1989] App no 14038/88 paras. 100–10.

[174] On the opportunity to interpret obligations to negotiate as duties of due diligence nature see Chapter 2, Section 2.4.3.

[175] *Legality of the Threat or Use of Nuclear Weapons*, paras. 263–4.

and obligations of result is often a source of misunderstanding. It is not always clear whether the court uses it by having Ago's or the civil law distinction in mind. In this respect, one should be wary of reading too much into the court's statement on Article IV's nature since it is far from sure what kind of 'distinction' the court had in mind.

Nonetheless, one may argue that what the court wished to declare by describing Article IV as an 'obligation of result requiring a particular course of conduct' was not really to deny the due diligence nature of this obligation. On the contrary, by resuming Ago's classification of obligations, the court indeed tried to underscore the *sui generis* character of the duty to negotiate nuclear disarmament. As a duty aimed at ensuring interests fundamental to the international community, this obligation demands 'heightened' efforts on the part of the binding states. In sum, one may reconcile the due diligence nature of the obligation to negotiate with the understanding that the level of efforts required of states in matters of nuclear disarmament is higher and more demanding.

3.3.3 The Level of State's Capabilities

A state's scientific, technical, or economic capacity is another factor that may influence the content of a primary rule of due diligence. The question of the extent to which a state's capabilities affect the due diligence content of a primary rule is salient in specific contexts. For instance, one of the most debated issues concerning states' obligation to prevent international terrorism and, more generally, the duty *alienum non laedas*, is how much a states' institutional capacities, financial abilities, and technological resources should affect the degree of the required due diligence. On the one hand, states with higher resources, including financial capacity and military expertise, are clearly in a better position to effectively prevent and suppress risks of terrorism emanating from their territory. As such, failure to act on their part to prevent terrorist acts should be evaluated more rigorously. On the other hand, leaning too much on state's capabilities when assessing a state's due diligence to prevent terrorism may incentivise terrorist groups to operate and base themselves on the territory of states with limited capacities.[176] Understanding in these cases how much capabilities are part of due diligence is crucial for assessing whether failure to prevent is the result

[176] K. Trapp, *State Responsibility for International Terrorism* (Oxford: Oxford University Press, 2011), 70–1.

of a state's *inability* to act (for insufficient capabilities) or a state's unwillingness to use diligently its apparatus.[177]

The level of a state's capability is generally considered relevant for due diligence obligations related to protecting the environment and human rights. In the context of environmental protection, the ILC commentary to the obligation to prevent transboundary harm notes the importance of scientific and technological development in shaping the degree of diligence required of a state: 'what may be considered appropriate and reasonable procedure, standard or rule at one point in time may not be considered as such at some point in the future. Hence, due diligence in ensuring safety requires a state to keep abreast of technological changes and scientific development.'[178]

Other conventional due diligence obligations related to the environment refer more or less explicitly to the level of the state's capabilities and the best available resources at the state's disposal. For example, Article 6 of the Convention on Biological Diversity provides that a state party to the convention shall adopt general measures for the conservation and sustainable use of biological resources 'in accordance with its particular condition and capabilities'. Article 2 of the 1972 Convention on the Prevention of Marine Pollution by Dumping of Wastes and Other Matters is even more explicit, calling upon states to take effective measures to protect and preserve the marine environment from pollution 'according to their scientific, technical, and economic capabilities'.[179]

In any case, whether and to what extent the level of a state's capability determines the required degree of due diligence is a matter of the primary rule. Thus, there may be cases where a state's financial and economic resources, the fact that the state is a developing economy, will have a major influence in determining the level of diligence due. This occurs, for example, because the primary rule is to be interpreted in light of the principle of 'common but differentiated responsibilities'.[180] In other circumstances, it may be irrelevant for the application of a due diligence

177 Again, in the context of prevention of terrorism, determining whether the territorial state was unable or unwilling to prevent a terrorist group from carrying out attacks against another state is pivotal for assessing the victim state's right to breach the territorial integrity of the harbouring state to use of force against terrorists, see Tancredi, 'Doctrinal Alternative', 69.

178 ILC Draft Articles on Prevention with commentary, 154.

179 Convention on the Prevention of Marine Pollution by Dumping of Wastes and Other Matters (adopted 29 December 1972, entered into force 30 August 1975) 1046 UNTS 120.

180 Birnie, Boyle, Redgwell, *International Law and the Environment*, 148–50.

rule whether the binding subject is a developed or a developing state. The ITLOS 2011 advisory opinion on the responsibility of sponsoring states for activities in the Area shed light on this point. The tribunal did recognise that due diligence varies in relation to new scientific and technological knowledge. This way, it implied that the level of effort expected by sponsoring states for their Area's activities should be commensurate to their technical and scientific know-how.[181] The tribunal also noted that, with regard to activities in the Area, the participation of developing states in these activities should duly be accounted for, considering their interests and needs.[182] However, the tribunal argued that considerations related to the needs and interests of developing states did not affect the content of the due diligence obligation 'to ensure' ex Article 139 of UNCLOS. The 'general provisions concerning the responsibility and liability of the sponsoring State' remain the same for both developed and developing states.[183]

Within the international human rights framework, some primary rules of due diligence may impose on states a different degree of effort depending on their economic and financial means. Human rights obligations of an economic, social, and cultural nature usually depend on a state's capabilities to fulfil them. For instance, so-called human rights obligations of 'progressive development' are typical examples of rules imposing states to take steps and adopt measures to achieve the realisation of rights 'to the maximum of their available resources'.[184] The weight to be afforded to resource availability must be assessed on a case-by-case scenario and depending on the obligation in question. For example, Article 2 of the ICESCR provides the adoption of states' positive obligations 'to the maximum of a State's available resources'. However, the Committee on Economic, Social, and Cultural Rights has clarified that not every measure to be taken by a state is subject to resource constraint. If resources are inadequate to ensure specific goals, states may be required to strive to obtain them through international assistance and cooperation.[185]

181 *Responsibility and Obligations of states Sponsoring Persons*, para. 117.

182 Ibid. paras. 151–7.

183 Ibid. para. 158.

184 International Covenant on Economic, Social and Cultural Rights (adopted 16 December 1966, entered into force 3 January 1976) 993 UNTS 3 Article 2; Convention on the Rights of Persons with Disabilities (adopted 13 December 2006, entered into force 3 May 2008) 2515 UNTS 3 Article 4(2).

185 See Committee on Economic, Social and Cultural Rights, 'General Comment no 3 on the Nature of State Parties Obligations' (1990) UNDOC/E/1991/23 para 11. Similarly, the

Distinguishing between a state's capability and other variables of a due diligence rule may sometimes prove a difficult task. In some instances, it seems plausible that resource and technological availability will have a bearing on the state's knowledge of the risk and power over its sources. These factors will also, in turn, affect the degree of diligence required in specific circumstances, making it more difficult to determine up to which point the state's capabilities effectively play a role in shaping a due diligence obligation.

The ICJ's decision in Military and Paramilitary Activities in Nicaragua clearly illustrates the entanglement of due diligence variables. In this case, one of the court's questions was whether Nicaragua had failed to prevent and put a stop to the arms flow from its territory in support of the armed opposition in El Salvador. From the decision, it is difficult to say whether the decisive factor for the court ruling out of Nicaragua's responsibility for failure to prevent was lack of knowledge of the arms flow occurring in its territory or the limited capabilities at the state's disposal in fighting this flow. At one point, the court affirms that it would have been unreasonable to demand of Nicaragua a high degree of diligence given the limited resources at its disposal compared with those deployed by the United States (which had also been unsuccessful in stopping the flow). Accordingly, the ICJ considered that 'it is scarcely possible for Nicaragua's responsibility for arms traffic taking place on its territory to be automatically assumed'.[186] At the same time, it appears that the court made these considerations primarily to pinpoint as plausible Nicaragua's lack of knowledge of arms flowing from its territory. Indeed, the court concludes its analysis considering it 'realistic . . . to recognize that an activity of that nature, if on a limited scale, may well be pursued unbeknown to the territorial government'.[187]

CEDAW Committee has affirmed in relation to state parties' obligation to ensure education for women and girls that, although the right to education is generally interpreted as requiring progressive implementation according to states' available resources, the committee requires states to immediately ensure the 'core' of this right, see UN Committee for the Elimination of All Forms of Discrimination against Women, 'General Recommendation No 28 on the core obligations of State Parties under article 2 of the Convention on the Elimination of All Forms of Discrimination Against Women' (2010) UN Doc. CEDAW/C/GC/28 para 29.

[186] *Case Concerning Military and Paramilitary Activities in and Against Nicaragua*, para. 157.

[187] Ibid.

3.3.4 Control over the Source of Risk

The beginning of this chapter focused on the state's PSR and how this power must be reconstructed from the circumstances of the case. In this regard, acts of state control over sources of risk may point to a higher degree of PSR and shape the scope of a duty to act with due diligence. Control may indeed be a *variable in the degree* of diligence required by the state in a particular case.

To clarify the matter entirely, one may consider the 2016 South China Sea Arbitration Award. One of the Philippines' allegations in this case against China concerned China's alleged failure to prevent its nationals and vessels from exploiting the resources in the exclusive economic zone (EEZ) of the Philippines. The Philippines argued that, at the time of the events under scrutiny, Chinese military vessels had escorted fishing vessels flying China's flag and engaged in fishing activities into the EEZ of the Philippines. The Philippines alleged that the Chinese conduct violated Article 56 of UNCLOS, which recognises the coastal state's sovereign rights in its EEZ to exploit marine living resources. Drawing on the 2016 ITLOS advisory opinion on states' obligations concerning illegal, unreported, and unregulated (IUU) fishing, the Philippines contended that Article 56 implies that states other than the coastal state are under the obligation to take measures necessary to prevent their nationals from exploiting the living resources in the EEZ of another state party.

The Arbitral Tribunal set to solve the dispute argued as follows. First, the tribunal confirmed that states other than the coastal state are under the duty to take all necessary measures to ensure that vessels flying their flag are not engaged in IUU fishing in the EEZ of other states. It also confirmed that this state's obligation is a due diligence duty. Second, the tribunal found evidence that Chinese fishing vessels had indeed engaged in fishing in some areas belonging to the Philippines' EEZ and that these vessels were often escorted by Chinese military vessels. At this point, the tribunal considered that China had failed to fulfil its obligation to ensure. It is worth reporting the entire passage of the tribunal's reasoning:

> 754. In many cases, *the precise scope and application of the obligation* on a flag State to exercise due diligence in respect of fishing by vessels flying its flag in the exclusive economic zone of another State *may be difficult to determine.* Often, unlawful fishing will be carried out covertly, far from any official presence, and it *will be far from obvious what the flag State could realistically have done to prevent it.* That, however, is not the case here.

755. Chinese fishing vessels have in all reported instances been closely escorted by government CMS vessels. . . . In any event, there can be no question that the officers aboard the Chinese Government vessels in question were fully aware of the actions being taken by Chinese fishermen and *were able to halt them had they chosen to do so.*[188]

This passage underscores that the close physical presence of Chinese military vessels in the EEZ where Chinese fishing vessels were operating led the tribunal to establish China's responsibility for failing to act. Put differently, this passage suggests that China's presence (through military vessels) *enhanced* its control over the source of risks (national vessels flying China's flag and engaged in IUU fishing). This acknowledgment gave the tribunal reason to conclude that, had China chosen to do so, the state would have been able to halt fishing vessels flying its flag from engaging in IUU fishing. This does not mean that China's duty to act with due diligence existed *because of* the control exerted by military vessels over Chinese fishing boats. Such duty had arisen because of the jurisdictional competence that states hold over vessels flying their flag, which gives them *power* (and, to a certain extent, control) and *means* to adopt 'diligent' measures. Yet, China's factual control in the particular circumstances of the case influenced the measuring of what the state could realistically have done to fulfil its duty.

Concluding Remarks

This chapter has argued that, despite each primary rules' specificity, due diligence obligations share a number of common characteristics in terms of content and scope of application. The operation of due diligence obligations is premised upon the possibility to act. This possibility implies, at minimum, the existence of the state's power over the source of risk linked to the due diligence rule and knowledge – or capacity to know under normal circumstances – of risks. In international law, the evaluation of due diligence obligations typically occurs when a relevant risk materialises, and there was a *prima facie* omission on the part of the state. Failing to act generally presupposes *inaction* on the part of the state; in other words, the circumstance that power over the source of risk has not been effected or activated over these sources. With omissions, power

[188] *In the Matter of South China Sea Arbitration (Republic of the Philippines* v. *The People's Republic of China)* PCA Case 2013–19 (2016) para. 754–5 (emphasis added).

often remains a dispositional concept, a hypothetical condition. This is what makes PSR in primary rules of due diligence challenging to assess. While the foundations of this power are evident with certain primary rules and in specific contexts (e.g. when the rule holds a territorial dimension and the state has territorial control), sometimes understanding the extent of a duty to act requires complex evaluations of facts and a certain degree of deductive inference.

As to the substance of due diligence, this is dictated by the primary rule's content and is typically appraised against the overarching parameter of reasonableness. As a normative standard imbued with legal and extra-legal elements, reasonableness harnesses the notion of due diligence and provides it with concreteness. On a more general level, the concept identifies the perimeter within which a state's choice of measures and actions are deemed sufficient to fulfil due diligence. In this regard, reasonableness has acquired such specificity in certain contexts that the perimeter within which states are allowed to make their choices has become narrower and defined precisely. In these cases, states are no longer expected to adopt measures that would equate to the standard of an ideal and generally 'well-administered' government. States are expected to perform duties and comply with standards and procedures that reflect a rather technical notion of 'good government' and progressively erode the reasonable concept of its extra-legal components. Finally, on a more personalised level, reasonableness entails appraising the content of due diligence against the circumstances of the case. From this perspective, common variables are identifiable in the practice of due diligence across international law. Their applicability and importance vary depending on the rule, yet identifying these common parameters supports the thesis of a general standard of due diligence across international law.

4

Due Diligence Obligations in the Law of International Responsibility

Introduction

This chapter analyses how an international wrongful act accrues from the violation of a due diligence obligation and its consequences. The history of due diligence in international law dovetails with the history of international responsibility. The root of due diligence lies in the old idea of state responsibility in connection with the acts of private individuals and, more generally, in the role of fault in the law of international responsibility.[1] However, with the 2001 adoption by the International Law Commission (ILC) of the Articles on Responsibility of States for Internationally Wrongful Acts (ARSIWA),[2] due diligence was excluded from the secondary rules of state responsibility and the concept 'migrated' to the level of primary rules. Walking the line traced by the ILC, this chapter discusses the application of secondary rules of ARSIWA to due diligence obligations. The following analysis is not concerned with identifying remnants of fault in the law of state responsibility[3] nor with how the concept of due diligence evolved in the history of codification of international responsibility.[4] Rather, the chapter focuses on the relationship between primary rules of due diligence and secondary rules of state responsibility.

The distinction between primary and secondary rules in ARSIWA is attributed to Special Rapporteur Ago. Ago remodelled the entire

[1] F. V. García-Amador, 'Second Report on State Responsibility' (1957) ILC YB II/2 122.

[2] ILC Draft articles on Responsibility of States for Internationally Wrongful Acts, with commentaries (2001) ILC YB II/2.

[3] See the discussion in Chapter 1. On the role of fault in ARSIWA A. Gattini, 'Smoking/No Smoking: Some Remarks on the Current Place of Fault in the ILC Draft Articles on State Responsibility' (1999) 10 EJIL 397; S. Besson, *La Due Diligence en Droit International* (2020) 409 RCADI 285–96.

[4] On this H. P. Aust, P. Feihle, 'Due Diligence in the History of the Codification of the Law of State Responsibility', in H. Krieger, A. Peters, L. Kreuzer (eds.), *Due Diligence in the International Legal Order* (Oxford: Oxford University Press, 2020), 42.

architecture of state responsibility that had been codified up to that point by previous Special Rapporteur García-Amador, who had combined it with the treatment of aliens. Ago's intent was to purge principles of international responsibility of aspects related to the content of international obligations. For this reason, he introduced the distinction between primary rules, that is, the substantive rules across various areas of international law, and secondary rules, which would determine whether a substantive rule was violated and the consequence of any such violation.[5]

The ARSIWA follow Ago's approach and include only principles related to secondary rules, namely 'general conditions under international law for the State to be considered responsible for wrongful actions or omissions, and the legal consequences which flow therefrom'.[6] Definitions and content of international obligations are left out. Yet, the conceptual grounds for the dichotomy between primary and secondary rules should not be overestimated, and the distinction should not be taken as a logical necessity, but rather as a functional tool.[7] In this regard, the relationship between primary and secondary rules is often one of mutual influence, since primary rules affect the application of secondary rules of responsibility inasmuch as secondary rules can influence the scope and content of primary rules.[8] This is especially true for Part I of ARSIWA, which sets out the conditions for an international wrongful act. However, the application of rules pertaining to the content of international responsibility, which are strictly secondary, can also change in relation to the scope and nature of international obligations.[9]

Against this backdrop, this chapter addresses the key points of the relationship between due diligence obligations and secondary rules of international responsibility. Accordingly, the largest part of the analysis is dedicated to examining the conditions for an international wrongful act arising out of a violation of due diligence obligations. This section focuses on aspects related to the breach, the relationship between due diligence and other grounds of responsibility, and circumstances precluding wrongfulness. Yet, issues of reparations and the content of international

[5] ILC YB (1971) II/1 200.
[6] ARSIWA Commentary at 31.
[7] J. Crawford, 'The ILC Articles on Responsibility of States for Internationally Wrongful Acts' (2002) 96 AJIL 874, 879.
[8] G. Gaja, 'Primary and Secondary Rules in the International Law on State Responsibility' (2014) 97 *Rivista di diritto internazionale* 981, 984.
[9] See for instance Articles 40 and 41 of ARSIWA.

responsibility arising out of violations of due diligence obligations are also considered.

4.1 The Existence of an International Wrongful Act Stemming from Violation of a Due Diligence Obligation

Article 2 of ARSIWA establishes that an international wrongful act arises out of two cumulative conditions: (i) conduct consisting of an action or omission attributable to the state, and (ii) in breach of an international obligation of that state. Hence, in assessing the responsibility of a state for failure to exercise due diligence, both elements must exist. Conduct consisting of a failure to act must be attributable to the state pursuant to one of the provisions set forth in Article 4 through Article 11 of ARSIWA and must be in breach of one of the state's primary obligations of due diligence.

Despite the silence of ARSIWA on the issue, scholars like Brigitte Stern contend that the sequence of the conditions set in Article 2 is logical, and therefore it is first necessary to ensure that an act is attributable to the state before examining whether that act is in conformity with what is required by international law.[10] In support of this thesis, one may recall that Special Rapporteur Ago – the creator of the architecture behind the international wrongful act – noted that 'the international legal order must be able to regard the action or omission concerned as an act of the state, if it is to be allowed ... to assume the creation of ... subjective legal situations'.[11] However, it is clear that in cases of international wrongful acts accruing from violations of due diligence obligations, one cannot attribute any conduct to the state unless the existence of an international obligation has been first established.[12] Indeed, when the question of state responsibility revolves around an alleged failure of due diligence, conduct to be attributed to the state consists of inaction, or better, an omission.[13]

[10] B. Stern, 'The Elements of An Internationally Wrongful Act', in J. Crawford, A. Pellet, S. Olleson (eds.), *The Law of International Responsibility* (Oxford: Oxford University Press, 2010), 201; contrary P. M. Dupuy, 'Infraction' (1998) *Répertoire de Droit International* para. 19.

[11] R. Ago, 'Second Report on State Responsibility' (1970) ILC YB II para. 37.

[12] One may correctly point that one thing is to affirm that an international obligation exists and is applicable in a particular case, whereas another is to determine whether this obligation has been breached. Yet, verifying the existence of an international obligation is part of the process of assessing its breach, see Article 12 of ARSIWA.

[13] On the distinction between inaction and omissions E. Weinryb, 'Omissions and Responsibility' (1980) 30 *The Philosophical Quarterly* 1, 6–7; see also J. Crawford, *State Responsibility: The General Part* (Cambridge: Cambridge University Press, 2013), 218.

Clearly, an omission is such ontologically only if the subject had a duty to act and disregarded it.[14] Identifying a duty to act necessarily implies establishing who owed this duty. For this reason, international wrongful acts arising out of a failure of due diligence generally raise no particular issues of attribution of conduct. If the basis of a claim of international responsibility rests on a state's alleged failure to act, attribution of conduct should be automatically satisfied.[15] Although attribution of conduct and the breach of an international obligation are two analytically distinct conditions, as sensibly pointed out by the commentary of ARSIWA, 'there is often a close link between the basis of attribution and the particular obligation said to have been breached'.[16]

This is not to deny that, in certain situations, issues of attribution of conduct may arise before assessing whether a state has failed to act with due diligence. On the contrary, claims of a state's responsibility for violations of due diligence obligations often arise in relation to internationally harmful acts carried out by third parties, including private ones. In such cases, the question of state responsibility for failure to act is normally preceded by whether the acts of these actors are attributable to the state. For instance, if a group of individuals carries out an attack against the embassy of a foreign diplomatic mission, assessing the territorial state's responsibility may first entail ascertaining whether the attackers' actions were attributable to the state – for example, because they occurred under the instruction, direction, or control of the state (Article 8) or because of the state's subsequent acknowledgement (Article 11). A claim of a state's breach of the obligation to protect the premises of the diplomatic mission may only arise if the preceding issues of attribution are not satisfied. Similarly, if a state sends its armed forces to the territory of another state with the latter's consent and from the second state they use force against the territorial integrity of a third state, it may be necessary to establish whether these armed forces remained under the authority of the sending state or whether they were under the orders of the territorial state (Article 6). The question of the territorial state's

[14] See F. Latty, 'Actions and Omissions', in Crawford, Pellet, Olleson, *The Law of International Responsibility*, 357.

[15] Reaching the same conclusions Crawford, 'First Report on State Responsibility' (1998) ILC YB II/2 para. 154; L. Condorelli, C. Kress, 'The Rules of Attribution: General Considerations', in Crawford, Pellet, Olleson, *The Law of International Responsibility*, 225; Latty, 'Actions and Omissions' 361; P. D'Argent, 'State Organs Placed at the Disposal of the UN, Effective Control, Wrongful Abstention and Dual Attribution of Conduct' (2014) 1 *QIL-Questions of International Law* 17, 28.

[16] ARSIWA Commentary to Chapter III, para. 4.

breach of a due diligence obligation would arise only under the first scenario.

In relation to the breach, it has just been argued that a breach of a due diligence obligation entails an omission. Jan Klabbers notes that it is better to talk about 'failure to act' than omission because breaches of due diligence obligations can consist not only of inaction by a state's organs but also of a state's acting badly or mistakenly.[17] A state's failure to comply with a due diligence obligation can result from a positive act, for example, because the state has taken measures that are deemed insufficient. In a similar vein, a state's failure to act can also accrue from a series of actions and omissions by a state's organs, which, taken together, allow one to conclude that the state failed to exercise the due diligence required by its obligation.[18] From this perspective, the concept of 'failure to act with due diligence' must be construed as a legal one, not as a notion stemming from the material conduct adopted by the organs of a state's apparatus.[19]

In analysing the elements of an international wrongful act stemming from a violation of due diligence obligations, the next subsections focus on the most relevant issues at stake. First, situations in which a claim of state responsibility arises in connection with harmful acts carried out by private actors are further clarified. These circumstances raise question about the relationship between rules of attribution of conduct and due diligence. The analysis will then move to arguably the most problematic aspect of establishing a state's responsibility for violation of a due diligence obligation, that is, the question of breach and the *momentum a quo* of the violation.

Finally, this section will conclude with the distinction between breaches of due diligence obligations and complicity. When a state is accused of having violated a due diligence obligation, the alleged failure to act is often assessed in connection with the action of another party.[20] This party may be another state or an international organisation committing an international wrongful act. In these cases, there is a question of whether the first state is responsible for the violation of its due diligence

17 J. Klabbers, 'Reflections on Role Responsibility: The Responsibility of International Organizations for Failing to Act' (2017) 28 EJIL 1133, 1153.

18 ARSIWA Art. 15.

19 Ago, 'Le délit international' (1939) 68 RCADI 415, 501.

20 As amply demonstrated in the previous chapters, this is not always the case. One of the constitutive elements of due diligence obligations is the connection with the concept of risk, but it does not matter whether the source of such risk is a third party, an activity, or a particular situation.

obligation or whether responsibility (also) accrues for the international wrongful act carried out by the second state or the international organisation. The relationship between due diligence and derivative responsibility (Articles 16, 17, and 18 of ARSIWA; Article 58 of ARIO) deserves specific attention when failure to act with due diligence conflates with conduct of aid or assistance by omission.[21]

4.1.1 The Recourse to Due Diligence Obligations as an Alternative Basis for State Responsibility: The Limits of Attribution of Conduct

The question of state responsibility for failing to act with due diligence invites preliminary considerations on the relationship between due diligence and rules of attribution of conduct. When state responsibility is evaluated in connection with acts of private parties, responsibility for failure to act is often alternatively examined with the application of (certain) rules of attribution of conduct.

Notably, rules of attribution of conduct fundamentally rest on the state organ principle and the public/private dichotomy.[22] Accordingly, acts of

[21] Aside from aid or assistance, the relationship of due diligence obligations with other grounds of derivative responsibility does not seem to pose particular issues. In relation to Article 17, there seems to be an incompatibility between a breach of a due diligence obligation and acts of control and direction toward another state in the commission of an international wrongful act. As specified by the commentary to ARSIWA, direction and control presuppose more than mere states' power, oversight or influence over the commission of the wrongful act, and require domination over the act, see ARSIWA at 69. On the contrary, states' power over the source of risk (which includes influence) is sufficient for 'harnessing' a state's duty to act with due diligence. On the distinction between power, control, and influence see Chapter 3. Similar considerations can be made about Article 18, since the attribution of responsibility implies in this case coercion by the state of the very act of the coerced state that is internationally wrongful. More interesting is instead the relationship between due diligence and circumvention as codified by Article 61 of the Draft Articles on the Responsibility of International Organizations (ARIO), (2011) ILC YB II/2. Specifically, it may be queried whether an act of circumvention can consist of a state's failure to exercise due diligence, notwithstanding the commentary's assertion that circumvention requires 'intention to avoid compliance' and not mere knowledge or constructive knowledge that an international wrongful act will be committed, see commentary to ARIO at 93. In my view however, this question does not say much about how a breach of a due diligence obligation comes to existence or how such breach is to be distinguished from cases of attribution of responsibility. Rather, the question regards the scope of application of Article 61. On the relationship between due diligence and circumvention, M. Starita, 'Négligence illicite et responsabilité multiples: partage ou cumul de responsabilités ?', in S. Cassella (ed.), *Le standard de due diligence et la responsabilité internationale* (Paris: Pedone, 2018), 297.

[22] On the state organ principle Condorelli, Kress, 'The Rules of Attribution', 226–33; F. Salerno, 'Genesi e usi della nozione di organo nella dottrina internazionalistica

a state emanate in principle from its organs and representatives, which are defined primarily, but not exclusively, by the law governing the internal organisation of the state.[23] Acts of private individuals are generally not attributable to the state as they are performed outside its authority. Yet, under certain circumstances, international law attaches legal significance to their conduct as well. Articles 8–11 of ARSIWA set forth the conditions under which conduct of a private agent or group is considered an act of state.

As international practice illustrates, the threshold of attribution of conduct of private agents to the state is very high. This is particularly true in relation to the standard of control set by Article 8 of ARSIWA: the level of control a state must exercise over a private agent's conduct in order to attribute that conduct to the state has been interpreted very strictly by the International Court of Justice (ICJ),[24] and it is always subject to much debate.[25] Furthermore, rules of attribution of conduct of private acts are not only difficult to satisfy, but they are also often hard to prove in a claim for international responsibility.[26] For this reason, it is often perceived that in an era of unprecedented growth of internationally harmful acts carried out by non-state actors (NSAs), the fact that certain relationships between the state and NSA fail the test of attribution leaves a gap in the law of state responsibility.

When the application of rules of attribution of conduct of private actors is unsuccessful and harmful acts of these agents are not attributed to the state, responsibility for failure to exercise due diligence can be

italiana' (2009) 92 *Rivista di diritto internazionale* 921; on the public/private distinction as a marker for the domain of the law of international responsibility C. Chinkin, 'A Critique of the Public/Private Dimension' (1999) 10 EJIL 387, 389.

23 ARSIWA Articles 4 to 7. According to international practice, state's organs are not only those defined *de jure* by the state's internal law, but may exceptionally be established de facto, see *Case Concerning Application of the Convention on the Prevention and Punishment of the Crime of Genocide (Bosnia Herzegovina* v. *Serbia and Montenegro)* (Merits) [2007] ICJ Rep, paras. 391–5; P. Palchetti, *L'organo di fatto dello Stato nell'illecito internazionale* (Milan: Giuffré, 2007).

24 *Military and Paramilitary Activities in and against Nicaragua (Nicaragua* v. *United States of America)* (Merits) [1986] ICJ Rep. 13, para. 115; *Genocide* case, para. 399.

25 Among the others J. Griebel, M. Plücken, 'New Developments Regarding the Rules of Attribution? The International Court Justice's Decision in *Bosnia* v. *Serbia*' (2008) 21 LJIL 601; G. Bartolini, 'Il concetto di "controllo" sulle attività di individui quale presupposto della responsabilità dello stato', in M. Spinedi, A. Gianelli, M. L. Alaimo (eds.), *La codificazione della responsabilità internazionale degli Stati alla prova dei fatti* (Milan: Giuffré, 2006), 27.

26 For instance, see the argument of the ICJ in the *Military and Paramilitary Activities*, paras. 115–16, 292.

a 'favoured' strategy[27] to avoid responsibility gaps. For example, in the Teheran Hostage case, the ICJ was faced with the question of Iran's responsibility for the taking over of the US Embassy by a group of Islamic militants. With regard to the events that occurred after the militants' occupation of the US Embassy and the seizure of the consulate, the court found a sufficient link for attributing the conduct of the militants directly to Iran. As for the series of events that preceded the occupation of the embassy and the detention of the hostages, the court noted that the fact that attribution could not operate 'does not mean that Iran is, in consequence, free of any responsibility in regards to those attacks'.[28] Iran was indeed deemed responsible for failing to prevent the attack on the US Embassy and failing to take appropriate steps to ensure the protection of the US personnel.[29]

Similarly, in the 2007 Bosnian Genocide case, the ICJ resorted to Serbia's due diligence obligations when rules of attribution of conduct fell short of connecting the acts of genocide perpetrated by the militia of the Republic of Srpska (VRS) in Srebrenica with the Serbian state. The court based its reasoning on three sequential alternatives. It first analysed Articles 4 and 8 of ARSIWA and concluded that the militia that carried out the genocide were neither de facto organs of Serbia nor had their acts been directed or controlled by the state.[30] Then, the court considered whether the degree of Serbia's involvement in the acts of these groups amounted to complicity by Serbia in the commission of genocide. After finding no sufficient proof that Serbia had provided aid and assistance to the militias carrying out genocide,[31] the court, as a last resort, relied on Serbia's obligation to prevent genocide. It concluded that due to the strength of Serbia's political, military, and financial links with the entities committing acts of genocide, Serbia had the capacity to influence their conduct but failed to act with the diligence due to avert or minimise acts of genocide.[32]

After 2001, the supplementary role of due diligence obligations has also been a much-debated topic in the context of international terrorist

[27] The expression is taken from K. E. Boon, 'Are Control Tests Fit for the Future? The Slippage Problem in Attribution Doctrines' (2014) 15 *Melbourne Journal of International Law* 330, 364.

[28] *United States Diplomatic and Consular Staff in Teheran (United States of America* v. *Iran)* (Merits) [1980] ICJ Rep 3, 61.

[29] Ibid. 63.

[30] *Genocide* case, paras. 391–5.

[31] Ibid. paras. 423–4.

[32] Ibid. para. 430.

activities carried out by NSAs. A state's involvement in acts of terrorism can take a variety of forms, from effectively controlling acts of terrorism carried out by NSAs to providing financial, logistic, and military support, or passively tolerating terrorist groups having a base or conducting activities from the state's territory. Since there are no special rules of attribution of conduct that apply to the terrorist context, the focus has been on ARSIWA, and in particular, on the application of the strict 'effective control' standard. The difficulty of attributing acts of terrorist groups to a state has led certain states,[33] the Security Council,[34] and international scholarship[35] to focus on the preventive obligations of territorial states, and in particular, on the general state obligation not to allow their territory to be used for acts that are contrary to the rights of other states. This issue has acquired a salient dimension particularly with regard to the lawful consequences that may ensue when a state fails to prevent or suppress the use of force by NSAs operating within its territory. In this sense, some affected states and a minority of scholarship have argued that victim states would be allowed to resort to self-defence not only when the acts of NSAs are attributable to a state – provided that they amounted to an armed attack – but also when there is no attribution, yet the state was *unwilling* or *unable* to prevent attacks from being organised in its territory.[36] In this author's view, these propositions are controversial: among other reasons,[37] they are based on an unprincipled approach

[33] For instance, UN Doc S/2001/246 (United States of America); UN Doc A/60/937- S/2006/515 (Israel); SC 5489th meeting 2006 at 6; UN Doc S/1998/780 (United States of America).

[34] Remarkably UNSC Res 1373 (11 September 2001) UN Doc S/RES/1373 para. 2(e); UNSC Res 2396 (21 December 2017) UN Doc S/RES/2396.

[35] F. Dubuisson, 'Vers un Renforcement des Obligations de Diligence en Matière de Lutte Contre le Terrorism ?', in K. Christakis-Bannelier, T. Christakis, O. Corten, B. Delcourt (eds.), *Le Droit International Face au Terrorisme* (Paris: Pedone, 2002) 145; P. M. Dupuy, C. Hoss, 'Trail Smelter and International Terrorism: International Mechanisms to Combat Transboundary Harm', in C. Walter, C. Vöneky, F. Schorkopf, V. Roeben (eds.), *Terrorism as a Challenge for National and International Law: Security versus Liberty?* (Berlin: Springer, 2004), 23.

[36] V. Joel-Proux, 'Babysitting Terrorists: Should States Be Strictly Liable for Failing to Prevent Transborder Attacks?' (2005) 23 *Berkeley Journal of International Law* 615; Y. Dinstein, *War, Aggression and Self-Defence* (Cambridge: Cambridge University Press, 2011), 224–7; A. Deeks, 'Unwilling or Unable: toward a Normative Framework for Extraterritorial Self-Defence' (2012) 53 *Virginia Journal of International Law* 483.

[37] Among the critics K. Trapp, *State Responsibility for International Terrorism* (Oxford: Oxford University Press, 2011), 58–62; A. Tancredi, 'Il problema della legittima difesa nei confronti di milizie non statali alla luce dell'ultima crisi tra Israele e Libano' (2007) 90 *Rivista di diritto internazionale* 969.

to due diligence obligations that construes them as duties of result and disregards the distinction between inability and unlawful behaviour.[38] Yet, these positions testify to the increasing reliance on due diligence obligations when there is no room for successfully applying rules of attribution of conduct by private agents.

Drawing on examples of international practice, certain authors suggest that state responsibility for failure of due diligence complements rules of attribution of conduct.[39] When private actors carry out internationally harmful acts and their conduct is considered an 'act of the state' pursuant to rules of attribution of conduct, responsibility is found in the violation of a primary rule that typically mandates the state to refrain from causing harm to such interests. If the conduct of these actors cannot be considered an 'act of the state', responsibility can still be found in the violation of a primary rule of due diligence that requires the state to prevent or protect from harm. This way, a 'seamless' connection is created between 'the theory' of attribution of conduct and that of due diligence so as to avoid a vacuum in the responsibility of states for acts of private actors.[40]

[38] Specifically, the unwilling or unable doctrine equates the situation in which a state fails to exercise best effort to prevent acts of terrorism, which would amount to a situation of wrongfulness on the part of the state for breaching its due diligence obligation; and the situation in which the state uses its best effort but it is incapable or unable to effectively prevent. As seen in Chapter 3, a state's inability should be the limit of due diligence, see Chapter 3 Section 3.1.

[39] C. Ryngaert, 'State Responsibility and Non-State Actors' in M. Noortmann, A. Reinisch, C. Ryngaert (eds.), *Non-State Actors and International Law* (London: Hart Publishing, 2015), 163; T. Dannenbaum, 'Public Power and Preventive Responsibility', in A. Nollkaemper, I. Plakokefalos (eds.), *The Practice of Shared Responsibility* (Cambridge: Cambridge University Press, 2017); this dimension has been explored in several legal contexts, including state security against acts of terrorism, the protection of human rights, the cyber domain: T. Becker, *Terrorism and the State: Rethinking the Rules of State Responsibility* (Portland: Hart Publishing, 2006); R. P. Barnidge, *Non-State Actors and Terrorism: Applying the Law of State Responsibility and the Due Diligence Principle* (Berlin: Springer, 2008); M. Hakimi, 'State Bystander Responsibility' (2010) 21 EJIL 341; A. Seibert-Fohr, 'From Complicity to Due Diligence: When Do States Incur Responsibility for Their Involvement in Serious International Wrongdoing?' (2017) 60 GYIL 667; N. Tsagourias, 'Cyber Attacks, Self-Defence and the Problem of Attribution' (2012) 17 *Journal of Conflict and Security Law* 229; M. N. Schmitt, 'In Defence of Due Diligence in Cyberspace' (2015) 125 *The Yale Law Journal Forum*; L. Chircop, 'A Due Diligence Standard of Attribution in Cyberspace' (2018) 67 ICLQ 643.

[40] The idea of using the 'attribution theory' and the 'due diligence theory' alternatively in order to create a 'seamless' responsibility framework that can cope with international harmful acts of non-state actors is taken from A. Kanehara, 'Reassessment of the Acts of the State in the Law of State Responsibility' (2019) 399 RCADI 29, 174–202.

Although powerful, this approach requires clarification. Methodologically, the perspective adopted is that of the 'internationally harmful act', that is, harm stemming from private actors – notoriously armed groups, private military companies, terrorist organisations, multinational corporations – and affecting interests protected by international law. The point of departure is, therefore, not *whether* a certain international wrongful act exists. Rather, the question is *which* international wrongful act has been committed by the state in relation to harm caused by private actors. This is important, as due diligence does not constitute a 'further' or 'missing element' in the rules of attribution of conduct. Due diligence is a concept that identifies the nature of a primary rule and does not operate at the level of secondary rules of responsibility.[41] Hence, due diligence forms the alternative basis for state responsibility when the conditions for the existence of a certain wrongful act are lacking but exist in relation to a different wrongful act. As pointed out by the commentary to ARSIWA, rules of attribution of conduct have a 'cumulative effect', such that if the conduct of private parties cannot be attributed to the state, responsibility for the 'effects' of such conduct can still accrue if the state failed to adopt the measures necessary to prevent them.[42] Yet, 'cumulative effects' concerns rules of attribution of conduct, not the relationship between attribution and due diligence.

In this regard, treating responsibility for due diligence as a supplementary tool when rules of attribution of conduct fall short of connecting the conduct of NSAs with the state runs the risk of conflating issues of secondary rules with questions on the substance of international obligations. Such 'risk' had already been identified by the ILC during the work on ARSIWA. Specifically, draft Article 11, which was adopted on the first reading by the commission, drew a connection between rules of attribution of conduct and due diligence obligations. It read:

> (1) The conduct of a person or a group of persons not acting on behalf of the State shall not be considered as an act of the State under International Law.
> (2) Paragraph 1 is without prejudice to the attribution to the State of any other conduct which is related to that of persons or groups of

[41] Stressing the distinction between primary and secondary rules and noting that due diligence cannot provide answer to the limits of attribution of conduct I. Plakokefalos, 'The Use of Force by Non-State Actors and the Limits of Attribution of Conduct: A Reply to Vladyslav Lanovoy' (2017) 28 EJIL 587, 590.

[42] ARSIWA Commentary to Chapter II, para. 4.

> persons referred to in that paragraph and which is to be considered as an act of the State by virtue of articles 5 to 10.[43]

The commentary to Paragraph 2 specified that the responsibility of a state would not be excluded simply by virtue of the impossibility of attributing to it acts of private individuals. A state could still be responsible for the omissions of its organs in relation to the acts carried out by NSAs.[44] Draft Article 11 was originally introduced by Special Rapporteur Ago in his study for the commission on the grounds for attribution of conduct in international law. In a somewhat circular argument, Ago first argued that conduct of private individuals was generally not considered an act of the state under international law. However, these acts could still amount to 'external events' catalysing wrongfulness of the state for failure to act.[45] In these cases, a state would not be responsible for the acts committed by NSAs; rather, state responsibility would accrue from the omission of its own organs in failing to prevent these acts.[46]

Ago's conceptualisation and draft Article 11 were rightly criticised during the subsequent readings of the draft articles on state responsibility. In particular, the tension between primary and secondary rules did not pass undetected before governments and the commission. Some states argued that draft Article 11 was only a 'pedantic' clarification of principles of attribution conduct, while others stressed that the article lacked any independent content.[47] During the second reading of ARSIWA, Special Rapporteur Crawford aptly observed that Article 11 'focus[ed] on the wrong question ... not whether the acts of private individuals as such are attributable to the state ... but rather, what is the extent of the obligation of the state to prevent or respond to those acts'.[48]

The analytical distinction between rules of attribution of conduct and due diligence does not only concern the (secondary and primary) nature of the two concepts. The distinction also involves the factual relationship between the acts of the private actors and the entity of the state. Attribution of acts of private actors to the state typically follows either a situation of necessity in which a private individual replaces the absence

43 Draft Articles on State Responsibility with Commentaries Thereto Adopted by the International Law Commission on First Reading (1996) ILC YB II/2 Draft Article 11.
44 Ibid. 50.
45 Ago, 'Fourth Report on State Responsibility' (1972) ILC YB II para. 65.
46 Ibid. paras. 141–2.
47 ILC YB (1980) II/1, Comment of China at 97 and Crawford, 'First Report', para. 243.
48 Crawford, 'First Report', para. 244.

or default of official authorities with his or her actions,[49] or situations in which there is an 'active' and distinct intervention by the state over the conduct of the person in question, whether in the form of instruction, direction, effective control, or subsequent acknowledgement of the conduct as the state's own.[50] When state responsibility is instead assessed for failure to exercise due diligence in connection with acts of private actors, the link between the state and these acts differs in degree and nature. This connection ensues from 'diffuse' power that the state holds vis-à-vis the source of risk (private individuals and their actions) and that determines the extent to which the state is expected to act upon it. As argued in Chapter 3, this power derives from the combination of both institutional links (i.e., territorial sovereignty, jurisdiction) and from the concrete circumstances in which the state finds itself. Contrary to rules of attribution of conduct, the factual connection between the state and acts of private actors does not need to be expressed through the state's tangible intervention. The connection exists even if a state retains its power over the source of risk and does not exercise that power through any form of control or intervention over private actors' conduct.

4.1.2 The Breach of Due Diligence Obligations

Most of the issues regarding state responsibility for violation of due diligence obligations arise in relation to the breach. It is difficult to discuss what constitutes a breach of an international obligation of due diligence without inevitably trespassing into the realm of primary rules. As stressed by the commentary to Chapter III of ARSIWA, '[t]here is no such thing as a breach of an international obligation in the abstract',[51] and in this sense, the principles set forth in Article 12 through Article 15 of ARSIWA only play an 'ancillary' role in determining the violation of an obligation.

Apart from preventive obligations,[52] ARSIWA is silent on what constitutes a breach of a due diligence obligation. The history of the codification of the articles reveals that the reason for this silence is twofold. First, during the ILC's second reading of the articles, it emerged that part of the codified rules related to breach that were previously adopted by the commission were either too complex or considered the content of

49 ARSIWA Article 9.
50 ARSIWA Articles 8, 11.
51 ARSIWA Commentary to Chapter III, para. 2.
52 See Section 4.1.3.

primary rules too much.[53] There was strong support within the ILC to delete some of the classifications of international wrongful acts proposed by Ago and to streamline the entire Chapter III.

Second, some ILC members felt that taxonomy between obligations of conduct and obligations of result that were adopted on the first reading did not adequately capture the reality of international obligations. In the articles adopted on the first reading, the distinction between obligations of conduct and obligations of result had reflected Ago's original conceptualisation.[54] Accordingly, obligations of conduct were described as obligations requiring states 'to adopt a particular course of conduct', the breach of which would arise 'when the conduct of that State is not in conformity with that required of it by that obligation'.[55] Obligations of result were instead presented as obligations requiring a state to achieve, by means of its own choice, a specific result. A breach of these obligations would arise if the state 'by the conduct adopted ... does not achieve the result required of it by that obligation'.[56]

Part of the commission considered Ago's distinction confusing because of the 'inversion' it had created of the 'traditional' civil law dichotomy between obligations of conduct and obligations of result.[57] In particular, some members expressed doubts as to whether Ago's taxonomy could accommodate the specificities of due diligence obligations.[58] Ago's distinction had focused on the more or less 'determinacy' of the content of an international obligation.[59] However, what was deemed more relevant for establishing a breach was not determinacy, but rather whether the obligation requires a state to guarantee a certain result or *only* to exercise best effort to attain it.[60] Some members argued for replacing Ago's taxonomy with the distinction between obligations 'to endeavour' and obligations 'to achieve', noting that the latter would be more helpful for determining the *momentum a quo* of a violation.[61]

[53] ILC YB (1999) II/2 60–3. Crawford, 'Second Report on State Responsibility' (1999) ILC YB II/2 20–8.

[54] The distinction was extensively discussed in Chapter 2.

[55] Draft Articles adopted on the first reading, Article 20.

[56] Ibid. Article 21.

[57] See extensively Chapter 2, Section 2.2.

[58] For a summary of the discussion within the commission, ILC YB (1999) II/2 para. 147–72; for the positions expressed by each member of the Commission see ILC YB (1999) I meetings 2569th; 2571st; 2573rd; 2574th.

[59] Crawford, 'Second Report', 22.

[60] See the Comment of Mr Rao, ILC YB (1999) I meeting 2571st para. 42.

[61] Ibid. para. 10, comment by Simma.

Others stressed the importance of codifying obligations of conduct as due diligence obligations and clarifying what would integrate a breach of the latter.[62] Those construing obligations of conduct as best-effort obligations all felt that a state bound by a due diligence obligation would be liable not because of its failure to achieve the result set by the rule of due diligence but for failure to adopt the necessary measures required by the rule.[63] From this perspective, draft Articles 20 and 21 did not elucidate on both the existence and the time aspects of the breach of due diligence obligations.

International case law has widely confirmed that a breach of due diligence obligations arises out of a state's failure to adopt the measures required to fulfil due diligence.[64] What counts is not whether the result envisaged by a primary rule of due diligence (e.g., prevention or protection from a given event; assurance of a certain goal) is *actually* achieved. What matters is the measure of diligence adopted by the state, which is violated when the state fails to reach the best-effort threshold required by the content of the primary rule.

These aspects were well explained by the International Tribunal of the Law of the Sea (ITLOS) in its 2015 advisory opinion submitted by the Sub-Regional Fisheries Commission (SRFC). One of the questions before the tribunal concerned the extent to which flag states are liable for illegal, unreported, and unregulated (IUU) fishing activities conducted by vessels sailing under their flags. To answer, the ITLOS first reasoned that

[62] ILC YB (1999) I meeting 2571st para. 24, 42; meeting 2573rd para. 26 comments by Mr He, Economides, and Rao.

[63] Ibid. See also the comment of Mr Al-Khawawneh, meeting 2573rd para. 29.

[64] *Genocide* case, para. 430; *Case Concerning Pulp Mills on the River Uruguay (Argentina* v. *Uruguay)* (Merits) [2010] ICJ Rep para. 197; *Responsibility and Obligations of States Sponsoring Persons and Entities with Respect to Activities in the Area (Request for an Advisory Opinion submitted to the Seabed Dispute Chamber)* ITLOS Reports 2011 para. 172; in the context of the protection of human rights see for instance *Goginashvili* v. *Georgia*, (Judgment) [2011] App no 47729/08 para. 71, noting:

> In its assessment of this issue, the Court considers that it must be guided by the due diligence test, since the State's obligation to cure a seriously ill detainee is one of means, not of result. Notably, the mere fact of a deterioration of the applicant's state of health, albeit capable of raising ... certain doubts concerning the adequacy of the treatment in prison, could not suffice, as such, for a finding of a violation of the State's positive obligations under Article 3 of the Convention, if, on the other hand, it can be established that the relevant domestic authorities have in timely fashion resorted to all reasonably possible medical measures in a conscientious effort to hinder development of the disease in question.

states are under the obligation 'to ensure that vessels flying their flag and engaged in fishing activities in the Exclusive Economic Zone (EEZ) of another State comply with the conservation measures and the conditions established by this State's laws and regulations'.[65] After labelling this obligation one 'of due diligence', the tribunal then recalled Article 2 of ARSIWA and noted:

> [The] liability of the flag State does not arise from a failure of vessels flying its flag to comply with the laws and regulations of the SRFC Member States concerning IUU fishing activities in their exclusive economic zones, as the violation of such laws and regulations by vessels is not *per se* attributable to the flag State. The liability of the flag State arises from its failure to comply with its 'due diligence' obligations concerning IUU fishing activities conducted by vessels flying its flag in the exclusive economic zones of the SRFC Member States.[66]

The tribunal stressed that a state is not automatically liable if vessels flying its flag engage in IUU fishing in the EEZ of other states. A state can only be responsible for a breach 'of its international obligations' when it fails to take 'all necessary and appropriate measures to meet its "due diligence" obligations to ensure that vessels … do not conduct IUU fishing activities'.[67] The ITLOS also underscored that the frequency of IUU fishing activities by vessels flying the state's flag is immaterial to the issue of whether there has been a breach of the state's due diligence obligations.[68] This aspect is important, as it clarifies that the way in which 'the event' takes place is irrelevant with respect to how the breach of the obligation accrues.

If a breach of a due diligence obligation consists of a failure to adopt measures set by the primary rule, one would expect the time of the breach to correspond to the moment a state fails to adopt the required measures. This, of course, is unless the primary obligation states otherwise, for example by conditioning the breach on the occurrence of damage.[69] Yet, when it comes to the *momentum a quo* of violations of due diligence, things get muddy. Some international decisions explicitly recognise that a breach of due diligence accrues *in itself* from a state's failure to act,

[65] *Request for an Advisory Opinion submitted by the Sub-Regional Fisheries Commission (SRFC)* (Case No. 21) ITLOS Reports 2015 para. 129.
[66] Ibid. para. 146
[67] Ibid. paras. 147–8.
[68] Ibid. para. 150.
[69] For example Article 139 of United Nations Convention on the Law of the Sea (UNCLOS) (adopted 10 December 1982, entered into force 16 November 1994) 1833 UNTS 3.

without any further requirement such as damage or the occurrence of a certain event.[70] Other cases instead subordinate the existence of the violation to the occurrence of an event that prima facie points to a state's failure to act. In these cases, although it is acknowledged that a violation of due diligence stems from a failure to adopt the required measures, in order for a breach to occur, an event contrary to the aim and objective of the primary rule of due diligence must first have materialised. Since this construction of the breach applies typically to preventive obligations, Section 4.1.3 addresses this aspect thoroughly.

4.1.3 *The Breach of Obligations to Prevent*

I *Pars Destruens*: The Genealogy of Article 14(3) and the Event as a Secondary Element of the Breach

Article 14(3) of ARSIWA deals with the extension in time of the breach of preventive obligations by saying:

> 'The breach of an international obligation requiring the state to prevent a given event occurs when the event occurs and extends over the entire period during which the event continues and remains not in conformity with that obligation.'

The commentary to the article specifies that obligations of prevention are usually construed as best-effort obligations requiring the state to take all reasonable and necessary measures to prevent a given event from occurring but without warranting that the event will not occur.[71] With this take, the commentary to ARSIWA seemingly considers the nature of preventive obligations of due diligence.

The assertion that a breach of preventive obligations requires the event to occur appears at odds with the due diligence nature of these obligations. As duties of best effort, due diligence obligations emphasise conduct adopted by the state to endeavour to realise the result set by the primary rule. Their violation should, in principle, be ascertained on a state's failure

[70] *United States Diplomatic and Consular Staff in Teheran (United States of America* v. *Iran)* (Merits) [1980] ICJ Rep 3, 33; in the *Responsibility and Obligations of Sponsoring States*, the ITLOS appeared to support this position. While the ITLOS recognised that Article 139 requires damage as a condition for a breach of the sponsoring states' due diligence obligations, the tribunal also noted: 'The failure by a sponsoring State to meet its obligations not resulting in material damage is covered by customary international law which does not make damage a requirement for the liability of States. . . . this is confirmed by the ILC Articles on State Responsibility' at 210.

[71] ARSIWA Commentary to Article 14 para. 14.

to adopt measures necessary to prevent and not depend on the occurrence of the event to be prevented. Indeed, a state that fails to prevent a certain event can still escape responsibility should it demonstrate to have met 'due diligence'. In the same vein, a state that fails to meet due diligence cannot assert as a defence that, had measures been taken, the event would have occurred anyway. The event should therefore be immaterial to the question of breach. Yet, by shifting the focus to the event, Article 14(3) overshadows considerations of the conduct at the origin of prevention and instead gives priority to the result to be achieved, that is, the non-occurrence of the event. The outcome is the conversion of preventive obligations into negative obligations of result: a violation accrues only if prevention, the goal set by the primary rule, is not achieved.

The paradox of the solution adopted by the ILC is explained by authoritative scholarship with the distinction between 'pure' obligations to prevent and preventive obligations of 'conduct'.[72] According to this division, pure obligations to prevent are duties whose primary objective is to avoid a given event from coming into existence. A typical example is the obligation to prevent genocide, which is intended to avoid the occurrence of genocide and therefore cannot be violated by a state unless genocide is committed. Pure preventive obligations are those regulated by Article 14(3) and their breach requires, other than failure to prevent by the state, the occurrence of the event in question. On the contrary, preventive obligations of conduct are duties whose fundamental focus is the adoption by a state of measures appropriate and necessary to ensure prevention. They are classic due diligence duties whose violation accrues regardless of the event and simply by evaluating conduct at the time of prevention.

Chapter 2 has already cast doubt upon the division between pure obligations to prevent and preventive obligations of conduct. It argued that the distinction is hard to draw conceptually and seems to be grounded exclusively on the *momentum a quo* of the violation – the occurrence of the event for pure preventive obligations or the failure to act with due diligence for preventive obligations of conduct. Furthermore, the separation does not find support in international practice. A cursory look at the ILC work on ARSIWA – where the distinction was suggested first by Special Rapporteur Ago[73] and then by Special

[72] The expression is taken from P. M. Dupuy, 'Reviewing the Difficulties of Codification: On Ago's Classification of Obligations of Means and Obligations of Result in Relation to State Responsibility' (1999) 10 EJIL 371; on the distinction between obligations to prevent of conduct nature and 'pure' preventive obligations Crawford, *State Responsibility*, 227–8.

[73] Ago, 'Seventh Report on State Responsibility' (1978) ILC YB II/2 35–6.

Rapporteur Crawford[74] – reveals much confusion into which obligations are deemed those of pure prevention and which are of a due diligence nature. The examples presented to the commission are often contradictory,[75] and the few cases in practice provided do not paint a clear picture as to a division of the categories of preventive obligations.

Rather, to grasp the rationale of Article 14(3) and its relationship to due diligence, one needs to critically revisit its genealogy and consider the paradigm shift from Ago's classification of obligations to Crawford's appreciation of Ago's distinction. The history of ILC work indeed shows not only much disagreement among the ILC members on the codification of the event as a condition for breaches of preventive obligations. It also illustrates that, despite Crawford's criticism of Ago's distinction between obligations of conduct and obligations of result, the final version of Article 14(3) is essentially a remnant of that division.

The codification of obligations to prevent in the ILC's ARSIWA work is down to Special Rapporteur Ago. In his Seventh Report to the Commission, Ago asserts that breaches of preventive obligations require two cumulative conditions: the occurrence of the event to be prevented and lack of vigilance and prevention by a state's organs.[76] Neither the occurrence of the event without state negligence nor negligence without the occurrence of the event are deemed sufficient to integrate a violation of preventive duties. For a breach to accrue both elements must exist and it must be established that the event was made possible by the state's lack of vigilance and prevention.

Ago's construction of preventive obligations fits coherently into his distinction between obligations of conduct and obligations of result. Obligations to prevent are presented by the Special Rapporteur as *sui generis* obligations of result. They set a certain 'negative' result – the non-occurrence of a given event – by giving states the freedom to decide the means of fulfilling prevention. As obligations of result, preventive obligations cannot be violated unless the result has not been achieved (i.e., the event has come into existence). At the same time, freedom of the choice of means does not signify that a state is responsible for every failure to prevent. Ago states clearly that only failures to prevent due to lack of adequate protection and vigilance make a state liable for a breach of preventive duty.

74 Crawford, 'Second Report', para. 134
75 See Chapter 2, Section 2.4.1.
76 Ago, 'Seventh Report', 32.

Two considerations suggest that the dogmatic foundations of Ago's depiction of preventive obligations are the result of a top-down approach rooted in his taxonomy of obligations. First, the evidence presented by the Special Rapporteur to sustain the view that breaches of preventive obligations require the occurrence of the event are either circumstantial or derived by logical inference. For example, Ago bases his considerations on obligations to prevent almost only on diplomatic practice without really engaging in a detailed analysis of case law. He notes that in the practice of arbitral commissions dealing with the protection of foreigners and their property, 'it is only after the occurrence of the event that a State invokes the breach of the obligation'.[77] In a subsequent part of the report, the Special Rapporteur simply registers that various writers have taken as a '*fait accompli*' the 'damage caused by private persons to foreign States or its nationals'.[78]

The other indication suggesting caution over Ago's approach is that his propositions on preventive obligations initially sparked a vivid debate among the members of the commission. Some warned that by making the occurrence of the event an essential condition for the breach, Ago had introduced the notion of damage into the elements of international responsibility.[79] Others cast doubt on the relationship between Ago's obligations of result and obligations to prevent a given event. Questions were also raised on the relationship between preventive obligations and due diligence and the correctness of an approach treating the event as a necessary element of the breach of preventive duties.[80]

This dissension notwithstanding, draft Article 23 adopted by the ILC on the first reading incorporated Ago's classification of obligations to prevent in the following terms: 'When the result required of a State by an international obligation is the prevention, by means of its own choice, of the occurrence of a given event, there is a breach of that obligation only if, by the conduct adopted, the State does not achieve that result'.[81] Ago's footprint in this formulation is apparent as preventive obligations are indeed treated by Article 23 as 'negative' obligations of result.[82] The commentary confirmed that a breach would arise solely from the occurrence of the event coupled with state conduct causally

[77] Ibid. 35.
[78] Ibid. 36.
[79] ILC YB (1978) I meeting 1476th para. 21, 33–4.
[80] Ibid. meeting 1477th para. 1, 29; meeting 1478th para. 6.
[81] Draft Articles adopted on the First Reading, 174.
[82] Ibid. 172–3.

linked to such event. To emphasise the need of a causal nexus, the commentary provided that 'said conduct may be regarded as a *sine qua non* of the event'.[83]

The paradigm shift occurred with Special Rapporteur Crawford and the revision of the draft articles on the second reading. Crawford's criticism of draft Article 23 ran along two lines. The first problem concerned the meaning of Ago's taxonomy of obligations, which the last Special Rapporteur deemed 'reversed'.[84] Second, for Crawford, the provision of draft Article 23 dug too much into the content of primary rules and created a presumption in their interpretation. According to Crawford, not all obligations to prevent a given event condition the breach on negligent conduct by the state. Some require states to provide an unconditional guarantee that the event will be averted, while others excuse a failure to prevent only in situations of force majeure. In its current formulation, draft Article 23 targeted only one type of obligations to prevent.

Against this criticism, the solution eventually reached with Article 14(3) developed as a sort of compromise of the opposing views that emerged within the commission. On the one hand, the majority of the ILC's members shared Crawford's scepticism around introducing into ARSIWA a theoretical distinction of obligations clearly touching upon the content of primary rules. For this reason, it was decided that reference in draft Article 23 to 'conduct adopted by the State' to prevent would be deleted, so as to avoid any allusion to the content of preventive obligations.[85] On the other hand, the event as a condition for the breach was maintained based largely upon the conviction that an event must occur before a state can be said to have violated its obligation to prevent it. To address the concerns raised by members who had stressed the link between due diligence and prevention, the distinction between pure obligations to prevent and preventive obligations of conduct was put forward.

Yet, the commission's final approach is not without shortcomings. Aside from the correctness of separating pure obligations to prevent from preventive obligations of conduct, a problem lies in the identification of the 'event' as a necessary secondary element of the breach. If, like Crawford suggested, preventive obligations are manifold and primacy in their interpretation should always be given to the content of the primary

83 Ibid. 176.
84 Crawford, 'Second Report', 22.
85 For a summary of the discussion see ILC YB (1999) I meetings 2569th; 2571st; 2573rd; 2574th.

rule, a principled approach would have deleted both the conditions set in draft Article 23. Instead, Article 14(3) maintains the event as a secondary element and is only silent on states' adoption of conduct to prevent. As a result, ARSIWA inevitably affects the scope and understanding of *all* obligations to prevent. In its current formulation, Article 14(3) precludes the interpretation of preventive obligations as strict obligations of conduct, whose focus is on state efforts toward achieving certain results and not on the ultimate result achieved. Overall, the article ends up doing exactly what the commission had feared, namely over codifying the content of primary rules.

II *Pars Construens*: The Event as a Factual Condition of the Breach and the Issue of Causality

I can now put forward the following considerations on the breach of preventive obligations. In light of the history of the codification of Article 14(3), the principle that makes the breach of preventive obligations necessarily contingent upon the occurrence of the event does not appear adequately supported.

First, there is nothing that impedes interpreting obligations to prevent a certain event as pure duties of best effort. On the contrary, in a number of cases, the most logical assertion is that a violation of an obligation to prevent arises the moment the state fails to adopt the required measures. In part, this emerged in the ICJ's reasoning in the Bosnian Genocide case. Notably, in that case, the court drew on Article 14(3) and affirmed that a state can be held responsible for breaching the obligation to prevent genocide only if genocide was actually committed.[86] Yet, the court fell into a contradiction when it subsequently noted:

> [T]his obviously does not mean that the obligation to prevent genocide only comes into being when perpetration of genocide commences: that would be absurd, since the whole point of the obligation is to prevent, or attempt to prevent, the occurrence of an act. In fact, a State's obligation to prevent, and the corresponding duty to act, arises the instance that the State learns of, or should normally have learned of, the existence of serious risk that genocide will be committed.[87]

The court construed the obligation to prevent genocide as a best-effort duty but then clearly frustrated its nature by invoking Article 14(3). Yet, as aptly put it by one author, 'if state responsibility is concerned with

[86] *Genocide* case, para. 431.
[87] Ibid. para. 432.

determining whether state behaviour is "wrong" or "unlawful", it should not matter whether genocide is carried out or not. The wrong here is . . . doing nothing in the face of imminent genocide'.[88] Hence, the occurrence of the event should not be treated as a *sine qua non* condition for breaches of preventive obligations. One fails to see why a state manifestly failing to prevent genocide when there is a serious risk that the latter will commence should not be liable because, for instance, genocide was eventually averted due to the intervention of other states.[89]

Dogmatic considerations aside, the apparent contradiction between the due diligence nature of preventive obligations and Article 14(3) is mitigated by the reality of international practice. By their nature, the content of due diligence obligations is difficult to establish in advance and in the abstract. Due diligence obligations are highly circumstantial and their assessment can hardly be done *a priori*. In the case of many obligations to prevent, it may be necessary to wait until the event has occurred to establish what the duty of due diligence entailed and whether it has been violated.

Furthermore, in international law, obligations to prevent are often conceived in relation to harmful activities of private individuals and third parties. Exercise of due diligence for these obligations usually implies, other than the adoption of the required measures of legislative and administrative character, the exercise of a certain vigilance over the activities of these subjects.[90] Yet, the assessment of a state's lack of vigilance can only take place when the event has occurred and then it must be established whether the state has failed to prevent it. This is what Ago meant when he described the occurrence of the event as a 'catalyst' for wrongfulness to accrue. In his report on obligations to prevent, Ago described the event to be prevented as the 'occasion' for the breach to arise and the element that 'when placed in contact with a given substance [the conduct of the state] provokes a reaction in the latter'.[91] From this

[88] S. Forlati, 'The Legal Obligation to Prevent Genocide: *Bosnia* v. *Serbia* and Beyond' (2011) 31 *Polish Yearbook of International Law* 189, 200.

[89] On the opportunity to interpret the obligation to prevent genocide as a 'classic' due diligence obligation, M. Longobardo, 'L'obbligo di prevenzione del genocidio e la distinzione fra obblighi di condotta e obblighi di risultato' (2019) *Diritti Umani e Diritto Internazionale* (2019) 237.

[90] *Case Concerning Pulp Mills on the River Uruguay (Argentina* v. *Uruguay)* (Merits) [2010] ICJ Rep, para. 197; *Responsibility and Obligations of Sponsoring States*, para. 136. The exercise of vigilance is clearly connected with the exercise of power of the state over the source of risk, see Chapter 3.

[91] Ago, 'Seventh Report', 46. At any rate, in Ago's writing, there is no real contradiction between due diligence obligations and obligations to prevent a given event. For Ago,

perspective, one may argue that, albeit wrongly codified as a legal element for a breach to accrue, the occurrence of the event often constitutes a necessary factual condition for a state's alleged omission to come to light.[92]

A problem may instead arise when the content of obligations to prevent is spelled out in a series of more direct and procedural duties, for example following the intervention of a court or a treaty body. This phenomenon, which is called 'proceduralisation' of due diligence obligations,[93] breaks down the obligation of due diligence by specifying which measures, procedures, and duties a state must fulfil to comply with the due diligence rule. When prevention becomes less circumstantial and is interpreted as imposing specific duties, it is clearly difficult to reconcile the solidification of due diligence into a set of clear and specific measures with the assertion that, unless the event has occurred, the obligation to prevent is not breached.[94]

In light of these considerations, we can now address the problem of causality between a state's failure to prevent and the event to be prevented. In drafting Article 23, Special Rapporteur Ago noted that 'it must be possible to establish the existence of a certain relationship of causality, at least indirect, between the conduct of State organs and the event; the conduct must have made possible the occurrence of an event which *otherwise* would not have occurred'.[95] The commentary to draft Article 23 adopted on the first reading espoused this approach, arguing that breaches of preventive obligations accrue if a state's failure to prevent was a *sine qua non* element of the event.[96] The current version of ARSIWA is silent on the question of causation. But it is logical that if obligations to prevent are best-effort duties and the event must occur for a breach to

obligations of due diligence are indeed either obligations of 'negative' result – that is, obligations that grant freedom in the choice of means to prevent a given event, and, as such, cannot be violated unless the result has not occurred – or obligations to adopt a particular course of conduct – that is, due diligence obligations which 'appear' flexible in nature but which effectively impose the adoption of 'specific means'. See Ago's observation in ILC YB (1978) I meeting 1478th, para. 46, noting: 'there were obligations of due diligence that were obligations of conduct [taken as obligations to adopt a particular course of conduct], and which might therefore be said to have been breached by the mere fact that requisite due diligence had not been exercised'.

92 Interpreting the event as a factual condition, G. Morelli, *Nozioni di Diritto Internazionale* (Padua: CEDAM, 1967), 349.

93 See Chapter 5.

94 Ibid. for a wider discussion on this issue.

95 Ago, 'Seventh Report', 35.

96 Draft Articles adopted on the First Reading, 176.

arise, some causality link must exist between failure to prevent and the event in question.

It is outside the scope of the present analysis to test against practice the validity of the commission's assertion that breaches of preventive obligations imply a *sine qua non* causal link between the event and the state's failure to prevent it. First, problems of causality are treated differently by international courts and tribunals depending on the primary rule in question and the legal regime to which the rule belongs.[97] Furthermore, when it comes to assessing breaches of preventive obligations, courts and tribunals often avoid explicit reference to causation and tend to resort to simplified tests that incorporate elements of causation along with other concepts. In relation to due diligence obligations, issues of causality are indeed often eluded by resorting to the test of foreseeability. Accordingly, the responsibility of a state for failure to act with due diligence is engaged if it is established that the event was within the foreseeable risk connected to the primary rule.[98] Additionally, the question of causality in international law is complicated by the fact that the very notion of cause in law depends largely on the legal tradition to which a judge belongs. While common law systems tend to treat legal causation from a more empirical perspective and largely as a question of policy,[99] civil law traditions have long construed causation in the law through conceptual theories and against the backdrop of systematic philosophy.[100] Hence, it is likely that judges adjudicating in international fora will be confronted with a diversity of approaches, which may eventually contribute to fragmentation in the criteria and principles applied to cases.

In any case, from a theoretical perspective, recourse to a 'but-for test' in the context of breaches of preventive obligations is quite problematic. Under the but-for test, a state does not breach its preventive obligation unless it is established that, had the state adopted the required due

[97] I. Plakokefalos, 'Causation in the Law of State Responsibility and the Problem of Overdetermination: In Search of Clarity' (2015) 26 EJIL 471.

[98] For example *F. G.* v. *Sweden* App (Judgment) [2016] App no 43611/11 para. 115; *Paposhvili* v. *Belgium* (Judgment) [2016] App no 41738/10 para 187; *Kindler* v. *Canada*, Human Rights Committee (1993) UN Doc CCPR/C/48/D/470/1991 para 13.2; *Wippermann case*, in J. B. Moore, *History and Digest of the International Arbitrations to which the United States Has Been a Party* (Washington: US Government Printing, 1943), vol. 3, 3041.

[99] Generally H. L. A. Hart, T. Honoré, *Causation in the Law* (Oxford: Oxford University Press, 1959); M. S. Moore, *Causation and Responsibility: An Essay in Law, Morals and Metaphysics* (Oxford: Oxford University Press, 2009).

[100] F. Carnelutti, *Teoria generale del diritto* (Milan: Edizioni Scientifiche, 1999).

diligence, the event would not have occurred. Yet, in cases of omission, causality between state conduct and the harmful event is always normative and hypothetical. When state responsibility is assessed in connection with an obligation to prevent a given event, the 'cause in fact' of the event is not a state's omission, but the action of another subject made possible by the state's failure to prevent. This is particularly true for preventive obligations conceived vis-à-vis the potentially harmful activity of third parties. Hence, claims of responsibility for failure to prevent usually involve a plurality of causes. The question then is not really whether without the state's omission the event would have not occurred. Rather, the issue is which causal contribution, if any, a state's failure to act provided to the occurrence of the event.

The 2007 Bosnian Genocide case is again illustrative of the struggle faced by international practice in dealing with causation in relation to breaches of preventive obligations. In broaching the question of Serbia's responsibility for failure to prevent genocide, the court avoided any reference to causality between the occurrence of genocide and Serbia's failure to act with due diligence to prevent it. The court noted that Serbia had the capacity to influence persons and entities carrying out genocide and that it had failed to intervene even though the genocide in Srebrenica was imminent.[101] Instead, at the reparation stage, the court had to ascertain whether and to what extent the injury caused by genocide was the consequence of Serbia's wrongful conduct. The court expressly addressed the problem of causality as follows:

> [The] question is whether there is a sufficiently direct and certain causal nexus between the wrongful act, the Respondent's breach of the obligation to prevent genocide, and the injury suffered by the Applicant ... Such a nexus could be considered established only if the Court were able to conclude from the case as a whole and with a sufficient degree of certainty that the genocide at Srebrenica would in fact have been averted if the Respondent had acted in compliance with its legal obligations. However, the Court clearly cannot do so ... [It] has not been shown that, in the specific context of these events, those means [at Serbia's disposal] would have sufficed to achieve the result which the Respondent should have sought.[102]

The court applied a strict but-for test to exclude a causal relationship between Serbia's omission and the commission of genocide. But it is clear that there is a difference between saying that 'had Serbia acted with due

[101] *Genocide* case, para. 436.
[102] Ibid. 462.

diligence, genocide would have been averted' or saying that 'had Serbia acted with due diligence, genocide would have occurred differently'. In the first case, we are treating Serbia's conduct as the exclusive cause of the event, while in the second we are conceding that multiple causes may have played a role but that Serbia's conduct may have also contributed to the occurrence of the event. The court's assertion appears slightly too categorical when confronted with the argument made by the court in relation to the breach of the obligation to prevent genocide. The notion of Serbia's capacity to influence is indeed a reminder of the concept of causality.[103] Albeit not explicitly, by stating that Serbia had 'undeniable' influence and 'power to prevent' the tragic events from taking shape,[104] the court de facto recognised a causal link between Serbia and genocide: the latter may have occurred in any case, but by acting diligently Serbia may have been able to mitigate its effects.[105]

4.1.4 The Distinction between Due Diligence Obligations and Complicity

It becomes necessary in some cases to distinguish conduct of a state in violation of a due diligence obligation from conduct that constitutes an act of complicity pursuant to Article 16 of ARSIWA or Article 58 of the Draft Articles on the Responsibility of International Organizations (ARIO). The issue arises only when a harmful act has been committed by a state or an international organisation and another state was under a duty to exercise due diligence to prevent it. In these circumstances, when the harmful act constitutes an international wrongful act, it may be queried whether the state's failure to exercise due diligence facilitated its commission to the point of making the state responsible for aid or assistance. The question is instead irrelevant when the state is under a due diligence obligation but the act injuring the interest protected by a primary rule and facilitated by a state's failure to act is carried out by a private subject. Unless special rules provide for these situations,[106]

[103] Conceptualising causation as linked to power and influence R. A. Dahl, 'The Concept of Power' (1957) 2 *Behavioral Science* 201.

[104] *Genocide* case, para. 438.

[105] As aptly noted by A. Gattini, 'Breach of the Obligation to Prevent and Reparation Thereof in the ICJ's Genocide Judgement' (2007) 18 EJIL 695, 710, the ICJ confused the notion of concurrent causes with that of exclusive cause.

[106] For instance Article III(e) of the Convention on the Prevention and Punishment of the Crime of Genocide (adopted 9 December 1948, entered into force 12 January 1951) 78 UNTS 277.

there is no general regime of a state's complicity into acts carried out by subjects different from states and international organisations.

Distinguishing between a state's responsibility for violation of a due diligence obligation and responsibility for complicity rests on a central premise, namely that complicity can be accomplished through omissions. In the 2007 Bosnian Genocide case, the ICJ rejected this possibility. Ruling on the scope of a state's responsibility for complicity in genocide, the court expressly referred to Article 16 of ARSIWA and observed:

> [Complicity] always requires that some positive action has been taken to furnish aid or assistance to the perpetrators of genocide, while a violation of the obligation to prevent results from the mere failure to adopt and implement suitable measures to prevent genocide from being committed. In other words, while complicity results from commission, violation of the obligation to prevent results from omission . . . .[107]

In the court's reasoning, complicity puts a state under a negative obligation – to refrain from actions that would make the state complicit in the wrongful act – whereas the duty to prevent places states under a positive obligation to ensure that something does not occur. Although criticised,[108] this position has found further support from scholars who question the usefulness of complicity as a form of derivative responsibility.[109] For them, the establishment of complicity pursuant to Article 16 is an operation '*théoriquement problématique*', which is avoided in practice.[110] Specifically, not only does complicity imply 'action' as opposed to the violation of a due diligence obligation, which implies 'omission', but in most cases, responsibility for complicity is overshadowed by responsibility for the failure of due diligence, since the latter is much more practical to establish both in terms of procedure and criteria to be met.

Despite the authoritativeness of these opinions,[111] the majority of scholarship does not question the applicability of Article 16 of ARSIWA and Article 58 of ARIO to omissions.[112] Furthermore, neither

[107] *Genocide* case, para. 432.

[108] V. Lowe, 'Responsibility for the Conduct of other States' (2002) 101 *Japanese Journal of International Law and Diplomacy* 1, 6; Gattini, 'Breach of the Obligation to Prevent', 703; P. Palchetti, 'State Responsibility for Complicity in Genocide', in P. Gaeta, *The UN Genocide Convention* (Oxford: Oxford University Press, 2009), 385.

[109] O. Corten, 'La "complicité" dans le droit de la responsabilité internationale: un concept inutile?' (2011) 57 AFDI 57.

[110] Ibid. 72–83.

[111] See also Crawford, *State Responsibility*, 403.

[112] H. P. Aust, *Complicity in the Law of State Responsibility* (Cambridge: Cambridge University Press, 2011), 227–8; M. Jackson, *Complicity in International Law* (Oxford: Oxford

the commentary to these provisions nor the history of the work of the ILC seem to exclude omissions from conduct giving rise to cases of aid or assistance in the commission of a wrongful act.[113] Hence, in the absence of indications to the contrary, one should apply the general rule recognising that wrongful conduct can consist of actions or omissions.

The superimposition of responsibility for violation of due diligence upon responsibility for complicity builds on the following reasons. First, complicity through omission can only accrue if the aiding or assisting state was originally bound by a primary rule of a positive nature. As stated at the outset, an omission is such only if there was a duty to act upon the subject who disregarded it. Complicity through omission cannot arise out of 'lawful inaction' by a state, as this would turn Articles 16 and 58 into catalysts for the creation of positive primary rules.[114] This means that in complicity through omission, the material element – conduct of aiding or assisting capable of generating responsibility for complicity – always corresponds to the violation of a positive rule, like a due diligence obligation. Typical examples are states failing to control their territory and allowing another state to commit an international wrongful act, such as temporary incursions into a third state, extra-judicial killings, or acts of aggression into a third state.[115]

Second, it is not possible to conceptually demarcate complicity through omission from responsibility for due diligence based on the subjective element of complicity. Articles 16 and 58 provide as conditions for complicity that the state that aids or assists does so 'with knowledge of the circumstances of the international wrongful act'. During the ILC work on ARSIWA, Special Rapporteur Ago argued that complicity necessarily presupposes 'intention' by the state to collaborate with the commission of the wrongful act.[116] The commentary to Article 16 partly retains this solution: albeit with a slight contradiction, the commentary first states that a state must be aware of the circumstances of the wrongful act and then affirms that the state is not responsible unless it '*intended* to facilitate the commission of the international wrongful act'.[117] In the Bosnian Genocide case, the ICJ drew

University Press, 2015), 157; V. Lanovoy, *Complicity and Its Limits in the Law of International Responsibility* (London: Hart Publishing, 2016), 184–5; G. Puma, *Complicitá di Stati nell'Illecito Internazionale* (Turin: Giappichelli, 2018), 74–84.

113 See ARSIWA Commentary to Article 16.

114 See Puma, *Complicità*, fn. 104.

115 For a review of practice Lanovoy, *Complicity*, 175–6.

116 Ago, 'Seventh Report', 56.

117 ARSIWA Commentary to Article 16, para. 5 (emphasis added).

a distinction between the subjective element of complicity and the 'subjective' condition for the breach of the obligation to prevent genocide. The court contended that while the violation of the obligation to prevent genocide requires that the state is aware or ought to be aware of the risk of genocide, complicity requires that state support for the commission of genocide is given with 'full knowledge of the facts'.[118] Yet, an interpretation based on the ordinary meaning of the texts of Articles 16 and 58 and a review of international practice does not support the idea that complicity necessarily requires a subjective element of stronger intensity than responsibility for failure of due diligence. Instances of complicity have often been invoked by raising the same subjective standard of due diligence, namely by showing that the aiding or assisting state was aware of the circumstances, or that the state had knowledge of the risk of the international wrongful act being committed by another state.[119]

Finally, it seems uneven to draw the line between complicity and responsibility for failure of due diligence based on the fact that aid or assistance must have facilitated the commission of the international wrongful act.[120] Such an approach would imply a distinction being made on the causal link between a state's material conduct and the international wrongful act committed by the third state or the international organisation. However, this seems both theoretically unsound and impractical. It is theoretically unsound because it was shown above that causality between state conduct and a harmful event materially committed by a third party is often a (factual) condition for the breach of due diligence obligations. Thus, the ascertaining of state responsibility may demand causality both for assessing complicity and for establishing a breach of a due diligence obligation. What is more, and from a practical standpoint, it appears that the type of causality sufficient to establish complicity resembles, to a great extent, the causal connection required for determining a state's failure of due diligence.[121] Both responsibility for failure of due diligence and

118 *Genocide* case, para. 432.

119 *El-Masri* v. *The Former Yugoslav Republic of Macedonia* (Judgment) (GC) [2012] App no 39630/09 25; *Al Nashiri* v. *Poland* and *Husayn (Abu Zubaydad)* v. *Poland* (Judgment) [2014] App no 28761/11 para. 442; see also, albeit with reference to aid or assistance of international organisations 'Thirtieth Report of the Secretary General on the United Nations Organization Mission in the Democratic Republic of the Congo', 2009, UN Doc. S/2009/623 para. 12. For a review of practice and its interpretation Lanovoy, *Complicity*, 222–40.

120 ARSIWA Commentary to Article 16 para. 3.

121 On how to construe causality in relation to aid or assistance Aust, *Complicity*, 210–19, 225; Puma, *Complicità*, 69–73.

responsibility for complicity require ascertaining the causal contribution of a state's omissive conduct to the event or the principal international wrongful act.

Despite these considerations, there is still room for distinguishing responsibility for the violation of a due diligence obligation from responsibility through complicity. To mark the distinction, some scholars have focused on the structural differences between due diligence and complicity. For example, it has been argued that due diligence obligations are more circumstantial as opposed to complicity, which is integrated by any state conduct that satisfies the conditions required by Articles 16 of ARSIWA and 58 of ARIO.[122] Furthermore, due diligence obligations are positive obligations of conduct, whereas Articles 16 and 58 impose upon states a negative obligation of result (to refrain from being complicit in the commission of a wrongful act).[123] Another structural difference rests in the fact that the evaluation of due diligence obligations focuses on a state's power over the source of risk, which typically consists of territorial control, or control over individuals and activities materialising risks. On the contrary, complicity is not contingent upon the assessment of state control over the state or the international organisation responsible for the main wrongful act.[124]

While there is merit in these arguments, in this author's view the distinction lies not so much in the nature of the obligations to exercise due diligence and to refrain from being complicit in a wrongful act. After all, as explained above, complicity through omission must be premised upon the violation of a positive duty. When this duty is a due diligence one, focusing on the different nature of the obligations behind the two notions does not really help determine whether the relevant situation is one of responsibility for complicity or responsibility for a failure of due diligence.

Instead, the difference can be grasped once it is recognised that complicity carries greater 'social disvalue' than responsibility for the violation of a due diligence obligation.[125] This greater social disvalue is to a certain extent linked to the shift in the law of international responsibility from an inter-state approach to a more communitarian and 'social' system in which the conceptualisation of wrongfulness is based on the breach and not the injury.[126] Drawing again on the Bosnian Genocide

122 Lanovoy, *Complicity*, 214.
123 Ibid. 214–16.
124 Puma, *Complicità*, 87.
125 Putting emphasis on this distinction Puma, *Complicità*, 96, 100.
126 A. Pellet, 'Remarques sur une révolution inachevée, le projet d'articles de la Commission du Droit International sur la responsabilité des Etats' (1996) AFDI 7, 11–12.

case, it seems that at the heart of the court's decision to find Serbia responsible for the obligation to prevent genocide, there were not only considerations on the structural differences of conduct integrating complicity. The impression is that the ICJ implicitly acknowledged that failing to prevent does not carry the same weight as being complicit in the act.[127] This impression also emerges from the reading of the ILC work on state responsibility, where it is affirmed on several occasions that complicitly of a territorial state in a wrongful act of another state entails something more than *mere* failure in the duty to protect or prevent.[128] In sum, complicitly would entail a stronger and intensified degree of a state's participation in the international wrongful act, while responsibility for due diligence would not. From this perspective, the choice between accusing a state of complicity or accusing it of failure to exercise due diligence would not really rest on structural discrepancies between these two forms of responsibility. The choice would be primarily dictated by the more or less 'social disvalue' that a court or the accusing state wishes to attach to the conduct of the responsible state.[129]

4.2 Due Diligence Obligations and Circumstances Precluding Wrongfulness

While consent (Article 20), self-defence (Article 21), countermeasures (Article 22), and necessity (Article 25) do not raise particular issues as justifications of conduct contrary to a due diligence obligation, questions arise as to the relationship between due diligence, force majeure (Article 23), and distress (Article 24).

Article 23 of ARSIWA provides that the wrongfulness of a state's act not in conformity with one of its international obligations is precluded if the act is due to force majeure. Force majeure is defined as an irresistible force or an unforeseeable event beyond the control of the state, making it materially impossible for the state to fulfil its obligation in the circumstances of the case. According to Article 23, force majeure does not apply if: (i) it is due, alone or in combination with other factors, to the conduct

[127] *Bosnian Genocide* case, para. 432 where complicity is opposed to 'mere' failure to prevent.

[128] Ago, 'Seventh Report', 50–1.

[129] While I think that, at least from a dogmatic perspective, the greater 'social disvalue' with which complicity is imbued is what primarily distinguishes complicity through omission from failure to exercise due diligence, I do acknowledge that, in the end, the distinction is blurred and much 'relative' in practice.

of the state invoking it; or (ii) the state has assumed the risk of the situation occurring.

The commentary explains that irresistible forces or unforeseeable events giving rise to a situation of force majeure can be natural or physical events, human interventions, or a combination of the two, which are beyond the control of the state.[130] These external events must have 'effectively compelled'[131] the state to act in a manner incompatible with its obligation, thus giving rise to a situation of 'material impossibility' of performance. Essentially, the force must be irresistible so that 'the State concerned has no real possibility of escaping its effects'. Situations in which the performance of an obligation has become only more difficult do not fall within the plea.[132]

To clarify when a state is 'in effect compelled to act in a manner not in conformity with its international obligation,' the commentary states that 'the conduct of the State which would be otherwise internationally wrongful is *involuntary* or, at least, *involves no element of free choice*'.[133] This explanation, which is mainly due to Special Rapporteur Crawford,[134] finds root in the theory of free will applied to international responsibility, according to which responsibility is premised on the existence of free will of the state or its voluntary act.[135] Accordingly, the conduct of a state is involuntary when the state has no power to act or capacity to choose its conduct due to the circumstances.[136] If a vessel is dragged by an irresistible current into prohibited foreign waters, the captain of the vessel has no power to act against this force and to prevent the vessel from entering such waters. Similarly, if a state has to return an object to another state but that object is unexpectedly destroyed by fire,

130 ARSIWA Commentary to Article 23, para. 3.

131 Ibid. para. 2.

132 Ibid. paras. 2–3.

133 Ibid. para. 1. Note that the original expression used by Ago was conduct 'involuntary or at least, unintentional', although the difference between the two concept is not clearly explained, Ago, 'Eighth Report on State Responsibility' (1979) ILC YB II/1 para. 103 (emphasis added).

134 Crawford eliminated any reference to 'fault' which was instead crippling in Ago's conceptualisation of force majeure, Ago, 'Eighth Report' paras. 123, 145; Crawford, 'Second Report', para. 262; the link between fault and force majeure was also underlined by Austria in the comments submitted by Governments, ILC YB (1980) II/1 89–90.

135 Ago, 'Third Report on State Responsibility' (1971) ILC YB II/1 para. 51; Crawford, *Brownlie's Principles of Public International Law* (Oxford: Oxford University Press, 2012), 556.

136 F. Paddeu, *Justification and Excuses in International Law: Concept and Theory of General Defences* (Cambridge: Cambridge University Press, 2018), 325–8.

the state has no capacity to choose and no available means to fulfil its obligation. This complete absence of power to act or capacity to choose in relation to one's conduct is what makes it 'materially impossible' for the state to comply with its obligation.

Recall from Chapter 3 that the 'possibility to act' is what distinguishes due diligence obligations from other types of international obligations, like obligations of result. Obligations of result do not integrate impossibility of performance into their fabric, insofar as their breach ensues simply from verifying that the state has failed to achieve the result required by the obligation. A state is thus responsible for violating an obligation of result as soon as the result is not attained, *unless* a secondary rule such as force majeure applies to the case and precludes such responsibility from arising. To the contrary, due diligence obligations are postulated around possibility and on at least two conditions. First, the state must have power over the source of risk, that is, have the capacity to affect the situation linked to the due diligence rule. Second, the state must have knowledge or constructive knowledge of the risk linked to due diligence.

Power over the source of risk and knowledge of the risk determine the sphere of voluntariness and freedom of choice with which a state must be equipped in order to act diligently. They also *tailor* the scope of a duty to act with due diligence, inasmuch as the level of diligence expected of a state by its obligation cannot exceed what was beyond the state's knowledge and capacity to affect. If the circumstances of the case made it impossible for a state to know about the risk or to act upon it the way that would normally be expected – for example, because an event occurred that was beyond a state's power to control – the degree of diligence is in fact automatically reduced and state conduct is not deemed incompatible with the primary obligation. Thus, if the material circumstances affect a state's possibility of acting in accordance with its due diligence obligation, there is no need to resort to any secondary rule like force majeure to exclude responsibility: the scope and content of the obligation in question will be curtailed and the state will have complied with its duty as long as the degree of diligence displayed matched what the state was able to exercise.[137]

[137] One may point out that the distinction between a rule precluding a breach and another (secondary) that precludes wrongfulness is only theoretical and it has no practical implications, in this regard Gaja, 'Primary and Secondary Rules', 985–8; yet, the distinction may have a bearing in light of the classification of a circumstance precluding

While this approach to force majeure and due diligence is top-down and builds mostly on the rationale of both concepts, support for this solution is found in international practice and in the history of the codification of ARSIWA. Starting from the work of the ILC, it was Special Rapporteur Ago who introduced the concept of circumstances precluding wrongfulness and the notion of force majeure. In his eighth report on state responsibility, Ago distinguished between force majeure and a fortuitous event, which has now been absorbed into Article 23 and is not treated as a separate defence. Ago understood force majeure and fortuitous events as defences also applicable to a typical category of due diligence obligations, namely obligations to prevent.[138] In support of this view, he referred to a number of arbitral cases, mostly from the late nineteenth century, which I will address shortly. In relation to force majeure, the report argued that a state is not responsible for a violation of an obligation to prevent if the circumstances – like loss of territorial control as a result of an insurrection – made it absolutely impossible for the state to fulfil prevention.[139] With regard to fortuitous events, they were conceptualised as supervenient circumstances making it impossible for the state to know that its conduct is not in conformity with its own obligation.[140] Ago explained that a fortuitous event may also preclude the wrongfulness of state conduct not in conformity with an obligation to prevent a harmful event. What is fortuitous in these cases may be the occurrence of the event itself: its unexpected and unforeseeable nature would make it impossible 'for the State organs to realise that their conduct might have been such as not to have the effect of preventing the event as the obligation required'.[141]

Despite conceiving force majeure and fortuitous events as defences applicable also to preventive obligations, Ago argued in a footnote:

> By this, we do not of course mean to limit the cases in which a State may not be accused of culpable negligence and held internationally responsible for not having prevented the occurrence of an event solely to those in which the event in question, because of its unexpected and unforeseeable nature, assume the appearance of a genuinely fortuitous event. *There may be other convincing reasons for excluding the presence of such negligence,*

wrongfulness as a justification or an excuse, see generally Paddeu, *Justification and Excuses*, 63–97.

138 Ago, 'Eighth Report', paras. 121–2, 145–52.

139 Ibid. paras. 121–3.

140 Ibid. para. 152.

141 Ibid. para. 145.

> *taking into account as well that the degree of diligence required for the purpose of prevention varies according to the content of the obligation and the specific features of each particular case.*[142]

This passage acknowledges the inextricable link between force majeure and due diligence and suggests that Ago was aware of the *sui generis* nature of these obligations in relation to this defence.

Furthermore, the idea that the question of force majeure and the level of due diligence required by a primary rule could overlap did not pass undetected before states and the ILC. During the debates within the ILC on the draft article on force majeure provisionally adopted by Ago, the issue was broached by one member of the commission, Willem Riphagen. For Riphagen, Ago had defined force majeure and fortuitous cases by a high level of abstraction, irrespective of the content of the obligation in question. Although this abstraction was justified in light of the draft articles' focus on secondary rules, Riphagen warned that both force majeure and fortuitous cases could require adaptation under certain primary rules.[143] Accordingly, the way Ago had developed these defences made it difficult to distinguish between 'fortuitous event as a circumstance precluding wrongfulness and determination of the degree of diligence required, which was a matter of the content of the obligation'.[144] In a similar fashion, in the observations made by governments in relation to the articles adopted on the first reading, Austria declared that draft Article 31 had 'far-reaching consequences' for the notion of due diligence.[145] Hence, efforts to avoid questions of primary rules coupled with a lack of adequate conceptualisation of due diligence during the ILC's work influenced the understanding of the relationship between due diligence and force majeure.

As for international practice, it is difficult to draw firm conclusions from the practice up to 1945. Most cases regarding due diligence obligations up to this point regarded the protection of foreigners and their property and the security of other states against acts of rebels or insurgents. In some cases, it appears that arbitral tribunals framed situations of impossibility for a state to fulfil its due diligence obligations as pleas of force majeure.[146] In other cases, supervenient events were addressed by

[142] Ibid. fn. 290 at 64 (emphasis added).

[143] ILC YB (1979) I meeting 1571st paras. 1–4.

[144] Ibid.

[145] Comments and observations received by Governments, A/CN.4/488 and Add. 1–3 133.

[146] *St Albans Raid* case (1878) in Moore, *History and Digest*, vol. 1, 4054; *Cresceri Case (Italy* v. *Peru)* (1901) 15 RIAA 451–2; *Sambiaggio (Italy* v. *Venezuela)* (1903) 10 RIAA 507, 509, 511.

tribunals as events outside the scope of a state's duty to act with due diligence.[147]

Contemporary practice on due diligence obligations seems to treat material impossibility of performance not as a secondary rule excluding the breach of the obligation. This is evident particularly in relation to human rights practice and practice on international investment. As for the former, international human rights courts and monitoring bodies normally understand the scope of states' human rights due diligence obligations as not going beyond states' capacity to act[148] and what was foreseeable under the circumstances.[149] The ECtHR, for instance, regularly reminds states that positive obligations to take measures to protect individuals from violations of human rights by other individuals or third parties must be interpreted 'in a way which does not impose an impossible or disproportionate burden on the authorities, bearing in mind the difficulties involved in policing modern societies, the unpredictability of human conduct and the operational choices which must be made in terms of priorities and resources'.[150] Thus, violations of human rights that were not within a state's power to prevent or were unforeseeable and accidental are not regarded as conditions triggering the application of a secondary rule of force majeure – they are conditions that prevent the breach of the state's due diligence obligation.

The same emerges in relation to the practice of investment tribunals. In cases concerning the duty to protect foreign investments from acts of civil strife, acts of revolutionary movements, or riots, which were outside a state's power to prevent or foresee, the question addressed by arbitrators is whether the scope of the obligation to guarantee full protection and security extends to these acts and not whether a plea of force majeure applies to the case.[151] Accordingly, it has been argued that circumstances

[147] *Prats* case in Moore, *History and Digest*, vol. 3, 2893–5; *Wipperman* case, 3040–3; *Brissot* case (1898) in Moore, *History and Digest*, vol. 3, 1949; for a review of practice ILC YB (1978) II/2 152–63.

[148] As argued in Chapter 3, for some human rights obligations 'capacity to act' is evaluated also by taking into account the level of economic, technological, and financial resources at a state's disposal. In relation to other obligations however, resource capability is irrelevant and it is expected that the state will have the means to fulfil at least part of the substance of its duty.

[149] *Catan and others* v. *Moldova and Russia* (Judgment) [2012] App no 43370/04, 8252/05, 18454/06 paras. 145–8; *Sargsyan* v. *Azerbaijan* (Judgment) [2015] App no 40167/06 paras. 124–31, 146, albeit there is certain confusion in this case between the concept of jurisdiction and that of the scope of Azerbaijan's positive obligations.

[150] *Mikayil Mammadov* v. *Azerbajan* (Judgment) [2009] App no 4762/05 paras. 99, 111–12.

[151] *Técnicas Medioambientales Tecmed, S.A.* v. *United Mexican States*, ICSID Case No. ARB(AF)/00/2 para. 176–7; *Karmer Marble* v. *Georgia*, ICSID Case No. ARB/08/19

in which a state was powerless in the face of sudden social unrest preclude a state from failing to comply with due diligence in the guarantee of full protection and security.[152]

Finally, considerations similar to the above apply to distress. Article 24 of ARSIWA provides that the wrongfulness of an act not in conformity with an international obligation is precluded 'if the author of the act has *no other reasonable way*, in a situation of distress, of saving the author's life or the lives of other persons entrusted to the author's care'. The article also specifies that distress does not apply if two conditions are cumulatively met, namely that the situation of distress is not due to the conduct of the state invoking it and that the act in question does not create a comparable or greater peril.

Situations of distress differs from situations of force majeure insofar as a state's impossibility of performance of its obligation is relative and not absolute.[153] The conduct of the state is in fact neither involuntary nor unintentional, but is dictated by the situations of peril in which the state finds itself.[154] Furthermore, distress can only be invoked when the agent acting on a state's behalf contravenes one of the state's international obligations in order to save their life or the life of other individuals under their care from an immediate danger, and provided that this danger outweighs the other interests at stake in the circumstances.[155] The relative impossibility of distress is thus to be distinguished from the plea of necessity, in which a state's choice is between complying with its obligation or saving one of its essential interests.

The connection between distress and a due diligence obligation lies in the concept of reasonableness. As seen in Chapter 3, due diligence obligations are typically interpreted in light of this overarching parameter. Hence, even when a state is required to adopt 'all measures at its disposal', or to do 'all that is possible' to achieve a given result, possibility is judged against what was reasonable in the circumstances of the case. If reasonableness is the limit of due diligence obligations, whatever is deemed unreasonable under the circumstances is not covered by due diligence. This means that if a state bound by a due diligence obligation is prevented from acting with the diligence normally required under the

para. 291; *Parkerings-Compagniet AS* v. *Republic of Lithuania*, ICSID Case No. ARB/05/08 paras. 356–7.

152 *Pantechniki* v. *The Republic of Albania*, ICSID Case No. ARB/07/21 paras. 75–84.

153 Ago, 'Eighth Report', para. 106.

154 ARSIWA Commentary to Article 24, para. 1.

155 Ibid. para. 6.

circumstances because the life of the relevant state's agent was in immediate danger and the interest protected by the obligation did not outweigh such danger, state conduct will not be deemed unreasonable. Like in the previous case, there is no need to resort to a secondary rule precluding wrongfulness. A situation of distress applied to due diligence obligations is a condition for the evaluation of the degree of diligence expected by the state under the circumstances.

4.3 The Content of Responsibility for Violation of Due Diligence Obligations

The breach of a due diligence obligation entails all the applicable consequences provided by Part II of ARSIWA. However, there is at least one aspect of the content of the responsibility for the violation of a due diligence obligation that deserves separate analysis. It relates to the question of reparations for failing to exercise the diligence required by the primary rule and, in particular, on aspects of the causal link.

Article 31 of ARSIWA provides that the responsible state is under a duty to make full reparation for any injury caused by the international wrongful act and that injury includes any damage, moral and material, caused by the state's wrongful act. The commentary clarifies that material and moral damages must be broadly understood, with the only exclusion being abstract concerns or general interests of the state affected by the breach.[156] Generally, 'material' damages are damages to property and other interests of the state and its nationals that are assessable in financial terms, while 'moral' damages include individual pain and suffering, loss of loved ones, or personal affronts to one's private life. The question of whether the injury will effectively include moral and material damage is determined by the primary rule, since some international wrongful acts may only injure a state's non-material interests and limit reparations to this aspect.[157]

Article 31 specifies that there must be a causal link between the international wrongful act and the injury. According to the commentary, reparations cover only an injury 'resulting from and ascribable to the wrongful act, rather than any and all consequences flowing from [it]'.[158] The commentary explains that causality between the injury and the

156 Ibid. para. 5
157 Ibid.
158 Ibid. para. 9.

wrongful act is legal causality and not a historical process. Hence, although the wrongful act must be a cause in fact of the injury, legal considerations may play a role and exclude from reparations elements of the injury deemed 'too remote', 'unforeseeable', or not sufficiently 'proximate' to the wrongful act.[159]

In relation to due diligence obligations, reparations are required for any injury that 'results from and is ascribable' to a state's failure to adopt the measures of due diligence set by the primary rule. In many circumstances, injuries consist of harmful events and reparation requires a causal link between these events and the state's failure to prevent or protect from them. In other cases, such as when the due diligence obligation is devised to ensure a particular goal, injuries may arise out of the state of affairs created by the non-fulfilment of said goal; a causal connection will therefore be required between the failure to act and the state of affairs affecting the rights and interests of the injured state or party. To be sure, causality at this point is not required to verify the breach of a due diligence obligation but to ascertain the extent to which the state's wrongful omission has contributed to the injury.[160]

One question that arises is how to construe the causal link between a state's failure to act with due diligence and the resulted injury. Specifically, the question arises as to whether the fact that a state's wrongful omission is typically a 'concomitant cause' of the injury should affect the amount of reparations due. By 'concomitant cause', one intends a cause that plays a decisive yet not exclusive role in generating damage. Since the rationale of a plethora of due diligence obligations is to require action vis-à-vis the 'danger' posed by third parties' activities, injuries stemming from the breach of these obligations are usually the result of activities of third parties combined with the state's negligence. Should the responsible state in these cases provide full reparations, or should reparations be reduced in light of the state's partial contribution to the injury?

The short answer based on ARSIWA is that wrongful failure to act with due diligence compels the state to provide full reparation of the injury regardless of 'concomitant' causes. This solution is regarded by the commentary as the most in line with international practice, and particularly with obligations that require states to exercise due diligence vis-à-vis

[159] Ibid. para. 10.

[160] There seems to be a certain confusion in the ARSIWA Commentary however between this distinction, see commentary to Article 31 para. 6.

private individuals.[161] Concomitant causes must be considered only when the injury is the result of a state's wrongful conduct combined with a wilful or negligent action or an omission by the injured state.[162] In these circumstances, considerations of equity and fairness require limiting reparations to what was effectively caused by the responsible state.[163]

The solution adopted by ARSIWA is the most practical and avoids complex causal issues. However, it has been critically revisited both by more recent international practice and by a doctrine that has tested its appropriateness in light of situations of multiple or 'shared' responsibilities. On the one hand, specifically with reference to due diligence obligations, international practice post-2001 does not necessarily follows ARSIWA's approach.[164] The irrelevance of concomitant causes in the final version of ARSIWA was due to Special Rapporteur Crawford. His most convincing argument built on reference to a number of international decisions, including the Corfu Channel and the United States Diplomatic and Consular Staff in Teheran decisions, in which reparations were awarded by the ICJ for the entire injury, irrespective of third parties' actions.[165] And yet, in the Armed Activities in the Territory of the Congo, the ICJ hinted that compensation may require adjustment when

[161] *Alabama* case in Moore, *History and Digest*, vol. 29, 125–34; *Teheran Hostage* case, 45; *Corfu Channel Case (UK* v. *Albania)* (Merits) [1949] ICJ Rep 23.

[162] ARSIWA Article 39.

[163] Crawford, *State Responsibility*, 500–1; contrary Stern, 'The Obligation to Make Reparation', in Crawford, Pellet, Olleson, *The Law of International Responsibility*, 563.

[164] ARSIWA Commentary to Article 31 para 12. Besides the examples taken from the practice of the ICJ, some considerations can be made also in relation to the practice of the European Court of Human Rights. It is correct to state that rules of reparation in the practice of the European court in principle do not fall under Article 31, since rules of reparation in ARSIWA regard only situations in which the injury has been caused to (an) other state(s), as set by Article 33. However, the practice of Article 41 of the European Convention on Human Rights (adopted 4 November 1950, entered into force 3 September 1953) 213 UNTS 221, presents elements of analogy with rules of ARSIWA, see for instance *Cyprus* v. *Turkey* (Judgment) [2014] App no 25781/94 para. 46 quoting the ICJ's *Guinea* v. *Democratic Republic of the Congo* case [2012] ICJ Rep 344. With regard to the ECtHR's decisions that construe reparation for a state's failure to act according to the contribution of the state to the injury see for instance *E. and Others* v. *United Kingdom* (Judgment) [2002] App no 33218/96 para. 128. But see *Responsibility and Obligations of Sponsoring States*, paras. 195, 201–2, 205.

[165] Crawford, 'Second Report', 34. The other arguments proposed by Crawford built on comparisons with national law and on the fact that concurrent causes were not included in the text of the draft articles. Jacob describes the practice of full reparation in relation to due diligence obligations as a form of '*elargissement*' of responsibility, see D. Jacob, 'Le contenu de la responsabilité de l'Etat négligent', in Cassella, *Le standard de due diligence*, 283–6.

it is sought in relation to a state's failure to act. The court appeared to suggest that a state's responsibility for removing property from the premises of a foreign diplomatic mission entails different consequences at the reparation stage with respect to responsibility for failing to prevent removal by a third party.[166]

In the Bosnian Genocide case, the court was clearly confronted with the shortcomings of an approach to reparations that is insensitive to concomitant causes. In this case, the ICJ dealt with causality between Serbia's conduct and the commission of genocide both in relation to the breach of Serbia's obligation to prevent genocide, and in relation to the amount due in reparations. As for the breach of the obligation to prevent genocide, the court implicitly found a connection between Serbia's failure to act with due diligence and the genocide in Srebrenica in the state's capacity to influence the conduct of the militia carrying out acts of genocide.[167] When charged with the question of reparations, however, the court faced a crossroads – either acknowledging causality between Serbia's omission and genocide and consequently affording reparations to Bosnia for the integral damage caused by genocide in Srebrenica, or mitigating the consequences of Serbia's responsibility by denying causality between its failure to prevent and the commission of genocide. The court famously opted for the second alternative and argued that it could not be established with certainty that the genocide in Srebrenica would have taken place even if Serbia had attempted to prevent it by employing all means at its disposal.[168] On the one hand, the decision was rightly criticised for applying the strict *sine qua non* test and failing to recognise that Serbia's omission was one of the causes leading to the genocide.[169] At the same time, had the court established causality, a principled approach to ARSIWA would have implied making Serbia liable for the integral damage and disregarding the issue of concomitant causes.

In this regard, the history of the codification of state responsibility shows that the principle of full reparation for injuries stemming from concomitant causes did not find unanimous support from the beginning. Special Rapporteur Arangio-Ruiz included concomitant causes in the set of

[166] *Case Concerning Armed Activities on the Territory of the Congo (Democratic Republic of the Congo* v. *Uganda)* (Merits) [2005] ICJ Rep 168, para. 342. As of March 2021, the question of reparation is currently pending in a separate proceeding before the Court.

[167] *Genocide* case, para. 430.

[168] Ibid. para. 462. Similarly see *Construction of a Road in Costa Rica along the San Juan River (Nicaragua* v. *Costa Rica)* [2015] ICJ Rep 665, para. 226.

[169] Section 4.1.3.

elements to be considered for establishing reparations.[170] In his view, whenever damage was partly due to causes other than the international wrongful act, compensation should be reduced accordingly. This solution initially found criticism within the Drafting Committee of the ILC, which regarded Arangio-Ruiz's proposal as failing to distinguish among different scenarios of concomitant causes. Specifically, and in relation to cases in which an independent cause unknown to the wrongdoing state had aggravated the harm, the committee had argued that 'the wrongdoing State should be liable for all the harm caused, irrespective of the role which external causes might have played in aggravating the harm'.[171] However, in the draft articles adopted on the first reading, the commentary upholds Arangio-Ruiz's observations and notes that 'innumerable elements, of which actions of third parties ... are just a few, may contribute to the damage as concomitant causes'. In these situations, 'to hold the author State liable for compensation would be neither equitable nor in conformity with a proper application of the causal link criterion'.[172]

Furthermore, and on a broader level, the bilateral inter-subjective perspective that still informs principles of reparations in ARSIWA has been questioned by alternative methodological approaches that build upon the notion of an 'international harmful outcome' or 'indivisible injury', rather than on the international wrongful act.[173] According to these positions, principles of ARSIWA would offer little or no guidance when a plurality of states and/or international organisations have contributed to an 'indivisible injury' through the commission of one or more international wrongful acts.[174] In these situations of 'shared' responsibility, a principled approach would require distinguishing the position of each international person depending on its causal contribution to the indivisible harmful outcome. As a result, the law of international responsibility would be faced with situations of (i) *individual* contribution to the injury, where one contribution attributable to multiple international persons suffices to cause the injury;[175] (ii) situations of *concurrent*

[170] G. Arangio-Ruiz, 'Second Report on State Responsibility' (1989) ILC YB II/1 draft Article 8(5); see also paras. 44–51.

[171] ILC YB (1992) I para. 20.

[172] Draft Articles adopted on the First Reading, 290.

[173] See A. Nollkaemper, D. Jacobs, 'Shared Responsibility in International Law: A Conceptual Framework' (2013) 34 MJIL 359; A. Nollkaemper, J. d'Aspremont, C. Ahlborn, et al., 'Guiding Principles on Shared Responsibility in International Law' (2020) 31 EJIL Principle 2(1).

[174] Nollkamper, d'Aspremont, et al., 'Guiding Principles', Introduction to the commentary.

[175] Ibid. commentary to Principle 2, para. 6

contributions, in which each of the respective actions or omissions of multiple international persons is sufficient to produce the injury;[176] or (iii) situations of *cumulative* responsibility, in which multiple international wrongful acts accumulate and jointly produce an injury.[177] For each of these scenarios, reparations should be accorded in proportion to the contribution to the injury of each responsible state or international organisation.[178]

International practice on shared responsibility is still scarce and some of the solutions suggested by the supporting scholarship have yet to achieve the status of *lex lata.* However, these alternative methodological approaches may have a bearing on the consequences of a state's responsibility for breaches of due diligence obligations, at least in those situations where the duty to act arises in relation to the acts of other states or international organisations. After all, it has been illustrated that responsibility for the failure to exercise due diligence occurs to a large extent in connection with the action of third parties, which at times may be also other states or international organisations.[179] It is then likely that violations of primary rules of due diligence may give rise to situations of concurrent or cumulative responsibilities in which the causal contribution of a state's failure to act will have to be assessed in light of another international wrongful act committed by a state or an international organisation.

Concluding Remarks

This chapter has examined the key points of the relationship between due diligence obligations and secondary rules of international responsibility. As expected, most of the specificities of due diligence obligations when appraised against the ARSIWA framework emerge in relation to the conditions for the existence of an international wrongful act. In this

[176] Ibid. para.7

[177] Ibid. para. 8.

[178] P. D'Argent, 'Reparation, Cessation, Assurance and Guarantees of Non-Repetition', in A. Nollkaemper, I. Plakokefalos (eds.), *Principles of Shared Responsibilities in International Law* (Cambridge: Cambridge University Press, 2014), 224–31.

[179] Think, for instance, about the case of a state which tolerates that its territory is used by another state to carry out an international wrongful act. If one accepts the arguments about complicity and due diligence provided above, this situation may classify, depending on the circumstances, either as a form of complicity through omission, or as a situation of 'mere' state's responsibility for failure to control its territory in connection with the acts of another state.

regard, much of this chapter's analysis was devoted to the discussion of the conditions for the breach of due diligence obligations. The issue is arguably the most salient, not only because ARSIWA is silent on how a breach of due diligence obligations accrues, but especially because of the difficult relationship between due diligence and Article 14(3). A critical reappraisal of the history of codification of this rule has attempted to demonstrate that Article 14(3) should not preclude the interpretation of obligations to prevent as due diligence obligations that are breached the moment a state fails to display the effort required by the primary rule.

Overall, the analysis conducted confirms the initial premise, namely there is mutual influence between primary rules and secondary rules contained in ARSIWA. In relation to due diligence obligations, this influence not only concerns the way in which due diligence obligations affect the application of relevant secondary rules. Most notably, the influence is appreciable in the way in which secondary rules of responsibility affect our understanding and interpretation of due diligence obligations.

5

The Proceduralisation of Due Diligence Obligations

Introduction

This chapter investigates the phenomenon of 'proceduralisation' of due diligence obligations. The chapter first defines proceduralisation and introduces the relevant legal questions that this process brings about. The second part of the chapter analyses the impact of proceduralisation on the nature and content of due diligence obligations. Drawing from examples of proceduralisation in international practice, the chapter tests the proceduralisation of due diligence obligations against the taxonomy of international obligations laid down in Chapter 2 and investigates how proceduralisation affects the conduct nature of due diligence primary rules. The chapter also illustrates that the proceduralisation of due diligence obligations often result in their content-expansion. Finally, this chapter also illustrates the consequences of proceduralisation on the conditions of wrongfulness and the application of secondary rules of state responsibility.

5.1 Definition and *Problématique*

From the outset, the definition of proceduralisation and what it means for a due diligence obligation to be subject to this process must be clarified. The following is a working definition of the concept

> Proceduralisation consists fundamentally in the process that progressively erodes the 'reasonable' standard traditionally linked to due diligence and substitutes it with more specific legal parameters. Through proceduralisation, the content of due diligence obligations is spelled out into a series of 'sub'-duties, technical standards or direct obligations (including procedural ones) whose fulfilment is required for assessing compliance with the standard of due diligence of the 'principal' obligation.

Proceduralisation is, therefore, a way to operationalise due diligence by objectifying its content and by crystallising the substance of primary rules of this character. From a phenomenological perspective, the proceduralisation of due diligence obligations can occur mainly as a result of treaty law or following the interpretative practice of international courts, tribunals, and treaty bodies. Through proceduralisation, the elements of flexibility traditionally ingrained in due diligence, such as reasonableness, knowledge, capability, good governance, give way to procedural obligations, standardised practices, direct duties and objectified measures which together inform the substance of a due diligence obligation.

From this viewpoint, the proceduralisation of due diligence must be distinguished from other emerging international legal processes that call attention to the role of procedures and standards in international lawmaking and practice. Specifically, we are not concerned with exploring the extent to which international law is making a turn toward proceduralisation by accommodating forms of lawmaking alternative to the prism of formal sources and based on standardised practices or cooperative and informal procedures.[1] Similarly, this chapter's intent is not to investigate whether the treaty-making practice is shifting from substantive to procedural obligations, and whether, at least in some international law areas, procedural obligations are surpassing substantive ones.[2] Although there is certainly a connection between these issues and the proceduralisation of due diligence obligations,[3] the latter is a different phenomenon. The proceduralisation of due diligence obligations captures indeed the tendency to solidify through formal legal parameters the notion of reasonableness traditionally associated with due diligence.

A first way to proceduralise due diligence obligations is via treaties. This form of proceduralisation is more straightforward and occurs when treaty provisions clarify in legal terms what it means for a state to comply with the standard of reasonableness linked to certain international

[1] In this regard see Y. Radi, *La standardisation et le droit international: contours d'une théorie dialectique de la formation du droit* (Brussels: Bruylant, 2013).

[2] For an evaluation of this process in the environmental context see J. Brunnée, 'Procedure and Substance in International Environmental Law' (2020) 405 RCADI 87; M. Lemoine-Schonne, 'Substance et procédure en droit international du climat', in I. Prezas (ed.), *Substance and procédure en droit international public: dialectique et influences croisées* (Paris: Pedone, 2019), 19; more generally K. Krieger, A. Peters, 'Due Diligence and Structural Change in the International Legal Order', in K. Krieger, L. Kreuzer, A. Peters (eds.), *Due Diligence in the International Legal Order* (Oxford: Oxford University Press, 2020), 363–5.

[3] As argued at the end of this section, due diligence obligations tend to thrive in contexts where states relinquish on negotiating treaty texts with hard and determinate rules and favour open-ended standards or rules of procedures which shift the underpinning conflict among parties at a later stage.

obligations 'to protect' internationally recognised values and 'to ensure' or 'to prevent' harmful practices. New generation treaties in the area of human rights provide for some good examples of international agreements that progressively standardise the content of state parties' protective obligations and solidify the concept of reasonableness and good governance linked to due diligence. Take the example of the 2000 Palermo Protocol to Prevent, Suppress and Punish Trafficking in Persons.[4] Article 6 sets a general obligation of state parties to assist and protect victims of trafficking and protect their privacy and identity. To this end, Article 6(1) provides that 'in *appropriate cases* and to *the extent possible* under its domestic law, each State Party shall *protect* the privacy and identity of victims of trafficking in persons, including, inter alia, by making legal proceeding relating to such trafficking confidential'.[5] Owing to its flexible content and its 'conduct' nature, this obligation can be classified as of due diligence.[6] Under Article 6, however, states are not completely free to decide which measures of protection for victims of trafficking are to be deemed the most appropriate. In fact, the subsequent paragraphs of this provision, namely Article 6(2) and 6(3), pre-emptively formalise 'reasonableness' and specify the types of measures that states are expected to take in order to comply with their duty to protect. For example, Article 6(3) states that in pursuing protection of victims of trafficking, states shall provide for measures that ensure physical, psychological, and social recovery of victims of trafficking, including appropriate housing (Article 6(3)(a)); counselling and information on their rights as victims (Article 6(3)(b)); medical psychological and material assistance (Article 6(3)(c)); employment and education opportunities (Article 6(3)(d)). From a dogmatic perspective, all the measures required by Article 6(3)(a)(b)(c) can be regarded either as 'direct' duties imposed upon a state party, as well as the 'specification' of the content of the principal obligation to exercise due diligence in ensuring assistance and protection of victims.

The second form of proceduralisation takes place through the interpretative work of international courts, tribunals, or through specialised

[4] Protocol to Prevent, Suppress and Punish Trafficking in Persons, Especially Women and Children, supplementing the United Nations Convention against Transnational Organized Crime (adopted 15 November 2000, entered into force 25 December 2003) 2237 UNTS 319.

[5] Ibid. (emphasis added).

[6] See Chapter 2 for the analysis of which international obligations can fall under the due diligence 'label'.

treaty bodies' decisions and resolutions. When assessing whether a state has fully discharged its obligation to act with due diligence, these bodies may objectify what is 'due' by pointing to international standards, procedural duties, and international measures developed by relevant treaty mechanisms or through interpretative practice. This way, the variability of due diligence is gradually eroded and replaced with the identification of more specific obligations, sets of good practices and international measures that crystallise the content of the due diligence primary rule.

Sometimes, the treaty itself refers back to internationally agreed standards to solidify and inform the content of due diligence. For example, Article 210 of United Nations Convention on the Law of the Sea (UNCLOS) incorporates into the due diligence obligation to prevent pollution reference to international rules and standards developed by competent international supervising mechanisms.[7] In this case, although the treaty itself does not specify which measures states have to comply with to fulfil due diligence, it formally delegates to competent international bodies the task of progressively define its content. In other cases, the text of the treaty does not expressly refer to internationally agreed standards and measures to clarify the substance of a due diligence obligation. Yet, the content of such obligation may still be operationalised through the adoption of best practices, technical standards, guidelines, and resolutions progressively developed by treaty monitoring mechanisms and other relevant international bodies. While these instruments have formally a soft-law character,[8] they may be employed in certain circumstances by international courts or supervising bodies to concretise due diligence and determine whether a state is in breach of its obligation.[9]

7 United Nations Convention on the Law of the Sea (UNCLOS) (adopted 10 December 1982, entered into force 16 November 1994) 1833 UNTS 3, Article 210. On the specific international standards employed to set the standard of due diligence of Article 210 see P. Birnie, A. Boyle, C. Redgwell, *International Law & The Environment* (Oxford: Oxford University Press, 3rd ed., 2009), 149–50, 389–90.

8 Following the lines sketched by Klabbers, rather than constituting a third genus of international legal sources, soft law can actually be recast into the traditional sources of international law, J. Klabbers, 'The Redundancy of Soft Law' (1996) 65 *Nordic Journal of International Law* 167; for a critique of this position C. Chinkin, 'Normative Development in the International Legal System', in D. Shelton (ed.), *Commitment and Compliance: The Role of Non-binding Norms in the International Legal System* (Oxford: Oxford University Press, 2003), 21.

9 For instance, on how international standards and guidelines developed by UNESCO and the World Heritage Committee can inform the content of rules of due diligence contained in the World Heritage Convention see G. Bartolini, 'Cultural Heritage and Disasters', in

The proceduralisation of due diligence obligations through international courts and treaty bodies' intervention begs the enduring question of international judicial and quasi-judicial institutions from law-applying actors to lawmakers. The problem seems confined to the proceduralisation of treaty-based due diligence obligations. Indeed, in relation to international customary law, courts and tribunals' interpretative practice contributes to creating what must be found.[10] However, with treaty-based due diligence obligations, proceduralisation through interpretative practice often implies that the vague and indeterminate content of these obligations is filled with a substance going well beyond the original text of the rule. This may induce onlookers to inquiry about the legitimacy of this process or, at least, to raise questions about its limits.

In certain international legal areas, it is a well-established and accepted practice that international courts or treaty bodies 'spell out' progressively the content of state's due diligence obligations.[11] For instance, in the human rights arena, the intervention of judicial bodies like the European

F. Francioni, A. F. Vrdoljak (eds.), *The Oxford Handbook of International Cultural Heritage Law* (Oxford: Oxford University Press, 2020), 150–5; similar observations are made by the same author on how international standards developed by the World Health Organisation provide concreteness to due diligence obligations set in the 2005 International Health Regulation, G. Bartolini, 'The Failure of "Core Capacities" under the WHO International Health Regulations' (2020) 70 ICLQ 233; further, on how international standards developed through a mutual and reiterative reinforcing process between NGOs, adjudicating bodies, treaty bodies, and expert working groups may solidify the content of due diligence rules, especially in the human rights context, A. Boyle, C. Chinkin, *The Making of International Law* (Oxford: Oxford University Press, 2007), 84–5.

10 See the ILC draft conclusions on the 'Identification of Customary International Law' adopted by the Drafting Committing on second reading, UN Doc A/CN.4/L.908, conclusion no. 13. In this regard, Jean d'Aspremont has distinguished between 'content-determinant' and 'law ascertainment' interpretation. Content-determinant interpretation is the process by which the judge or any other interpreter, interprets the law 'she is empowered to apply with the view to determining . . . the applicable standard of behaviour or the normative guideline for the case of which she is seized'. Law-ascertainment interpretation occurs instead when the professional is called to interpret the pedigree of the rule 'in order to ascertain whether a given rule can claim to be part of the international legal order', J. d'Aspremont, 'The Multidimensional Process of Interpretation', in A. Bianchi, D. Peat, M. Windsor (eds.), *Interpretation in International Law* (Oxford: Oxford University Press, 2015), 117.

11 On how human rights treaty bodies contribute to the evolution of concepts enshrined in human rights treaties L. Crema, 'The Interpretative Work of Treaty Bodies: How They Look at Evolutionary Interpretation, and How Other Courts at Them', in G. Abi-Saab, K. Keith, G. Marceau, C. Marquet (eds.), *Evolutionary Interpretation and International Law* (London: Hart Publishing, 2019), 77.

Court of Human Rights (ECtHR) and the Inter-American Court of Human Rights (IACtHR), as well as monitoring bodies like the Human Rights Committee or the Committee on Economic, Social and Cultural Rights continuously solidifies state parties' general commitments to human rights protection. The interpretation of a plethora of states' obligations to ensure and protect human rights now requires states to show compliance with a set of procedural and substantive duties, which together inform the overall concept of 'acting with due diligence' vis-à-vis the protection of specific human rights.[12]

In other contexts, however, the proceduralisation of the due diligence rule and its departure from the text is seen as more problematic.[13] One example is the South China Sea Arbitration case and the Arbitral Tribunal interpretation of Article 192 of UNCLOS. Specifically, the tribunal was called to assess China's compliance with the due diligence obligation to 'protect and preserve the marine environment'. The tribunal refrained from treating the question of China's due diligence mainly as a matter of facts and instead used the standard to develop legal norms.[14] Drawing on the corpus of international law related to the environment and on the provisions of the Convention on International Trade in Endangered Species of Wild Fauna and Flora (CITIES),[15] of which both the Philippines and China are parties, the tribunal indeed affirmed that the obligation to protect and preserve the marine environment includes the duty to prevent the harvesting of marine species that are recognised to be internationally at risk of extinction. Although China's obligations under the CITIES were not under scrutiny, a systemic interpretation of Articles 192 in light of these provisions allowed the arbitrators to derive a novel obligation to prevent the harvesting of species at risk from the due diligence obligation to protect the marine environment.

To be sure, there is no necessary correlation between the proceduralisation of due diligence obligations and interpretative methods provided by

[12] Section 5.2.2.

[13] See P. d'Argent, A. de Vaucleroy, 'Le contenu de l'omission illicite: la non utilisation de moyens raisonnables', in S. Cassella (ed.), *Le standard de due diligence et la responsabilité internationale* (Paris: Pedone, 2018), 272–3 ; S. Besson, *La Due Diligence en Droit International* (2020) 409 RCADI 261–4.

[14] This shift is captured by M. Möise Mbengue, 'The South China Sea Arbitration: Innovations in Marine Environmental Fact-Finding and Due Diligence Obligations' (2016) 110 AJIL Unbound 285.

[15] *In the Matter of South China Sea Arbitration (Republic of the Philippines* v. *The People's Republic of China)* PCA Case 2013–19 (2016) paras. 944–5; 950–6.

the Vienna Convention on the Law of Treaties.[16] Some interpretative methods more than others side well with the technique of proceduralisation, like evolutionary or systemic interpretations of treaty provisions.[17] However, there is no hard-and-fast rule. The reason is that general rules on interpretation do not dictate interpretative outcomes but are merely instruments through which an intended result is achieved.[18]

Regardless of the interpretative means, the output of proceduralisation may be hard to square with orthodox positivist views that separate interpretation from lawmaking and construe the latter as an expression of state consent. Positivist approaches to international law assert that lawmaking processes occur only through rules of recognition and posit state consent as the exclusive basis for legal validity. Once the rule is set out, the interpreter's function is to discover its meaning and dispel the penumbra of indeterminacy that may eclipse its hard core. Sure, positivist views do not exclude that rules may be vague in content and concede that such vagueness grants the interpreter more leeway in finding the rule's *true* meaning.[19]

However, even when the parties have opted for more vague and indefinite norms, the scope of 'content-determinant' interpretation may still be subject to debate. In relation to due diligence, one thing is indeed to fill the substance of a due diligence rule with other open-ended concepts like reasonableness or good governmentality. Resorting to

[16] Vienna Convention on the Law of Treaties (adopted 23 May 1969, entered into force 27 January 1980) 1155 UNTS 331, Articles 31–3.

[17] On how evolutionary interpretation sides well with treaties rules designed by the party to accommodate developments in international law see *Dispute Regarding Navigational and Related Rights (Costa Rica* v. *Nicaragua)* [2009] ICJ Rep 213, para. 64.

[18] One may argue the same about judicial activism, which is a highly contextualised as well as a shifting phenomenon, F. Zarbiyev, 'Judicial Activism in International Law: A Conceptual Framework for Analysis' (2012) 3 *Journal of International Dispute Settlement* 247.

[19] Hans Kelsen had already been critical of classic positivist views which understood interpretation merely as an act of clarification and understanding of the legal rule. For Kelsen, interpretation is an act of will and cognition of the legal rule, a choice the interpreter makes when applying the rule, see H. Kelsen, *Pure Theory of Law* (Berkeley: University of California Press, 2nd ed., 1970), 349–51; on positivist accounts that see interpretation, regardless of the indeterminacy or uncertainty of the legal rule, as an act of law-application distinct from lawmaking C. Focarelli, *International Law as Social Construct: The Struggle for Global Justice* (Oxford: Oxford University Press, 2012), 317–18; A. Pellet, D. Müller, 'Article 38', in A. Zimmermann, C. Tams, K. Oeller-Frahn (eds.), *The Statute of the International Court of Justice: A Commentary* (Oxford: Oxford University Press, 3rd ed., 2019) paras. 324–6; G. Abi-Saab, 'Introduction: A Meta-Question', in Abi-Saab, Keith, Marceau, Marquet, *Evolutionary Interpretation*, 7–12.

these standards when concretising due diligence shapes the discourse about it as an *in casu* one, since what is reasonable, hence 'due', is normally and primarily assessed in terms of facts. From a strict positivist stand, such interpretation is respectful of states' consent, for it clarifies the meaning of an indeterminate rule without normatively impinging upon its flexibility. Instead, another thing is to crystallise the substance of a due diligence obligation into legal procedures and extract from this 'subsidiary' and other direct duties. In these cases, due diligence becomes the catalyser for the development of standards and duties which, as *legal* rather than factual parameters, can apply *in abstracto* to all states bound by the primary rule (of due diligence) and well beyond the circumstances of a single case. It is difficult to deny that, in these situations, proceduralisation comes close to creating (new) legal rules.

Differently, the 'interventionist' approach of international courts and treaty bodies toward proceduralisation appears less problematic if read through the lens of realist schools of thoughts or alternative methods to interpretative practice. The New Haven School has been among the first to move away from the 'myth' of the doctrine of sources and to argue that lawmaking neither starts nor ends with formal sources but is a process emerging from mediating a plethora of communicative streams. For instance, Michael Reisman has taught that 'any communication between elites and politically relevant groups which shape wide expectations about appropriate future behavior must be considered a functional lawmaking'.[20] This would certainly include international courts, tribunals, and technical treaty bodies called to assess states' due diligence obligations. In a similar vein, alternative approaches to lawmaking have drawn attention to the role that authoritative practice of interpretation plays in creating what it purports to find.[21] According to this thesis, even if the text of a rule was tied to states' consent, once the rule is out there, international courts, scholars, and other authoritative institutions make interpretative claims about its meaning and contribute to its

[20] W. M. Reisman, 'International Lawmaking: A Process of Communication' (1981) 75 *Proceedings of the Annual Meeting, American Society of International Law*, 113.

[21] See I. Venzke, *How Interpretation Makes International Law: On Semantic Change and Normative Twists* (Oxford: Oxford University Press, 2014), 17; G. Hernandez, 'Interpretative Authority and the International Judiciary', in Bianchi, Peat, Windsor, *Interpretation*, 166. Constitutional approaches to international law also regard the interpretative practice of international courts and tribunals as a form of lawmaking, see A. von Bogdandy, I. Venzke, 'Beyond Dispute: International Judicial Institutions as Lawmakers' (2011) 12 *German Law Journal* 979; J. Klabbers, A. Peters, G. Ulfstein, *The Constitutionalization of International Law* (Oxford: Oxford University Press, 2009), 127.

development. This lawmaking function cannot be adequately grasped by the doctrine of sources and rests on the practice of interpretation itself.[22]

Be as it may, this book takes an agnostic stand on which theory best captures the interpretative outcome of the proceduralisation of due diligence obligations. However, a few considerations on the underlying causes and effects of this process seem opportune. First, at least in some legal areas,[23] the proceduralisation of due diligence obligations – and, one may argue, the proceduralisation of international law – is not merely the connatural side of adjudicatory practice. Proceduralisation is instead the ramification of a broader phenomenon finding origin in the 'crisis' of traditional international lawmaking and, more specifically, in states' failure to negotiate in relevant fora 'hard' rules with determinate content.[24] Indeed, open-ended rules such as due diligence obligations camouflage with their vagueness the conflict among negotiating parties and testify to the lack of real power of those wishing to change the rules of the game.[25] With due diligence obligations, the parties' conflict is temporarily brought to a close by the rule's open-ended substance and is postponed to a later stage. This means that, once tested in practice, the vagueness of the rule will inevitably give rise to stronger synergies between law-creation and law-application processes. In other words, the more states are incapable of agreeing on precise rules, the more lawmaking functions are de facto delegated to law-application bodies.[26] These bodies intervene to provide concrete substance to the rules so that they can effectively monitor whether states are in compliance with or in breach of their commitments.

22 Venzke, *How Interpretation Makes International Law*, 30.

23 I am referring here especially to the international environmental legal field, see Brunnée, 'Procedure and Substance' 88, 106–9; sketching some of the reasons behind the proceduralisation of international environmental law D. Bodansky, J. Brunnée, E. Hey, 'International Environmental Law: Mapping the Field', in D. Bodansky, J. Brunnée, E. Hey (eds.), *The Oxford Handbook of International Environmental Law* (Oxford: Oxford University Press, 2007), 6–8.

24 Generally on the crisis of formal lawmaking and the rise of proceduralism as an antidote J. Pauwelyn, R. A. Wessel, J. Wouters, 'When Structures Become Shackles: Stagnation and Dynamics in International Lawmaking' (2014) 25 EJIL 733, 757–9; see also Y. Radi, 'Standardization: A Dynamic and Procedural Conceptualization of International Law-Making' (2012) 25 LJIL 283.

25 J. Salmon, 'Les notions à contenu variable en droit international public', in C. Perelman, R. Vander Elst (eds.), *Les Notions à contenu variables en droit* (Brussels: Bruylant, 1984), 266–8.

26 Radi, 'Standardization', 293.

Second, the intervention of law-application bodies in giving substance to vague rules goes hand-in-hand with the progressive 'technicisation' of the latter. That is, with proceduralisation not only is the content of 'proceduralised' due diligence obligations, formerly prescribed in terms of reasonableness, now defined according to procedural rules, standards, and, in some cases, direct duties. Since the content-determinant task is often entrusted to specialised treaty bodies, proceduralised due diligence obligations become increasingly more technical. In order to define the substance of due diligence, law-application bodies increasingly make *renvoi* to technical standards, guidelines, scientific evidence, or soft rules developed by experts or negotiated by other technical organs.

This technicisation has a number of advantages. It allows the replacement of the volatile concept of reasonableness with legal parameters, and in this sense, it contributes to more legal certainty in the future application of the rule. Simultaneously, the 'hard' fabric of the rule remains flexible, which means that the rule will be apt to accommodate changes in light of new developments and learning. Technical standards, guidelines, and soft rules informing the substance of due diligence can in fact be continuously rediscussed and updated in relevant fora. They 'reshape' the content of due diligence obligations following technological, scientific, and social developments.[27]

However, there is a darker side to this process. Martti Koskenniemi has warned against the redefinition of unsettled legal problems by reference to technical legal discourses and experts' 'language'. To begin with, there is a problem of democratic legitimacy in the transferring of decision-making powers from negotiating states to technical experts. If 'hard' rules remain open and flexible like due diligence obligations, states effectively devolve material regulation to actors, like specialised bodies, whose concern is primarily to pursue the interests of the functional context in which they operate.[28] Furthermore, the redefinition of legal questions by reference to specialised standards, technical 'soft' rules, or scientific evidence masks a political preference

[27] Brunnée, 'Procedure and Substance', 113–14; arguing, instead, that crystallising due diligence through standardisation may hinder legal changes Birnie, Boyle, Redgwell, *International Law & The Environment*, 150.

[28] M. Koskenniemi, 'International Law and Hegemony: A Reconfiguration' (2004) 17 *Cambridge Review of International Affairs* 197, 210–11; on how this problem of democratic legitimacy in international law can trigger sentiments of anti-globalism and populism J. Wouters, 'International Law, Informal Law-Making, Global Governance in Times of Anti-Globalism and Populism', in H. Krieger, G. Nolte, A. Zimmermann (eds.), *International Rule of Law: Rise or Decline?* (Oxford: Oxford University Press, 2019), 242.

under the guise of neutrality.[29] The apparent neutral language of 'technical reasoning' obscures the contingent nature of the choice made and 'solidifies the sense that questions of distribution and preference have already been decided elsewhere, so all that remains are technical questions, questions about how to smooth the prince's path'.[30]

Having set the general framework surrounding the proceduralisation of due diligence obligations, the next sections will discuss proceduralisation at micro-level and against the findings of the book's previous chapters. By replacing the flexibility traditionally ingrained in due diligence with objectified measures, proceduralisation affects both the nature and content of primary rules of this character. In terms of content, proceduralisation progressively replaces reasonableness as well as the variables traditionally linked to due diligence with defined duties. This process often results in the content-expansion of the primary rule, which becomes the source for identifying a multitude of substantive and procedural duties. In terms of nature, the identification of substantive and procedural duties derived from due diligence impinges upon the conceptual understanding of the 'principal' due diligence rule. That is, if read against the taxonomy of international obligations developed in Chapter 2, 'proceduralised' due diligence obligations give rise to some considerations on the 'conduct nature' of due diligence and their relationship with secondary rules of international responsibility.

5.2 The Effect of Proceduralisation on the *Nature* and *Content* of Due Diligence Obligations

Proceduralisation is a phenomenon that involves a plethora of due diligence obligations across international law. To explore the impact of proceduralisation on the nature and content of due diligence obligations, the next two sections focus on the general obligations to prevent transboundary environmental harm and on international human rights law. The reason for this choice is twofold. First, international environmental law and human rights are among the international legal areas in which the proceduralisation of due diligence obligations is more evident. In international environmental law, proceduralised due diligence

[29] M. Koskenniemi, 'The Politics of International Law: 20 Years Later' (2009) 20 EJIL 7, 15–17; warning against proceduralisation as a process that masks politics under the guise of technicalities, M. Koskenniemi, 'Peaceful Settlement of Environmental Disputes' (1991) 60 *Nordic Journal of International Law* 73.

[30] Ibid. 16.

obligations are increasingly common both in treaty practice and in relation to customary international law. With regard to international human rights law, human rights courts and monitoring bodies have played a great role in concretising the substance of state's obligations to protect human rights. They have continuously eroded the scope of states' discretion in choosing the measures necessary to ensure protection of human rights and have progressively replaced the concept of reasonableness with 'hard' legal criteria.

Second, the proceduralisation of due diligence in these areas is an excellent example of the complexities raised when the substance of due diligence is concretised in procedural and substantive duties that may end up having an independent existence of their own. The following analysis should capture well the relationship between the 'principal' rule of due diligence and proceduralised duties, and should illuminate how this relationship affects the application of secondary rules of international responsibility.

In any case, the role of these examples is not to cover exhaustively the way in which the proceduralisation of due diligence takes place in international law. Rather, the following analysis indicates to the reader the conceptual twist underpinning proceduralisation and the consequences that the phenomenon bears on the dogmatic foundations of due diligence primary rules. From this perspective, it is submitted that the following considerations on how proceduralisation affects the nature and content of obligations of due diligence may be translated to other international contexts, either *de lege lata* or *de lege ferenda*.

5.2.1 The Proceduralisation of the Customary Obligation to Prevent Transboundary Environmental Harm

One of the cornerstones of international environmental law is the general obligation to prevent transboundary harm. This obligation originates from the no-harm rule which found early crystallisation in international law in the Trail Smelter case and in the Corfu Channel dispute.[31] The obligation to prevent transboundary damage from hazardous activities, including activities affecting the environment, is now codified by the 2001 ILC draft Articles on Prevention of Transboundary Harm from

[31] *Trail Smelter* case *(United States* v. *Canada)* (1941) 3 RIAA 1965; *Corfu Channel Case (UK* v. *Albania)* (Merits) [1949] ICJ Rep 244, para. 22.

Hazardous Activities.[32] In the advisory opinion on the Legality of the Threat or Use of Nuclear Weapons, the ICJ has recognised that the duty to prevent transboundary harm is part of general international law and instructs states to ensure that activities within their jurisdiction and control respect the environment of other states as well as areas beyond national control.[33] With the Pulp Mills case, the court has expressly linked prevention of transboundary harm with due diligence, noting that the duty to prevent transboundary harm does not require states to guarantee that harm will be absolutely prevented, but rather to exercise best efforts to avoid the occurrence of harm.[34]

Along with the general obligation to prevent transboundary harm, international environmental law also includes procedural obligations that are seen as complementary to the substantive no harm rule.[35] They include the obligation to notify, warn, inform, and consult states potentially affected by transboundary harm, and the obligation to conduct an Environmental Impact Assessment (EIA). These duties are often found in international environmental agreements, but they are also part of general international law.[36] Starting from the Pulp Mills case and subsequently, in the Certain Activities and the Construction of a Road cases involving an environmental dispute between Costa Rica and Nicaragua, the ICJ has drawn a clear link between procedural obligations and the substantive duty to prevent transboundary harm. The court has confirmed that procedural obligations enjoy customary status and are part of the substantive duty to prevent harm. These are, in other words, duties that provide concreteness to due diligence and contribute to dispelling part of the vagueness traditionally associated with prevention.[37]

[32] ILC Draft Articles on Prevention of Transboundary Harm from Hazardous Activities, with commentaries (2001) ILC YB II/2.

[33] *Legality of the Threat or Use of Nuclear Weapons (Advisory Opinion)* [1996] ICJ Rep 226, para. 29.

[34] *Case Concerning Pulp Mills on the River Uruguay (Argentina* v. *Uruguay)* (Merits) [2010] ICJ Rep 14, paras. 101, 106.

[35] Procedural duties are considered both part of the due diligence rule and duties with a separate existence, see Section 2.1.1; see also I. Plakokefalos, 'Prevention Obligations in International Environmental Law' (2012) 23 *Yearbook of International Environmental Law* 5.

[36] ILC Draft Articles on Prevention of Transboundary Harm, Articles 3, 7, 8, 9; for a review of substance and procedure in international environmental law, Brunnée, 'Procedure and Substance', 87; see also P. Okowa, 'Procedural Obligations in International Environmental Agreements' (1997) 67 BYIL 275.

[37] L. Duvic-Paoli, *The Prevention Principle in International Environmental Law* (Cambridge: Cambridge University Press, 2018), 20–4.

While the general assertion that the due diligence solidifies into procedural duties does not raise particular issues, how the ICJ has operationalised the link between due diligence, prevention, and procedural duties has attracted criticism.[38] On the one hand, the court in Pulp Mills has asserted that procedural obligations are part of the substantive duty to prevent transboundary harm and have a separate existence of their own. The consequence of such a pronouncement is that a state responsibility can ensue even when significant transboundary harm has not materialised, yet the state has failed to comply with one of its procedural obligations, say, the obligation to conduct an EIA. This is an important stepping-stone in the evolution of general international environmental law since it testifies to the switch from a compensatory logic – crystallised by the Trail Smelter case – to a preventive paradigm that addresses risk and not damage.[39] Yet, both in Pulp Mills and then in the Costa Rica and Nicaragua disputes, the court did not take this argument to its full development. Specifically, the court refused to acknowledge that, if procedural obligations are part of a more concretised duty to prevent harm, the violation of a procedural duty necessarily entails the violation of due diligence, thus violating the obligation to prevent transboundary harm.

The court's reasoning in these decisions flashes out two important aspects of the proceduralisation of due diligence. The first is the complex and intertwined relationship between the 'principal' due diligence obligation and the specific duties that compose it. The second is the uneasiness that ensues from attempting to reconcile 'proceduralised' preventive obligations with Article 14(3) of ARSIWA. To further illustrate these points, the first prong of the analysis briefly reappraises the principal facts of these environmental cases. Then, the second prong of the argument critically assesses the ICJ's conceptualisation of proceduralised due diligence and makes some general consideration on this process.

I The Proceduralisation of Due Diligence in Pulp Mills and the Costa Rica and Nicaragua Disputes

The case of Pulp Mills concerned Uruguay's commissioning and construction of two pulp mills located on the River of Uruguay. In its

[38] Brunnée, 'Procedure and Substance'; L. Duvic-Paoli, *The Prevention Principle*, 336–9; Y. Kerbrat, 'Obligations procédurales et obligations de fond en droit international des dommages transfrontières', in Prezas, *Substance and procédure en droit international public*, 7.

[39] *Pulp Mills, Separate Opinion of Judges Al-Khasawneh and Simma*, para. 26; M. Möise Mbengue, *Essai sur une théorie du risqué en droit international public* (Paris: Pedone, 2009), 119–46.

submission before the ICJ, Argentina argued that the authorisation and operation of the mills violated a number of Uruguay's obligations under the 1975 Statute of the River Uruguay, of which both states were parties. These included the obligation to inform and notify Argentina about the construction and the obligations to avoid environmental harm to the river, protect its ecosystem, and contribute to its rational utilisation.

Instead of simply considering the violation of each obligation *ad seriatim*, the ICJ distinguished procedural and substantive obligations and considered their violation separately. The court identified procedural obligations in: Uruguay's obligation to inform Argentina, through the Administrative Commission for the River Uruguay (CARU), of its construction plans (Article 7, first paragraph); the obligation to notify Argentina of the plans (Article 7, second paragraph); and the obligation to negotiate and comply with the procedures outlined in Articles from 7 to 12 of the 1975 Statute. Substantive obligations were instead identified with the obligation to contribute to the optimum and rational utilisation of the river (Article 1); the obligation to ensure that the management of the soil and woodland did not impair the regime of the river and the quality of its waters (Article 35); and the obligation to protect and preserve the aquatic environment (Article 41).

The court explained the distinction between procedure and substance, stating that while substantive obligations are normally worded in broad terms, procedural obligations are narrower and more specific. Building on this dichotomy, the ICJ concluded that Uruguay had only violated procedural obligations under the 1975 Statute. It did not find any violation of substantive obligations to contribute to the river's optimum utilization and ensure its conservation and protection. Essentially, the lack of evidence that the construction of the mills had effectively impaired the quality of the waters and its ecosystem prevented the court from establishing a violation of substantive obligations.

During the proceedings, Argentina contended that procedural and substantive obligations are inevitably interconnected, suggesting that a breach of the former should entail a breach of the latter. In Argentina's view, procedural obligations laid down in Articles 7 to 12 of the 1975 Statute were aimed at ensuring the optimum utilisation of the river as well as its conservation and protection. Hence, any disregard of these procedural duties would clearly undermine the purpose and object of the 1975 Statute, pointing not only to a failure of procedure but also of substance. The court only partially espoused this argument. It did recognise a functional link between the procedural and substantive obligations laid down in the statute.[40] For example, in assessing Uruguay's failure to notify Argentina of its construction plans, the court regarded the obligation to notify as instrumental for cooperation between the parties, 'enabling them to assess the plan's impact on the river . . . and, if necessary, to negotiate the adjustments needed to avoid the potential damage that it might cause'.[41] That is, the court acknowledged that notification is an essential preventive measure to ensure protection from future environmental harm. Similarly, in relation to Uruguay's obligation to inform, the court drew a clear link with due diligence. It first noted that the principle of prevention has its origins in the due diligence that is required of a state in its territory, and that a state 'is thus obliged to use all the means at its disposal in order to avoid activities which take place in its territory, or in any other area under its jurisdiction, causing significant damage to the environment of another State'.[42] On this basis, the court deemed Uruguay's obligation to inform Argentina as essential 'for the initiation of co-operation between the Parties which is necessary in order to fulfil the obligation of prevention'.[43]

However, the court did not accept Argentina's argument that a breach of a procedural obligation automatically entails a breach of the corresponding substantive duty. The court noted that the 1975 Statute indicated neither that 'a party may fulfil its substantive obligations by complying solely with its procedural obligations' nor that 'a breach of procedural obligations automatically entails the breach of substantive ones'.[44] The judges of the world court also stressed that 'the fact that the parties have complied with their substantive obligations does not mean that they are deemed to have complied ipso facto with their procedural obligations, or are excused from doing so'.[45] While there is little doubt on the correctness of the first and the last assertion, the argument that a breach of procedural rule does not per se constitute a breach of due diligence raises more doubts.

The ICJ's decision to treat procedural obligations and substantive ones as conceptually distinct was presumably facilitated by the fact that Pulp Mills rested on compliance with treaty obligations laid down by the 1975 Statute. This made it easier for the court to argue that, despite the

40 *Pulp Mills*, para. 79.
41 Ibid. para. 113.
42 Ibid. para. 101.
43 Ibid. para. 102.
44 Ibid. para. 78.
45 Ibid.

interconnection, breaches of procedural and substantive obligations must be considered separately. Still, the court's reasoning points to a certain ambiguity in how the connection between procedural obligations and the duty to exercise due diligence should be construed. The most unsatisfying bit of the decision lies in the court's failure to bring the proceduralisation of due diligence to its logical consequences: if a procedural duty is part of an obligation to exercise due diligence, the violation of the former should entail by itself a breach of the principal substantive obligation.

This ambiguity was not dispelled and was rather magnified in Certain Activities Carried out by Nicaragua in the Border Area (*Costa Rica* v. *Nicaragua*) and the Construction of a Road in Costa Rica Along the San Juan River (*Nicaragua* v. *Costa Rica*), two cases jointly considered by the ICJ in 2015. The Certain Activities case involved Nicaragua's alleged violation of obligations under international environmental law in connection with dredging activities carried out over the Lower San Juan River, close to the border with Costa Rica. The Construction of a Road case concerned extensive road construction by Costa Rica along the border with Nicaragua, which, in Nicaragua's view, engendered serious environmental consequences. Following the methodology of Pulp Mills, the court resorted to the distinction between procedural and substantive obligations also in these two cases. Like in Pulp Mills, the ICJ did find violations of procedural obligations, and more specifically, of Costa Rica's obligation to carry out an EIA in relation to its construction along the border. It did not find any violation by either Nicaragua or Costa Rica of their substantive obligation to prevent transboundary environmental harm.

In the Certain Activities case and the Construction of a Road the ICJ did not deal with the violations of procedural and substantive treaty obligations, but rather with the breach of the customary obligation to prevent transboundary environmental harm. This contingency made the drawbacks of the court's reliance on a strict binarism between procedure and substance even more apparent. In particular, two arguments advanced by the court deserve scrutiny. First, drawing on Pulp Mills, the ICJ made it crystal-clear that the obligation to conduct an EIA is part of the due diligence obligation to prevent significant transboundary harm. It affirmed that to fulfil the obligation to exercise due diligence to preventing transboundary harm, 'a State must, before embarking on an activity having the potential adversely to affect the environment of another State, ascertain if there is a risk of significant transboundary harm, which would trigger the requirement to carry out an environmental impact assessment'.[46] The court then concluded that since Nicaragua's dredging programme planned in 2006 was not such as to give rise to a risk of significant transboundary harm, no obligation to carry out an EIA on the part of Nicaragua had arisen.[47]

Second, the court suggested that since procedural obligations are all part of the due diligence matrix, the violation of one of these duties makes it unnecessary to assess the violation of the others. More specifically, in the Construction of a Road, Nicaragua accused Costa Rica of a breach of the obligation to conduct an EIA and the obligations to notify and consult with Nicaragua in relation to the construction of the road along Nicaragua's borders. After finding that Costa Rica had indeed violated the duty to conduct an EIA, the court moved to the customary obligations to notify and consult, stating: '[T]he duty to notify and consult does not call for an examination by the Court in the present case, since the Court has established that Costa Rica has not complied with its obligation under general international law to perform an environmental impact assessment prior to the construction of the road.'[48]

This passage leans on a specific understanding of the relationship between procedural obligations and the due diligence paradigm. In sum, the court asserted that *because of* the violation of the duty to conduct an EIA, Costa Rica's failure to exercise due diligence had already occurred, making it unnecessary to evaluate breaches of the obligations to inform and to notify. The court's approach is therefore one that recognises the separate existence of procedural obligations, but links them with the due diligence required of a state to comply with the substantive preventive obligation.

[46] *Certain Activities Carried Out by Nicaragua in the Border Area (Costa Rica* v. *Nicaragua)* [2015] ICJ Rep 665, para. 104.

[47] Ibid. para. 108. Judge Dugard was critical of this position and submitted a Separate Opinion to the judgment declaring: 'The danger of viewing the due diligence obligation as the source of the obligation to perform an environmental impact assessment is that it allows a State to argue, retrospectively, that because no harm has been proved at the time of the legal proceedings, no duty of due diligence arose at the time the project was planned.' Dugard was sceptical about reading the obligation to conduct an environmental impact assessment as an obligation dependent on the obligation of a state to exercise due diligence in preventing transboundary harm. Rather, he construes due diligence as a general standard of conduct that states must show at all times to prevent transboundary harm, including in its decision to conduct an environmental impact assessment. See *Separate Opinion of Judge Dugard*, paras. 9–10.

[48] *Construction of a Road in Costa Rica along the San Juan River (Nicaragua* v. *Costa Rica)* [2015] ICJ Rep 665, para. 217.

In light of these findings, one would have expected the court to conclude that Costa Rica's violation of the procedural obligation to conduct an EIA also entailed the violation of the obligation to prevent transboundary harm. And yet, the court refrained again to do so, noting that there was insufficient evidence that Costa Rica's dredging programme had caused significant transboundary harm upon the Colorado River. As aptly noted by Jutta Brunnée, the ICJ judges essentially ended up drawing an artificial separation between the obligation *to prevent* transboundary harm and the obligation *not to cause* transboundary harm.[49] The first would imply due diligence as expressed through the procedural obligations to conduct an EIA, to consult and inform, and would be breached by a state's failure to comply with one or more of these procedural duties. The obligation not to cause transboundary harm would instead correspond to the substantive part of the duty to prevent: its breach would be contingent upon the occurrence of transboundary environmental damage.

II Critical Analysis

Overall, we can draw the following observations based on the court's approach in Pulp Mills and in the Nicaragua and Costa Rica disputes. First, the 'spelling out' of the due diligence principle into concretised duties clearly increases the grip of the obligation imbued with this concept. The notion of 'acting with due diligence' loses a bit of its elusiveness, since part of the contours of due diligence are now defined *in abstracto* and in relation to specific duties. The relationship between due diligence and these obligations is multifaceted and complex. On the one hand, procedural duties like the obligation to conduct an EIA or to notify are considered part of the principal obligation to exercise due diligence. They are, in other words, components of the due diligence rule. At the same time, these procedural duties may also have a separate existence on their own.

If one wished to resurrect Ago's classification of international obligations, one could argue that the relationship between the procedural duties which compose due diligence and the principal due diligence

[49] This has been argued by Brunnée, 'International Environmental Law and Community Interests', in E. Benvenisti, G. Nolte (eds.), *Community Interests Across International Law* (Oxford: Oxford University Press, 2018), 158–9. Interestingly, the reading of the *Certain Activities* and *Construction of a Road* cases also supports this view, with the court speaking specifically throughout the judgment of substantive obligations *not to cause* environmental harm.

obligation is captured by the category of obligations 'to adopt a particular course of conduct'. Recall from Chapter 2 that the distinction between obligations of conduct and obligations of result introduced by Special Rapporteur Ago rested on the criterion of determinacy. Accordingly, Ago classified obligations of result as those leaving states freedom regarding the choice of means for attaining the result set by the primary rule. On the contrary, obligations to adopt a particular course of conduct were defined as obligations prescribing the state a particular behaviour, the violation of which would automatically entail a breach. Although in Ago's original conceptualisation of 'conduct' and 'result' determinacy rested upon the relationship between international law and domestic law, international practice has resorted to the concept of obligation to adopt a particular course of conduct also when the primary rule prescribes the adoption of specific means at the international rather than national level.[50]

As illustrated by international practice, obligations to adopt a particular course of conduct carry analytical value when courts aim to underscore that the achievement of the objective set by a primary rule depends on a *specific* a course of conduct taken by the state.[51] This is exactly the function served by procedural duties – and potentially any other duty in which due diligence concretises – with respect to the principal obligation to prevent transboundary harm. Procedural duties crystallise the courses of conduct that a state must comply with in order to fulfil due diligence. They are characterised by more 'determinacy' than the vaguer due diligence notion and, in fact, their violation give rise to state responsibility even in absence of material damage. The 'determinacy' of procedural obligations is relative to the principal due diligence rule.

The second observation stemming from the ICJ's reasoning in Pulp Mills and *Nicaragua* v. *Costa Rica* regards the relationship between the best-effort nature of the obligation to prevent transboundary harm and Article 14(3) of ARSIWA. By confirming that a breach of the obligation to prevent transboundary harm cannot arise unless transboundary damage has occurred, the court has clearly adhered to the conclusion reached by the ILC in ARSIWA. Chapter 3 has illustrated the genealogy of Article 14(3) and argued that, although there is room to criticise the soundness of the commission's approach, the tension between due diligence and this article is often mitigated by international practice. Since due diligence

50 *Legality of the Threat or Use of Nuclear Weapons*, para. 20. See extensively Chapter 2, Section 2.2.

51 Chapter 2, Section 2.2.4.

obligations, including preventive ones, are by nature vague and flexible in content, their assessment is typically highly circumstantial. That is, it is often the occurrence of a harmful event that will trigger the evaluation of a due diligence primary rule and will allow adjudicators to determine *ex post facto* which measures should have been taken by the state to avoid harm.

However, the more that flexibility and vagueness of due diligence are replaced by legal standards, procedural, and substantive duties, the more the assessment of due diligence can be done *a priori*. In the context of prevention of transboundary harm, the shift from the logic of compensation for environmental damage to risk-anticipation has led to the progressive identification of the preventive international measures required to manage risks. This shift not only concretises due diligence, but makes the conflict between its rationale and Article 14(3) even more apparent. In the words of the ICJ, prevention finds source in the duty to exercise due diligence. Under this premise, failure to comply with a procedural duty, which is also part of due diligence, should be nothing less than proof of a state's failure to exercise due diligence in preventing transboundary harm. Judge Donoghue explains this paradox well in her Separate Opinion in Construction of a Road case:

> The requirement to exercise due diligence, as the governing primary norm, is an obligation of conduct that applies to all phases of a project . . . In the planning phase, a failure to exercise due diligence to prevent significant transboundary environmental harm can engage the responsibility of the State of origin even in the absence of material damage to potentially affected States. This is why (as in *Nicaragua* v. *Costa Rica*) a failure to conduct an environmental impact assessment can give rise to a finding that a State has breached its obligations under customary international law without any showing of material harm to the territory of the affected States. If, at a subsequent phase, the failure of the State of origin to exercise due diligence in the implementation of the project causes significant transboundary harm, the primary norm that is breached remains one of due diligence, but the reparation due to the affected State must also address the material damage caused to the affected State (For these reasons, I do not find it useful to draw distinctions between 'procedural' and 'substantive' obligations, as the Court has done).[52]

If one wishes to go beyond the obligation to prevent transboundary environmental harm, one could argue the same about any other preventive obligations of due diligence which are externalised into specific

[52] Ibid., *Separate Opinion of Judge Donoghue*, para. 9.

substantive or procedural duties. Once due diligence is concretised, at least in part, into legal parameters, the focus shifts from the (harmful) event to conduct taken by the state. This shift is hard to square with the understanding that, unless the event occurs, a breach of due diligence does not accrue.

5.2.2 'Objectivised' Due Diligence in the International Human Rights Context

Obligations of due diligence in the context of international human rights offer a further example of the progressive replacement of the concept of reasonableness linked to due diligence obligations with substantive and procedural duties.

The due diligence dimension of states' human rights obligations must be carved into their wide-ranging obligations *to protect* or *to ensure* human rights.[53] Obligations to protect human rights are obligations of conduct which typically require states to adopt measures necessary to ensure that the human rights of individuals are respected. Protection in international human rights does not indeed imply an absolute guarantee that a person's human rights will be ensured at all times and at all costs. It implies a duty to put in place an adequate legal and administrative framework and to make sure that domestic authorities exercise their best effort to guarantee individuals' rights. For example, with regard to the scope of the positive obligations to protect life as enshrined in Article 2 of ECHR, the ECtHR has noted:

> [This] State's obligation extends beyond its primary duty to secure the right to life by putting in place effective criminal-law provisions to deter the commission of offences against the person backed up by law-enforcement machinery for the prevention, suppression and punishment of breaches of such provisions. *Article 2 may also imply in certain well-defined circumstances a positive obligation on the authorities to take preventive operational measures* to protect an individual whose life is at risk from the criminal acts of another individual. That does not mean,

[53] On the due diligence nature of these obligations see Chapter 2, Sections 2.4.1 and 2.4.2. See also L. Lavrysen, *Human Rights in a Positive State: Rethinking the Relationship between Positive and Negative Obligations under the European Convention on Human Rights* (Cambridge: Intersentia, 2016), 156–8; B. Baade, 'Due Diligence and the Duty to Protect Human Rights', in H. Krieger, A. Peters, L. Kreuzer (eds.), *Due Diligence in the International Legal Order* (Oxford: Oxford University Press, 2020), 92; D. Shelton, A. Gould, 'Positive and Negative Obligations', in D. Shelton (ed.), *The Oxford Handbook on International Human Rights Law* (Oxford: Oxford University Press, 2013), 577.

> however, that a positive obligation to prevent every possibility of violence can be derived from this provision. *Such an obligation must be interpreted in a way which does not impose an impossible or disproportionate burden on the authorities*, bearing in mind the difficulties involved in policing modern societies, the unpredictability of human conduct and the operational choices which must be made in terms of priorities and resources.[54]

This characterisation clearly makes the positive obligation to protect life under the ECHR an obligation of conduct, hence, an obligation of due diligence.[55] Similar conclusions have been reached by the IACtHR in relation to obligations to protect under the Inter-American Convention, and by international human rights treaty bodies.[56]

Positive obligations to protect human rights stand in opposition to states' negative obligations *to respect* human rights. The latter obligate the state to refrain from interfering with the rights of individuals without adequate justification. Instead, obligations to protect instruct states to act upon human rights risks, and in particular against risks coming from non-state actors. As stressed by the Human Rights Committee, 'the positive obligations of States Parties ... will be only fully discharged if individuals are protected ... also against acts committed by private persons or entities that would impair the enjoyment of Covenant rights'.[57] While positive obligations are conceived primarily to protect the human rights of individuals against infringements by non-state actors, they are now also applied against infringements caused by natural hazards[58] or by official misconduct.[59]

Like other due diligence obligations, obligations to protect in the context of human rights are usually assessed against the parameter of reasonableness and in light of the circumstances of the case.[60] As

[54] *Mastromatteo* v. *Italy* (Judgment) [2012] App no 37703/97 paras. 68–9 (emphasis added).

[55] On the overlapping of obligations of conduct and obligations of due diligence see Chapter 2, Section 2.3.2.

[56] *Case of the 'Street Children' (Villagran-Morales et al.)* v. *Guatemala*, IACHR Series C no 77, 26 May 2001, paras. 144–6; *Environment and Human Rights*, Advisory Opinion OC-23/17 of November 15 (2017) IACHR paras. 108–9; Committee on Economic, Social and Cultural Rights, 'General comment No. 24 (2017) on State obligations under the International Covenant on Economic, Social and Cultural Rights in the context of business activities' (2017) UN Doc. E/C.12/GC.24 para. 16.

[57] Human Rights Committee, 'General Comment No. 31 on the Nature of the General Legal Obligation Imposed on States Parties to the Covenant ' (2004) UN Doc. CCPR/C/21/Rev.1/Add.13, para. 8.

[58] *Budayeva* v. *Russia* (Judgment) [2008] App no 15339/02 paras. 136, 156.

[59] *Mikahil Mammadov* v. *Azerbajan* (Judgment) [2009] App no 4762/05 paras. 117–33; *Giuliani and Gaggio* v. *Italy* (Judgment) (GC) [2011] App no 23458/02, paras. 58–68.

[60] *Osman* v. *United Kingdom* (Judgment) [1998] App no 87/1997/871/1083 para. 115. See also Baade, 'Due Diligence and the Duty to Protect', 97.

Chapter 3 has explained, reasonableness must be intended as the over-arching parameter against which due diligence obligations are assessed.[61] That is, human rights treaty and practice may point to various qualifying terms when prescribing the type of measures states are required to take to fulfil protection. For example, the ECtHR uses different expressions to determine the scope of states' obligations to protect, ranging from situations in which it imposes states to adopt 'adequate', 'sufficient', 'reasonable' measures, to situations in which measures are required to be 'effective' or 'necessary'.[62] In any case, and regardless of the specific qualifying standard used by the court, the ECtHR consistently reminds that the evaluation of a state's obligations to protect must be done 'in view of the circumstances'[63] and in a way not impose an 'excessive burden on the authorities'.[64]

Thanks to international human rights practice, the understanding of reasonableness in the context of states' human rights protective obligations has undergone significant change. The 'reasonable' state is traditionally considered to be one which, at a minimum, develops a legal and administrative framework to adequately protect the rights guarantee by a human rights treaty or by a convention.[65] Scholars and practitioners stress that states hold, at a minimum, positive duties to enact adequate legislation incorporating international human rights; duties to maintain an adequate administrative apparatus capable of protecting human rights and deter abuses; and duties to ensure remedies for the victims. Note that some of these scholars highlight the 'result' nature of these duties, stressing, for instance, that the duty of a state to provide for a specific legislation is a duty of result not subject to the due diligence rule.[66] Accordingly, they argue that obligations to protect human rights have a twofold nature, since they encompass both duties of result, such as those

[61] See generally Chapter 3, Section 3.2.2.

[62] For a review of the use of these qualifying terms in the practice of the ECtHR Lavrysen, *Human Rights in a Positive State*, 160–3.

[63] *Kemaloğlu* v. *Turkey* (Judgment) [2012] App no 19986/06 para. 33.

[64] Ibid. para. 36.

[65] See generally L. Lavrysen, 'Protection by the Law: The Positive Obligation to Develop a Legal Framework to Adequately Protect ECHR', in Y. Haeck, E. Brems (eds.), *Human Rights and Civil Liberties in the 21st Century* (Berlin: Springer, 2014).

[66] V. Stoyanova, 'Due Diligence versus Positive Obligations: Critical Reflections on the Council of Europe Convention on Violence Against Women', in J. Niemi, L. Peroni, V. Stoyanova (eds.), *International Law and Violence Against Women* (London: Routledge, 2020), 95; R. Pisillo-Mazzeschi, 'Responsabilité de l'état pour violation des obligations positives relatives aux droits de l'homme' (2008) 333 RCADI 187.

described above, and duties of diligent conduct – like duties to use a state's administrative or enforcement apparatus to prevent violations by non-state actors – which are effectively duties of a best-effort nature.[67]

While I do not dispute that a duty to enact legislation or a duty to equip the state with an adequate administrative apparatus is a duty of result, I argue that conceptualising obligations to protect as duties of twofold nature seems too artificial. The reasons is that, even though the enactment of a legislation is a duty of result, the application of this duty to individual cases is typically done by courts within the broader framework of reasonable protection.[68] In other words, a court's assessment of what a state should have reasonably done in the circumstances of the case to protect the human rights of an individual implies, inter alia, evaluating whether that state had an adequate apparatus or enacted the necessary required legislation to protect that individual. From this perspective, duties to enact legislation or to provide adequate administrative and operational frameworks are very much part of the due diligence content of obligations to protect.

To illustrate this further, the next subsections show how it is indeed the concept of the 'reasonable' state in human rights law that has progressively been formalised with legal parameters. What is reasonable or appropriate in the context of human rights protection is less and less devolved to the choice of states, and is gradually being replaced with legal duties, procedures, and international standards to which states must conform. Obligations to protect human rights are increasingly 'objectified' and their flexible and open-ended content concretised in more substantive and procedural obligations. Three examples have been picked to describe this process.

I The Proceduralisation of Reasonableness through Treaty Law

First, human rights treaties may provide more concreteness to due diligence by specifying the measures states shall adopt to comply with their obligations to protect from human rights abuses. Some recent human rights treaties perfectly reflect the 'proceduralisation' of states' due diligence human rights obligations. For example, the 2011 Council of Europe Convention on Preventing and Combating Violence Against

[67] Pisillo-Mazzeschi, 'Responsabilité de l'état pour violation des obligations positives', 297, 311–424.

[68] Lavrysen, *Human Rights in a Positive State*, 155–7.

Women and Domestic Violence[69] includes numerous provisions which spell out the content of more wide-ranging due diligence obligations of state parties.

The convention addresses violence against women (VAW) and aims at protecting women from violence and at preventing, prosecuting, and eliminating VAW. Article 5 of the convention provides a general due diligence obligation of states to ensure that women are free from violence and prescribes the adoption of all the *necessary legislative and other measures* to prevent, investigate, punish, and provide reparation for acts of VAW by non-state actors (note that the convention expressly use the term due diligence). The general obligation to prevent VAW is then reiterated at Article 12, which instructs states to take all necessary measures to prevent all forms of violence against women at various levels, including the social, cultural, and legislative level.

Yet, the convention does not grant much leeway to states in the choice of *necessary* measures. Chapter III of the convention indeed lists a variety of more specific duties that states must implement to comply with prevention requirements.[70] This way, the convention concretises due diligence and pre-emptively formalises the test of reasonableness ingrained in this notion. Accordingly, Article 13 provides for the duty to promote and conduct awareness-raising campaigns or programmes to increase the understanding of VAW among the general public; Article 14 provides for the obligation to include lessons on equality between men and women and non-stereotyped gender roles in teaching material; Article 15 requires states to provide appropriate training for professionals who deal with victims of violence, perpetrators of violence, or acts of violence; Article 16 provides for a duty to take all necessary measures to set up programmes aimed at teaching perpetrators of domestic violence to adopt non-violent behaviour in interpersonal relationships. The same applies to Chapter IV of the convention, which first provides for a general obligation to protect and support victims of VAW from further violence, and then spells out the more specific duties states need to adopt to meet their protection requirements (Articles 19–26).

[69] Council of Europe Convention on Preventing and Combating Violence Against Women and Domestic Violence (adopted 11 May 2011, entered into force 1 August 2014) CETS No 210.

[70] See explanatory report of the convention para. 83, which states: ‘the article comprises a number of general preventive measures which lay the foundation and represent overarching principles for more specific obligations contained in the subsequent articles of this chapter’.

Some of these duties are themselves framed as due diligence obligations, others instead are reminders of duties of result (Article 26(2)).

Another example regards some of the provisions of the Convention on the Rights of Persons with Disabilities.[71] Article 4 of this convention sets the general obligation of state parties to ensure and promote the full realisation of human rights of persons affected by disabilities. To this end, a number of specific sub-obligations are listed to ensure that states implement effective measures and act with due diligence in protecting and promoting the rights of persons with disabilities. Specifically, states are required to design policies and programmes that take into account the protection of people with disabilities (Article 4(1)(c)), to promote research and provide goods, services, facilities, and equipment for people affected by disabilities (Article 4(1)(f)), to provide accessible information to people with disabilities about mobility aids, devices, and assistive technology (Article 4(1)(h)), and to promote the training of professionals and staff working with people affected by disabilities (Article 4(1)(i)).

Overall, some human rights treaties tend to externalise at least part of the due diligence content of state's positive obligations to protect human rights. This process decreases the vagueness and the flexible contours of due diligence into operational duties 'spelt out' by treaty provisions. States are thus provided with more specific and direct obligations, whether obligations of means or obligations of result, that together inform the broader meaning of 'acting with due diligence' linked to general obligations to protect.

II The Proceduralisation of Reasonableness through Interpretative Practice

Another way of formalising reasonableness in the context of international human rights law is through proceduralising its meaning. The concept of proceduralisation in international human rights law and particularly in the context of the European Convention on Human Rights holds a specific meaning. Proceduralisation generally refers to two distinct phenomena. On the one hand, it points to the practice of courts like the ECtHR, which, instead of performing substantive reviews on the boundaries of a specific right under the convention, may limit itself to supervise the quality of national procedures in the application of

[71] Convention on the Rights of Persons with Disabilities (adopted 13 December 2006, entered into force 3 May 2008) 2515 UNTS 3.

said right and accepts their substantive outcome.[72] In these cases, the court scrutinises the decision-making process at the domestic level and, if it concludes that fundamental rights were adequately considered, the court refrains from making its own substantive review. On the other hand, proceduralisation may also consist of reading procedural requirements and duties into the substance of different conventional provisions.[73] This type of proceduralisation is intimately connected with due diligence.[74] Procedural human rights obligations are indeed often expounded from the interpretation of positive obligations to protect human rights. In concretising the meaning of reasonable and appropriate steps to be taken to fulfil human rights, courts or treaty bodies may establishes procedural duties and consider them part of a state's obligation to protect human rights.

Within the ECtHR context, many procedural obligations have been inferred through the 'positive obligations' matrix, that is, from expansive interpretations of states' due diligence obligations to protect and ensure human rights. One of the most important procedural obligations developed under both the ECtHR and the IACtHR is the state authorities' duty to investigate when individuals have been killed either by state agents or by non-state actors. In the context of the ECHR, the procedural duty to investigate was originally articulated in relation to Article 2 and the positive duty to protect the right to life. The obligation to protect the right to life under this provision [Article 2], read in conjunction with the state's general duty under Article 1 of the convention to 'secure to everyone within their jurisdiction the rights and freedoms defined in [the] Convention', requires by implication that there should be some form of effective official

[72] On this form of proceduralisation see T. Kleinlein, 'The Procedural Approach of the European Court of Human Rights: Between Subsidiarity and Dynamic Evolution' (2019) 68 ICLQ 91; O. M. Arnardóttir, 'The "Procedural Turn" under the European Convention on Human Rights and Presumptions of Convention Compliance' (2017) 15 *International Journal of Constitutional Law*9.

[73] On this second type of proceduralisation N. Le Bonniec, *La procéduralisation des droits sibstantiels par la Cour européenne des droits de l'homme: réflexion sur le côntrole juridictionnel du respect des droits garantis par la Convention européenne des droits de l'homme* (Brussels: Bruylant, 2017); E. Brems, 'Procedural Protection', in E. Brems, J. Gerards (eds.), *Shaping Rights in the ECHR: The Role of the European Court of Human Rights in Determining the Scope of Human Rights* (Cambridge: Cambridge University Press, 2013), 137–8.

[74] Note that the first type of proceduralisation may also intersect with due diligence, for example when the review of the quality of the national decision-making process by the ECtHR has an effect on the review of reasonableness of a contested due diligence measure, see S. Besson, *La Due Diligence*, 366.

investigation when individuals have been killed as a result of the use of force by, *inter alios*, agents of the state.[75]

Similarly, the IACtHR has derived the obligation to investigate from the general obligation of states to guarantee the right to life protected by the American Convention. Accordingly, this duty 'entails the need for conduct by the Government that ensures the genuine existence of an effective guarantee of free and full exercise of human rights'.[76] While originating from the obligation to protect the right to life, procedural investigative obligations have been applied by the ECtHR also in the context of individuals' rights to be free from torture, inhuman and degrading treatments,[77] forced labour or human trafficking,[78] or breaches of the physical integrity of individuals in relation to Article 8 of the European Convention.[79]

The procedural obligation under Article 2 has been inferred from the scope of the positive obligation of states to protect the right to life. Yet, it is now a separate free-standing duty applied coextensively to positive and negative obligations under the convention. Hence, the duty to investigate is both autonomous and at the same time part of the assessment of the general due diligence obligation to protect the right to life. Interestingly, this duty has also been subject to some form of further proceduralisation. Within the ECHR framework, the ECtHR has consistently affirmed the due diligence nature of the obligation to conduct an investigation, noting that 'this is not an obligation of result, but of means', and that authorities 'must have taken the reasonable steps available to them' to fulfil it.[80] In cases where cross-border or transnational investigations are to be undertaken, the court has declared that the reasonableness and effectiveness of the investigation must be assessed against the 'sub-procedural' duty of state parties to cooperate or seek cooperation in obtaining evidence or punishing the perpetrators.[81]

Other examples of procedural obligations inferred through the scope of states' positive obligations to protect human rights include duties to provide access to effective remedies. The ECtHR usually develops these

[75] *Hugh Jordan* v. *United Kingdom* (Judgment) [2001] App no 24746/94 para. 107.
[76] *Case of Anzualdo Castro* v. *Perù*, IACHR Series C no 160, 22 September 2009, para. 123.
[77] *El-Masri* v. *FYROM* (Judgment) [2012] App no 39630/09 para. 182.
[78] *Rantsev* v. *Cyprus and Russia* (Judgment) [2010] App no 25965/04 para. 288.
[79] *M. C.* v. *Bulgaria* (Judgment) [2003] App no 39272/98 paras. 152–3.
[80] *Hugh Jordan* v. *United Kingdom*, para. 107.
[81] *Güzelyurtlu and others* v. *Cyprus and Turkey* (Judgment) (GC) [2019] App no 36925/07 para. 229.

procedural duties in connection with the substantive obligations of states under the convention.[82] For example, in the context of the right to private and family life or the protection of private property, the ECtHR has noted that states have a duty to enact procedures and legal mechanisms to which individuals may appeal to have their rights effectively protected. Essentially, failure to provide for these procedures amounts to a state's failure to comply with its positive obligations to protect the right to family life or the right to property.[83] Similarly, in relation to situations where life is at risk due to natural hazards, the court has established that states have a duty to adopt a regulatory framework that guarantees transparent procedures by relevant authorities and public access to information. At times, this duty has been framed by the court as a procedural obligation arising out of the positive obligation of states to protect the right to life.[84] In other circumstances, it was simply noted that, in assessing whether the respondent state has complied with positive obligations, 'the Court must considered the particular circumstances of the case, regard being had, among other elements, to the domestic legality of the authorities acts or omissions, the domestic decision-making process, including the appropriate investigations and studies, and the complexity of the issue'.[85]

III Other Forms of Proceduralisation of Reasonableness

Finally, human rights courts may use other techniques to concretise due diligence and diminish the margin of liberty granted to states in the choice of measures. At times, courts circumscribe the notion of reasonableness by having recourse to international minimum standards adopted by other technical bodies. Reference to 'external' legal standards formalises reasonableness inasmuch as it allows courts to avoid the

82 The procedural obligation to provide an effective remedy is distinct from the obligations set in Article 13 of the European Convention, which has a broader and different scope, according to the ECtHR. However, the distinction between the two is not always clear, see Lavrysen, *Human Rights in a Positive State*, 66–74.

83 *Tysiac* v. *Poland* (Judgment) [2007] App no 5410/03 paras. 117–18; *Kotov* v. *Russia* (Judgment) [2012] App no 54522/00 para. 114.

84 *Brincat and others* v. *Malta* (Judgment) [2014] App no 60908/11 para. 101. See also *Di Sarno and others* v. *Italy* (Judgment) [2012] App no para. 107 noting: 'As to the procedural obligations under Article 8, the Court reiterates that it attaches particular importance to public access to information that enables them to assess the risks to which they are exposed', noting that in the particular circumstances of the case Italy had discharged its positive procedural obligations under the convention.

85 *Budayeva* v. *Russia*, paras. 136, 156.

hyper-contextualisation of this concept when applied to the individual case at hand. In fact, when courts draw on international standards to concretise due diligence in a specific case, they are implicitly stating that what is 'due' and 'reasonable' only in part depends on the circumstances and can be inferred from broader legal parameters.

For instance, in a case concerning the duty to protect life from excessive or illegal use of force by police officers, the ECtHR affirmed that state parties must ensure that policing operations are sufficiently regulated to provide effective safeguards against arbitrariness and abuse of powers.[86] To develop this duty and to provide more concreteness to its content, the court drew on the UN Basic Principles on the Use of Force and Firearms by Law Enforcement Officials. Similarly, the IACtHR has expressly referred to the General Recommendations of the Committee of the Convention on the Elimination of All Discriminations Against Women to indicate which measures state parties shall adopt to comply with the duty to protect the life of women from violence.[87]

To reduce the margin of appreciation granted to states when exercising due diligence, the ECtHR has also made reference to other own-developed standards, like the European consensus doctrine. European consensus is generally described as the practice of European states in relation to human rights and which reflects common values.[88] It is a 'strategy' used by the ECtHR to interpret the convention in light of political, cultural, and societal change and to reduce or enlarge states' margin of appreciation in implementing the rights of the convention. European consensus is not used exclusively for interpreting due diligence, but is employed more generally for giving substantive meaning to international standards and principle employed by the court like reasonableness, proportionality, fair balance etc.[89] In relation to due diligence, however, the European court has used it to harness the scope of some positive obligations and to clarify what it means to be a 'reasonable' state under the convention. For example, in a case involving the rape of a woman, Bulgaria was accused of having failed to protect the victim under Articles 3 and 8 of the convention for failing to prosecute the attackers. While acknowledging that states enjoy a wide margin of appreciation as to the means to ensure protection against rape, the court

86 *Makaratzis* v. *Greece* (Judgment) [2004] App no 50385/99 paras. 56–72.

87 *Case of Gonzàlez and others* v. *Mexico*, IACHR Series C no 205, 16 November 2009, 70–2.

88 *Demir and Baykara* v. *Turkey* (Judgment) [2008] App no 34503/97 para. 85.

89 For a review see D. Peat, *Comparative Reasoning in International Courts and Tribunals* (Cambridge: Cambridge University Press, 2019), 140–77.

observed that this margin may be limited by the changing conditions within the state parties and the evolving convergence as to the standards to be achieved.[90] Accordingly, the court drew on a comparative survey regarding other European states and affirmed that

> '[i]n accordance with contemporary standards and trend in the area, the member States' positive obligations under Articles 3 and 8 ... must be seen as requiring the penalisation and effective prosecution of any non-consensual sexual act, including in the absence of physical resistance by the victim'.[91]

The court used this finding to note that Bulgarian legislation in relation to acts of rape was defective and required amendments.

Overall, courts' indications of which measures states should apply to comply with reasonableness and due diligence may not ultimately result in the development of new free-standing duties or autonomous procedural obligations. Yet, these techniques do reflect the progressive objectivisation of due diligence in human rights practice.

This is why, from a structural perspective, conceptualising obligations to protect human rights as duties of a twofold nature adds an unnecessary layer of complexity to the foundations of these obligations. The examples above show that it is primarily the concept of reasonableness linked to due diligence that is acquiring progressively more concreteness by being interpreted according to legal, rather than factual, parameters. Sometimes, the increasing solidification of due diligence will develop into the 'externalisation' of direct duties, some of which may well be duties of result (for example the duty to adopt certain criminal legislation to address systematic violations of certain rights). As for the proceduralisation of the obligations to prevent harm, one may read the 'externalised' duties required to display due diligence as obligations 'to adopt a particular course of conduct'. For instance, from the perspective of states' broader positive obligations to protect the right to life, the duty to investigate prescribes to adopt 'a particular course of conduct' that states need to undertake to display due diligence.

Concluding Remarks

This chapter has explored the phenomenon of proceduralisation of due diligence obligations. By proceduralisation of due diligence, this chapter

[90] *M. C.* v. *Bulgaria*, paras. 154–5.
[91] Ibid.

has meant the process of progressively concretising due diligence by replacing reasonableness and the flexible variables traditionally linked to due diligence with legal parameters. From a phenomenological standpoint, this chapter has demonstrated that proceduralisation can appear in a variety of forms. At times, states themselves are willing to delimit the flexibility of due diligence *ab origine* and to delineate its boundaries within specific legal parameters. In these cases, proceduralisation derives from treaties themselves, which identify more or less stringent duties that together inform the understanding of what must be deemed due and diligent. In other circumstances, proceduralisation takes place through the interpretative practice of international courts, tribunals or treaty bodies. These bodies may concretise due diligence in different ways. They may resort to technical international standards and shift the evaluation of reasonableness from the factual to the legal plane, or they may derive from more general due diligence obligations specific duties, whether substantive of procedural, of self-standing nature.

It is proceduralisation through interpretative practice of courts and international bodies that brings about the most pressing legal questions around due diligence. Overall, these processes certainly raise issues with regard to their legitimacy and limits. When courts derive 'new' substantive and procedural duties from broader due diligence obligations, their action may come close to creating new legal rules. Likewise, the increasing reliance on technical standards and procedures to define the concept of reasonableness may be reflective of other broader critical phenomena of the international legal order, such as its 'managerialism' and its focus on 'compliance rather than (normative) analysis of what there is to comply with'.[92]

Yet, from the perspective of a book aiming to explore the theoretical foundations of due diligence obligations, proceduralisation is critical inasmuch as it fundamentally tests their dogmatic structure. Drawing on two case studies in the environmental and human rights context, this chapter has shown how proceduralisation affects the nature and content of due diligence obligations. When the flexible and open-ended character of due diligence is progressively solidified into more stringent duties, part of the 'conduct' nature of these obligations is lost in the transition: the risk structurally linked to due diligence is more objectified and, along with it, the measures required to address it. Both in the case of the obligation to prevent transboundary environmental harm and in human rights practice, this ultimately results into the creation of

[92] Koskenniemi, *The Politics of International Law*, 15.

procedural obligations that acquire a self-standing character. As this chapter has attempted to argue, these procedural duties may be construed as duties to adopt a particular course of conduct, since they crystallised the specific steps to be taken by states to fulfil due diligence. This solidification further exposes the paradox of conceptualising obligations to prevent as negative obligations of result whose breach depends on the occurrence of the harmful event. The more the interpretation of due diligence obligations shifts from an *ex post facto* and compensatory logic to a risk-anticipation one, the more the application of the rationale behind Article 14(3) to these obligations appears far-fetched.

Conclusion

This book began by laying down some of the most common arguments about due diligence obligations. It was noted that obligations of due diligence are often described as 'weak', 'elusive', as rules that operate in an opaque realm and are difficult to be examined a priori and in the abstract. The preceding chapters have explored the conceptual foundations of due diligence obligations with the view of testing these assumptions and providing more clarity into the nature, content, and scope of operation of these rules.

Part of the elusiveness surrounding due diligence obligations stems from the very concept of due diligence. Scholars have grappled with explaining the function and the exact place due diligence occupies in international law. The position that construes due diligence as a notion pertaining to the realm of state responsibility or a concept sitting in between primary and secondary rules continues to find appeal in doctrine. However, this approach stands in stark contrast with the letter of ARSIWA as well as with scholars who sees in this notion merely a standard of conduct applicable to certain primary rules. The terminology adopted to define due diligence adds a further layer of complexity to the debate. Legal literature and international practice have described due diligence with various terms, taking it as a 'rule', a 'standard of conduct', a 'general principle', and an 'obligation'. Behind the use of each term usually lies a different ideological opinion on the status of due diligence and the function due diligence should serve in the international legal order.

As Chapter 1 demonstrates, the history of due diligence is inextricably linked with some of the most problematic and contentious aspects concerning international responsibility. Retracing the genealogy of due diligence in international law means dealing with the foundations and development of state responsibility and requires understanding the relationship between due diligence and associated concepts, such as fault, the notion of states' responsibility in connection with acts of private individuals, and the concept of international liability. Hence, there is a genetic connection between due diligence and the law of international responsibility, one that often resurfaces in international practice and the writings of legal scholars.

However, this book has demonstrated that it is best to construe due diligence as an *identifier* for certain primary rules and not as a principle of state responsibility or a notion escaping the dichotomy primary/secondary rules. First, the approach that places due diligence at the level of primary rules has now become the orthodoxy in international law. It is followed by the ILC both in ARSIWA, which explicitly excludes due diligence from the range of secondary rules, and in the draft Articles on Prevention of Transboundary Harm from Hazardous Activities, which interprets due diligence as an element of the obligation to prevent transboundary harm. It is also the approach generally followed by international courts and tribunals like the ICJ and the ITLOS, which had used due diligence as a tool to provide substance, meaning, and rationale to international obligations of different content and kind. Second, construing due diligence as a *qualifier* for certain primary rules does not mean to deny the intimate link that exists between due diligence and international responsibility. On the contrary, this book has demonstrated that the very identification of a category of primary rules 'of due diligence' serves essentially to make normative considerations about how a state's responsibility for the violation of one of these rules can accrue. I will come back to this point shortly.

Finally, using due diligence as a *qualifier* for primary rules avoids thorny questions about the status of due diligence as a general principle of international law. The book has argued that the answer to such a problem depends on the meaning one attaches to due diligence and to general principles under international law. In international law, there are at least two ways to use due diligence: one is to describe a *standard of conduct* required by certain international obligations; the other is to understand due diligence as a *process* to be undertaken by a state, an international organisation or by a non-state actor as part of one or more of their obligations.[1] In the same vein, the question of what are general principles and what function they serve in the international legal order remains unsettled. That is why analysing due diligence as a principle clarifies little of the general debate on this notion unless one provides a precise definition of general principles and the role they serve in international law.

[1] See Chapter 1, Section 1.4.

The book has shown that situating due diligence within the theory of international obligations implies critically revisiting the taxonomy between obligations of conduct and obligations of result developed by the ILC during the work on state responsibility. As Chapter 2 as illustrated, speaking of due diligence obligations means speaking of flexible obligations which grant states leeway in the performance of the duty and call them to exercise best efforts toward a certain result. As such, due diligence obligations are obligations of conduct, as opposed to obligations of result, which are more stringent and require states to attain given results. The book has shown that the structural features of due diligence obligations make them suitable to proliferate in a risk-based society and to be invoked in the regulation of hazardous activities not prohibited under international law or activities carried out by non-state actors. As duties of conduct, due diligence obligations are postulated around the concept of risk and the idea that the realisation of certain results in international society cannot be absolutely guaranteed. Hence, when the goal set by a primary rule is outside the state's power to guarantee, what matters is the adoption of measures and the degree of effort displayed by the state toward that goal.

However, in international law the distinction between obligations of conduct and obligations of result is a source of much ambiguity because it does not necessarily refer to a dichotomy built around the criterion of *risk*. The distinction between obligations of conduct and obligations of result was originally introduced by the ILC to distinguish international obligations based on the *determinacy* of the content set by a primary rule. Accordingly, obligations of conduct were conceived as obligations describing with more precision the course of conduct and the type of measures to be adopted by a state in performing its duty; conversely, obligations of result were conceived as obligations allowing states a margin of manoeuvre in the choice of means necessary to perform the obligation.

A debate started during the second reading of the ILC articles on state responsibility and continued afterwards on which understanding of conduct–result carries more value in international law and should be retained. Chapter 2 has argued that this is a false debate, to the extent that both distinctions carry analytical value and are still employed in international practice to describe certain externalities of international obligations. The real issue is rather to understand their normative force, namely the capacity of each distinction to be used as a conceptual grid for making normative assumptions about the functioning of obligations. In this regard, Chapter 4 has shown that although the ILC eventually rejected the distinction conduct–result based on determinacy, some articles of ARSIWA are still built upon its logic. Article 14(3) of ARSIWA, dealing with the temporal element of the breach of obligations to prevent a given event, is a case in point: this provision conceptualises obligations to prevent a given event based on the dichotomy elaborated by the ILC, putting emphasis on the 'negative' result to be achieved by the state, that is, the non-occurrence of the event to be prevented. This dogmatic construction creates a permanent tension in how obligations to prevent a given event are operationalised in international practice. On the one hand, international courts and tribunals seems to converge toward the interpretation of obligations to prevent as duties of a best-effort nature, thus giving prominence to the element of risk around which prevention is to be understood. On the other hand, the letter of Article 14(3) appreciates prevention through a completely different logic – that of the more or less margin of liberty granted to a state to perform its duties.

The book has argued that what unifies due diligence obligations as a typology of primary rules is not just their nature of obligations of conduct, but also their content and scope of operation. Chapter 3 illustrated that due diligence operates indeed as a catalyser that injects meaning and rationale to a certain class of international obligations. Without downplaying the specificity of each primary rule, this chapter has shown that construing obligations through the lens of due diligence allows dogmatic considerations to be made about their scope and content. In this regard, the book argues that the scope of operation of due diligence obligations builds around the concept of possibility to act. Accordingly, a state bound by a primary rule of due diligence is expected to act with the required effort so long as two factual conditions are cumulatively met: the state must have power over the source of risk linked to the due diligence rule and it must have knowledge of such risk. Chapter 3 has shown that the difficulty of assessing a state's power over the source of risk is what makes complex the evaluation of a state's compliance with a due diligence obligation. Power over the source of risk is a dispositional concept and, as such, it often remains a potential. This means that the assessment of how much of this power a state holds – and, consequently, how far the state should act – will often require complex evaluations of facts and a certain degree of deductive inference. Yet, Chapter 3 argued that understanding power over the source of risk is crucial for adequately conceptualising due diligence obligations and avoiding confusion with notions that are only apparently similar, like control or jurisdiction.

The book has also discussed the content of due diligence obligations. The book has shown that the parameter of reasonableness along with a set of factual and legal variables are what inform the substance of due diligence obligations across international law. Reasonableness is simultaneously the strength and the weakness of obligations of due diligence. As a normative standard imbued with legal and extra-legal elements, reasonableness injects concreteness to the substance of due diligence obligations while maintaining their flexible and open-ended nature. These characteristics make due diligence obligations appealing to states when they are called to negotiate international rules in relevant fora. Opting for a due diligence rule de facto means 'agreeing to disagree' on the content of the rule in question and shifting the related conflict at the stage of law application. Furthermore, the expectation that what is 'reasonable' always implies a factual appraisal makes due diligence obligations highly adaptable and sensible to change over time. Due diligence obligations are dynamic because reasonableness is a variable concept, therefore 'measures considered sufficiently diligent at a certain moment in time may become not diligent enough in light, for instance, of new scientific or technological knowledge'.[2] At the same time, reasonableness as the overarching parameter of due diligence obligations is the main reason behind the understanding of such obligations as 'weak' or 'elusive'. Interpreting due diligence through reasonableness means that what is expected of a state bound by a due diligence rule cannot be established pre-emptively or *in abstracto*, and that the assessment of what was 'due' will always be influenced by the subjective evaluation of each state.

This book argued that the phenomenon of 'proceduralisation' of due diligence obligations is a way to increase legal certainty and overcome the ambiguity surrounding reasonableness. The book defined the proceduralisation of due diligence obligations as a process which progressively erodes the extra-legal elements of reasonableness by replacing them with 'hard' legal parameters. Through proceduralisation, the open-ended substance of due diligence obligations is spelled out into a series of 'sub'-duties, technical standards, and direct obligations whose fulfilment make up the content of the due diligence rule.

[2] *Responsibility and Obligations of States Sponsoring Persons and Entities with Respect to Activities in the Area (Request for an Advisory Opinion submitted to the Seabed Dispute Chamber)* ITLOS Reports 2011 para. 117.

Chapter 5 critically engaged with this process and argued that proceduralisation fundamentally tests the dogmatic foundations of due diligence obligations. If, on the one hand, proceduralisation injects 'objectivity' and legal certainty into the interpretation of a due diligence rule, on the other hand the process raises questions of legitimacy: the more international courts, tribunals, and monitoring bodies replace reasonableness with legal parameters, the more their action results in creating new legal rules. Additionally, the very understanding of due diligence obligations as best-effort duties as opposed to more stringent obligations of result falters when proceduralisation occurs. Once primary rules of due diligence solidify into specific and 'objectified' duties, there is no point in keeping on construing them as flexible obligations of conduct built around the criterion of risk.

Overall, this book demonstrated that a dogmatic reconstruction of due diligence obligations serves a cognitive as well as a normative purpose. The theoretical perspective of obligations chosen to examine due diligence has allowed to provide more clarity around the nature and content of due diligence obligations and the way in which these obligations are operationalised in practice. At the same time, this analysis has shown that conceptualising due diligence obligations as an autonomous typology of primary rules supplies a normative function in the context of international responsibility. It is in this realm that the peculiarities of due diligence obligations emerge more forcefully. When interpreters use the lens of due diligence to identify international obligations, they make normative evaluations about the content of these obligations with the view of defining conduct expected of a state and, consequently, the conditions for a breach to accrue. This leaves us with a final consideration on ARSIWA and the relationship between primary and secondary rules. On the one hand, the commission was probably right in dropping the taxonomy of obligations originally introduced in the first version of the articles on state responsibility. Keeping the distinction would have signified encapsulating primary rules into predeterminate grids, with the risk of stiffening the entire architecture of international responsibility. As this book illustrated, it can be hard to situate obligations within a unique taxonomy, inasmuch different classifications may be able to capture different externalities of obligations, each one useful for a different analytic purpose. Furthermore, the limit of keeping with certain dogmatic classifications has become apparent with the analysis of Article 14(3) of ARSIWA. The logic behind this provision has created an *aporia* with the now-consolidated interpretation of preventive obligations as duties of due diligence. Hence, from this perspective, the choice of the commission has proved wise.

On the other hand, this book has made apparent the understanding that certain dogmatic classifications, like the one of 'due diligence', allow for general statements to be made that do guide the interpreter in the application of the law of state responsibility.[3] If this is the case, however, by deciding to leave the 'character' of international obligations out of questions of secondary rules,[4] the impression is that ARSIWA has overlooked an important aspect of the equation of state responsibility. The task of filling this gap and providing more clarity to this relationship is therefore entrusted to legal doctrine.

[3] G. Gaja, 'Primary and Secondary Rules in the International Law on State Responsibility' (2014) 97 *Rivista di diritto Internazionale* 981, 991.

[4] ILC Draft articles on Responsibility of States for Internationally Wrongful Acts, with commentaries (2001) ILC YB II/2, Article 12: 'There is a breach of an international obligation by a State when an act of that State is not in conformity with what is required of it by that obligation, *regardless of its origin or character*' (emphasis added).

BIBLIOGRAPHY

Abi-Saab G., 'Introduction: A Meta-Question', in G. Abi-Saab, K. Keith, G. Marceau, C. Marquet (eds.), *Evolutionary Interpretation and International Law* (London: Hart Publishing, 2019).

Ago R., 'La colpa nell'illecito internazionale', in *Scritti Giuridici in Onore di Santi Romano* (Padua: CEDAM, 1940), vol. 3.

Ago R., 'Le délit international' (1939) 68 *Recueil des Course de l'Académie de Droit International de la Haye* 415.

Ago R., 'Positive Law and International Law' (1957) 51 *American Journal of International Law* 691.

Ambrus M., Rayfuse R., Werner W. (eds.), *Risk and the Regulation of Uncertainty in International Law* (Oxford: Oxford University Press, 2017).

Andenas M., Chiussi L., 'Cohesion, Convergence and Coherence of International Law', in J. Wouters, M. Andenas, M. Fitzmaurice, A. Tanzi (eds.), *General Principles and the Coherence of International Law* (Leiden: Brill, 2019).

Anzilotti D., 'La responsabilité internationale des Etats à raison des dommages soufferts par des étrangers' (1906) 13 *Revue Générale de Droit International Public* 5.

Anzilotti D., *Teoria generale della responsabilità dello Stato*, Part 1 (Florence: Lumachi Libraio Editore, 1902).

Arangio-Ruiz G., 'Dualism Revisited: International Law and Interindividual Law' (2003) 86 (Supplement to issue 1) *Rivista di diritto internazionale*, 909.

Arangio-Ruiz G., 'State Fault and the Forms and Degrees of International Responsibility: Questions of Attribution and Relevance', in *Mélanges Michel Virally: Le droit international au service de la paix de la justice et du développement* (Paris: Pedone, 1991).

Arangio-Ruiz G., 'State Responsibility Revisited: The Factual Nature of the Attribution of Conduct to the State' (2017) 100 (Supplement to issue 1) *Rivista di diritto internazionale* 1.

Arangio-Ruiz V., *Istituzioni di Diritto Romano* (15th ed., Naples: Jovene Editore, 2006).

Arcari M., 'La responsabilité en droit international: un "systeme"?', in V. Tomkiewicz (ed.), *Organisation mondiale du commerce et responsabilité* (Paris: Pedone, 2014).

Arcari M., 'Le juge et la codification du droit de la responsabilité: quelques remarques concernant l'application judiciaire des articles de la CDI sur la responsabilité de l'État pour fait internationalement illicite', in N. Boschiero, T. Scovazzi, C. Pitea, C. Ragni, *International Courts and the Development of International Law: Essays in Honour of Tullio Treves* (The Hague: Asser Press, 2013).

Arnardóttir O. M., 'The "Procedural Turn" under the European Convention on Human Rights and Presumptions of Convention Compliance' (2017) 15 *International Journal of Constitutional Law* 9.

Aust H. P., 'The UN Human Rights Due Diligence Policy: An Effective Mechanism against Complicity of Peacekeeping Forces?' (2014) 20 *Journal of Conflict & Security Law* 61.

Aust H. P., *Complicity in the Law of State Responsibility* (Cambridge: Cambridge University Press, 2011).

Aust H. P., Feihle P., 'Due Diligence in the History of the Codification of the Law of State Responsibility', in H. Krieger, A. Peters, L. Kreuzer (eds.), *Due Diligence in the International Legal Order* (Oxford: Oxford University Press, 2020).

Azaria D., *Treaties on Transit of Energy via Pipelines and Countermeasures* (Oxford: Oxford University Press, 2015).

Baade B., 'Due Diligence and the Duty to Protect Human Rights', in H. Krieger, A. Peters, L. Kreuzer (eds.), *Due Diligence in the International Legal Order* (Oxford: Oxford University Press, 2020).

Barnidge R., 'The Due Diligence Principle Under International Law' (2006) 8 *International Community Law Review* 81.

Barnidge R., *Non-State Actors and Terrorism: Applying the Law of State Responsibility and the Due Diligence Principle* (Berlin: Springer, 2008).

Bartolini G., 'Cultural Heritage and Disasters', in F. Francioni, A. F. Vrdoljak (eds.), *The Oxford Handbook of International Cultural Heritage Law* (Oxford: Oxford University Press, 2020).

Bartolini G., 'Il concetto di "controllo" sulle attivitá di individui quale presupposto della responsabilitá dello stato', in M. Spinedi, A. Gianelli, M. L. Alaimo (eds.), *La codificazione della responsabilitá internazionale degli Stati alla prova dei fatti* (Milan: Giuffré, 2006).

Bartolini G., 'The Failure of "Core Capacities" under the WHO International Health Regulations' (2020) 70 *International and Comparative Law Quarterly* 233.

Bartolini G., 'The Historical Roots of the Due Diligence Standard', in H. Krieger, A. Peters, L. Kreuzer (eds.), *Due Diligence in the International Legal Order* (Oxford: Oxford University Press, 2020).

Beck U., *Risk Society: Towards a New Modernity*, trans. M. Ritter (London: Sage Publishing, 1992).

Becker T., *Terrorism and the State: Rethinking the Rules of State Responsibility* (Portland: Hart Publishing, 2006).

Belli P., *De Re Militari et Bello Tractactus*, trans. H. C. Nutting, *The Classics of International Law* (Oxford: Clarendon Press, 1936).

Benninger-Budel C. (ed.), *Due Diligence and Its Application to Protect Women from Violence* (Leiden: Brill, 2008).

Bennouna M., 'Le droit international entre la lettre et l'esprit: cours général de droit international public' (2017) 383 *Recueil des Course de l'Académie de Droit International de la Haye* 1.

Berkes A., 'The Standard of "Due Diligence" as a Result of Interchange between the Law of Armed Conflict and General International Law' (2018) 23 *Journal of Conflict and Security Law* 433.

Besson S., 'Les obligations de protection de droit fondamentaux: un essai en dogmatique comparative' (2003) 1 *Revue de Droit Suisse* 49.

Besson S., 'The Extraterritoriality of the European Convention on Human Rights: Why Human Rights Depend on Jurisdiction and What Jurisdiction Amounts To' (2012) 25 *Leiden Journal of International Law* 857.

Besson S., 'La "Due Diligence" en droit international' (2020) 409 *Recueil des Course de l'Académie de Droit International de la Haye* 153.

Bingham T., 'The Alabama Claims Arbitration' (2005) 54 *International and Comparative Law Quarterly* 1.

Birnie P., Boyle A., Redgwell C., *International Law and the Environment* (3rd ed., Oxford: Oxford University Press, 2007).

Blanco S. M., *Full Protection and Security in International Law* (Berlin: Springer, 2018).

Bleckmann A., 'General Theory of Obligations under Public International Law' (1995) 38 *German Yearbook of International Law* 26.

Bodansky D., Brunnée J., Hey E., 'International Environmental Law: Mapping the Field', in D. Bodansky, J. Brunnée, E. Hey (eds.), *The Oxford Handbook of International Environmental Law* (Oxford: Oxford University Press, 2007).

Bodansky D., Crook J. R., 'Symposium: The ILC'S State Responsibility Articles Introduction and Overview' (2002) 96 *American Journal of International Law* 773.

Bonafé B., Palchetti P., 'Relying on General Principles in International Law', in C. Brölmann, Y. Radi (eds.), *Research Handbook on the Theory and Practice of International Lawmaking* (Cheltenham: Edward Elgar, 2016).

Bonfanti A., 'Attacchi cibernetici in tempo di pace e intrusioni nelle elezioni presidenziali alla luce del diritto internazionale' (2019) 102 *Rivista di diritto internazionale* 694.

Bonnitcha J., McCorquodale R., 'The Concept of "Due Diligence" in the Guiding Principles on Business and Human Rights' (2017) 28 *European Journal of International Law* 899.

Boon K. E., 'Are Control Tests Fit for The Future? The Slippage Problem in Attribution Doctrines' (2014) 15 *Melbourne Journal of International Law* 330.

Borchard E. M., 'Theoretical Aspects of the International Responsibility of States' (1929) 1 *Zeitschrift für ausländisches öffentliches Recht und Völkerrecht* 225.

Borchard E. M., *The Diplomatic Protection of Citizens Abroad* (New York: The Banks Law Publishing Company, 1915).

Bowman M., Davies P., Redgwell C., *Lyster's International Wildlife Law* (2nd ed., Cambridge: Cambridge University Press, 2011).

Boyle A., 'Liability for Injurious Consequence of Acts not Prohibited by International Law', in J. Crawford, A. Pellet, S. Olleson, K. Parlet (eds.), *The Law of International Responsibility* (Oxford: Oxford University Press, 2010).

Boyle A., 'State Responsibility and International Liability for Injurious Consequences of Acts not Prohibited by International Law: A Necessary Distinction?' (1990) 39 *International and Comparative Law Quarterly* 12.

Boyle A., Chinkin C., *The Making of International Law* (Oxford: Oxford University Press, 2007).

Brems E., 'Procedural Protection', in E. Brems, J. Gerards (eds.), *Shaping Rights in the ECHR : The Role of the European Court of Human Rights in Determining the Scope of Human Rights* (Cambridge: Cambridge University Press, 2013).

Brown D., 'Use of Force Against Terrorism After September 11th: State Responsibility, Self- Defence and Other Responses' (2003–2004) 11 *Cardozo Journal of International and Comparative Law* 13.

Brownlie I., *Principles of International Law* (6th ed., Oxford: Oxford University Press, 2003).

Brownlie I., *System of the Law of Nations, State Responsibility, Part I* (Oxford: Oxford University Press, 1983).

Brunnée J., 'International Environmental Law and Community Interests', in E. Benvenisti, G. Nolte (eds.), *Community Interests Across International Law* (Oxford: Oxford University Press, 2018).

Brunnée J., 'Procedure and Substance in International Environmental Law' (2020) 405 *Recueil des Course de l'Académie de Droit International de la Haye* 87.

Buergenthal T., 'Self-Executing and Non-Self-Executing Treaties in National and International Law' (1992) 235 *Recueil des Course de l'Académie de Droit International de la Haye* 303.

Calvo C., *Le droit international theorique et pratique* (Paris: Nabu Press, 1923).

Campbell E., Dominic E., Stadnik S., Wu Y., 'Due Diligence Obligations of International Organizations under International Law' (2018) 50 *New York University Journal of International Law and Politics* 541.

Cannizzaro E., 'Considerazioni in merito al ruolo della ragionevolezza e della proporzionalità nel diritto internazionale' (2002) 7 *Ars Interpretandi* 347.

Cannizzaro E., *Il principio della proporzionalità nell'ordinamento internazionale* (Milan: Giuffrè, 2000).

Carnelutti F., *Teoria generale del diritto* (Naples: Edizioni Scientifiche, 1999).

Caron D., 'The Basis of Responsibility: Attribution and Other Trans-Substantive Rules', in R. B. Lillich, D. B. Magraw (eds.), *The Iran-United States Claims Tribunal: Its Contribution to the Law of State Responsibility* (New York: Transnational Publishers, 1998).

Cassella S., 'Le travaux de la Commission du droit international sur la responsabilité internationale et le standard de due diligence' in S. Cassella (ed.), *Le standard de due diligence et la responsabilité internationale* (Paris: Pedone, 2018).

Cazala J., *Le principe de précaution en droit international* (Paris: Librairie générale de droit et de jurisprudence, 2006).

Cheng B., *General Principles of Law as Applied by International Courts and Tribunals* (Cambridge: Cambridge University Press, 2006).

Chinkin C., 'A Critique of the Public/Private Dimension' (1999) 10 *European Journal of International Law* 387.

Chinkin C., 'Normative Development in the International Legal System', in D. Shelton (ed.), *Commitment and Compliance: The Role of Non-binding Norms in the International Legal System* (Oxford: Oxford University Press 2003).

Chircop L., 'A Due Diligence Standard of Attribution in Cyberspace' (2018) 67 *International and Comparative Law Quarterly* 643.

Chiussi L., 'Corporate Human Rights Due Diligence: From Process to the Principle', in M. Buscemi, N. Lazzerini, L. Magi, D. Russo (eds.), *Legal Sources in Business and Human Rights: Evolving Dynamics in International and European Law* (Leiden: Brill, 2020).

Clapham A., *Human Rights Obligations of Non-State Actors* (Oxford: Oxford University Press, 2006).

Combacau J., 'La responsabilité internationale', in H. Thierry, J. Combacau, S. Sur, C. Vallée (eds.), *Droit International Public* (Paris: Editions Mont-Chrestien, 1981).

Combacau J., 'Obligations de résultat et obligations de comportement: Quelques questions et pas de réponse', in *Le droit international: unité et diversité. Melanges offerts à Paul Reuter* (Paris: Pedone, 1981).

Condorelli, L., 'The Imputability to States of Acts of International Terrorism' (1989) 19 *Israel Yearbook of Human Rights* 233.

Condorelli L., Kress, C., 'The Rules of Attribution: General Considerations', in J. Crawford, A. Pellet, S. Olleson, K. Parlet (eds.), *The Law of International Responsibility* (Oxford: Oxford University Press, 2010).

Conforti B., 'Obblighi di mezzo e obblighi di risultato nelle convenzioni di diritto uniforme' (1989) 25 *Rivista di diritto privato e processuale* 373.

Corten O., 'La "complicité" dans le droit de la responsabilité internationale: Un concept inutile?' (2011) 57 *Annuaire Français de Droit International* 57.

Corten O., *L'utilisation du "raisonnable" par le juge international: Discours juridique, raison et contraditions* (Bruxelles: Bruylant, 1997).

Corten O., 'Reasonableness' in *Max Planck Encyclopedia of International Law* (Oxford: Oxford University Press 2013).

Corten O., 'The Notion of "Reasonable" in International Law: Legal Discourse, Reason and Contradiction' (1999) 48 *International and Comparative Law Quarterly* 613.

Corten O., Klein O., 'The limits of complicity as a ground for responsibility: Lessons learned from the Corfu Channel case', in K. Bannelier, T. Christakis, S. Heathcote (eds.), *The ICJ and the Evolution of International Law: The Enduring Impact of the Corfu Channel Case* (London: Routledge, 2012).

Crawford J., 'The ILC's Articles on Responsibility of States for Internationally Wrongful Acts: A Retrospect' (2002) 96 *American Journal of International Law* 874.

Crawford J., 'The System of International Responsibility', in J. Crawford, A. Pellet, S. Olleson (eds.), *The Law of International Responsibility* (Oxford: Oxford University Press, 2010).

Crawford J., Grant T., Messineo F., 'Toward an International Law of Responsibility: Early Doctrine', in L. Boisson de Chazournes and M. Kohen (eds.), *International Law and the Quest of its Implementation: Liber Amicorum Vera Gowlland-Debbas* (Leiden: Brill, 2010).

Crawford J., *State Responsibility: The General Part* (Cambridge: Cambridge University Press, 2013).

Crawford J., *The International Law Commission's Articles on State Responsibility: Introduction, Text and Commentaries* (Cambridge: Cambridge University Press, 2002).

Crawford J., Watkins J., 'International Responsibility', in S. Besson, J. Tasioulas (eds.), *The Philosophy of International Law* (New York: Oxford University Press, 2010).

Crema L., 'The Interpretative Work of Treaty Bodies: How They Look at Evolutionary Interpretation, and How Other Courts Look at Them', in G. Abi-Saab, K. Keith, G. Marceau, C. Marquet (eds.), *Evolutionary Interpretation and International Law* (London: Hart Publishing, 2019).

d'Argent P., 'Les principes généraux à la Cour internationale de Justice', in S. Besson, P. Pichonnaz (eds.), *Les principes de droit européen* (Paris: Librairie Général de Droit et de Jurisprudence, 2011).

d'Argent P., 'Reparation, Cessation, Assurance and Guarantees of Non-Repetition ', in A. Nollkaemper, I. Plakokefalos (eds.), *Principles of Shared Responsibilities in International Law* (Cambridge: Cambridge University Press, 2014).

d'Argent P. , 'State Organs Placed at the Disposal of the UN, Effective Control, Wrongful Abstention and Dual Attribution of Conduct' (2014) 1 *QIL–Questions of International Law* 17.

d'Argent P. , De Vaucleroy A. , 'Le contenu de l'omission illicite: La non utilisation de moyens raisonnables', in S. Cassella (ed.), *Le standard de due diligence et la responsabilité internationale* (Paris: Pedone, 2018).
d'Aspremont J., 'The Multidimensional Process of Interpretation', in A. Bianchi, D. Peat, M. Windsor (eds.), *Interpretation in International Law* (Oxford: Oxford University Press, 2015).
Dahl R. A., 'The Concept of Power' (1957) 2 *Behavioral Science* 201.
Dailler P., Forteau M., Pellet A., *Droit International Public* (Paris: Librairie Général de Droit et de Jurisprudence, 2009).
Dannenbaum T., 'Public Power and Preventive Responsibility', in A. Nollkaemper, I. Plakokefalos (eds.), *Distribution of Responsibilities in International Law* (Cambridge: Cambridge University Press, 2015).
Daugirdas K., 'Member States' Due Diligence Obligations to Supervise International Organizations', in H. Krieger, A. Peters, L. Kreuzer (eds.), *Due Diligence in the International Legal Order* (Oxford: Oxford University Press, 2020).
David E., 'Primary and Secondary Rules', in J. Crawford, A. Pellet, S. Olleson, K. Parlett (eds.), *The Law of International Responsibility* (Oxford: Oxford University Press, 2010).
De Brabandere E., 'Host States' Due Diligence Obligations in International Investment Law' (2015) 42 *Syracuse Journal of International and Comparative Law* 319.
De Sena P., 'Condotta di singoli organi e condotta dell'apparato statale in tema di colpa nell'illecito internazionale' (1988) 71 *Rivista di diritto internazionale* 525.
De Sena P., 'La "due diligence" et le lien entre le sujet et le risqué qu'il faut prévenir: quelques observations', in S. Cassella (ed.), *Le standard de due diligence et la responsabilité internationale* (Paris: Pedone, 2018).
De Sena P., *La nozione di giurisdizione statale nei trattati sui diritti dell'uomo* (Turin: Giappichelli, 2020).
De Vaucleroy A., 'Les obligations de comportement en droit international public. Due diligence et responsabilité internationale', PhD thesis, Université catholique de Louvain (2021).
Deeks A., 'Unwilling or Unable: toward a Normative Framework for Extraterritorial Self-Defence' (2012) 53 *Virginia Journal of International Law* 483.
Delerue F., *Cyber Operations and International Law* (Cambridge: Cambridge University Press, 2020).
Demogue R., *Traité des Obligations en General* (Paris: Librairie Arthur Rousseau, 1925).
Desierto D. A., 'Due Diligence in World Bank and Project Financing', in H. Krieger, A. Peters, L. Kreuzer (eds.), *Due Diligence in the International Legal Order* (Oxford: Oxford University Press, 2020).

Diggelmann O., 'Fault in the Law of State Responsibility: Pragmatism *ad Infinitum*' (2006) 49 *German Yearbook of International Law* 293.

Dinstein Y., *War, Aggression and Self-Defence* (Cambridge: Cambridge University Press, 2011).

Donati D., *I trattati internazionali nel diritto costituzionale* (Turin: Unione tipografico-editrice torinese, 1906).

Dubuisson F., 'Vers un Renforcement des Obligations de Diligence en Matière de Lutte Contre le Terrorism ?', in K. Christakis-Bannelier, T. Christakis, O. Corten, B. Delcourt (eds.), *Le Droit International Face au Terrorisme* (Paris: Pedone 2002).

Dupuy P. M., 'Faute de l'Etat et "fait internationalement illicite"' (1987) 5 *Droit* 54.

Dupuy P. M., 'Infraction', in *Répertoire de Droit International* (Paris: Dalloz, 1999).

Dupuy P. M., 'La diligence due dans le droit international et la résponsabilité' in Organisation de coopération and développement économique (ed.), *Aspects Juridiques de la Pollution Transfrontière* (Paris: OECD, 1977).

Dupuy P. M., 'Le fait générateur de la responsabilité internationale des Etats' (1984) 188 *Recueil des Course de l'Académie de Droit International de la Haye* 9.

Dupuy P. M., 'Reviewing the Difficulties of Codification: On Ago's Classification of Obligations of Means and Obligations of Result in Relation to State Responsibility' (1999) 10 *European Journal of International Law* 371.

Dupuy P. M., Hoss C., 'Trail Smelter and International Terrorism: International Mechanisms to Combat Transboundary Harm', in C. Walter, C. Vöneky, F. Schorkopf, V. Roeben (eds.), *Terrorism as a Challenge for National and International Law: Security versus Liberty?* (Berlin: Springer, 2004).

Duvic-Paoli L. A., *The Prevention Principle in International Environmental Law* (Cambridge: Cambridge University Press, 2018).

Dworkin R., 'The Modes of Rules I', in *Taking Rights Seriously: New Impression with a Reply to Critics* (London: Duckworth, 1977).

Eagleton C., *Responsibility of States in International Law* (New York: New York University Press, 1928).

Fauchille P., *Traité de Droit International Public* (Paris: Rousseau & C., 1922).

Fiandaca G., Musco E., *Diritto Penale: Parte Generale* (Bologna: Zanichelli Editore, 2014).

Fitzmaurice G., 'The General Principles of International Law Considered from the Standpoint of the Rule of Law' (1957) 92 *Recueil des Course de l'Académie de Droit International de la Haye* 7.

Fitzmaurice M., 'International Responsibility and Liability', in D. Bodansky, J. Brunnée, E. Hey (eds.), *The Oxford Handbook of International Environmental Law* (Oxford: Oxford University Press, 2007).

Fitzmaurice M., 'Legitimacy of International Environmental Law' (2017) 77 ZaöRV 339.

Focarelli C., *International Law as Social Construct: The Struggle for Global Justice* (Oxford: Oxford University Press, 2012).

Forlati S., 'L'objet des différentes obligations primaires de diligence: prévention, cessation, répression . . . ?', in S. Cassella (ed.), *Le standard de due diligence et la responsabilité internationale* (Paris: Pedone, 2018).

Forlati S., 'The Legal Obligation to Prevent Genocide: *Bosnia* v. *Serbia* and Beyond' (2011) 31 *Polish Yearbook of International Law* 189.

Gaja G., 'Do States Have a Duty to Ensure Compliance with Obligations *Erga Omnes* by Other States?', in M. Ragazzi (ed.), *International Responsibility Today: Essays in Memory of Oscar Schachter* (Leiden: Brill, 2005).

Gaja G., 'General Principles of Law', in *Max Planck Encyclopedia of International Law* (Oxford: Oxford University Press 2012).

Gaja G., 'Primary and Secondary Rules in the International Law on State Responsibility' (2014) 97 *Rivista di diritto internazionale* 981.

Garcìa Mora M. R., *International Responsibility for Hostile Acts of Private Persons Against Foreign States* (Leiden: Martinus Nijhoff, 1962).

Gasbarri L., 'The European Union is not a State: International Responsibility for Illegal, Unreported and Unregulated Fishing Activities' (2020) 7 *Maritime Safety and Security Law Journal* 54.

Gattini A., 'Breach of International Obligations', in A. Nollkaemper, I. Plakokefalos (eds.), *Principles of Shared Responsibility: An Appraisal of the State of the Art* (Cambridge: Cambridge University Press, 2014).

Gattini A., 'Breach of the Obligation to Prevent and Reparation Thereof in the ICJ's Genocide Judgement' (2007) 18 *European Journal of International Law* 695.

Gattini A., 'Smoking/No Smoking: Some Remarks on the Current Place of Fault in the ILC Draft Articles on State Responsibility' (1999) 10 *European Journal of International Law* 397.

Gentili A., *De Legationibus Libri Tres, Vol II*, trans. J. Laing, *The Classics of International Law* (Oxford: Clarendon Press, 1924).

Gianelli A., 'Il contributo della dottrina italiana al tema della responsabilitá internazionale degli Stati per fatto illecito: qualche osservazione' (2016) 99 *Rivista di diritto internazionale* 1042.

Grans L., 'The Concept of Due Diligence and the Positive Obligations to Prevent Honour-Related Violence: Beyond Deterrence' (2018) 22 *The International Journal of Human Rights* 733.

Griebel J., Plücken M., 'New Developments Regarding the Rules of Attribution? The International Court Justice's Decision in *Bosnia* v. *Serbia*' (2008) 21 *Leiden Journal of International Law* 601.

Grotius H., *De Jure Belli Ac Pacis Libri Tres*, trans. by Kelsey, *The Classics of International Law* (Oxford: Clarendon Press, 1925).

Hackworth H., 'Responsibility of States for Damages Caused in Their Territory to the Person or Property of Foreigners' (1930) 24 *American Journal of International Law* 500.

Hakimi M., 'State Bystander Responsibility' (2010) 21 *European Journal of International Law* 341.

Hall W. E., *A Treatise on International Law* (Oxford: Oxford University Press, 1924).

Hart H. L. A., Honoré T., *Causation in the Law* (Oxford: Oxford University Press, 1959).

Harvard Law School Project, 'The Law of Responsibility of States for Damage Done in Their Territory to the Persons or Property of Foreigners' (1929) *American Journal of International Law* 131.

Hathaway O. A., Chertoff E. et al., 'Ensuring Responsibility: Common Article 1 and State Responsibility for Non-State Actors' (2017) 95 *Texas Law Review* 539.

Hautefeuille L. B., *Des droits et des devoirs des nations neutres en temps de guerre maritime, Tome premier* (Paris: Guillaumin et C, Libraires, 1858).

Heathcote S., 'State Omission and Due Diligence: Aspects of Fault, Damage, and Contribution to Injury in the Law of State Responsibility', in K. Bannelier, T. Christakis, S. Heathcote (eds.), *The ICJ and the Evolution of International Law: The Enduring Impact of the Corfu Channel Case* (London: Routledge, 2012).

Heieck J., *A Duty to Prevent Genocide: Due Diligence Obligations Among the P5* (Northampton: Edward Elgar Publishing, 2018).

Hernandez G. , 'Interpretative Authority and the International Judiciary', in A. Bianchi, D. Peat, M. Windsor (eds.), *Interpretation in International Law* (Oxford: Oxford University Press, 2015).

Hershey A. S., *The Essentials of International Public Law* (New York: The Macmillan Company, 1912).

Hessbruegge J. A., 'The Historical Doctrine of Attribution and Due Diligence in International Law' (2004) 36 *New York University Journal of International law and Politics* 265.

Higgins R., *Problems and Process: International Law and How We Use It* (Oxford: Clarendon Press, 1995).

Hollis D. H., 'The Existential Function of Interpretation in International Law', in A. Bianchi, D. Peat, M. Windsor (eds.), *Interpretation in International Law* (Oxford: Oxford University Press, 2015).

Horbach N. L. J. T., 'The Confusion about State Responsibility and International Liability' (1991) 4 *Leiden Journal of International Law* 47.

Hull D., 'Taxonomy', in E. Craig, *Routledge Encyclopedia of Philosophy* (London: Routledge, 1998).

Hyde C., 'Concerning Damages Arising from Neglect to Prosecute' (1928) 22 *American Journal of International Law* 140.

ILA Study Group on Due Diligence in International Law, 'Due Diligence in International Law: Second Report' (Johannesburg, 2016).

Jackson M., *Complicity in International Law* (Oxford: Oxford University Press, 2015).

Jacob D., Le contenu de la responsabilité de l'Etat négligent', in S. Cassella (ed.), *Le standard de due diligence et la responsabilité internationale* (Paris: Pedone, 2018).

Jinks D., 'State Responsibility for the Acts of Private Harm Groups' (2003) 4 *Chicago Journal of International Law* 83.

Joel-Proux V., 'Babysitting Terrorists: Should States Be Strictly Liable for Failing to Prevent Transborder Attacks' (2005) 23 *Berkeley Journal of International Law* 615.

Kamminga M., 'Due Diligence Mania: The Misguided Introduction of and Extraneous Concept into Human Rights Discourse' (2011) Maastricht Faculty of Law Working Paper No. 07.

Kanehara A., 'Reassessment of the Acts of the State in the Law of State Responsibility' (2019) 399 *Recueil des Course de l'Académie de Droit International de la Haye* 9.

Kelsen H., *Principles of Public International Law* (New York: Rinehart & Company, 1952).

Kelsen H., *Pure Theory of Law* (2nd ed., University of California Press, 1970).

Kerbrat Y., 'Le standard de due diligence, catalyseur d'obligations conventionnelles et coutumières pour les Etats', in S. Cassella (ed.), *Le standard de due diligence et la responsabilité internationale* (Paris: Pedone, 2018).

Kerbrat Y., 'Obligations procédurales et obligations de fond en droit international des dommages transfrontières', in I. Prezas (ed.), *Substance and procédure en droit international public: dialectique et influences croisées* (Paris: Pedone, 2019).

Klabbers J., 'Reflections on Role Responsibility: The Responsibility of International Organizations for Failing to Act' (2017) 28 *European Journal of International Law* 1133.

Klabbers J., 'The Redundancy of Soft Law' (1996) 65 *Nordic Journal of International Law* 167.

Klabbers J., Peters A., Ulfstein G., *The Constitutionalization of International Law* (Oxford: Oxford University Press, 2009).

Kleinlein T., 'The Procedural Approach of the European Court of Human Rights: Between Subsidiarity and Dynamic Evolution' (2019) 68 *International and Comparative Law Quarterly* 91.

Koivurova T., 'Due Diligence', in *Max Planck Encyclopedia of International Law* (Oxford: Oxford University Press 2010).

Koivurova T., 'What is the Principle of Due Diligence?', in J. Petman, J. Klabbers (eds.), *Nordic Cosmopolitanism: Essays in International Law for Martti Koskenniemi* (Leiden: Brill, 2003).

Kolb R., 'Reflections on Due Diligence Duties in Cyberspace' (2015) 58 *German Yearbook of International Law* 114.

König D., 'The Elaboration of Due Diligence Obligations as a Mechanism to Ensure Compliance with International Legal Obligations by Private Actors', in ITLOS (ed.), *The Contribution of the International Tribunal for the Law of the Sea to the Rule of Law: 1996–2016* (Leiden: Brill, 2018).

Koskenniemi M., 'International Law and Hegemony: A Reconfiguration' (2004) 17 *Cambridge Review of International Affairs* 197.

Koskenniemi M., 'Peaceful Settlement of Environmental Disputes' (1991) 60 *Nordic Journal of International Law* 73.

Koskenniemi M., 'The Politics of International Law: 20 Years Later' (2009) 20 *European Journal of International Law* 7.

Krieger H., Nolte G., 'The International Rule of Law: Rise or Decline? Points of Departure' (KFG Working Paper Series No 1 2016) 12.

Krieger H., Peters A., 'Due Diligence and Structural Change in the International Legal Order', in H. Krieger, A. Peters, L. Kreuzer (eds.), *Due Diligence in the International Legal Order* (Oxford: Oxford University Press, 2020).

Krieger H., Peters A., 'Due Diligence in the International Legal Order', in H. Krieger, A. Peters, L. Kreuzer (eds.), *Due Diligence in the International Legal Order* (Oxford: Oxford University Press, 2020)

Kulesza J., *Due Diligence in international Law* (Leiden: Brill, 2016).

Lagrange E., 'La responsabilité des organisations internationales pour violation d'une obligation de diligence', in S. Cassella (ed.), *Le standard de due diligence et la responsabilité internationale* (Paris: Pedone, 2018).

Lanovoy V., 'The Use of Force by Non-State Actors and the Limits of Attribution of Conduct' (2017) 28 *European Journal of International Law* 587.

Lanovoy V., *Complicity and Its Limits in the Law of International Responsibility* (London: Hart Publishing, 2016).

Latty F., 'Actions and Omissions', in J. Crawford, A. Pellet, S. Olleson (eds.), *The Law of International Responsibility* (Oxford: Oxford University Press, 2010).

Lauterpacht H., 'Revolutionary Activities by Private Persons Against Foreign States' (1928) 22 *American Journal of International Law* 105.

Lavrysen L., 'Protection by the Law: The Positive Obligation to Develop a Legal Framework to Adequately Protect ECHR', in Y. Haeck, E. Brems (eds.), *Human Rights and Civil Liberties in the 21st Century* (Berlin: Springer, 2014).

Lavrysen L., *Human Rights in a Positive State: Rethinking the Relationship between Positive and Negative Obligations under the European Convention on Human Rights* (Cambridge: Intersentia, 2016).

Lawrence W. B., 'Opinion exprimé sur les Trois Règles de Washington' (1974) 27 *Revue de Droit International et de Législation Comparée* 570.

Le Bonniec N., *La procéduralisation des droits substantiels par la Cour européenne des droits de l'homme: réflexion sur le côntrole juridictionnel du respect des droits garantis par la Convention européenne des droits de l'homme* (Brussels: Bruylant, 2017).

Lemoine-Schonne M., 'Substance et procédure en droit international du climat', in I. Prezas (ed.), *Substance and procédure en droit international public: dialectique et influences croisées* (Paris: Pedone, 2019).

Lévy D., 'La responsabilité pour omission et la responsabilité pour risque en droit international public' (1961) 65 *Revue Générale de Droit International Public* 744.

Linderfalk U., 'State Responsibility and the Primary-Secondary Rules Terminology: The Role of Language for an Understanding of the International Legal System' (2009) 78 *Nordic Journal of International Law* 53.

Longobardo M., 'L'obbligo di prevenzione del genocidio e la distinzione fra obblighi di condotta e obblighi di risultato' (2019) 2 *Diritti Umani e Diritto Internazionale* 237.

Longobardo M., 'The Relevance of the Concept of Due Diligence for International Humanitarian Law' (2019) 37 *Wisconsin International Law Journal* 44.

Lowe V., 'Responsibility for the Conduct of other States' (2002) 101 *Japanese Journal of International Law and Diplomacy* 1.

Luzzatto R., 'Responsabilitá e colpa in diritto internazionale' (1968) 51 *Rivista di diritto internazionale* 53.

Maiorca C., 'Colpa (teoria generale)', in *Enciclopedia del diritto* (Milan: Giuffré, 1960).

Mallory C., *Human Rights Imperialists: The Extraterritorial Application of the European Convention on Human Rights* (London: Hart Publishing, 2020).

Mann F. A., 'The Doctrine of Jurisdiction in International Law' (1964) 111 *Recueil des Course de l'Académie de Droit International de la Haye* 1.

Marchesi A., 'The Distinction Between Obligations of Conduct and Obligations of Result Following its Deletion from the Draft Articles on State Responsibility', in *Studi in onore di Gaetano Arangio-Ruiz* (Naples: Editoriale Scientifica, 2004), vol. 2.

Marchesi A., *Obblighi di Condotta e obblighi di risultato: Contributo allo studio degli obblighi internazionali* (Milan: Giuffré, 2005).

Mbengue M. M., 'The South China Sea Arbitration: Innovations in Marine Environmental Fact-Finding and Due Diligence Obligations' (2016) 110 *American Journal of International Law Unbound* 285.

Mbengue M. M., *Essai sur une théorie du risqué en droit international public* (Paris: Pedone, 2009).

McCormick N., *Legal Reasoning and Legal Theory* (Oxford: Clarendon Press 1978).

McDonald N., 'The Role of Due Diligence in International Law' (2019) 68 *International and Comparative Law Quarterly* 1041.

McDougal M. S., 'Law and Power' (1952) 46 *American Journal of International Law* 102.

Mendelson M., 'The International Court of Justice and the Sources of International Law', in V. Lowe, M. Fitzmaurice (eds.), *Fifty Years of the International Court of Justice: Essays in Honour of Sir Robert Jennings* (Cambridge: Cambridge University Press, 1996).

Milano E., 'Occupation', in A. Nollkaemper, I. Plakokefalos (eds.), *The Practice of Shared Responsibility in International Law* (Cambridge: Cambridge University Press, 2017), 733.

Milanović M., *Extraterritorial Application of Human Rights Treaties* (Oxford: Oxford University Press, 2011).

Milanović M., Papić T., 'The Applicability of the ECHR in Contested Territories' (2018) 67 *International and Comparative Law Quarterly* 779.

Monaco R., 'La responsabilità internazionale dello Stato per fatti degli individui' (1939) 18 *Rivista di diritto internazionale* 3.

Moore J. B., *History and Digest of the International Arbitrations to which the United States Has Been a Party* (Washington: US Government Printing, 1943).

Moore M. S., *Causation and Responsibility: An Essay in Law, Morals and Metaphysics* (Oxford: Oxford University Press, 2009).

Morelli G., *Nozioni di diritto internazionale* (Padua: CEDAM, 1967).

Morriss P., *Power: A Philosophical Analysis* (Manchester: Manchester University Press, 1987).

Newcombe A., Paradell L., *Law and Practice of Investment Treaties: Standards of Treatment* (Alphen aan den Rijn: Kluwer Law International, 2009).

Nielsen F. K., *American-Turkish Claims Settlement under the Agreement of December 24, 1923, and Supplemental Agreements Between the United States and Turkey, Opinions and Reports* (Washington: US Government Printing Office, 1937).

Nollkaemper A., 'Power and Responsibility', in A. di Stefano (ed.), *Un diritto senza terra? Funzioni e limiti del principio di territorialitá nel diritto internaizonale e dell'Unione Europea? A Lackland Law? Territory, Effectiveness and Jurisdiction in International and European Law* (Turin: Giappichelli, 2014).

Nollkaemper A., d'Aspremont J., et al., 'Guiding Principles on Shared Responsibility in International Law' (2020) 31 *European Journal of International Law* 15.

Nollkaemper A., Jacobs D., 'Shared Responsibility in International Law: A Conceptual Framework' (2013) 34 *Michigan Journal of International Law* 359.

Okowa P., 'Procedural Obligations in International Environmental Agreements' (1997) 67 *British Yearbook of International Law* 275.

Ollino A., 'A "Missed" Secondary Rule? Causation in the Breach of Preventive and Due Diligence Obligations', in G. Kajtar, B. Çali, M. Milanovic (eds.), *Attribution, Causality and Evidentiary Rules: Secondary Rules of Primary Importance* (Oxford: Oxford University Press 2021).

Oppenheim L., *International Law: A Treatise, Vol II War and Neutrality* (London: Longmans, Green & Co, 1912).

Österdahl I., 'Due Diligence in International Anti-Terrorism Law: Developments in the Resolutions of the UN Security Council', in H. Krieger, A. Peters, L. Kreuzer (eds.), *Due Diligence in the International Legal Order* (Oxford: Oxford University Press, 2020).

Ouedraogo A., 'La due diligence en droit international: de la règle de la neutralité au principe général' (2012) 42 *Revue Général de Droit* 641.

Ouedraogo A., 'La neutralité et l'emergence du concept de due diligence en droit international : l'affaire de l'Alabama revisité' (2011) 13 *Journal of the History of International Law* 307.

Paddeu F., *Justification and Excuses in International Law: Concept and Theory of General Defences* (Cambridge: Cambridge University Press, 2018).

Palchetti P., 'La violation par l'Union européenne d'une obligation de diligence', in S. Cassella (ed.), *Le standard de due diligence et la responsabilité internationale* (Paris: Pedone, 2018).

Palchetti P., *L'organo di fatto dello Stato nell'illecito internazionale* (Milan: Giuffré, 2007).

Palchetti P., 'State Responsibility for Complicity in Genocide', in P. Gaeta, *The UN Genocide Convention* (Oxford: Oxford University Press, 2009).

Palchetti P., 'The Role of General Principles in Promoting the Development of Customary International Rules', in J. Wouters, M. Andenas, M. Fitzmaurice, A. Tanzi (eds.), *General Principles and the Coherence of International Law* (Leiden: Brill, 2019).

Palmisano G., 'Colpa dell'organo e colpa dello Stato nella responsabilitá internazionale: Spunti critici di teoria e di prassi' (1992) 19 *Comunicazioni e Studi* 623.

Palmisano G., 'Fault', in *Max Planck Encyclopedia of International Law* (Oxford: Oxford University Press 2007).

Papanicolopulu I., 'Due Diligence in the Law of the Sea' in H. Krieger, A. Peters, L. Kreuzer (eds.), *Due Diligence in the International Legal Order* (Oxford: Oxford University Press, 2020).

Paparinskis M., *The International Minimum Standard and Fair and Equitable Treatment* (Oxford: Oxford University Press, 2013).

Pauwelyn J., Wessel R. A., Wouters J., 'When Structures Become Shackles: Stagnation and Dynamics in International Lawmaking' (2014) 25 *European Journal of International Law* 733.

Peat D., *Comparative Reasoning in International Courts and Tribunals* (Cambridge: Cambridge University Press, 2019).

Pellet A., 'Les Articles de la CDI sur la responsabilité de l'État pour faits internationalement illicite : suite – et fin?' (2002) 48 *Annuaire Français de Droit International* 1.

Pellet A., 'Remarques sur une révolution inachevée, le projet d'articles de la Commission du Droit International sur la responsabilité des Etats' (1996) *Annuaire Français de Droit International* 7.

Pellet A., Müller D., 'Article 38', in A. Zimmermann, C. Tams, K. Oeller-Frahn (eds.), *The Statute of the International Court of Justice: A Commentary* (3rd ed., Oxford: Oxford University Press, 2019).

Perassi G., *Introduzione alle scienze giuridiche* (Cittá di Castello: Unione Arti Grafiche, 1938).

Perelman C., 'The Rational and the Reasonable', in C. Perelman (ed.), *The New Rhetoric and the Humanities* (Berlin: Springer, 1989).

Pineschi L., 'The Duty of Environmental Impact Assessment in the First ITLOS Chamber's Advisory Opinion: Towards the Supremacy of the General Rule to Protect and Preserve the Marine Environment as a Common Value?', in N. Boschiero, T. Scovazzi, C. Pitea, C. Ragni (eds.), *International Courts and the Development of International Law: Essays in Honour of Tullio Treves* (The Hague: Asser Press, 2013).

Pisillo-Mazzeschi R., *Due diligence e responsabiitá internazionale degli stati* (Milan: Giuffré, 1989).

Pisillo-Mazzeschi R., 'Le chemin étranger de la due diligence: d'un concept mystérieux à un concept surévalué', in S. Cassella (ed.), *Le standard de due diligence et la responsabilité internationale* (Paris: Pedone, 2018).

Pisillo-Mazzeschi R., 'Responsabilité de l'état pour violation des obligations positives relatives aux droits de l'homme' (2008) 333 *Recueil des Course de l'Académie de Droit International de la Haye* 175.

Pisillo-Mazzeschi R., 'The Due Diligence Rule and the Nature of International Responsibility of States' (1992) 35 *German Yearbook of International Law* 9.

Plakokefalos I., 'Causation in the Law of State Responsibility and the Problem of Overdetermination: In Search of Clarity' (2015) 26 *European Journal of International Law* 471.

Plakokefalos I., 'Prevention Obligations in International Environmental Law' (2012) 23 *Yearbook of International Environmental Law* 5.

Plakokefalos I., 'The Use of Force by Non-State Actors and the Limits of Attribution of Conduct: A Reply to Vladyslav Lanovoy' (2017) 28 *European Journal of International Law* 587.

Pradier-Fodéré P., *Traité de Droit International Public Européen et Américain* (Paris: Pedone, 1885–1906).

Puma G., *Complicitá di Stati nell'Illecito Internazionale* (Turin: Giappichelli, 2018).

Quadri R., *Diritto internazionale pubblico* (Naples: Liguori, 1968).

Radi Y., *La standardisation et le droit international: contours d'une théorie dialectique de la formation du droit* (Paris: Bruylant, 2013).

Radi Y., 'Standardization: A Dynamic and Procedural Conceptualization of International Law-Making' (2012) 25 *Leiden Journal of International Law* 283.

Ragazzi M., *The Concept of International Obligations Erga Omnes* (Oxford: Oxford University Press, 2000).

Raible L., *Human Rights Unbound: A Theory of Extraterritoriality* (Oxford: Oxford University Press, 2020).

Rajput A., 'Due Diligence in International Investment Law', in H. Krieger, A. Peters, L. Kreuzer (eds.), *Due Diligence in the International Legal Order* (Oxford: Oxford University Press, 2020).

Rawl J., 'The Idea of Public Reason Revisited' (1997) 64 *The University of Chicago Law Review* 765.

Redgwell C., 'General Principles of International Law', in S. Vogenauer, S. Weatherill (eds.), *General Principles of Law: European and Comparative Perspectives* (London: Hart Publishing, 2017).

Reisman W. M., 'International Lawmaking: A Process of Communication' (1981) 75 *Proceedings of the Annual Meeting, American Society of International Law* 101.

Reuter P., 'De l'obligation de negocier' (1975) 14 *Comunicazioni e Studi* 711.

Reuter P., 'Principes de droit international public' (1961) 103 *Recueil des Course de l'Académie de Droit International de la Haye* 431.

Roucounas E., *A Landscape of Contemporary Theories of International Law* (Leiden: Brill, 2019).

Ryngaert C., 'State Responsibility and Non-State Actors', in M. Noortmann, A. Reinisch, C. Ryngaert (eds.), *Non-State Actors and International Law* (London: Hart Publishing, 2015).

Salerno F., 'Genesi e usi della nozione di organo nella dottrina internazionalistica italiana' (2009) 92 *Rivista di diritto internazionale* 921.

Salmon J., 'Le Concept de raisonnable en droit international public', in *Le droit international, unite et diversité: mélanges offerts à Paul Reuter* (Paris: Pedone, 1981).

Salmon J., 'Le fait étatique complexe: un notion contestable' (1982) 28 *Annuaire Français de Droit International* 709.

Salmon J., 'Les notions à contenu variable en droit international public', in C. Perelman, R. Vander Elst (eds.), *Les notions à contenu variable en droit* (Paris: Bruylant, 1984).

Schachter O., *International Law in Theory and Practice* (Dordrecht: Martinus Nijhoff Publishers, 1991).

Schachter O., 'Toward a Theory of International Obligation' (1968) 8 *Virginia Journal of International Law* 300.

Scheinin M., 'Just Another World? Jurisdiction in the Roadmaps of State Responsibility and Human Rights', in M. Langford, W. Vandenhole, M. Scheinin (eds.), *Global Justice, State Duties: The Extraterritorial Scope of Economic, Social and Cultural Rights in International Law* (Cambridge: Cambridge University Press, 2013).

Schmitt M., 'In Defence of Due Diligence in Cyberspace', (2015) 125 *The Yale Law Journal Forum* 68.

Schmitt M., 'Sovereignty in Cyberspace: *Lex Lata Vel Non*' (2017) 111 *American Journal of International Law Unbound* 213.

Schmitt M. (ed.), *Tallinn Manual 2.0 on the International Law Applicable to Cyber Operations* (Cambridge: Cambridge University Press, 2017).

Seibert-Fohr A., 'From Complicity to Due Diligence: When Do States Incur Responsibility for Their Involvement in Serious International Wrongdoing?' (2017) 60 *German Yearbook of International Law* 667.

Seminara L., 'Risk Regulation and the European Convention on Human Rights' (2016) 4 *European Journal of Risk Regulation* 733.

Seršić M., 'Due Diligence: Fault-Based Responsibility of Autonomous Standard?', in R. Wolfrum, M. Seršić, T. Šošić (eds.), *Contemporary Developments in International Law: Essays in Honour of Budislav Vukas* (Leiden: Brill, 2015).

Shany Y., *The Extraterritorial Application of International Human Rights Law* (2020) 409 *Recueil des Course de l'Académie de Droit International de la Haye* 9.

Shelton D., Gould A., 'Positive and Negative Obligations', in D. Shelton (ed.), *The Oxford Handbook on International Human Rights Law* (Oxford: Oxford University Press, 2013).

Shibatam A., 'The Court's Decision *In Silentium* on the Sources of International Law', in K. Bannelier, T. Christakis, S. Heathcote (eds.), *The ICJ and the Evolution of International Law: The Enduring Impact of the Corfu Channel Case* (London: Routledge, 2012).

Shue H., *Basic Rights: Subsistence, Affluence, and US Foreign Policy* (Princeton: Princeton University Press, 1980).

Sicilianos L., 'The Classification of Obligations and the Multilateral Dimension of the Relations of International Responsibility' (2002) 13 EJIL 1127.

Sperduti G., *Contributo alla teoria delle situazioni giuridiche soggettive* (Milan: Giuffré, 1944).

Sperduti G., 'Sulla colpa in diritto internazionale' (1950) 3 *Comunicazioni e Studi* 93.

Starita M., 'Négligence illicite et responsabilité multiples: partage ou cumul de responsabilités?', in S. Cassella (ed.), *Le standard de due diligence et la responsabilité internationale* (Paris: Pedone, 2018).

Stern B., 'The Elements of An Internationally Wrongful Act', in J. Crawford, A. Pellet, S. Olleson, K. Parlet (eds.), *The Law of International Responsibility* (Oxford: Oxford University Press, 2010).

Stern B., 'The Obligation to Make Reparation', in J. Crawford, A. Pellet, S. Olleson, K. Parlet (eds.), *The Law of International Responsibility* (Oxford: Oxford University Press, 2010).

Stoyanova V., 'Causation between State Omission and Harm within the Framework of Positive Obligations under the European Convention on Human Rights' (2018) 18 *Human Rights Law Review* 309.

Stoyanova V., 'Due Diligence versus Positive Obligations: Critical Reflections on the Council of Europe Convention on Violence Against Women', in J. Niemi, L. Peroni, V. Stoyanova (eds.), *International Law and Violence Against Women* (London: Routledge, 2020).

Stoyanova V., 'Fault, Knowledge and Risk Within the Framework of Positive Obligations under the European Convention on Human Rights' (2020) *Leiden Journal of International Law* 1.

Talbot Jensen E., 'Cyber Sovereignty: The Way Ahead' (2015) 50 *Texas International Law Review* 275.

Talmon S., 'Determining Customary International Law: The ICJ's Methodology between Induction, Deduction and Assertion' (2015) 26 *European Journal of International Law* 417.

Tams C., *Enforcing Obligations* Erga Omnes *in International Law* (Cambridge: Cambridge University Press, 2005).

Tancredi A., 'Doctrinal Alternatives to Self-Defence Against Non-State Actors' (2017) 77 *Zeitschrift für ausländisches öffentliches Recht und Völkerrecht* 69.

Tancredi A., 'Il problema della legittima difesa nei confronti di milizie non statali alla luce dell'ultima crisi tra Israele e Libano' (2007) 90 *Rivista di diritto internazionale* 969.

Tanzi A., 'Liability for Lawful Acts', in *Max Planck Encyclopedia of International Law* (Oxford: Oxford University Press 2013).

Tanzi A., Kolliopoulos A., 'The No-Harm Rule', in A. Tanzi, O. McIntyre, A. Kolliopoulos, A. Rieu-Clarke, R. Kinna (eds.), *The UNECE Convention on the Protection and Use of Transboundary Watercourses and International Lakes: Its Contribution to International Water Cooperation* (Leiden: Brill, 2015).

Thirlway H., *The Sources of International Law* (Oxford: Oxford University Press, 2014).

Tomuschat C., 'Obligations Arising for States without or against Their Will' (1993) 241 *Recueil des Course de l'Académie de Droit International de la Haye* 209.

Tomuschat C., 'What Is a "Breach" of the European Convention on Human Rights?', in R. Lawson, M. de Blois (eds.), *The Dynamics of the Protection of Human Rights in Europe: Essays in Honour of Henry G. Schermers* (Dordrecht: Martinus Nijhoff, 1994).

Tonkin H., *State Control over Private Military and Security Companies in Armed Conflict* (Cambridge: Cambridge University Press, 2011).

Townley S., 'The Rise of Risk in International Law' (2016) 18 *Chicago Journal of International Law* 594.

Trapp K., *State Responsibility for International Terrorism: Problems and Prospects* (Oxford: Oxford University Press, 2011).

Treves T., '"Due Regard" Obligations under the 1982 UN Convention on the Law of the Sea: The Laying of Cables and Activities in the Area' (2019) 34 *International Journal of Marine Coastal Law* 167.

Treves T., 'Environmental Impact Assessment and the Precautionary Approach: Why Are International Courts and Tribunal Reluctant to Consider Them as General Principles of Law?', in M. Andenas, M. Fitzmaurice, A. Tanzi, J. Wouters (eds.), *General Principles and the Coherence of International Law* (Leiden: Brill, 2019).

Triepel E., *Völkerrecht und landesrecht*, trans. by R. Brunet, *Droit international et droit interne* (first published 1899, Oxford: Pedone, 1920).

Tsagourias N., 'Cyber Attacks, Self-Defence and the Problem of Attribution' (2012) 17 *Journal of Conflict and Security Law* 229.

Tsagourias N., 'State Obligations in Cyber Operations' (2015) 14 *Baltic Yearbook of International Law* 71.

Tzevelekos V. P., 'Reconstructing the Effective Control Criterion in Extraterritorial Human Rights Breaches: Direct Attribution of Wrongfulness, Due Diligence and Concurrent Responsibility' (2014) 36 *Michigan Journal of International Law* 129.

Valentine S, Sprague R., 'Due Diligence', in *Encyclopedia Britannica*, www.britannica.com/topic/due-diligence.

Vattel E., *The Law of Nations, Or, Principles of the Law of Nature, Applied to the Conduct and Affairs of Nations and Sovereigns, Book II*, ed. by B. Kapossy, R. Whatmore (first published 1758, Carmel: Liberty Fund, 2008).

Venzke I., *How Interpretation Makes International Law: On Semantic Change and Normative Twists* (Oxford: Oxford University Press, 2014).

Violi F., 'The Function of the Triad "Territory", "Jurisdiction" and "Control" in Due Diligence Obligations', in H. Krieger, A. Peters, L. Kreuzer (eds.), *Due Diligence in the International Legal Order* (Oxford: Oxford University Press, 2020).

von Bogdandy A., Venzke I., 'Beyond Dispute: International Judicial Institutions as Lawmakers' (2011) 12 *German Law Journal* 979.

Vordermayer M., 'The Extraterritorial Application of Multilateral Environmental Agreements' (2018) 59 *Harvard International Law Journal* 59.

Weinryb E., 'Omissions and Responsibility' (1980) 30 *The Philosophical Quarterly* 1.

Westlake J., *International Law, Part II, War* (Cambridge: Cambridge University Press, 1913).

White N., 'Due Diligence, the UN, and Peacekeeping', in H. Krieger, A. Peters, L. Kreuzer (eds.), *Due Diligence in the International Legal Order* (Oxford: Oxford University Press, 2020).

Wilde R., 'Compliance with Human Rights Norms Extraterritoriality: Human Rights Imperialism?', in L. Boisson de Chazournes, M. Kohen (eds.), *International Law and the Quest for Its Implementation: Liber Amicorum Vera Gowlland-Debbas* (Leiden: Brill, 2010).

Wolfrum R., 'General International Law (Principles, Rules, and Standards)', in *Max Planck Encyclopedia of International Law* (Oxford: Oxford University Press 2010).

Wolfrum R., 'International Law of Cooperation', in R. Bernhardt (ed.), *Encyclopedia of Public International Law* (Amsterdam: Elsevier, 1995).

Wolfrum R., 'Obligations of Result Versus Obligation of Conduct: Some Thoughts About the Implementation of International Obligations', in M. H. Arsanjani, J. Cogan, R. Sloane, S. Wiessner (eds.), *Looking into the Future: Essays on International Law in Honor of W. Michael Reisman* (Leiden: Brill, 2010).

Wouters J., 'International Law, Informal Law-Making, Global Governance in Times of Anti-Globalism and Populism', in H. Krieger, G. Nolte, A. Zimmermann (eds.), *International Rule of Law: Rise of Decline?* (Oxford: Oxford University Press, 2019).

Xenos D., *The Positive Obligations of the State under the European Convention on Human Rights* (London: Routledge, 2012).

Zannas P. A., *La responsabilité internationale des Etats pour les actes de négligence* (Montreaux: Ganguin & Laubscher, 1952).

Zarbiyev F., 'Judicial Activism in International Law: A Conceptual Framework for Analysis' (2012) 3 *Journal of International Dispute Settlement* 247.

INDEX

Printed in the United Kingdom by TJ Clays Ltd.